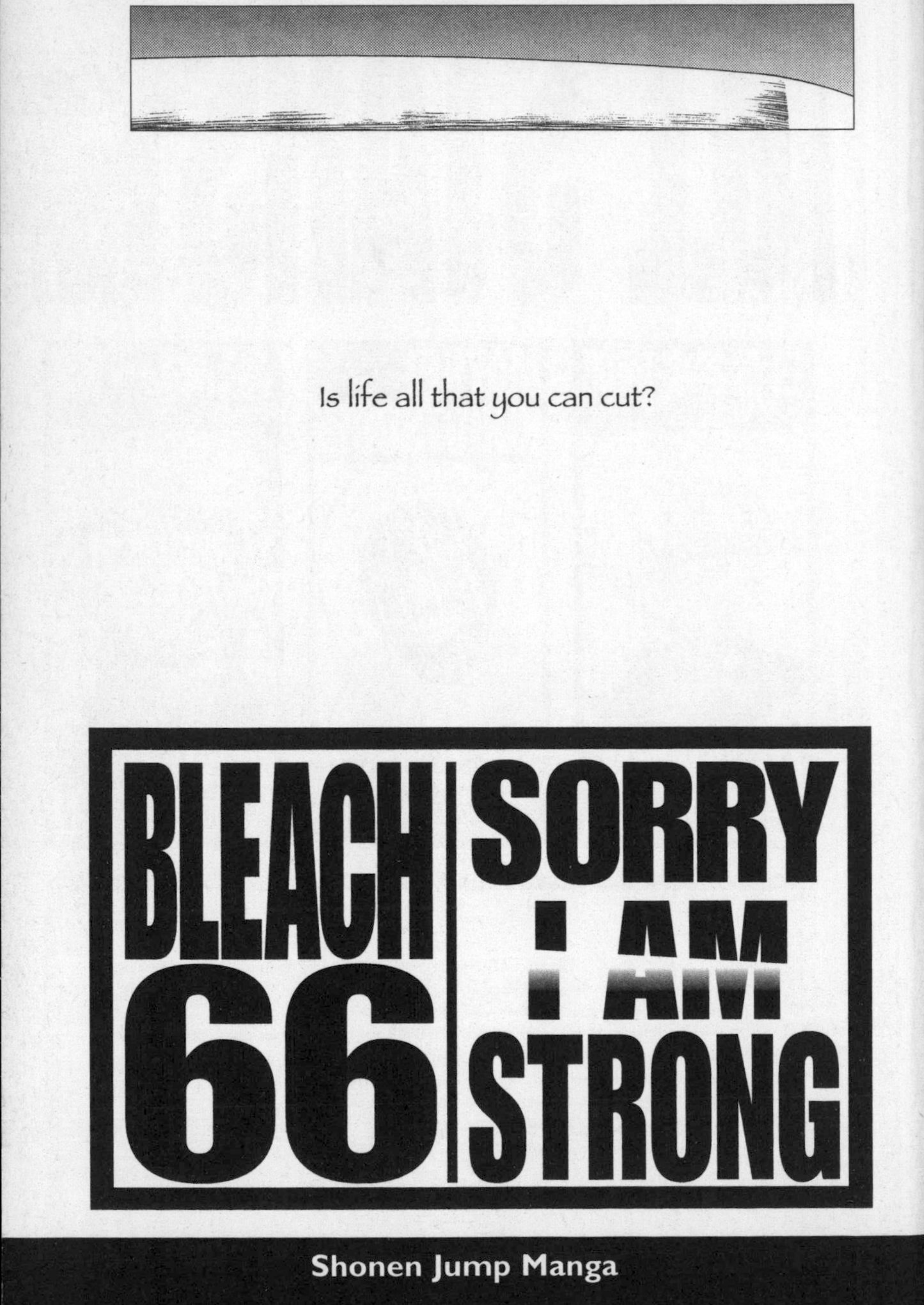

Is life all that you can cut?

BLEACH 66

SORRY I AM STRONG

Shonen Jump Manga

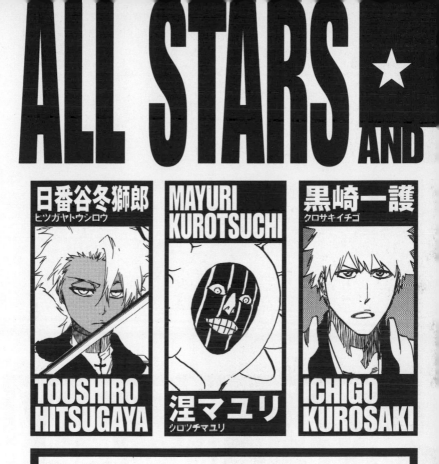

ALL STARS AND

日番谷冬獅郎
ヒツガヤトウシロウ

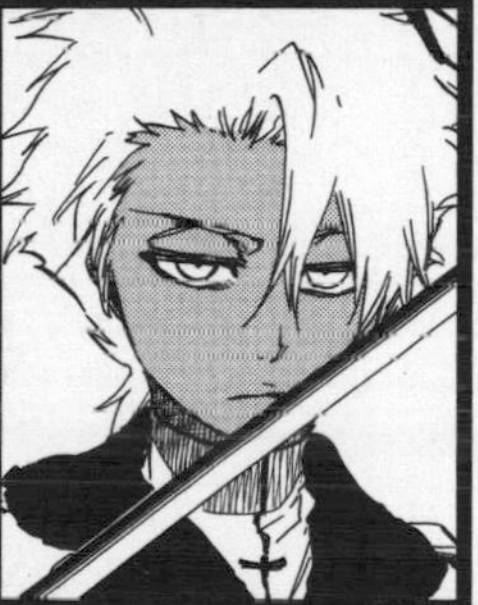

TOUSHIRO
HITSUGAYA

MAYURI
KUROTSUCHI

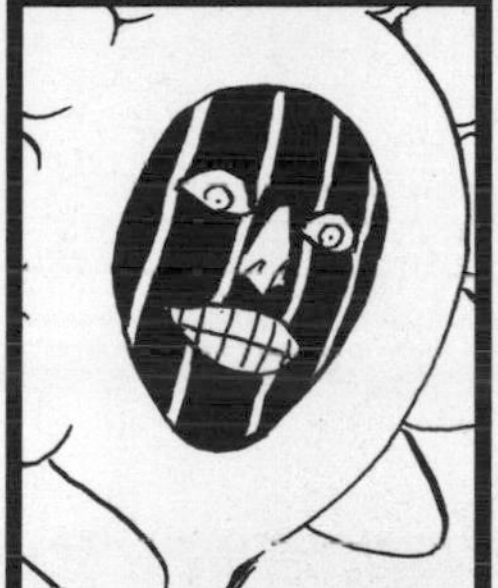

涅マユリ
クロツチマユリ

黒崎一護
クロサキイチゴ

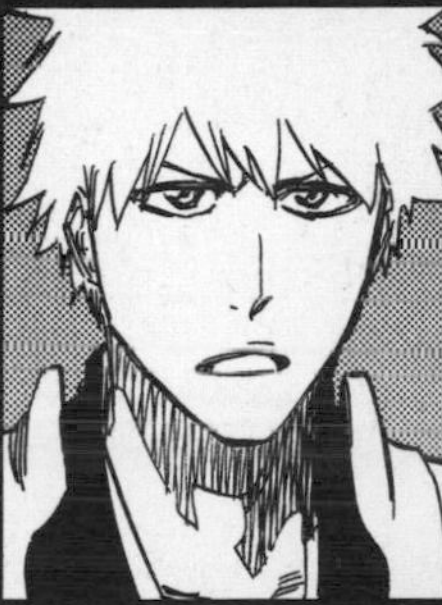

ICHIGO
KUROSAKI

plot

Ichigo Kurosaki meets Soul Reaper Rukia Kuchiki and ends up helping her eradicate Hollows. After developing his powers as a Soul Reaper, Ichigo befriends many humans and Soul Reapers and grows as a person...

Yhwach leads his Quincy army, the Stern Ritters, in an invasion of the Soul Society. The Court Guards stand in their way, but Kenpachi soon finds himself in trouble. Ichigo then returns from Reiokyu to save him, but Yhwach uses that opportunity to make his move. With Uryu at his side, he begins his grand attack on the royal palace. Meanwhile, Gigi and her zombie army face off against Mayuri's revived Arrancars. Gigi then brings out her newest zombie...

BLEACH

YHWACH

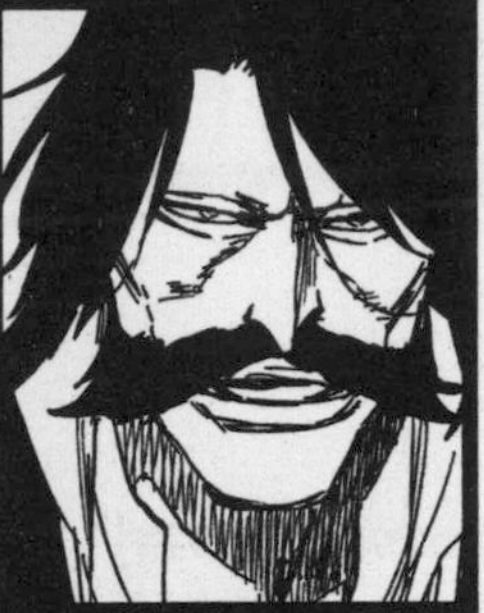

ユーハバッハ

修多羅千手丸

シュタラセンジュマル

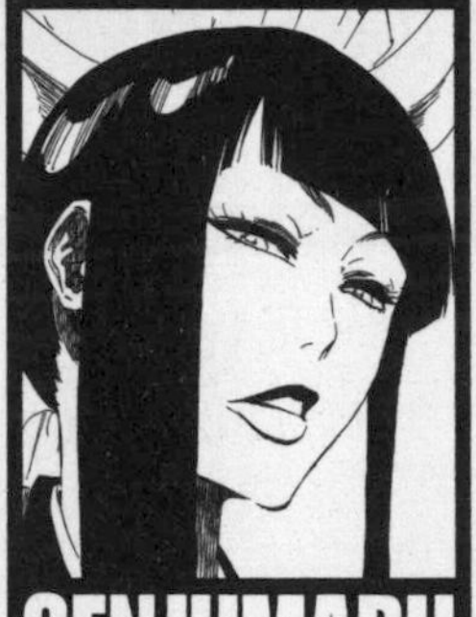

SENJUMARU SHUTARA

OH-ETSU NIMAIYA

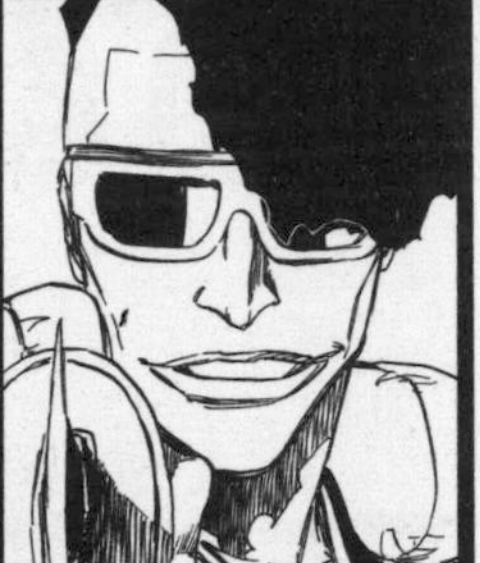

二枚屋王悦

ニマイヤオウエツ

STORIES

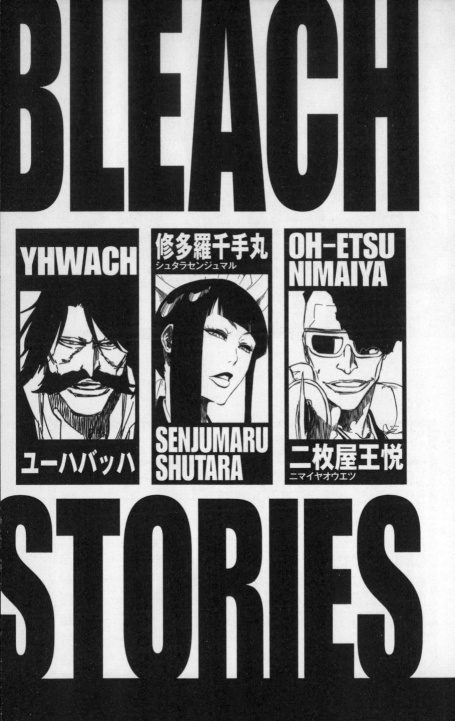

BLEACH 66

SORRY I AM STRONG

CONTENTS

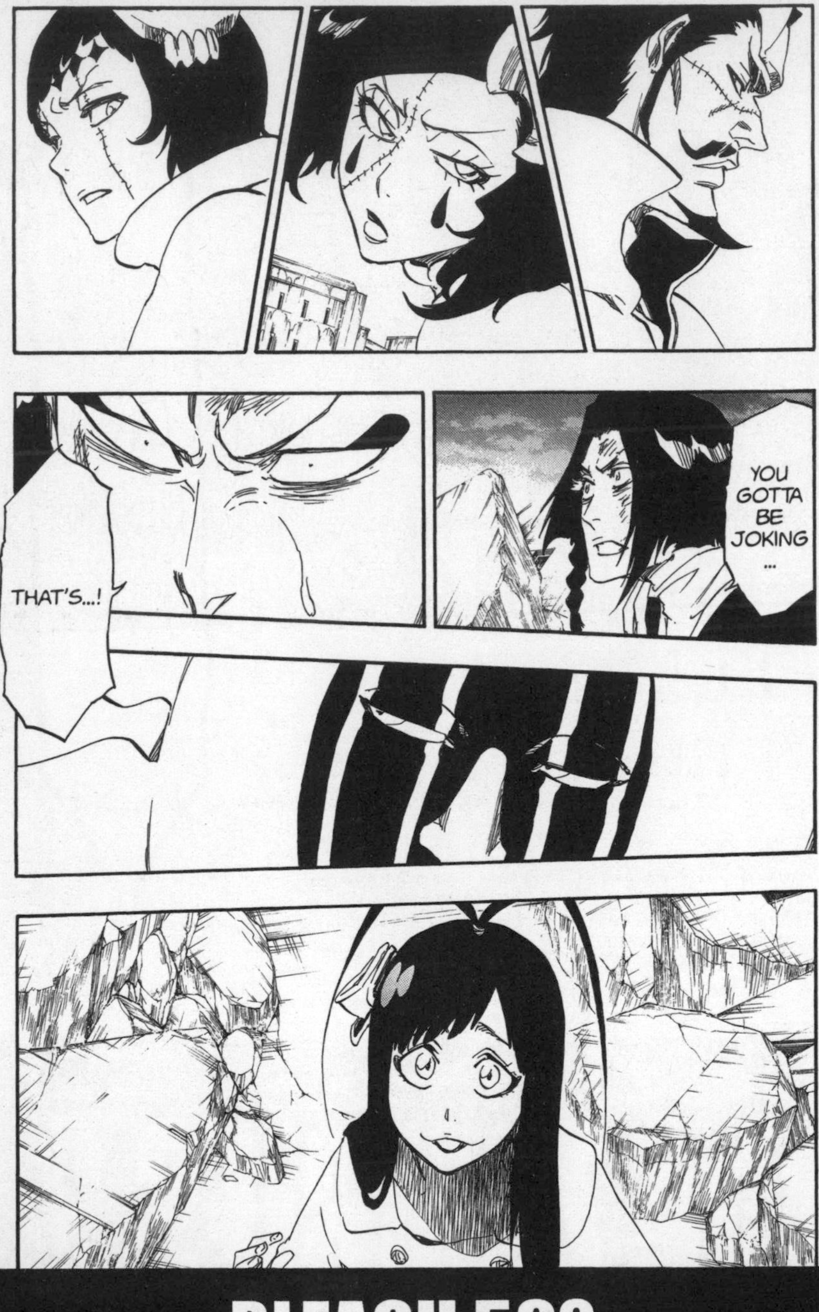
YOU GOTTA BE JOKING ...
THAT'S...!

BLEACH 592.

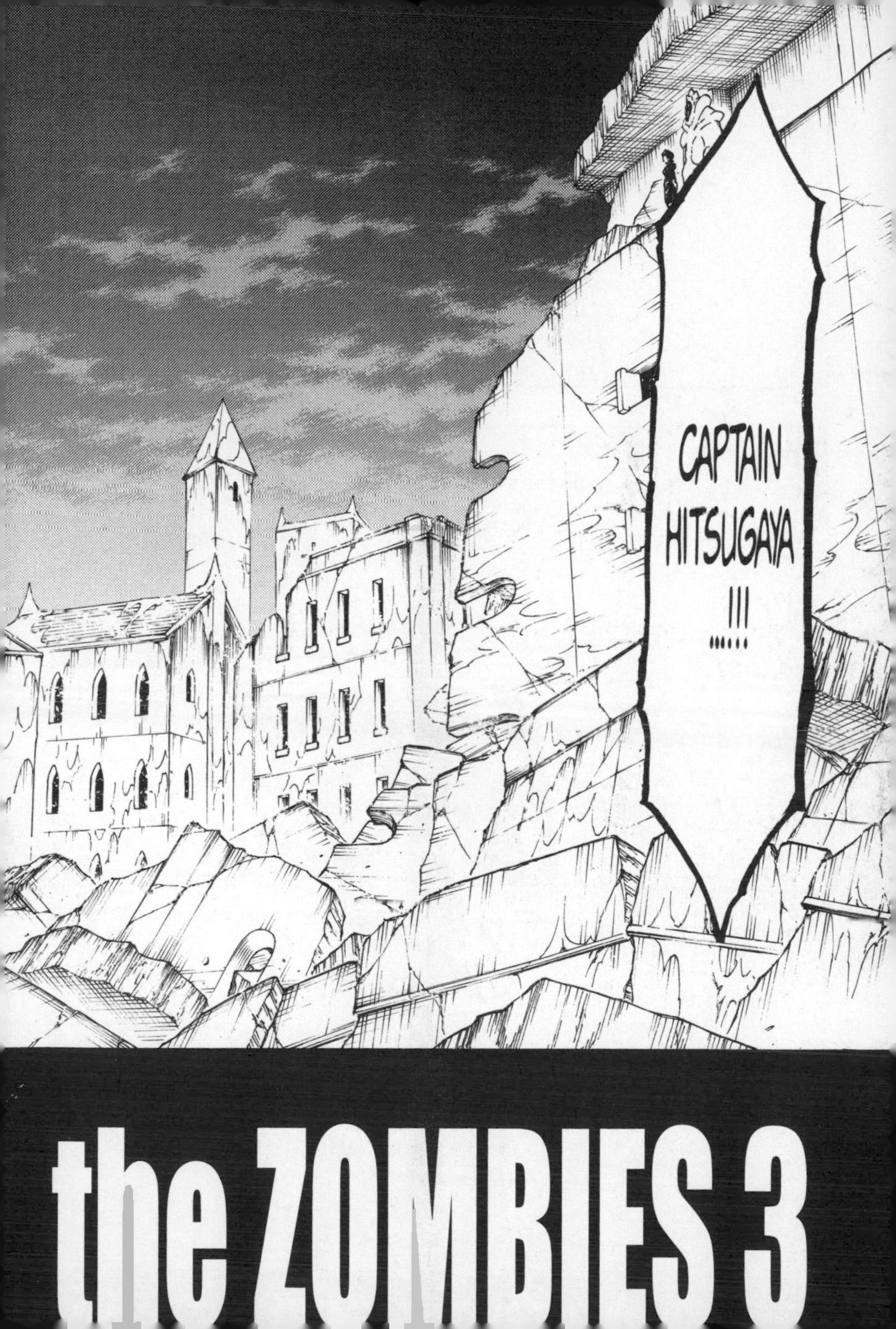
CAPTAIN HITSUGAYA ......!!!

the ZOMBIES 3

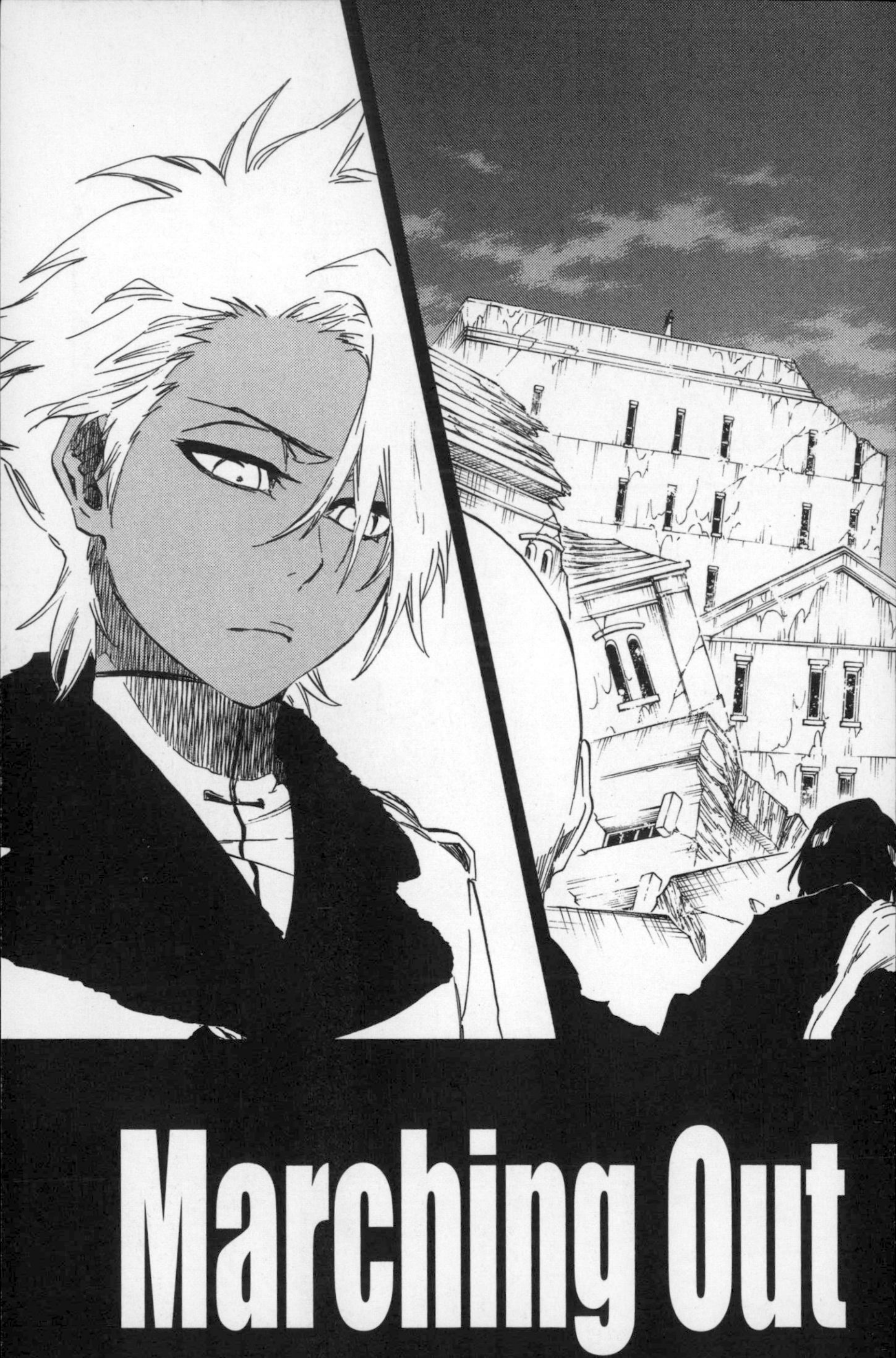

Marching Out

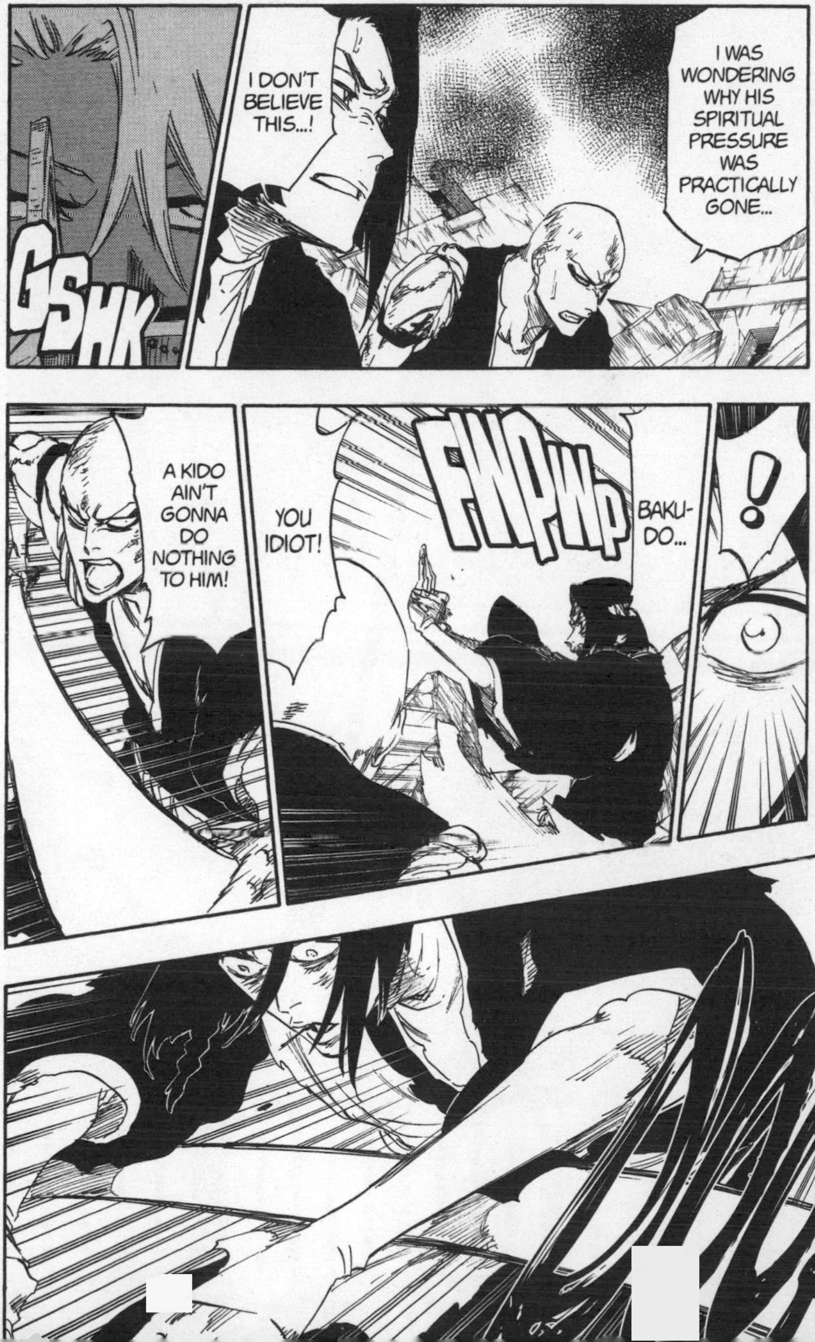
I WAS WONDERING WHY HIS SPIRITUAL PRESSURE WAS PRACTICALLY GONE...
I DON'T BELIEVE THIS...!
GSHK
!
BAKU-DO...
YOU IDIOT!
A KIDO AIN'T GONNA DO NOTHING TO HIM!

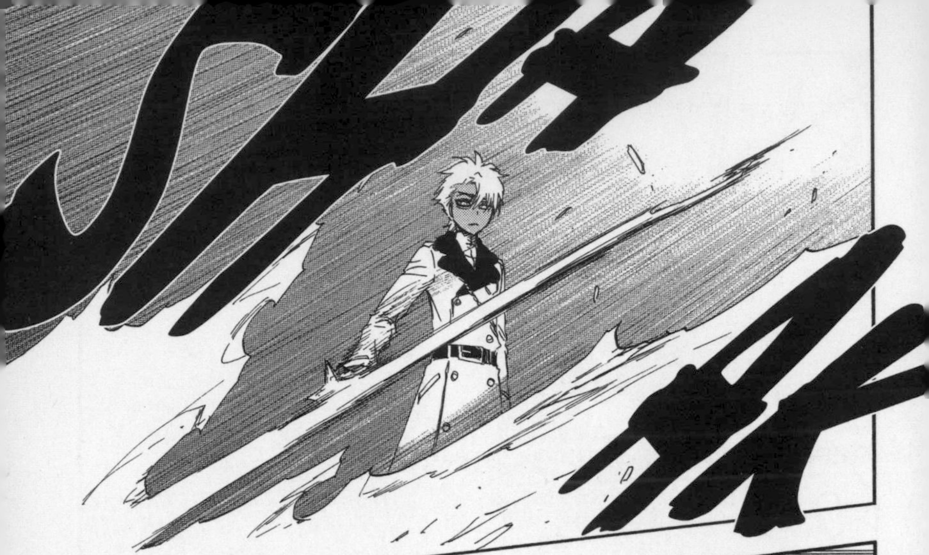

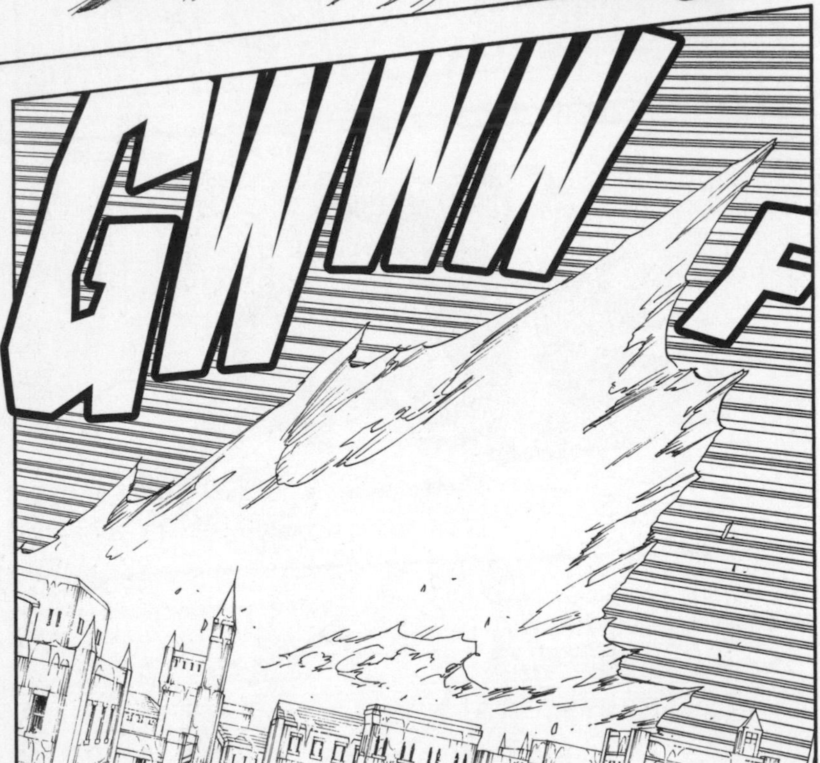
GWNNF

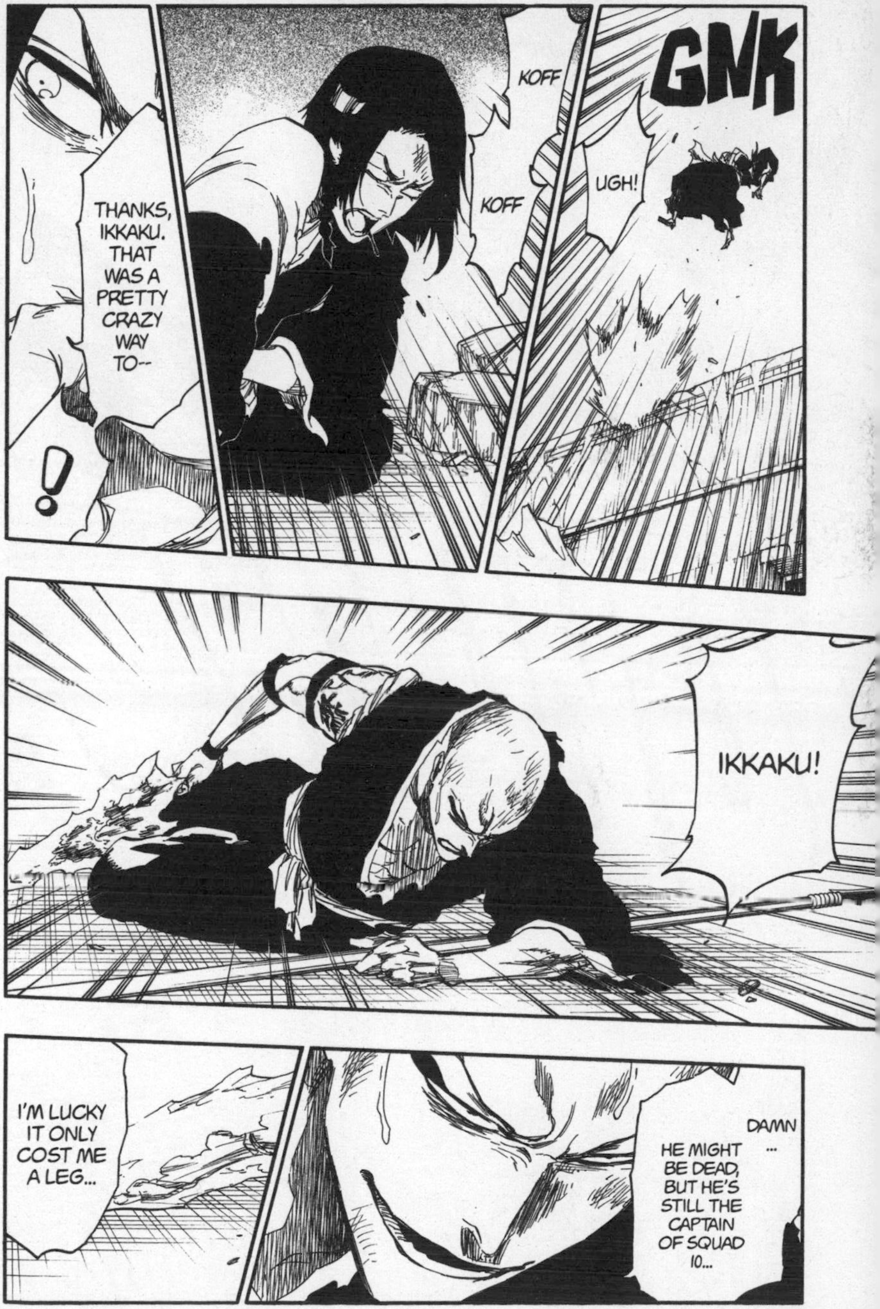
GNK
UGH!
KOFF
KOFF
THANKS, IKKAKU. THAT WAS A PRETTY CRAZY WAY TO--
!
IKKAKU!
DAMN...
HE MIGHT BE DEAD, BUT HE'S STILL THE CAPTAIN OF SQUAD 10...
I'M LUCKY IT ONLY COST ME A LEG...

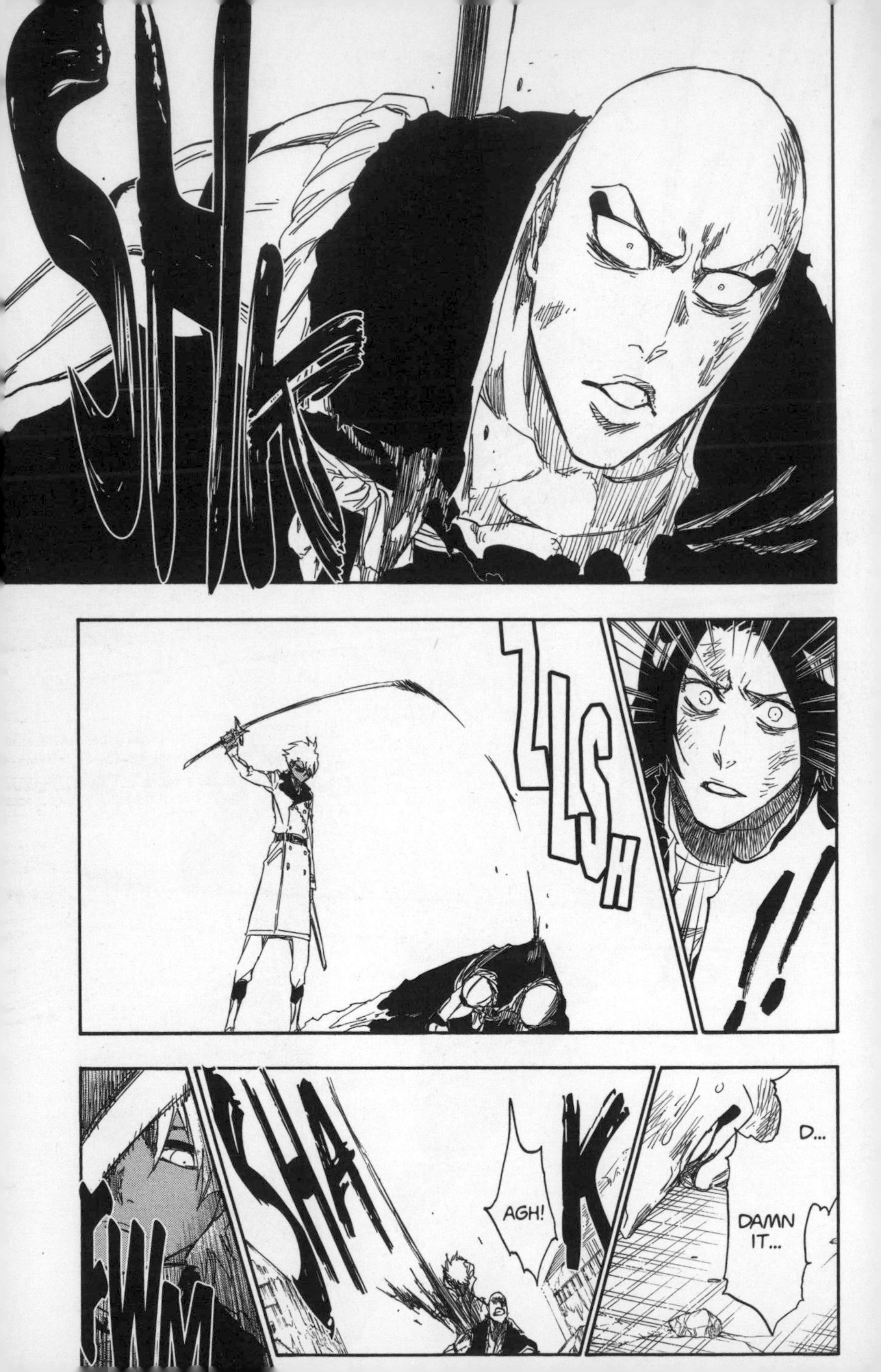
SHUK
!!
ZLSH
D...
DAMN IT...
AGH!

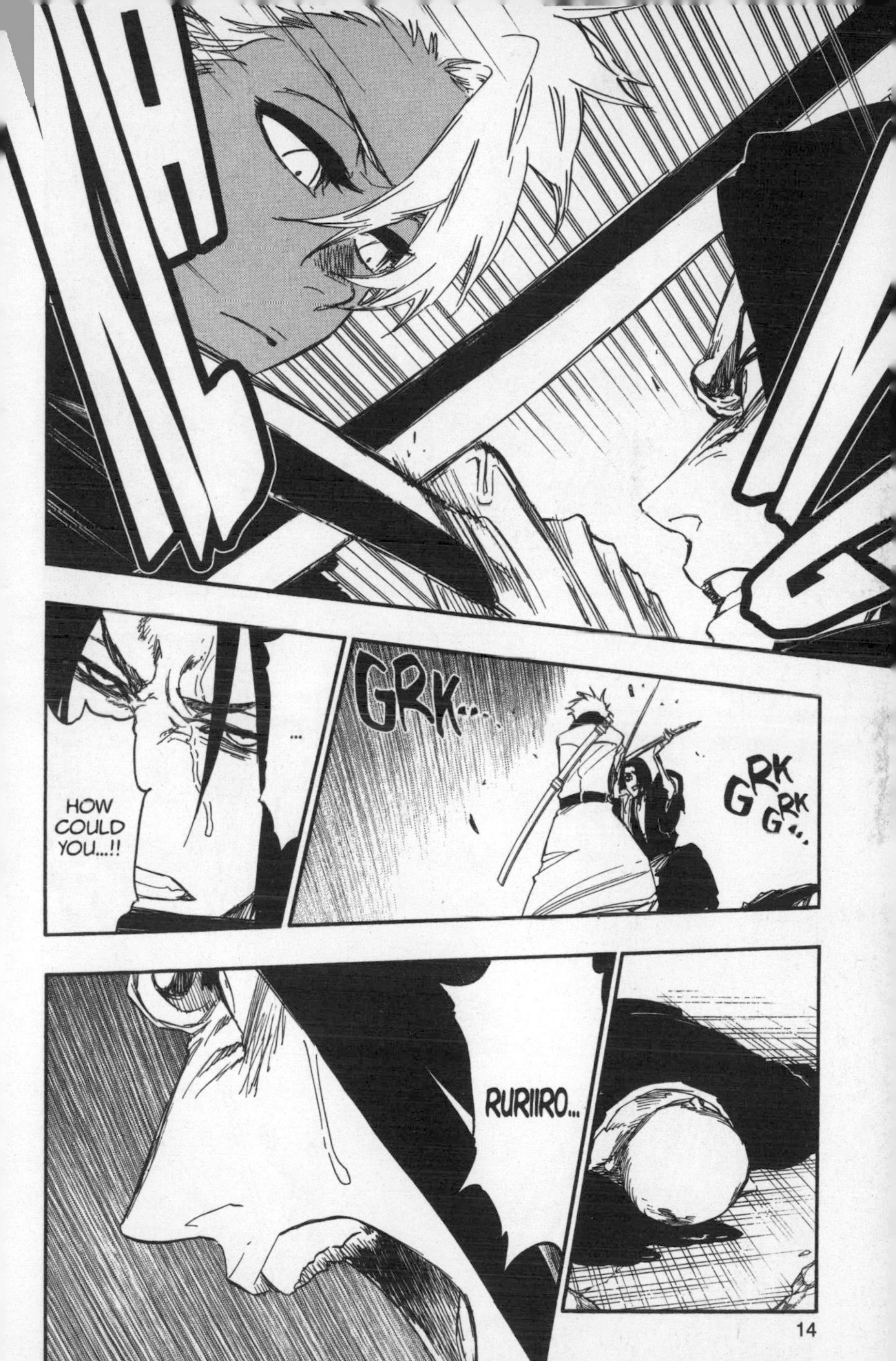
GRK GRK...
GRK...
...
HOW COULD YOU...!!
RURIIRO...

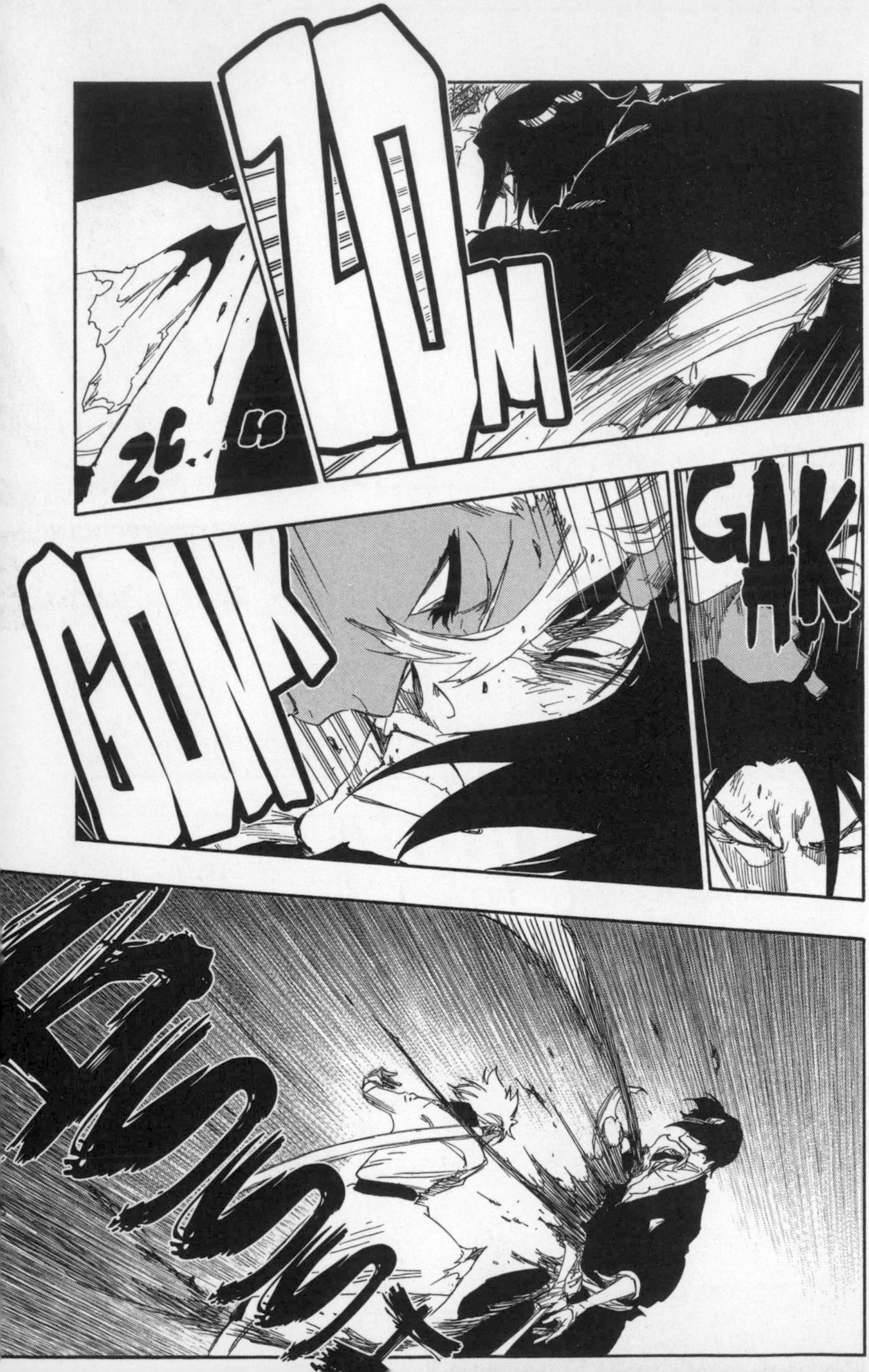
ZOOM
GAK
GDUK

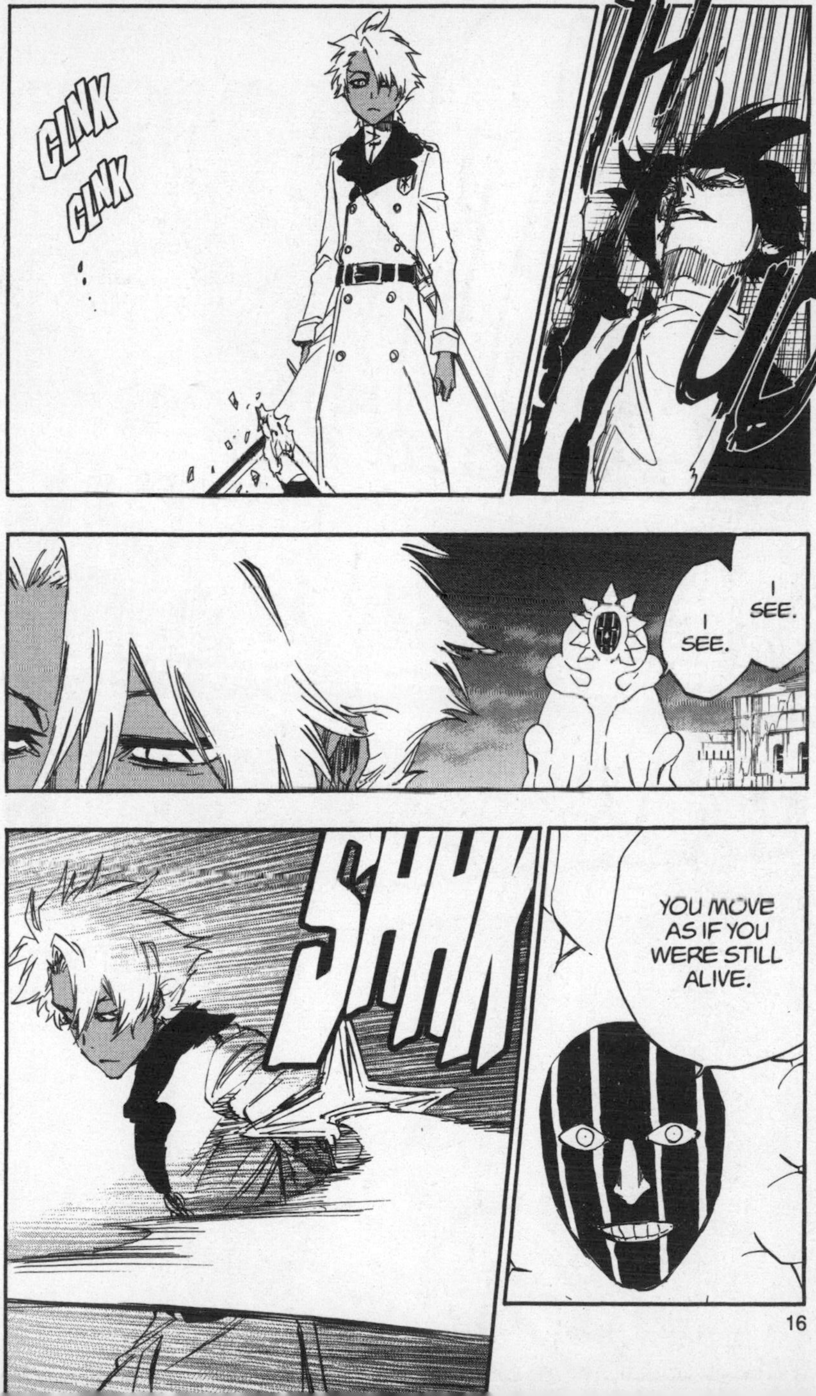
THUD
CLINK CLINK
I SEE. I SEE.
YOU MOVE AS IF YOU WERE STILL ALIVE.
SHHK

READ THIS WAY

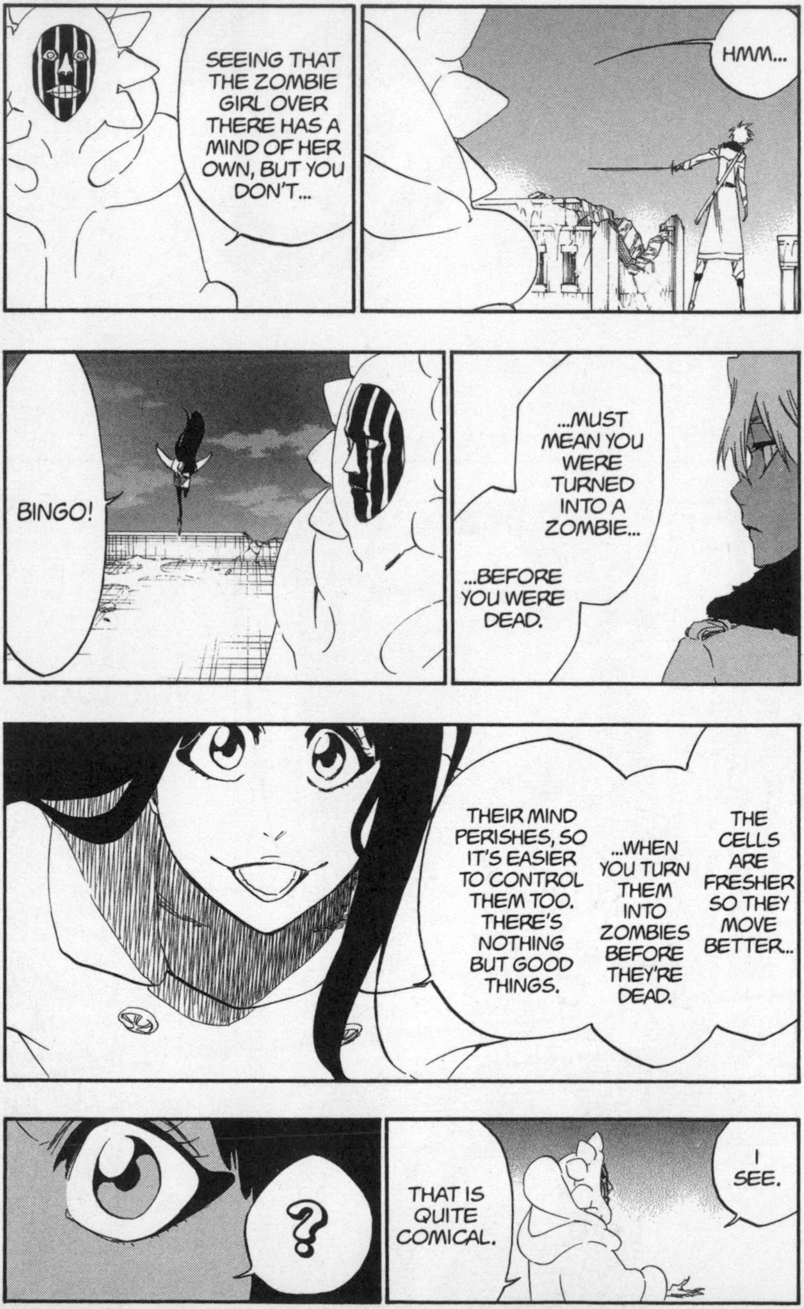
HMM...
SEEING THAT THE ZOMBIE GIRL OVER THERE HAS A MIND OF HER OWN, BUT YOU DON'T...
...MUST MEAN YOU WERE TURNED INTO A ZOMBIE...
...BEFORE YOU WERE DEAD.
BINGO!
THE CELLS ARE FRESHER SO THEY MOVE BETTER...
...WHEN YOU TURN THEM INTO ZOMBIES BEFORE THEY'RE DEAD.
THEIR MIND PERISHES, SO IT'S EASIER TO CONTROL THEM TOO. THERE'S NOTHING BUT GOOD THINGS.
I SEE.
THAT IS QUITE COMICAL.
?

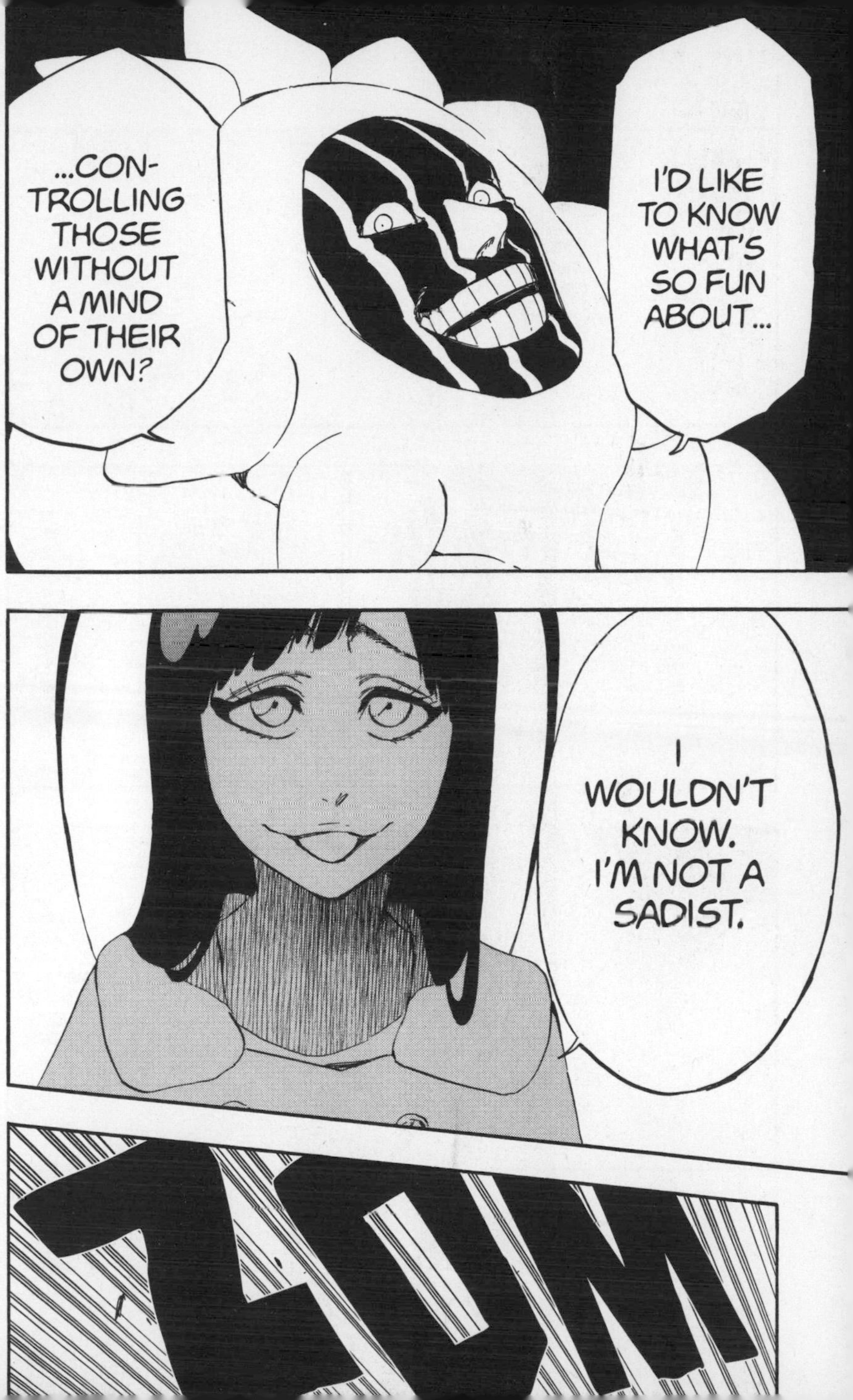
I'D LIKE TO KNOW WHAT'S SO FUN ABOUT...
...CON-TROLLING THOSE WITHOUT A MIND OF THEIR OWN?
I WOULDN'T KNOW. I'M NOT A SADIST.

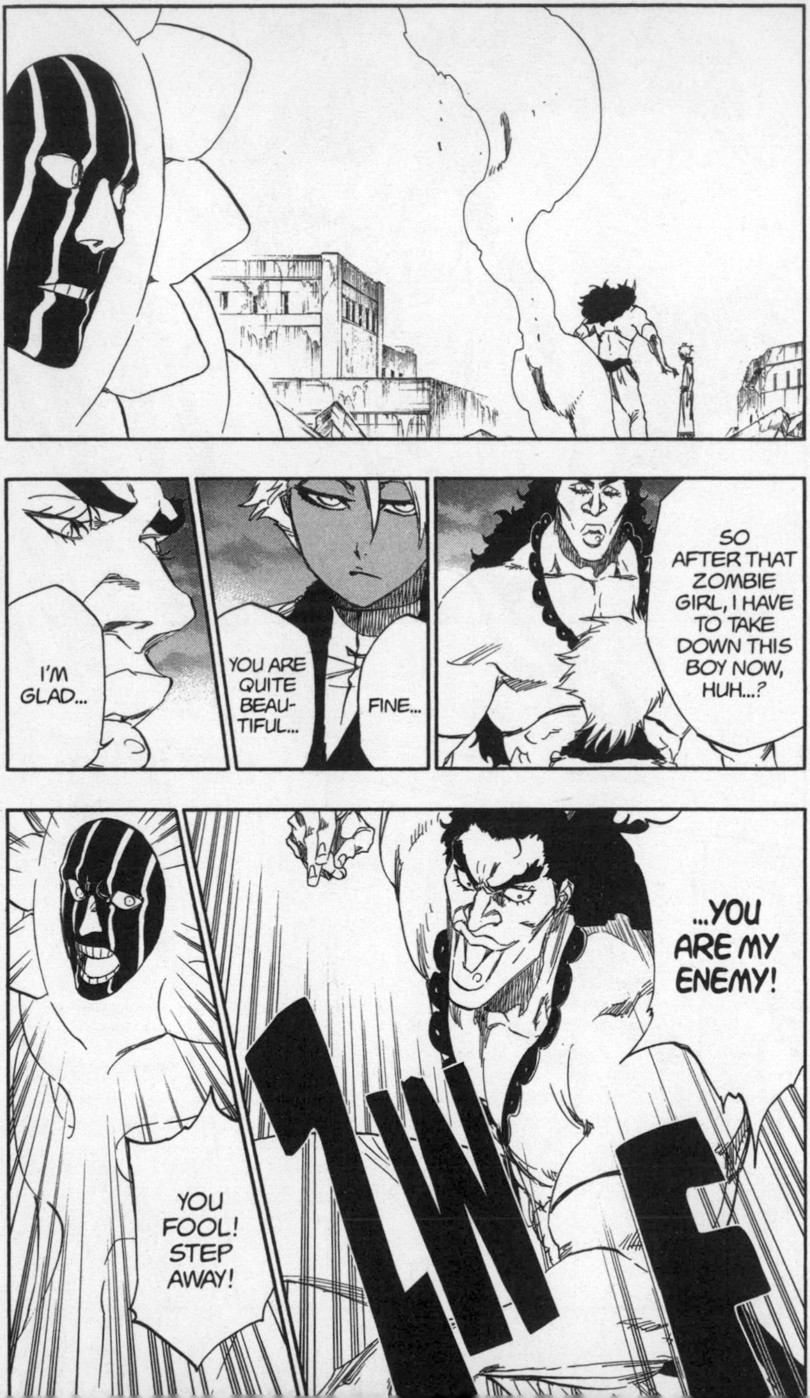
SO AFTER THAT ZOMBIE GIRL, I HAVE TO TAKE DOWN THIS BOY NOW, HUH...?
FINE...
YOU ARE QUITE BEAU-TIFUL...
I'M GLAD...
...YOU ARE MY ENEMY!
ZWF
YOU FOOL! STEP AWAY!

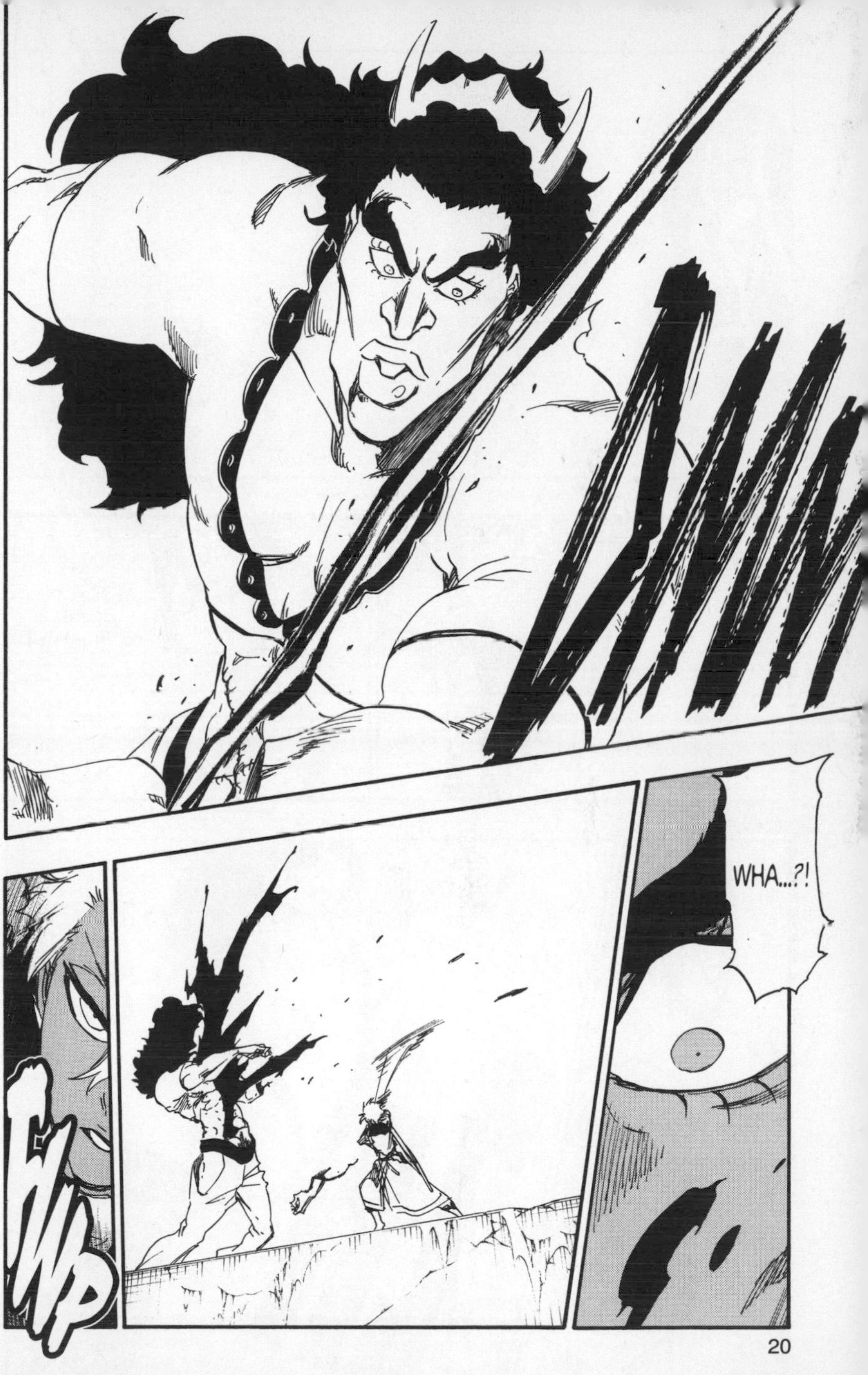
WHA...?!

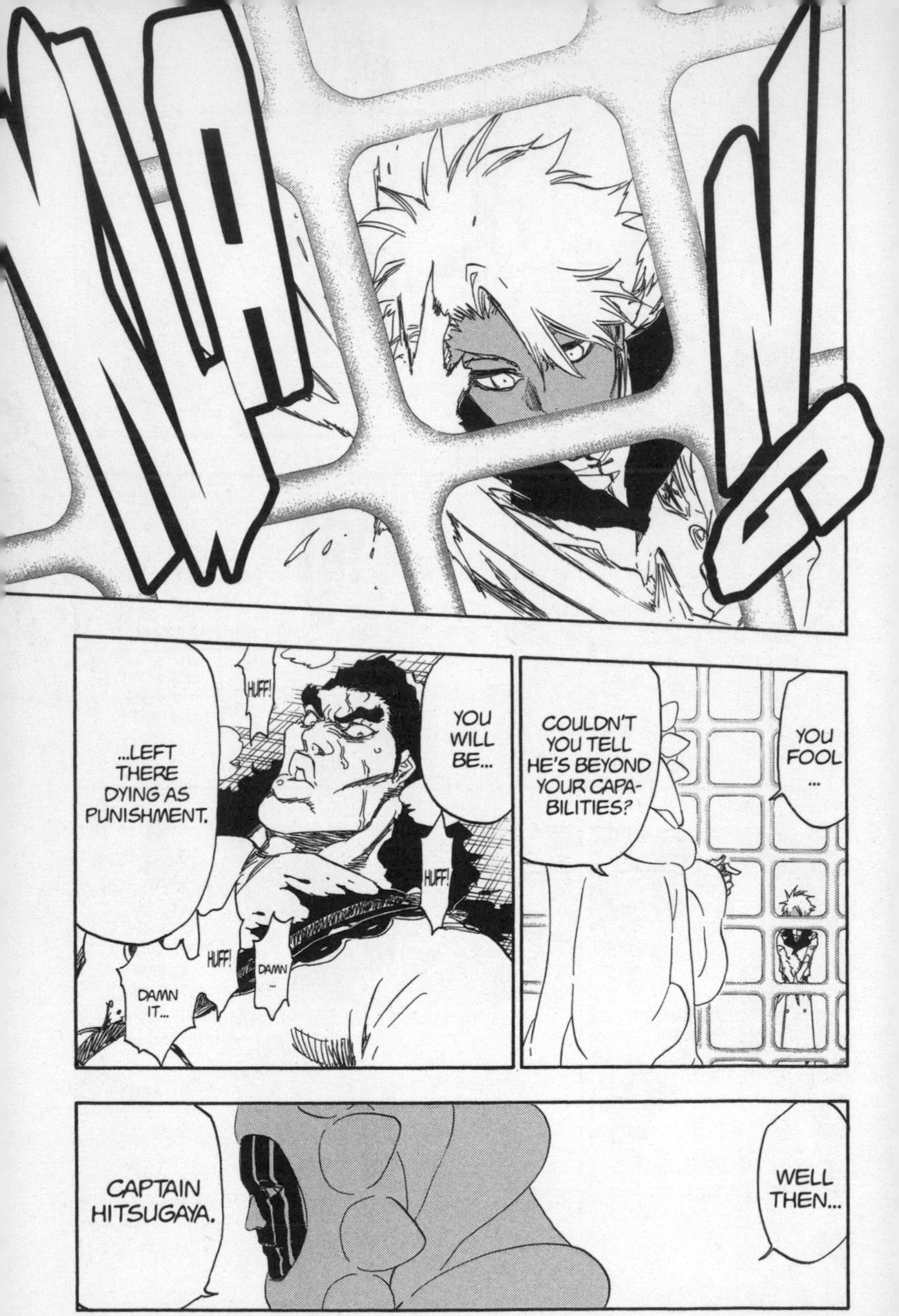
YOU FOOL ...
COULDN'T YOU TELL HE'S BEYOND YOUR CAPA-BILITIES?
YOU WILL BE...
...LEFT THERE DYING AS PUNISHMENT.
HUFF!
HUFF!
HUFF!
DAMN ...
DAMN IT...
WELL THEN...
CAPTAIN HITSUGAYA.

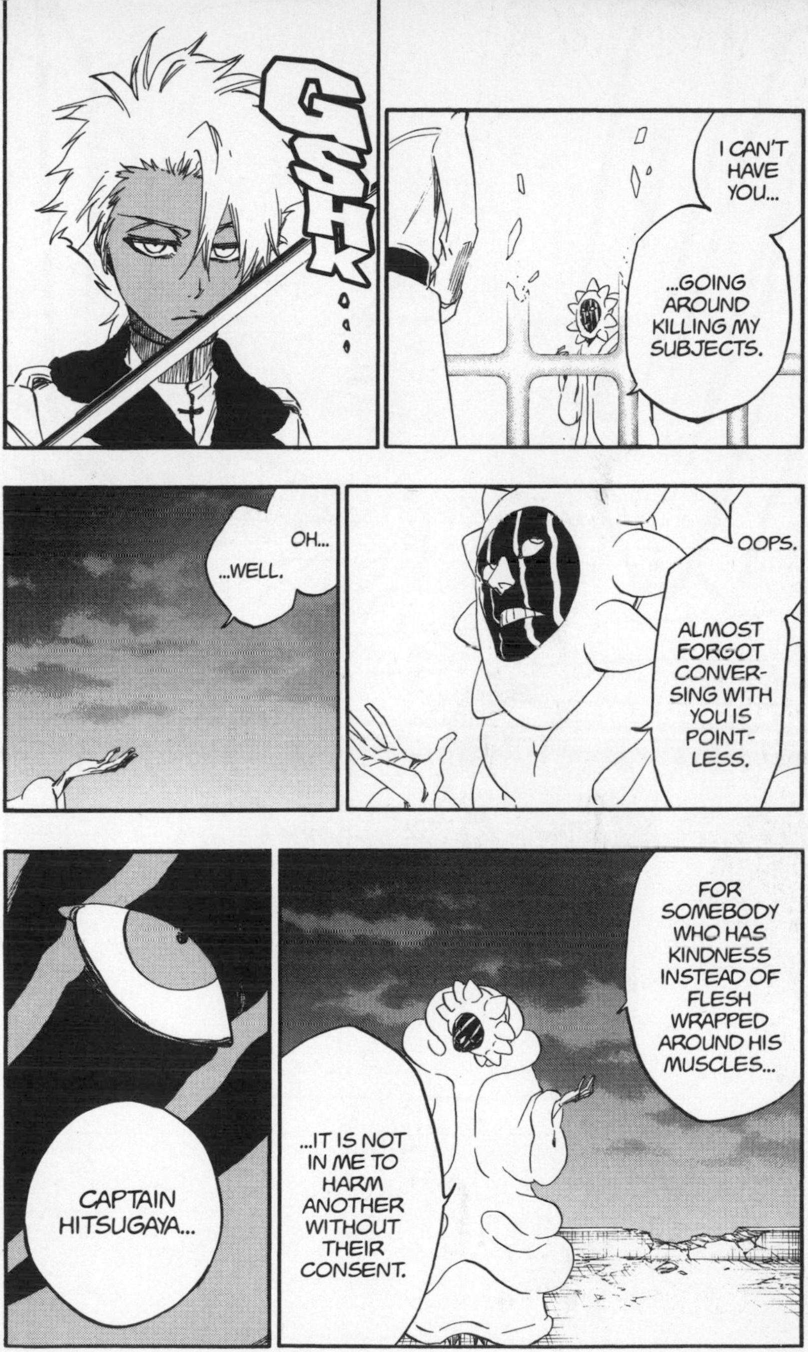
I CAN'T HAVE YOU...
...GOING AROUND KILLING MY SUBJECTS.
GSHK
OOPS.
ALMOST FORGOT CONVER-SING WITH YOU IS POINT-LESS.
OH...
...WELL.
FOR SOMEBODY WHO HAS KINDNESS INSTEAD OF FLESH WRAPPED AROUND HIS MUSCLES...
...IT IS NOT IN ME TO HARM ANOTHER WITHOUT THEIR CONSENT.
CAPTAIN HITSUGAYA...

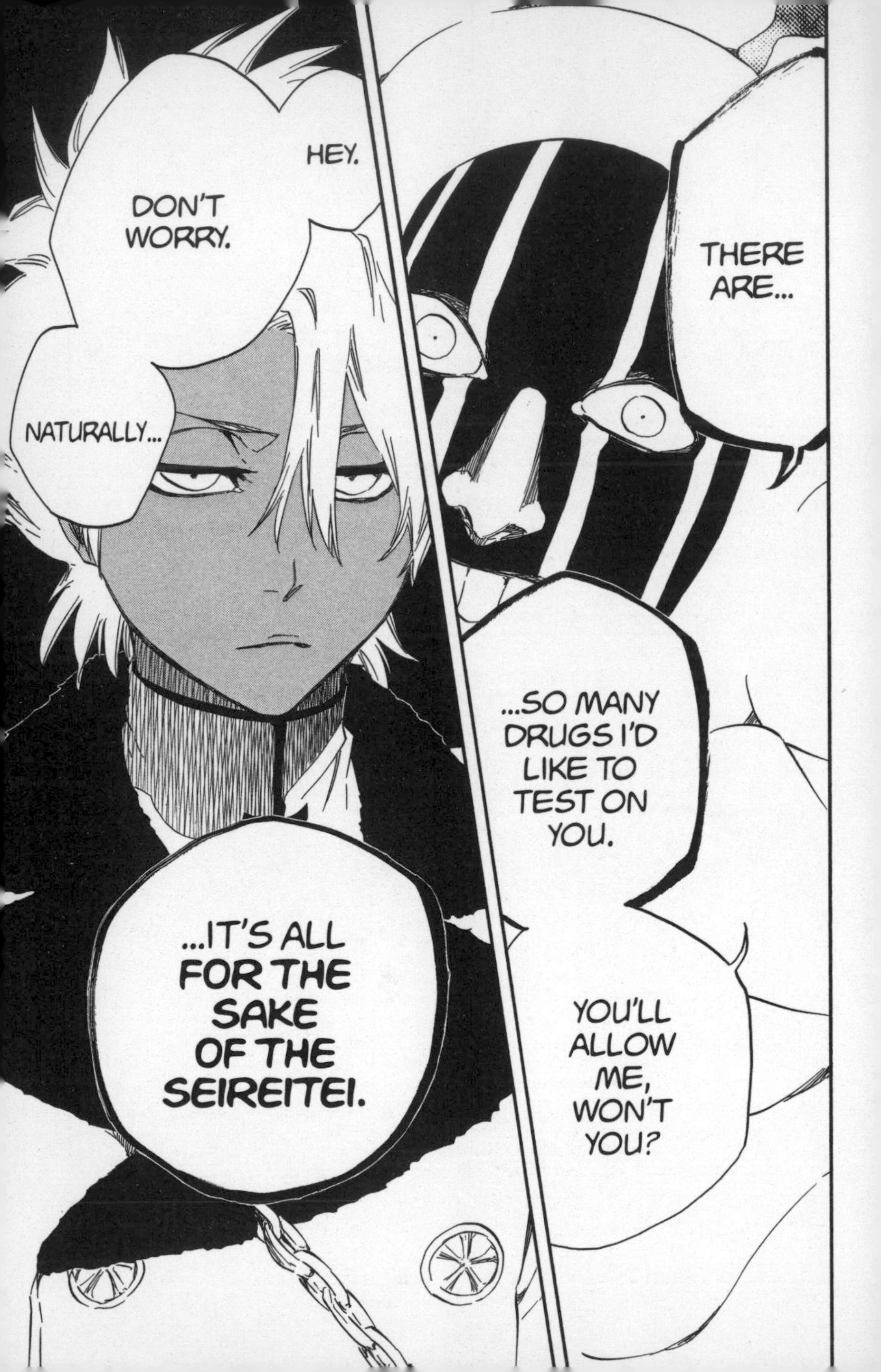
THERE ARE...
...SO MANY DRUGS I'D LIKE TO TEST ON YOU.
YOU'LL ALLOW ME, WON'T YOU?
HEY.
DON'T WORRY.
NATURALLY...
...IT'S ALL FOR THE SAKE OF THE SEIREITEI.

NOW THAT I
THINK ABOUT IT...
DON'T I LOOK SEXY
WHEN I'M INJURED
AND BREATHING
SO HEAVILY...?

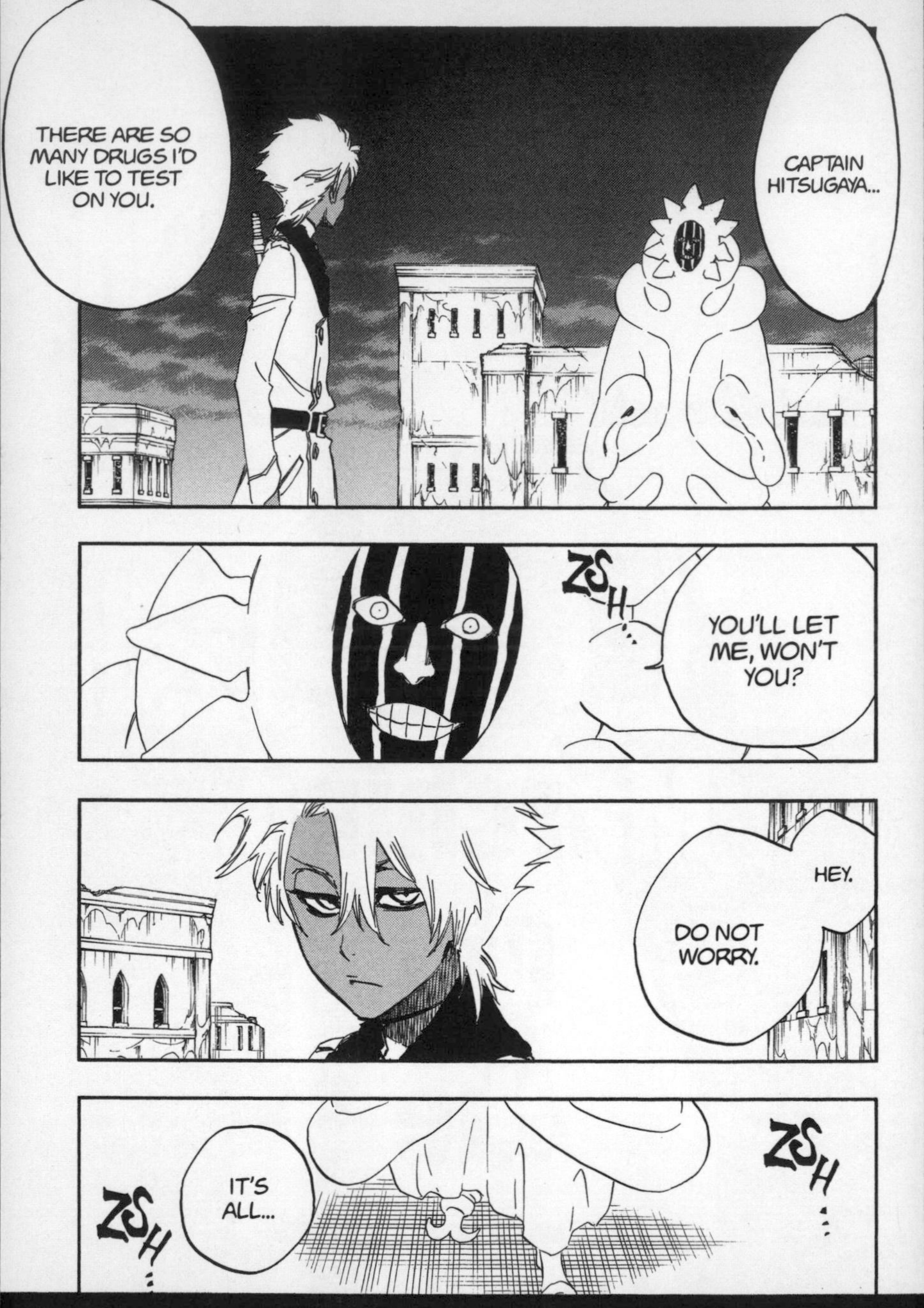
CAPTAIN HITSUGAYA...
THERE ARE SO MANY DRUGS I'D LIKE TO TEST ON YOU.
ZSH...
YOU'LL LET ME, WON'T YOU?
HEY.
DO NOT WORRY.
ZSH...
IT'S ALL...
ZSH...

BLEACH 593.

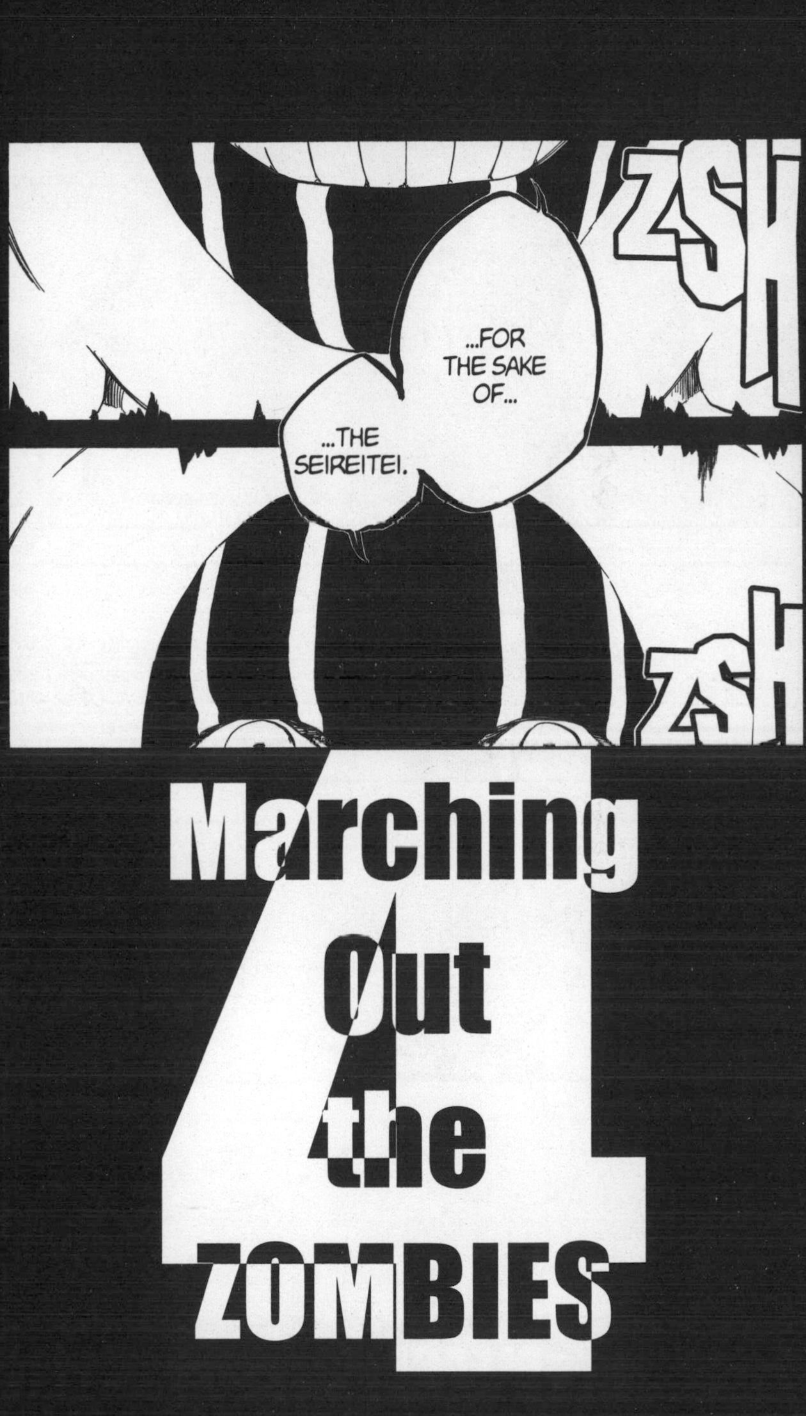
ZSH
...FOR THE SAKE OF...
...THE SEIREITEI.
ZSH

4 Marching Out the ZOMBIES

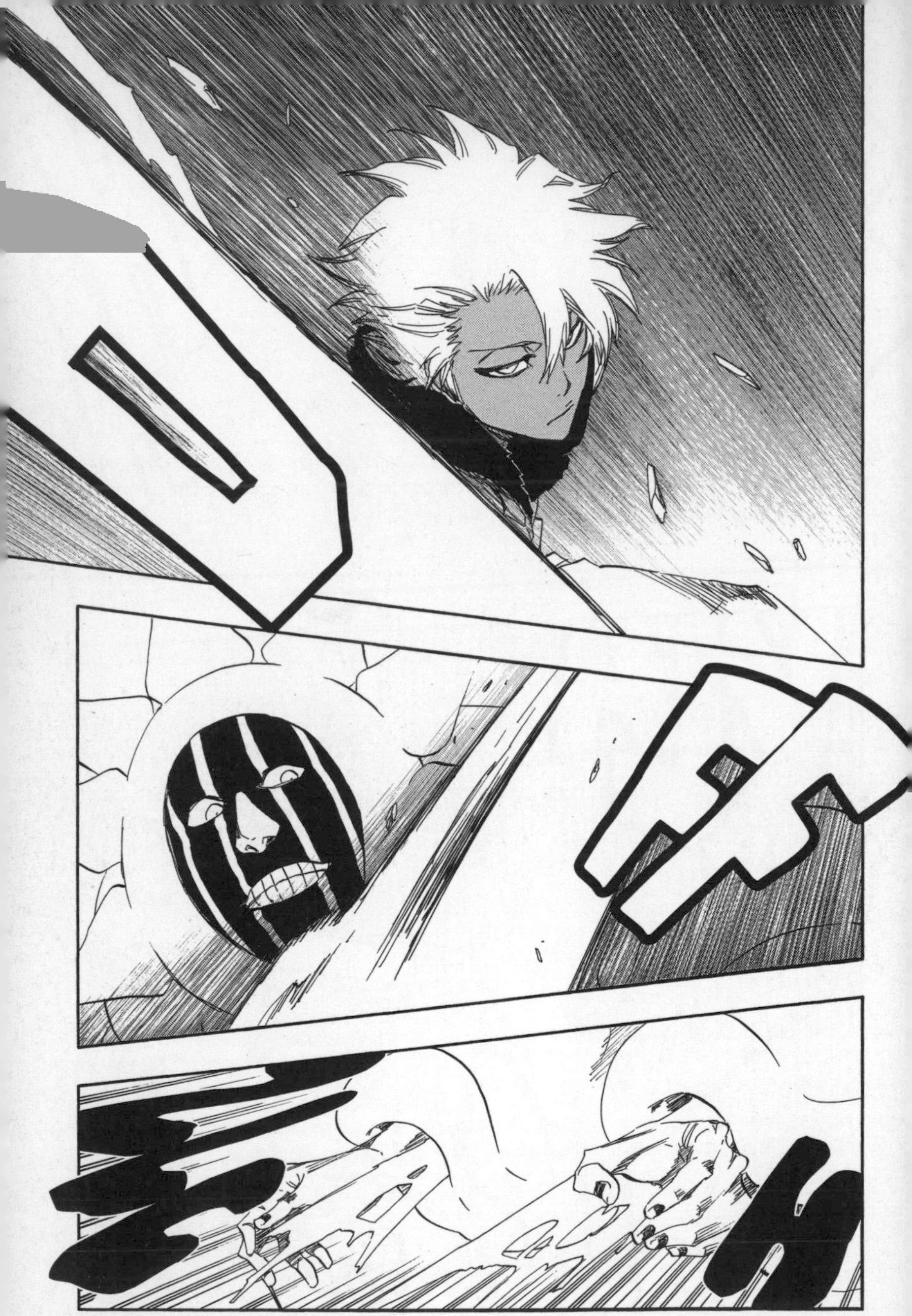

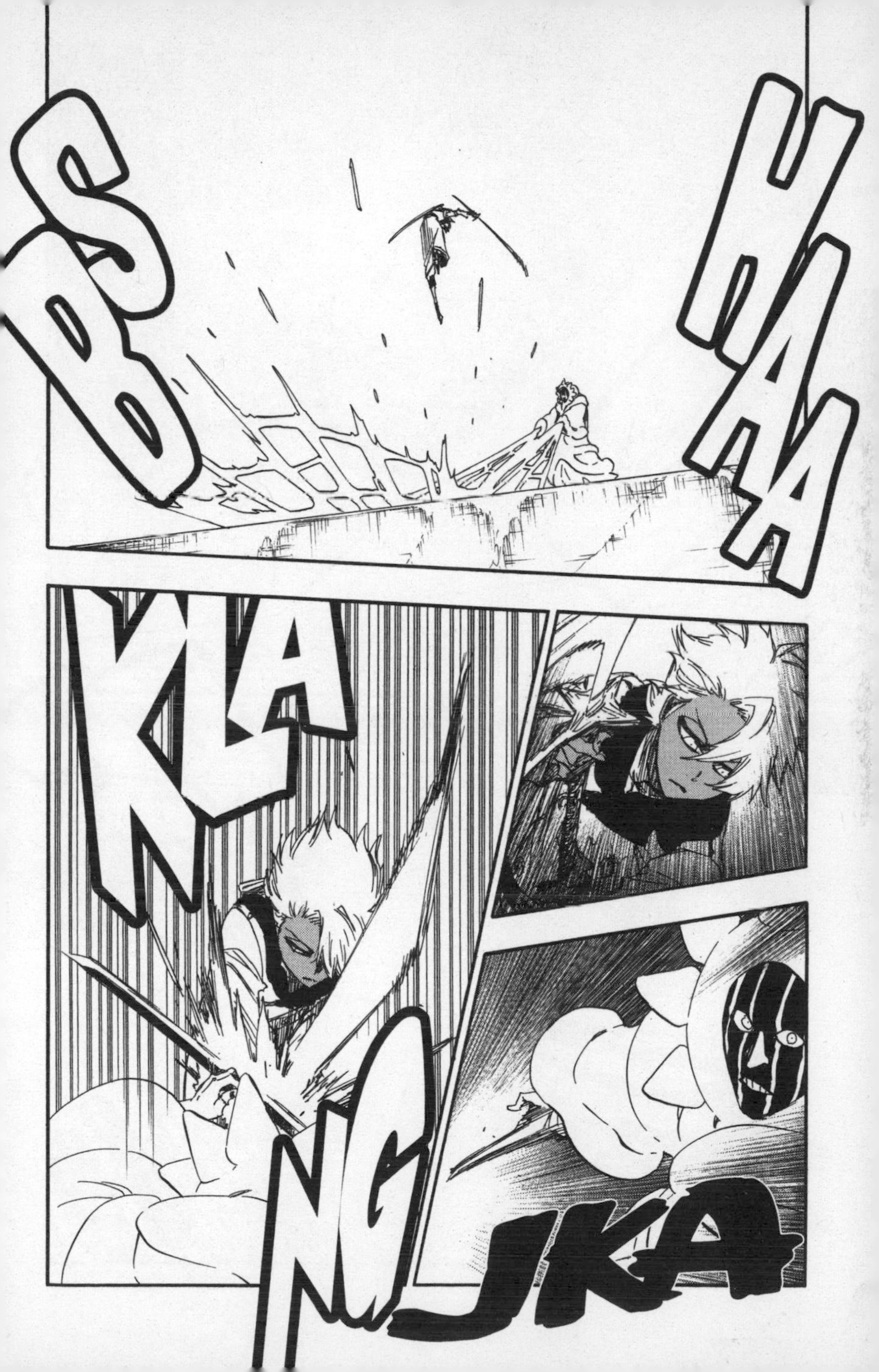
BSHAA
JKA
KLANG

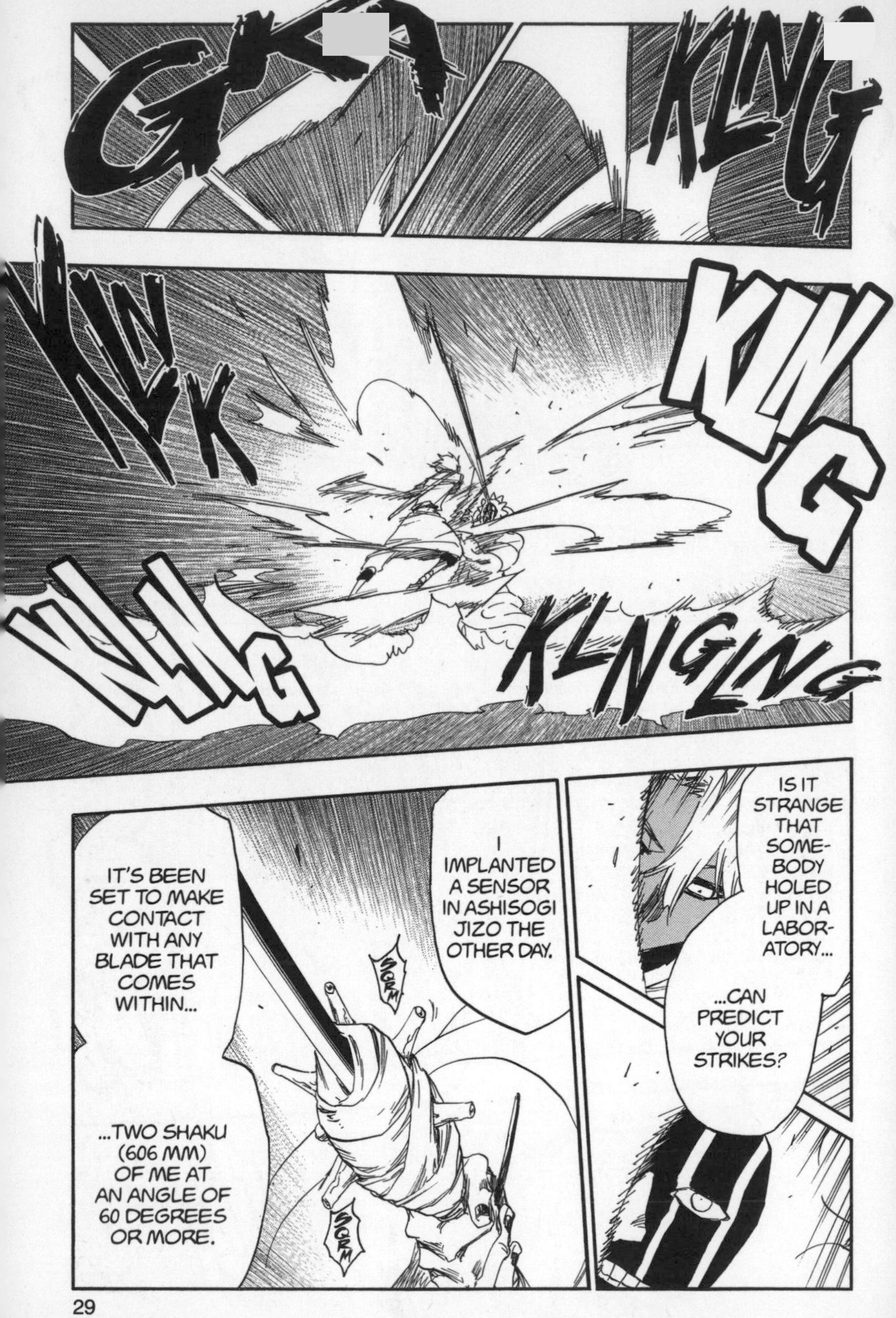
KLING
GKA
KLING
KLINK
KLNGLING
VWING
IS IT STRANGE THAT SOME-BODY HOLED UP IN A LABOR-ATORY...
...CAN PREDICT YOUR STRIKES?
I IMPLANTED A SENSOR IN ASHISOGI JIZO THE OTHER DAY.
IT'S BEEN SET TO MAKE CONTACT WITH ANY BLADE THAT COMES WITHIN...
SGRM
SGRM
...TWO SHAKU (606 MM) OF ME AT AN ANGLE OF 60 DEGREES OR MORE.

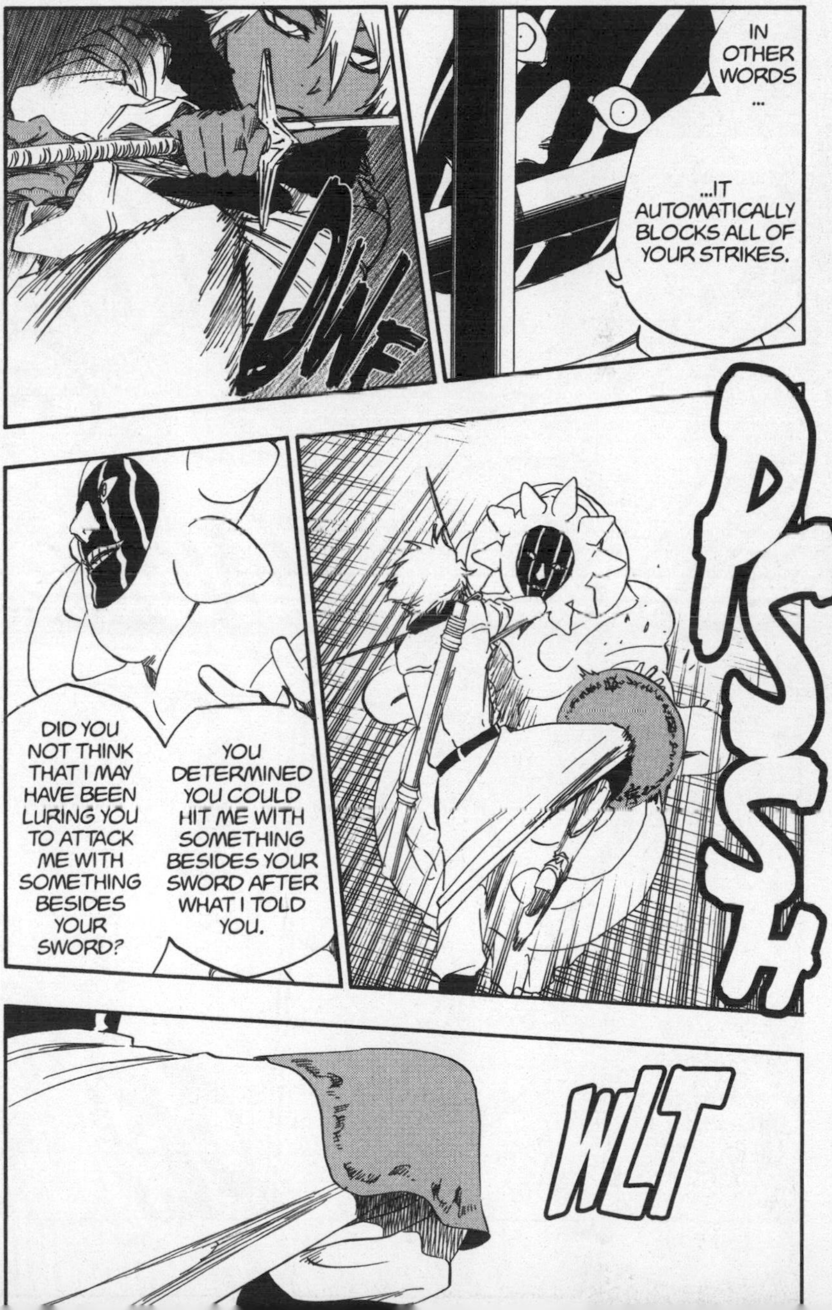
IN OTHER WORDS ...
...IT AUTOMATICALLY BLOCKS ALL OF YOUR STRIKES.
DWF
PSSH
YOU DETERMINED YOU COULD HIT ME WITH SOMETHING BESIDES YOUR SWORD AFTER WHAT I TOLD YOU.
DID YOU NOT THINK THAT I MAY HAVE BEEN LURING YOU TO ATTACK ME WITH SOMETHING BESIDES YOUR SWORD?
WLT

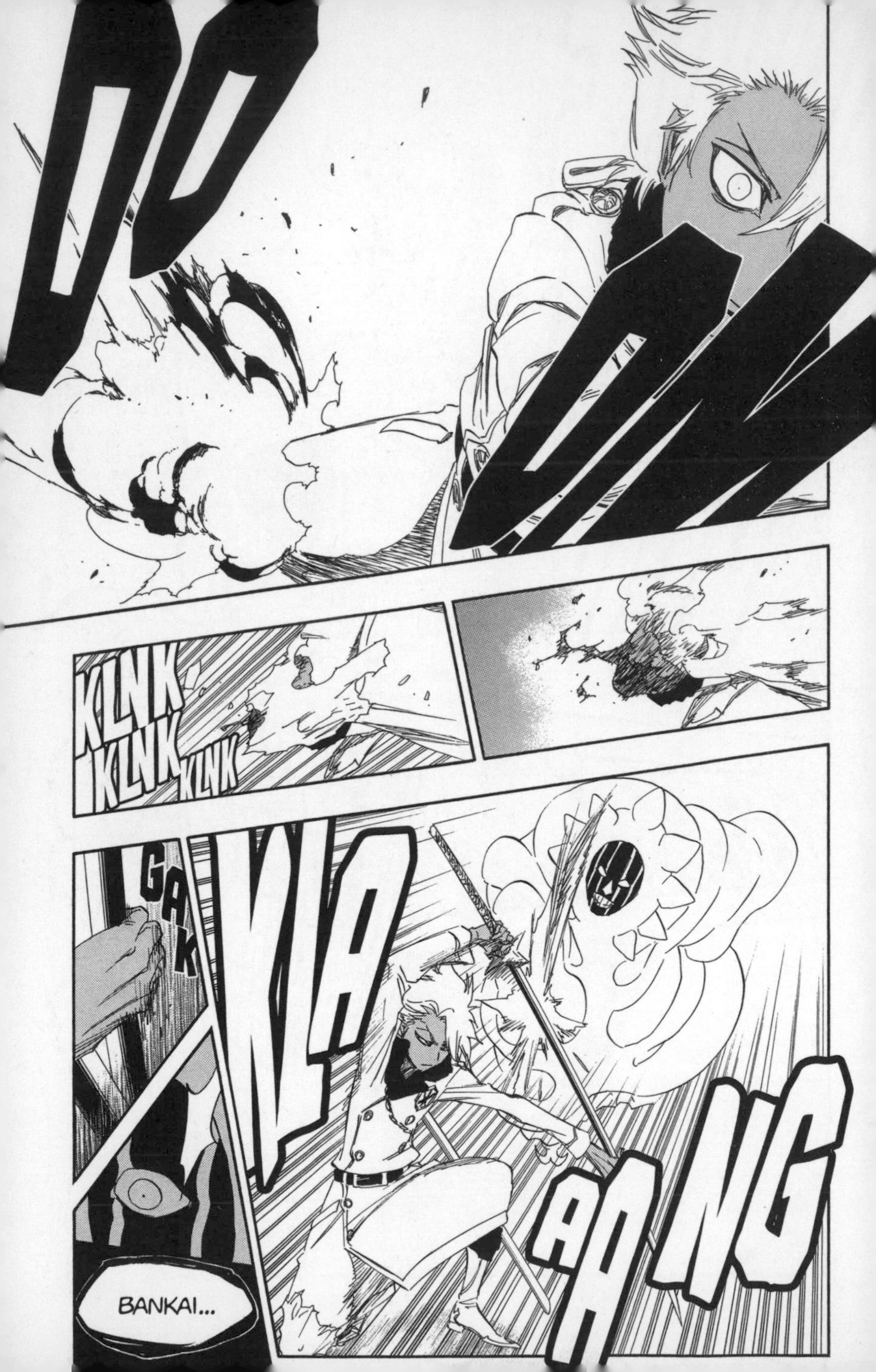
KLNK
KLNK
KLNK
GAK
BANKAI...

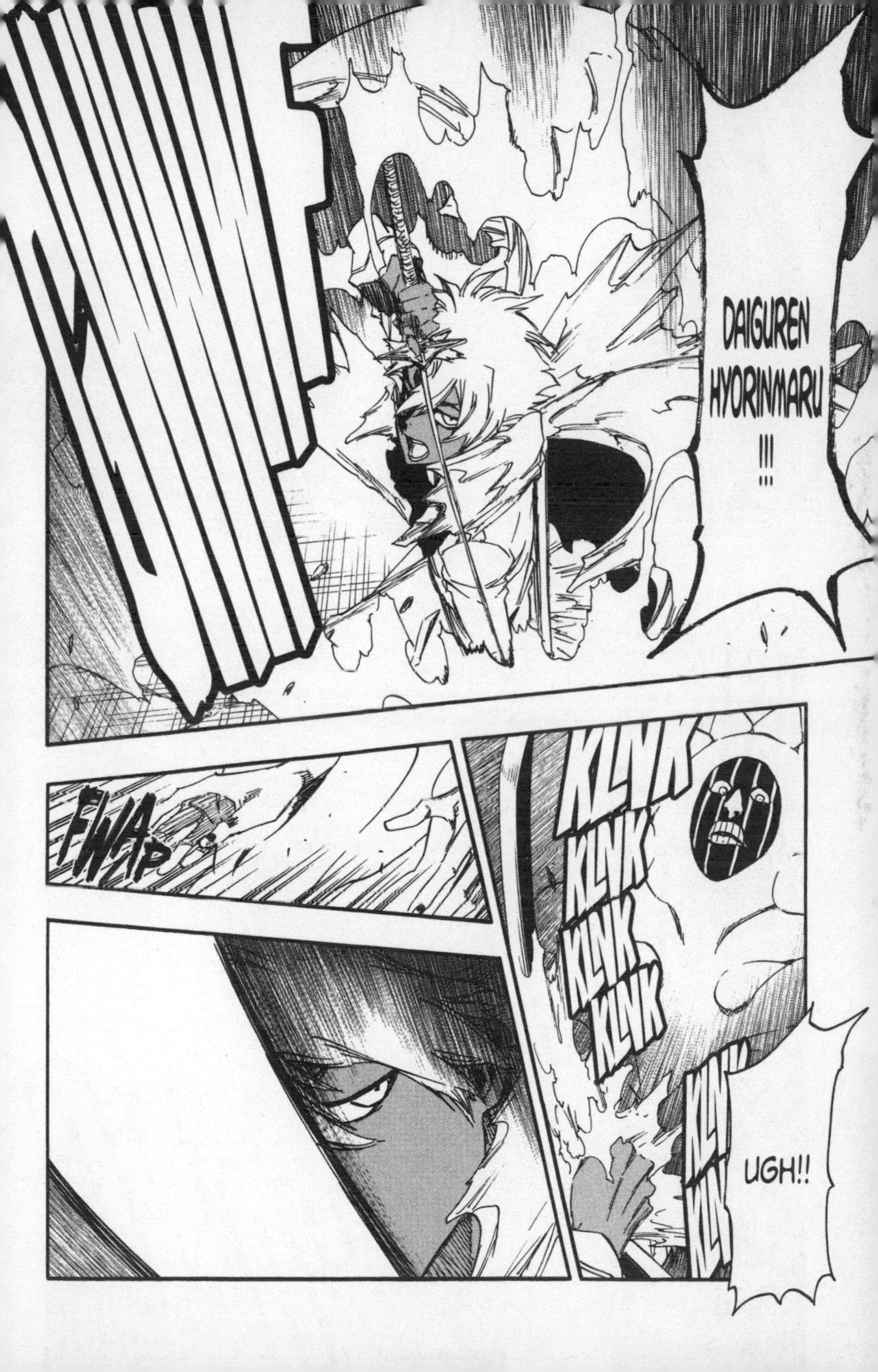
DAIGUREN HYORINMARU !!!
KLNK KLNK KLNK KLNK KLNK
KLNK
UGH!!
FWAP

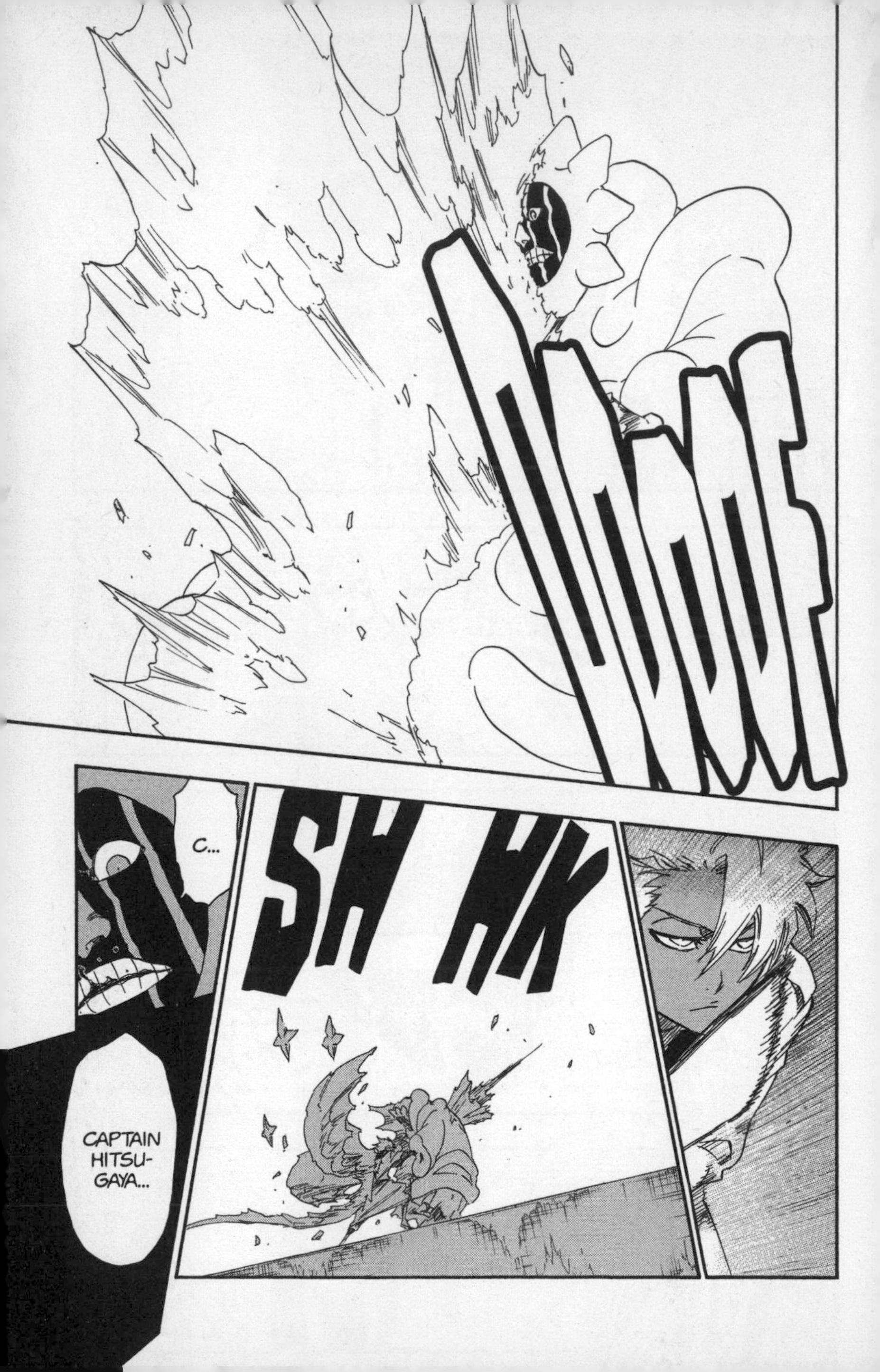
SH HK
C...
CAPTAIN HITSU-GAYA...

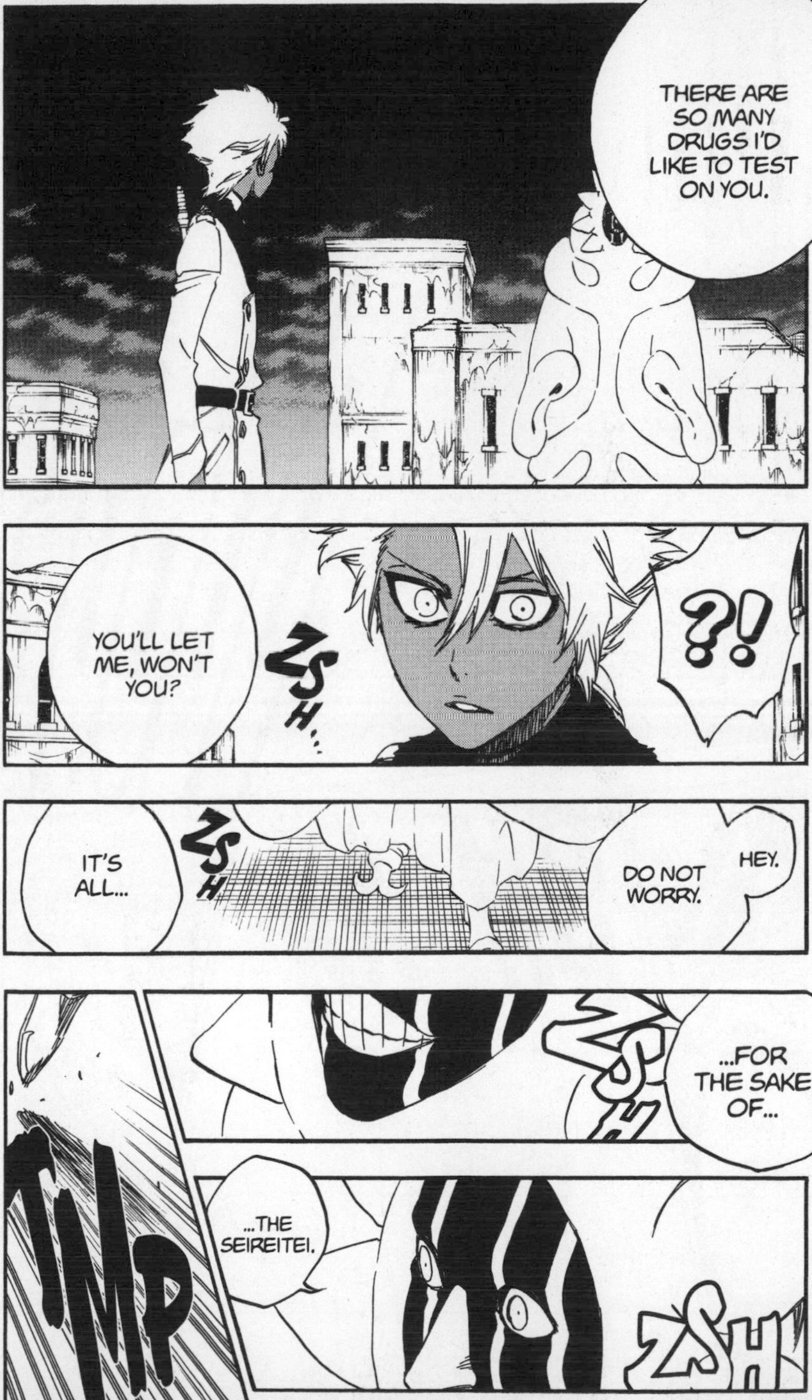
THERE ARE SO MANY DRUGS I'D LIKE TO TEST ON YOU.
?!
ZSH...
YOU'LL LET ME, WON'T YOU?
HEY.
DO NOT WORRY.
ZSH
IT'S ALL...
...FOR THE SAKE OF...
ZSH
ZSH
...THE SEIREITEI.
TMP

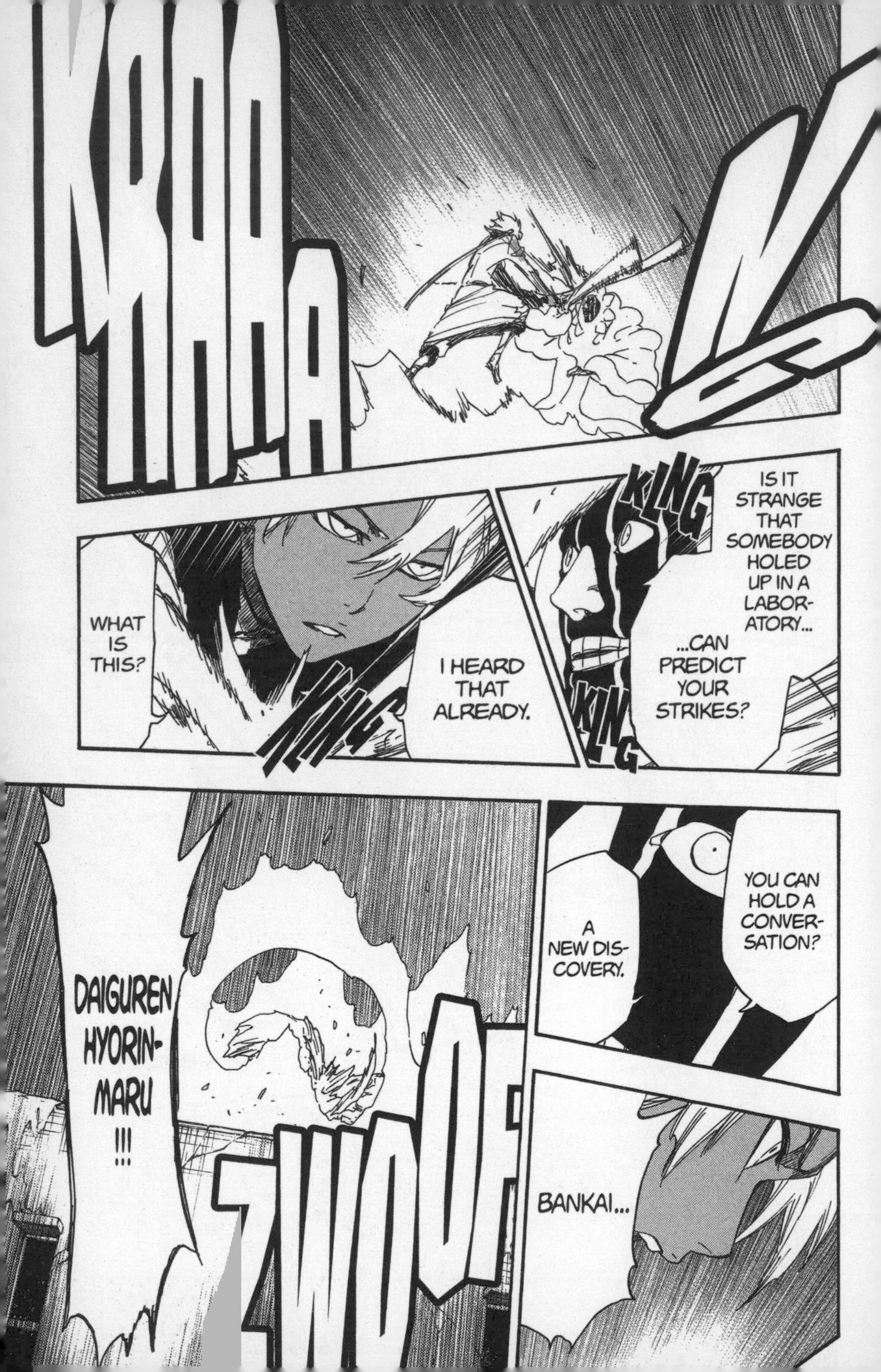
KLING
IS IT STRANGE THAT SOMEBODY HOLED UP IN A LABOR-ATORY...
...CAN PREDICT YOUR STRIKES?
KLING
I HEARD THAT ALREADY.
KLING
WHAT IS THIS?
YOU CAN HOLD A CONVER-SATION?
A NEW DIS-COVERY.
BANKAI...
DAIGUREN HYORIN-MARU !!!
ZWOOF

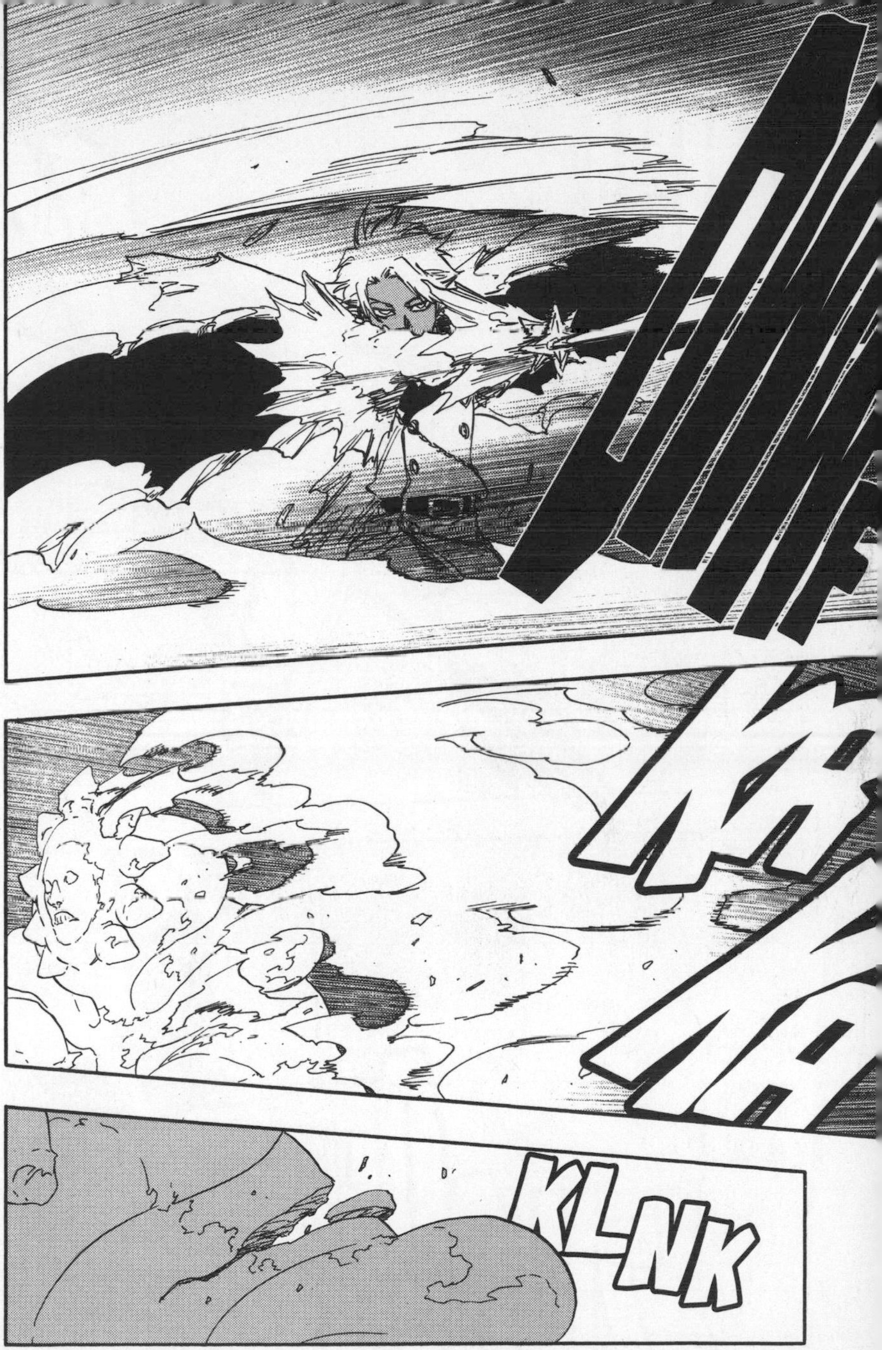
KLNK

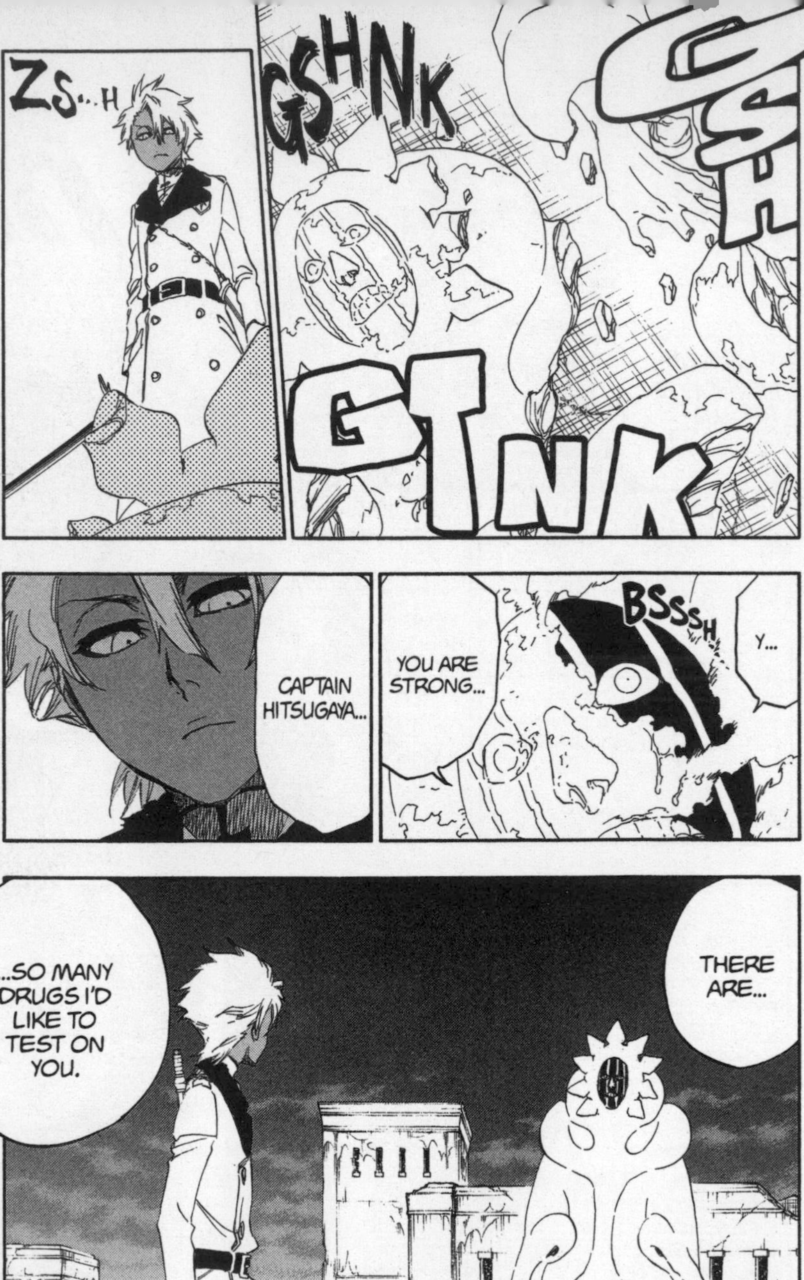
GSH
GSHNK
GTNK
ZS...H
Y...
BSSSH
YOU ARE STRONG...
CAPTAIN HITSUGAYA...
THERE ARE...
...SO MANY DRUGS I'D LIKE TO TEST ON YOU.

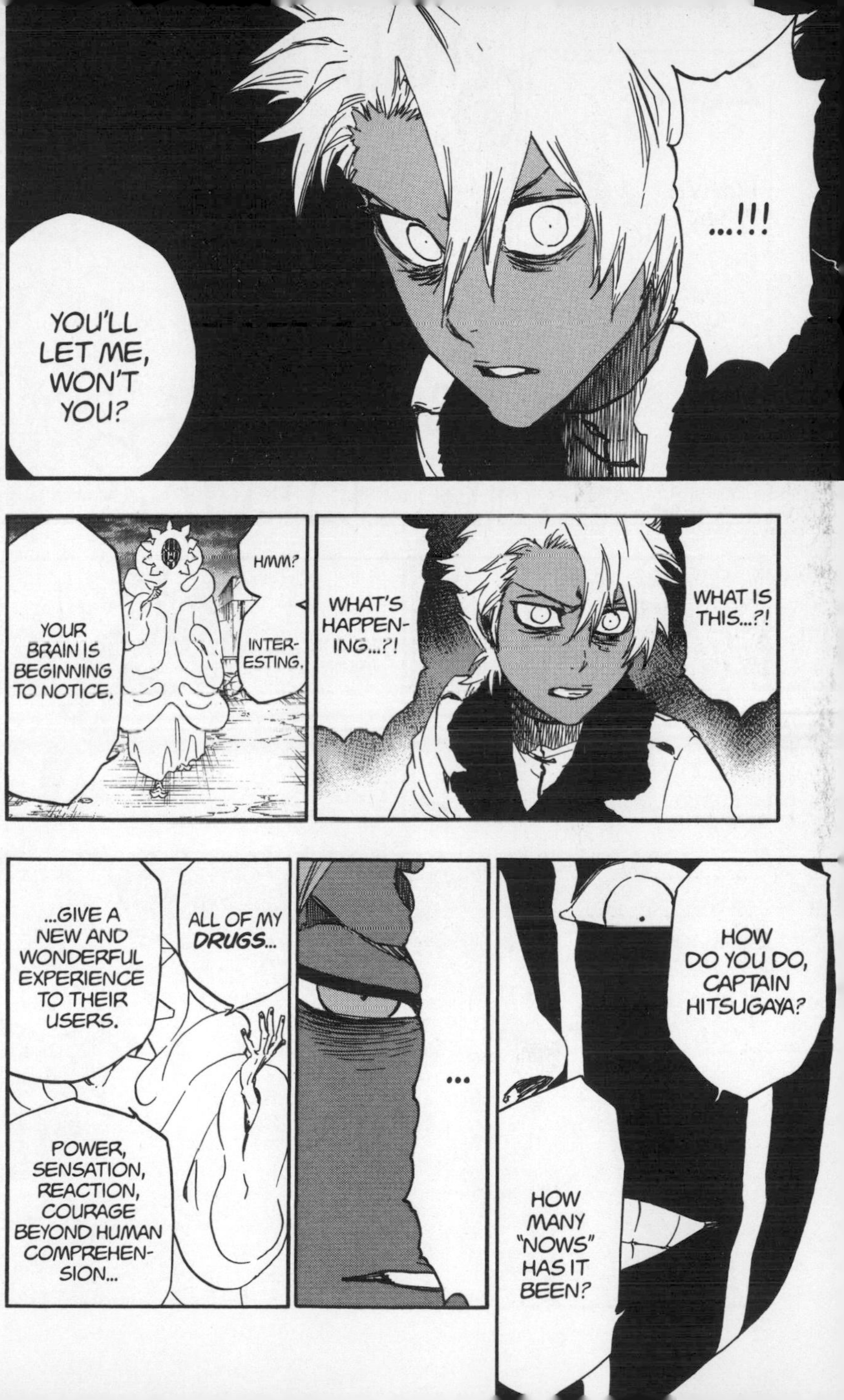

...!!!
YOU'LL LET ME, WON'T YOU?
WHAT IS THIS...?!
WHAT'S HAPPEN-ING...?!
HMM?
INTER-ESTING.
YOUR BRAIN IS BEGINNING TO NOTICE.
HOW DO YOU DO, CAPTAIN HITSUGAYA?
HOW MANY "NOWS" HAS IT BEEN?
...
ALL OF MY **DRUGS**...
...GIVE A NEW AND WONDERFUL EXPERIENCE TO THEIR USERS.
POWER, SENSATION, REACTION, COURAGE BEYOND HUMAN COMPREHEN-SION...

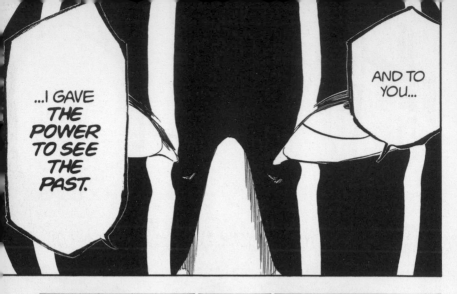

AND TO YOU...
...I GAVE THE POWER TO SEE THE PAST.
EVERY TIME YOU CROSS A CERTAIN POINT OF THE BATTLE...
...YOU RETURN TO A MOMENT IN THE PAST.
THAT POINT IS...
...WHEN YOU KILL ME.
IN OTHER WORDS, IF YOU DO NOT KILL ME, YOUR FUTURE WILL CONTINUE ON FOREVER.
IF YOU DO KILL ME, YOUR FUTURE CEASES AT THAT MOMENT.
TROUBLING, ISN'T IT?
IF YOU DO NOT DEFEAT THE ENEMY, YOU CANNOT MOVE FORWARD.
BUT IF YOU DO, YOU MOVE BACKWARD.
HOWEVER...
...THE IMPERFECTION OF THIS DRUG IS...
...THAT IT ONLY WORKS ON THE BRAIN'S HIPPOCAMPUS, WHICH CONTROLS SHORT-TERM MEMORY.
BECAUSE OF THAT, ITS USERS CANNOT REMEMBER HOW MANY TIMES THEY'VE RETURNED TO THE PAST.
AND...
...WHEN THEY JOURNEY BACK TO THE PAST OVER TEN TIMES...

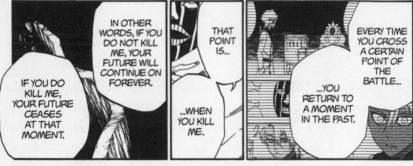

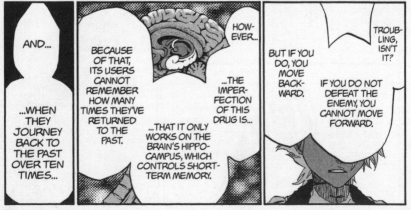

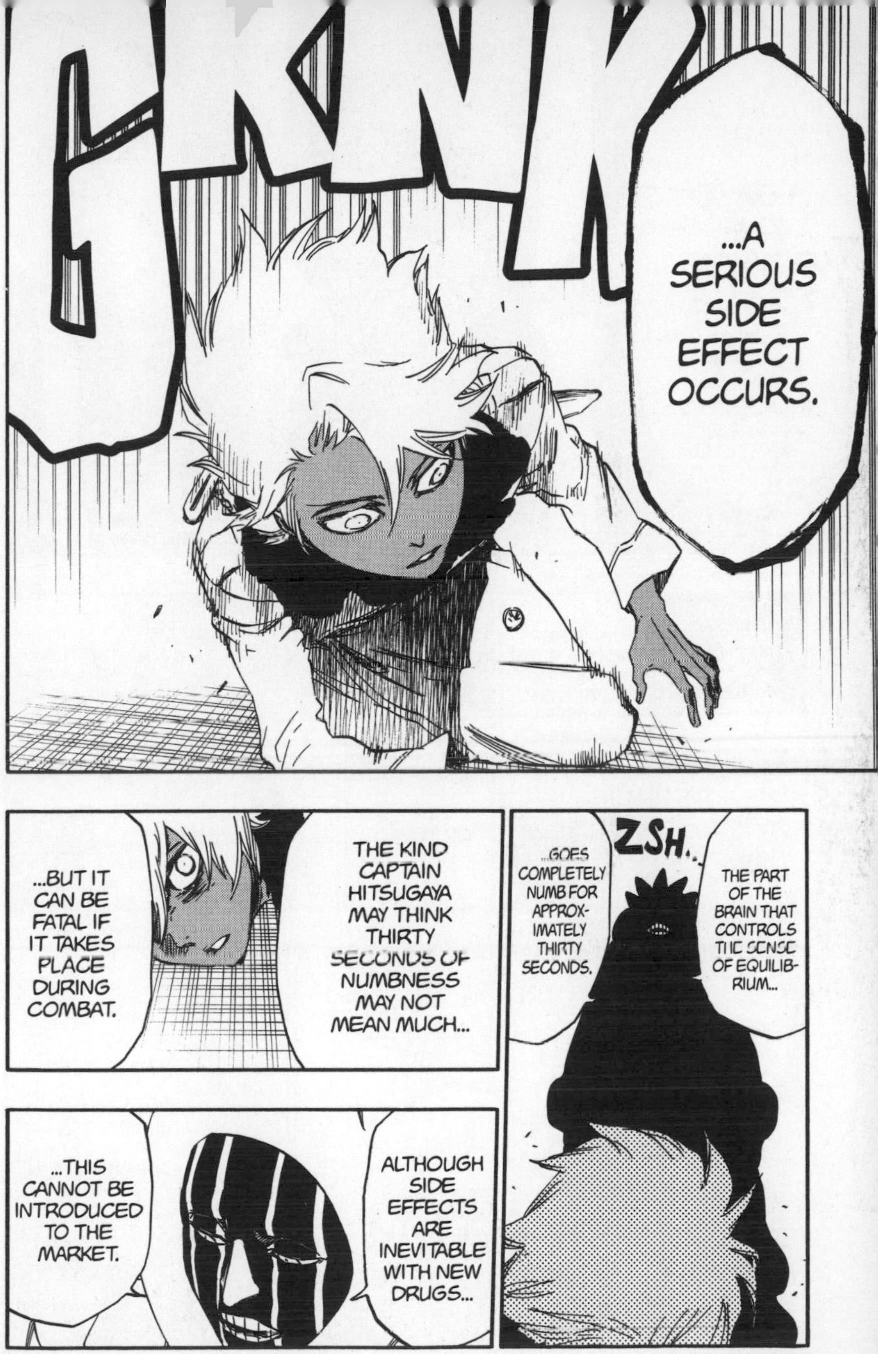
...A SERIOUS SIDE EFFECT OCCURS.
ZSH...
THE PART OF THE BRAIN THAT CONTROLS THE SENSE OF EQUILIBRIUM...
...GOES COMPLETELY NUMB FOR APPROXIMATELY THIRTY SECONDS.
THE KIND CAPTAIN HITSUGAYA MAY THINK THIRTY SECONDS OF NUMBNESS MAY NOT MEAN MUCH...
...BUT IT CAN BE FATAL IF IT TAKES PLACE DURING COMBAT.
ALTHOUGH SIDE EFFECTS ARE INEVITABLE WITH NEW DRUGS...
...THIS CANNOT BE INTRODUCED TO THE MARKET.

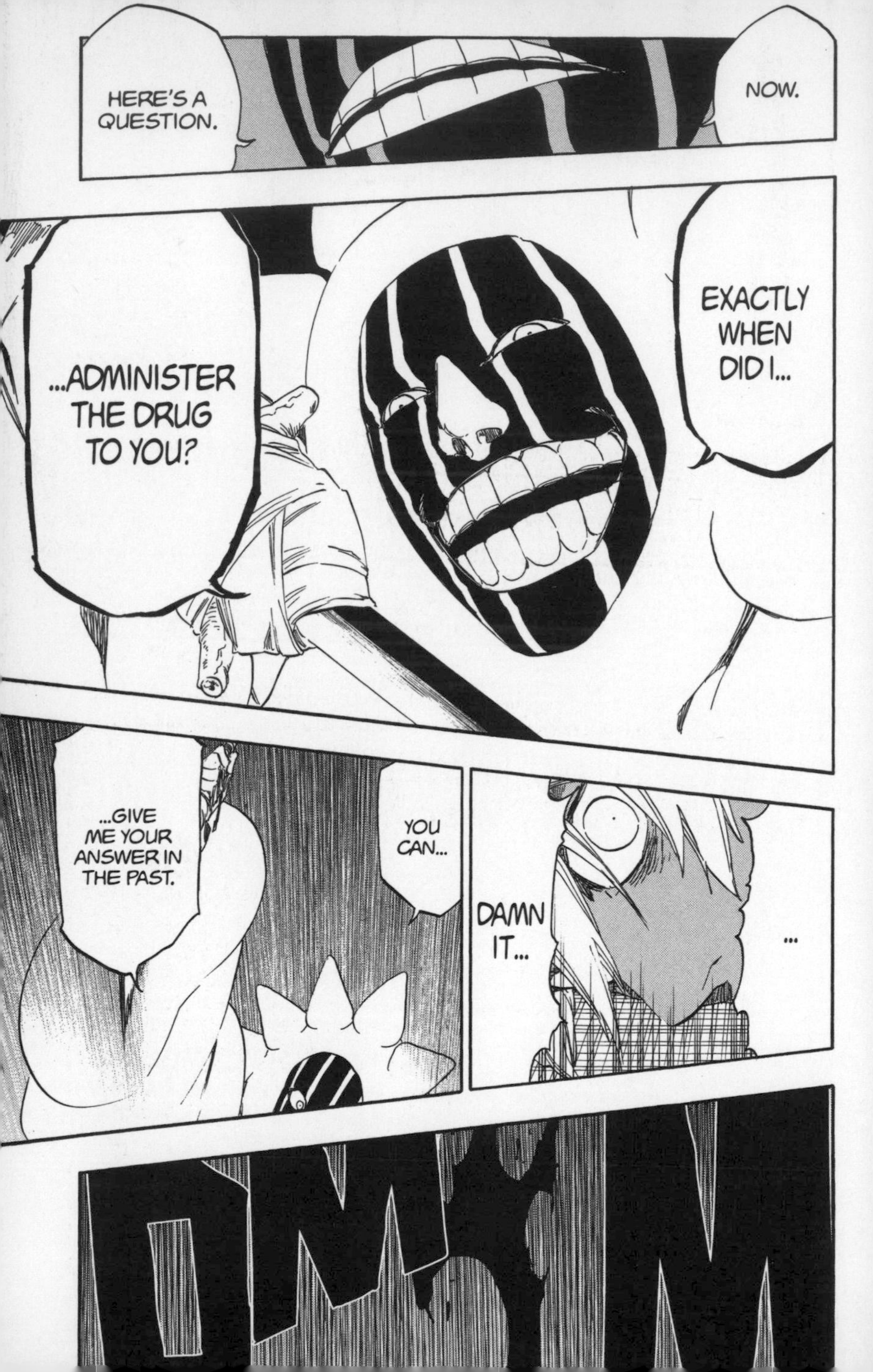
NOW.
HERE'S A QUESTION.
EXACTLY WHEN DID I...
...ADMINISTER THE DRUG TO YOU?
...
DAMN IT...
YOU CAN...
...GIVE ME YOUR ANSWER IN THE PAST.

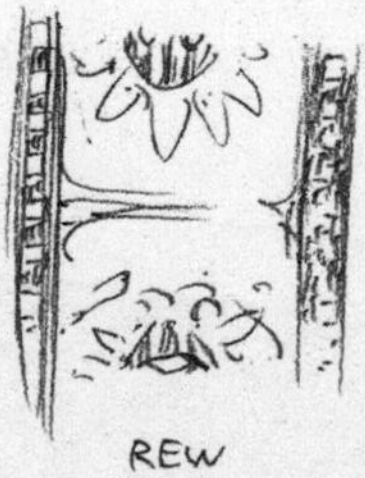

REW

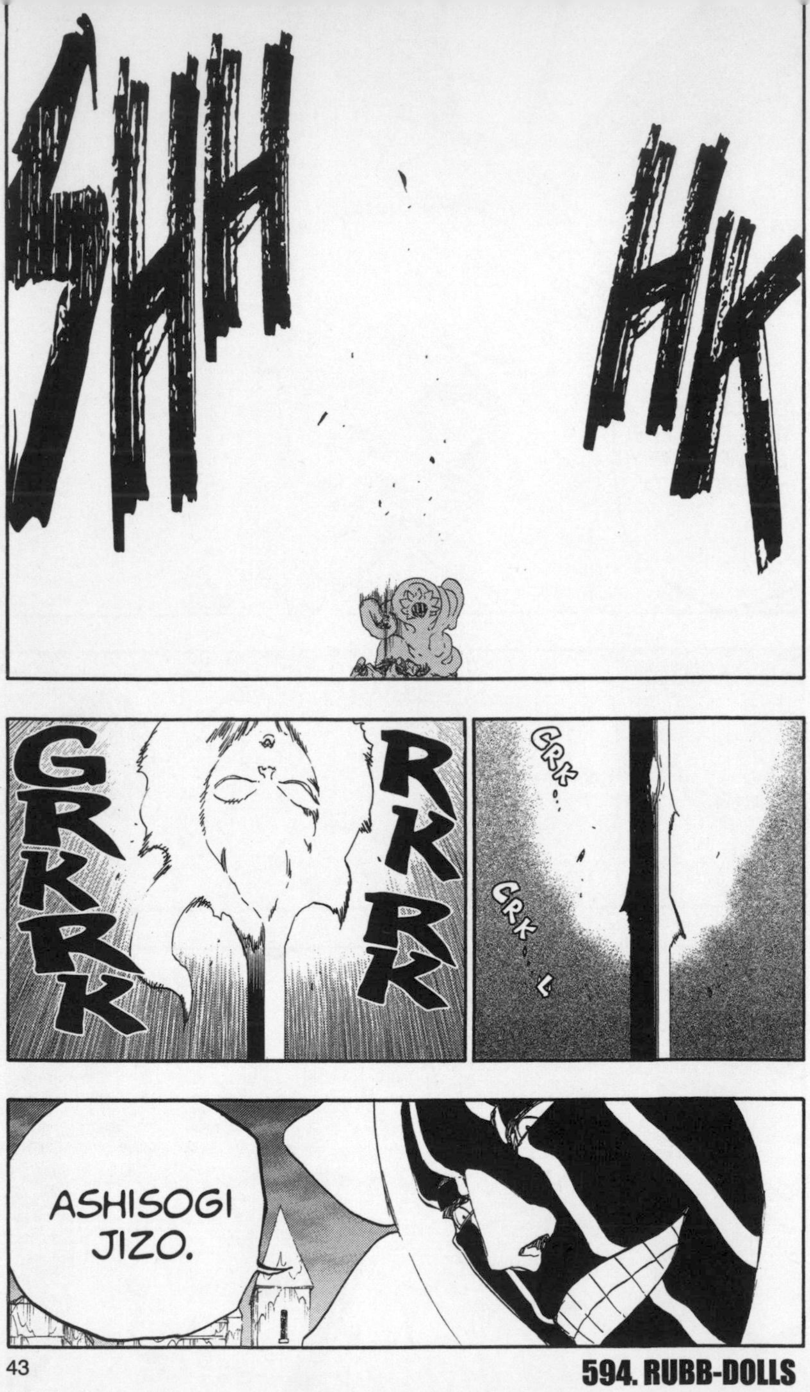
SHHH
HHK
CRK...
CRK...L
GRKRK
RKRK
ASHISOGI JIZO.

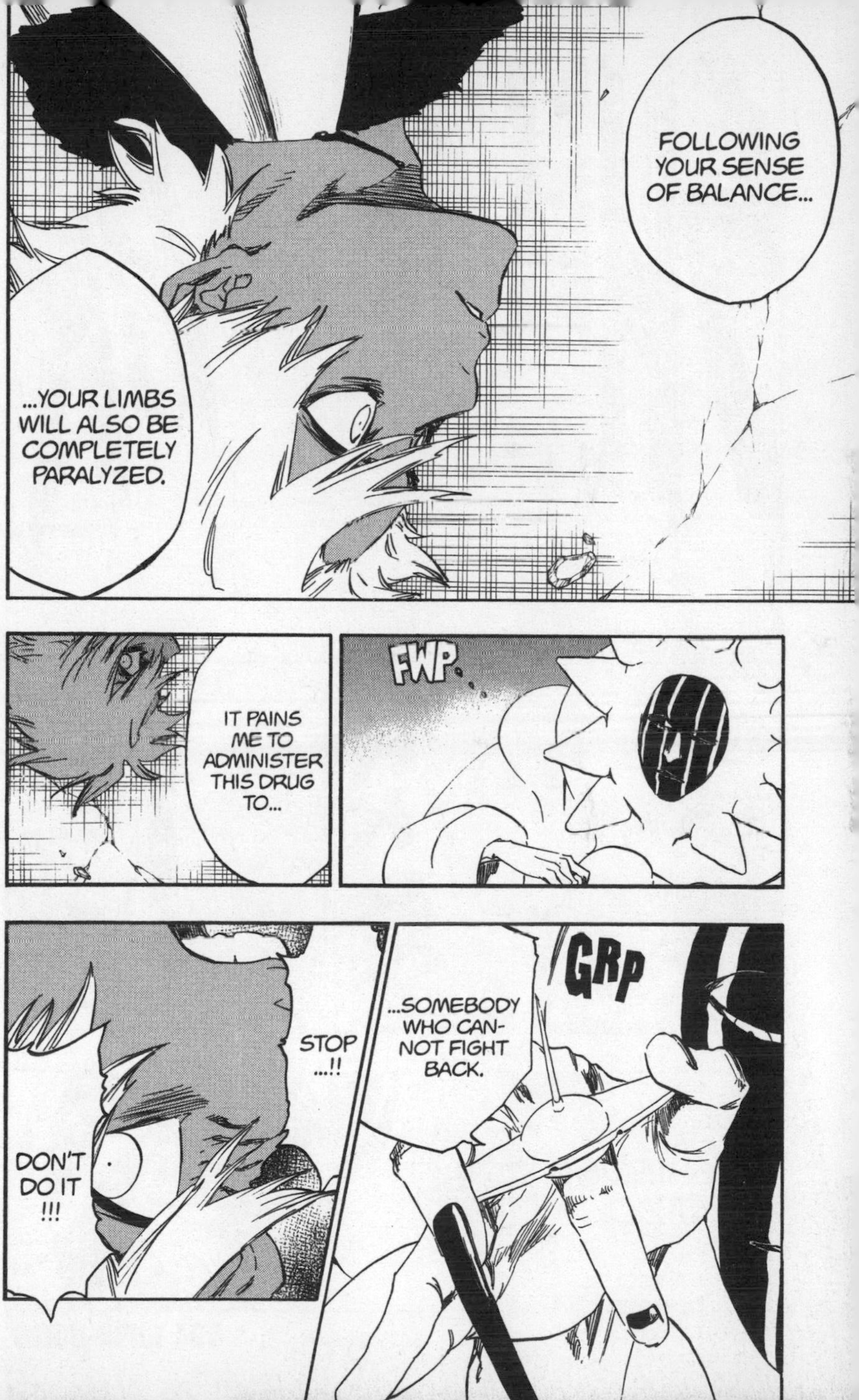

FOLLOWING YOUR SENSE OF BALANCE...
...YOUR LIMBS WILL ALSO BE COMPLETELY PARALYZED.
FWP...
IT PAINS ME TO ADMINISTER THIS DRUG TO...
GRP
...SOMEBODY WHO CAN-NOT FIGHT BACK.
STOP ...!!
DON'T DO IT !!!

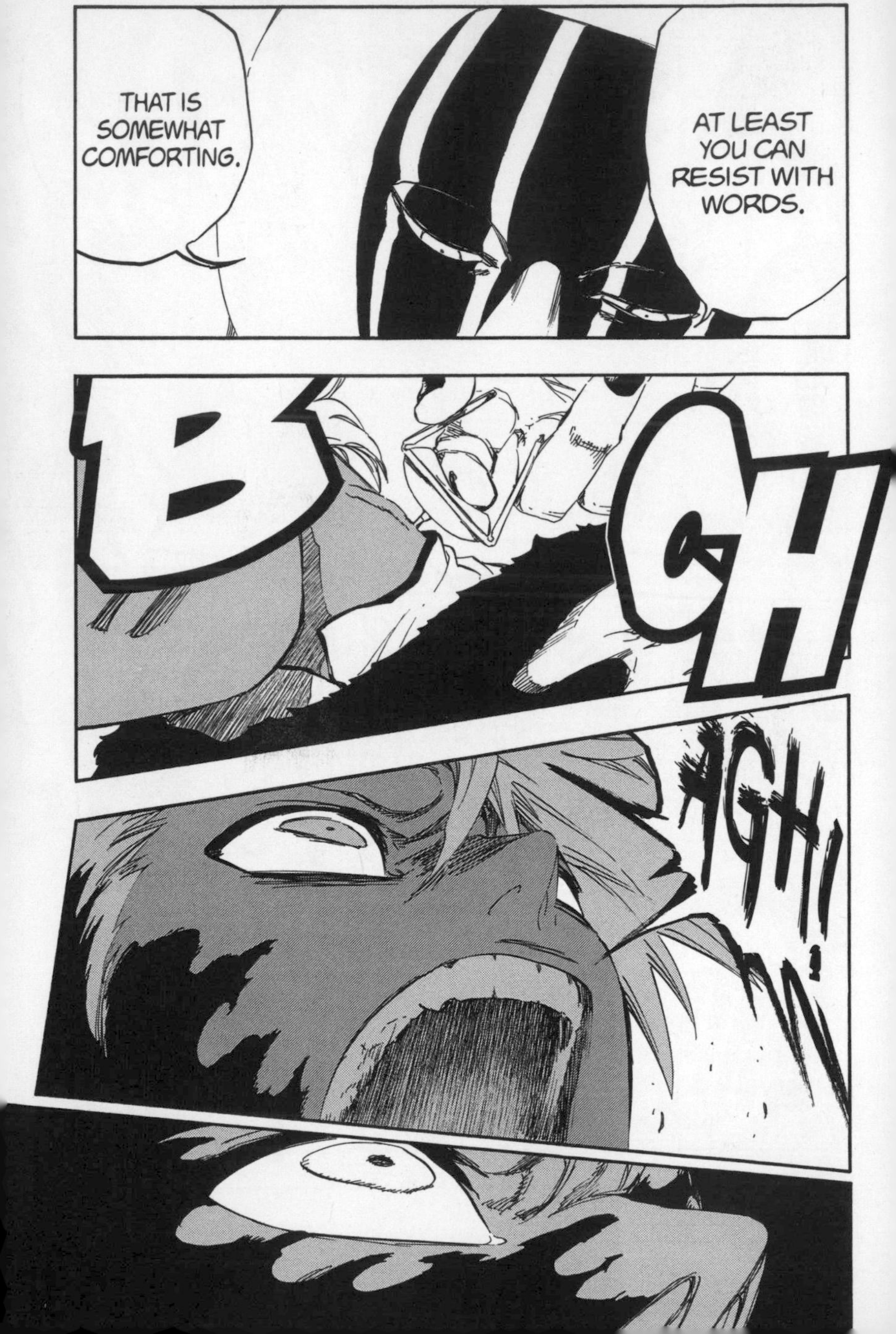
AT LEAST YOU CAN RESIST WITH WORDS.
THAT IS SOMEWHAT COMFORTING.
B CH
AGH!!

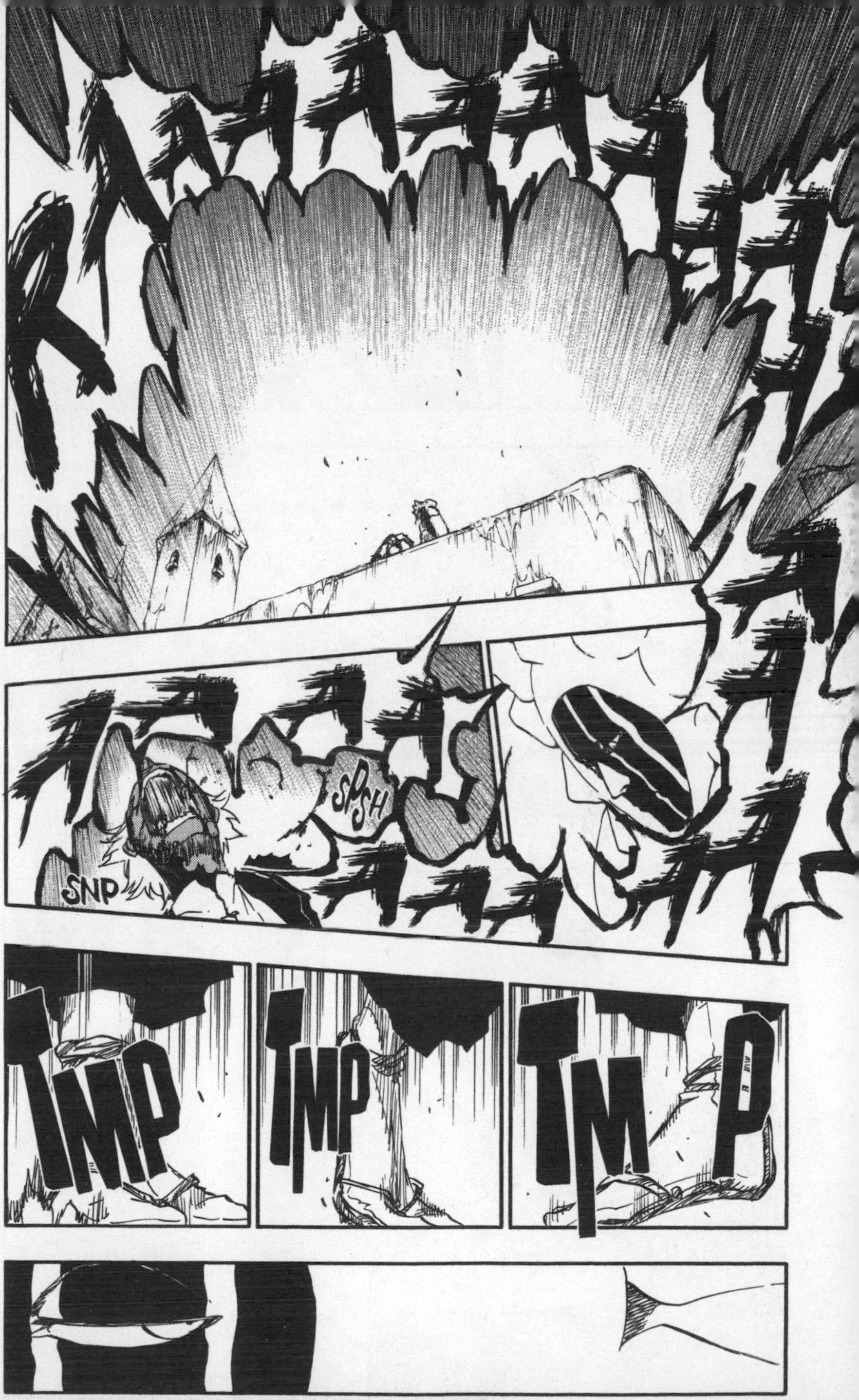
SPSH
SNP
TMP
TMP
TMP

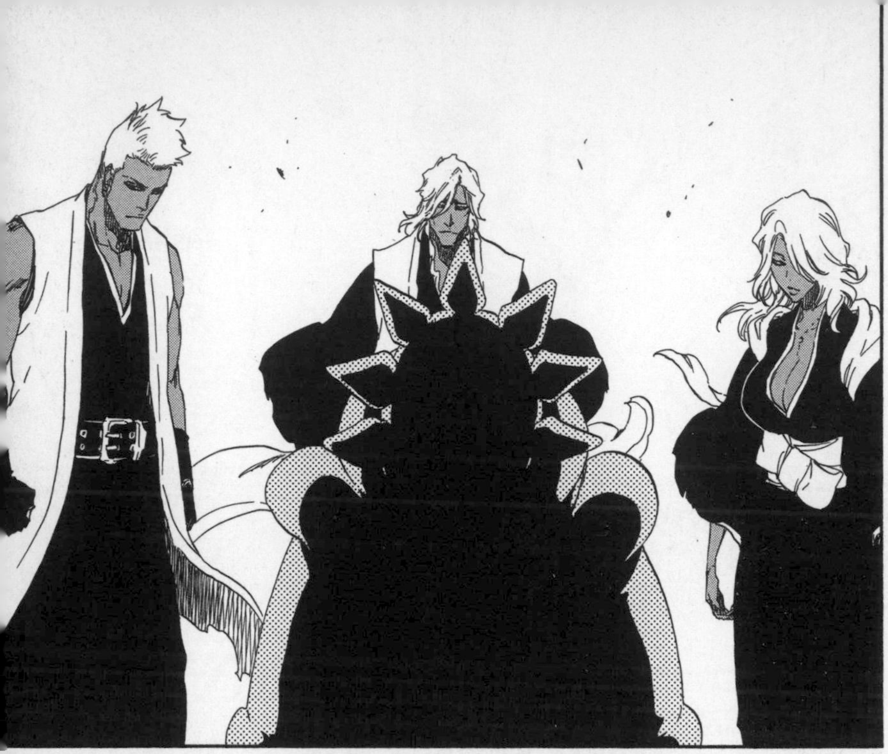

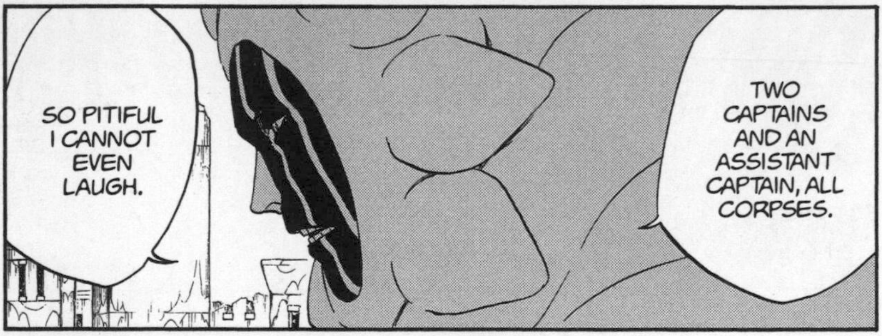
TWO CAPTAINS AND AN ASSISTANT CAPTAIN, ALL CORPSES.
SO PITIFUL I CANNOT EVEN LAUGH.

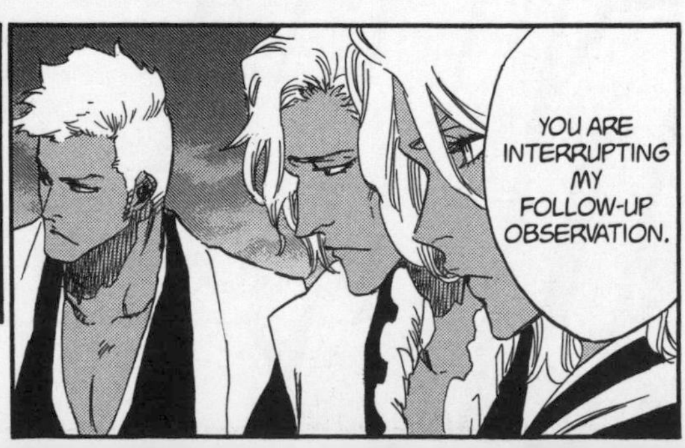
YOU ARE INTERRUPTING MY FOLLOW-UP OBSERVATION.

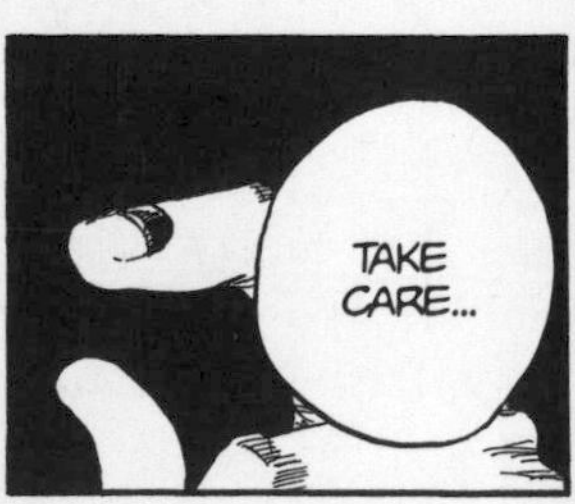
TAKE CARE...

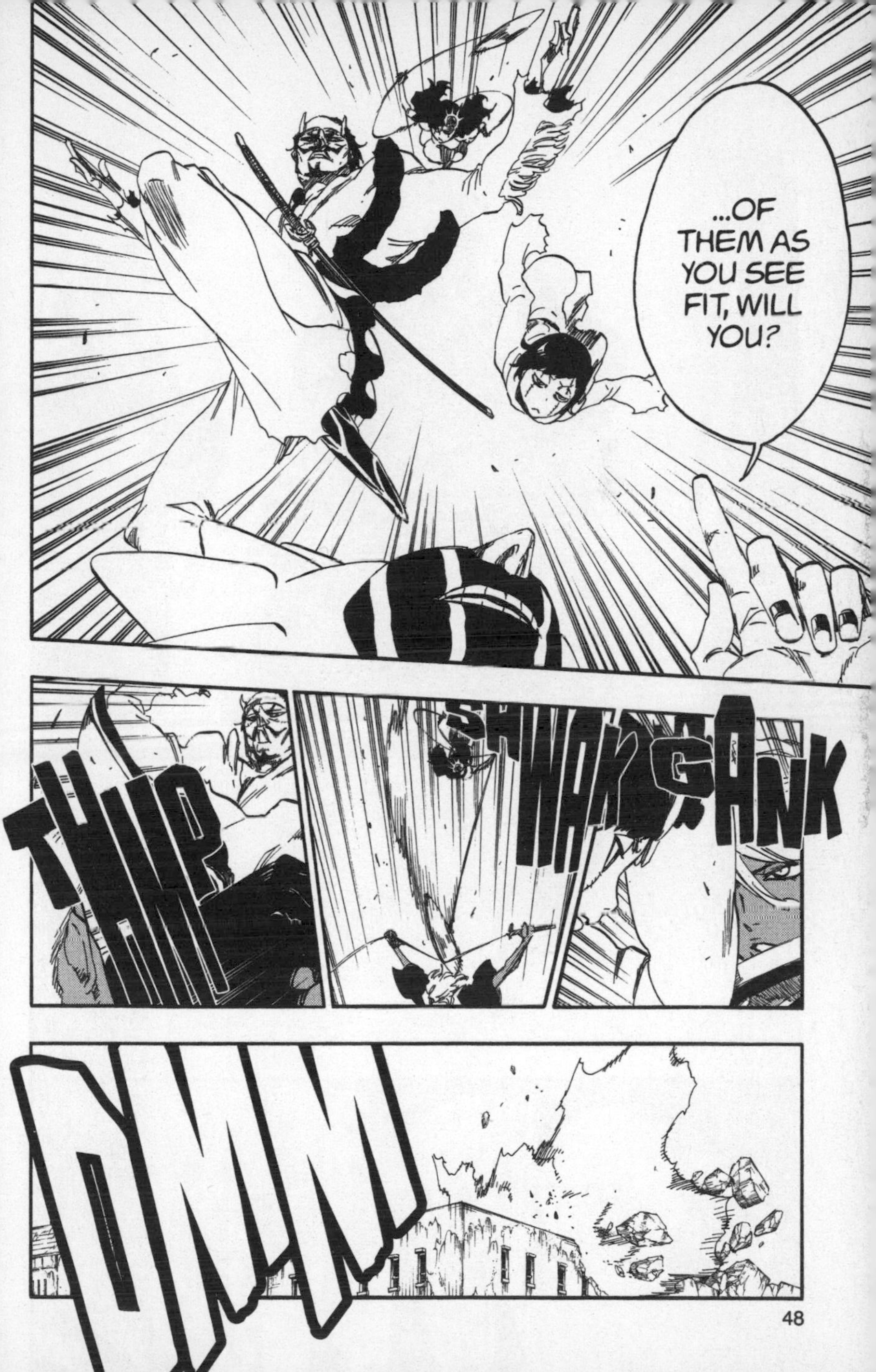
...OF THEM AS YOU SEE FIT, WILL YOU?
GANK
SHWAK
THMP
DMM

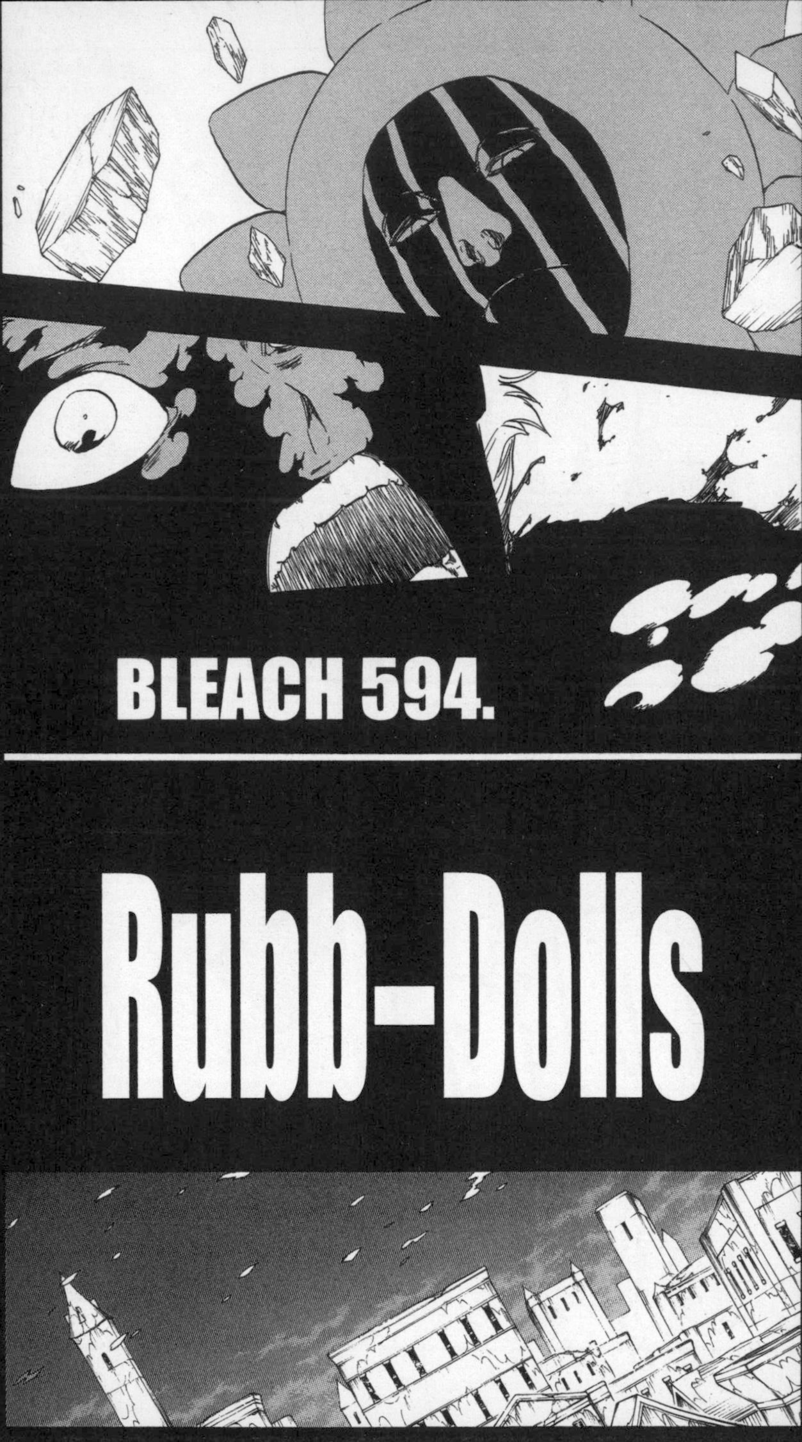
BLEACH 594.
Rubb-Dolls

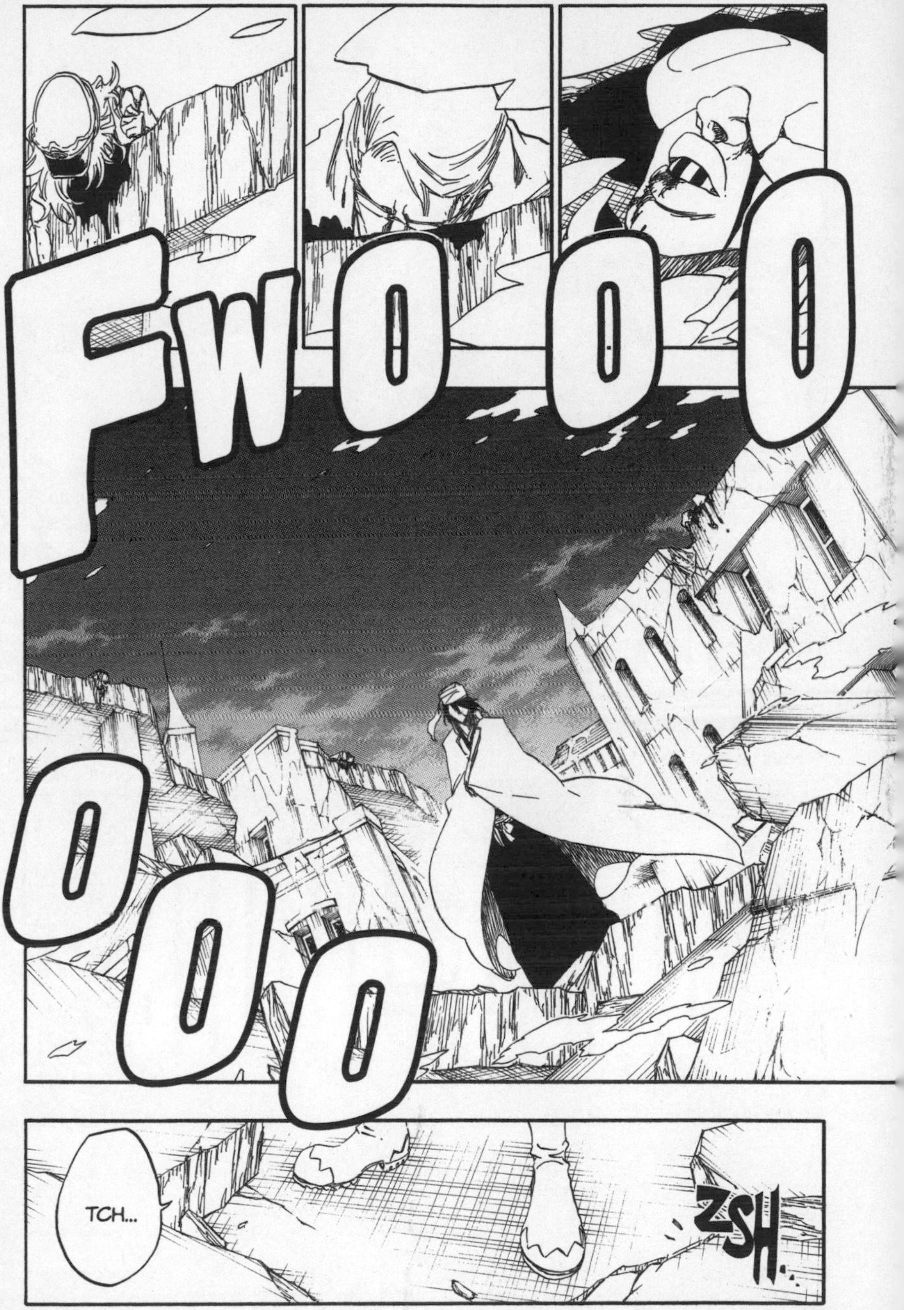
FWOOOOOOO
TCH...
ZSH...

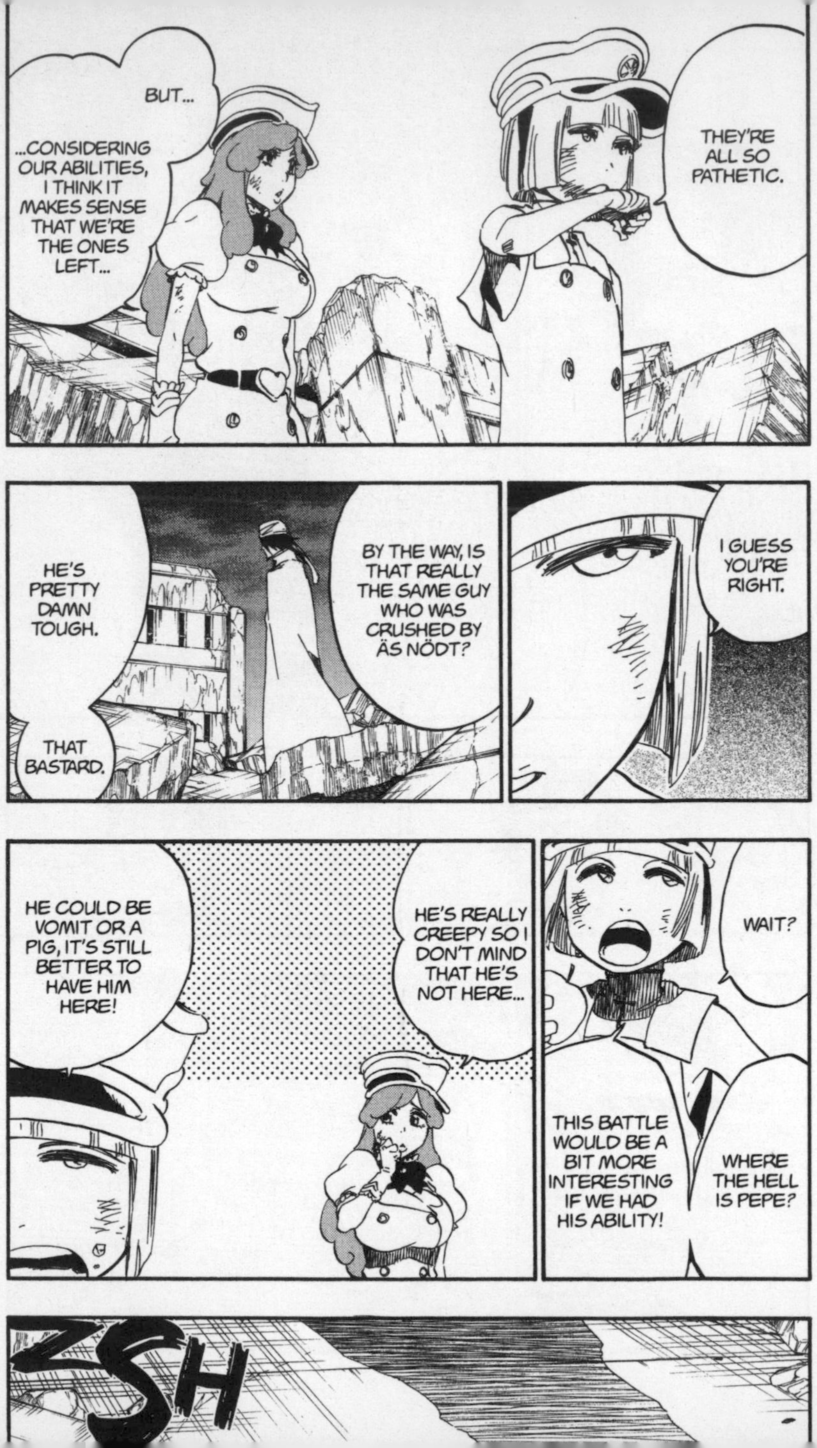
THEY'RE ALL SO PATHETIC.
BUT...
...CONSIDERING OUR ABILITIES, I THINK IT MAKES SENSE THAT WE'RE THE ONES LEFT...
I GUESS YOU'RE RIGHT.
BY THE WAY, IS THAT REALLY THE SAME GUY WHO WAS CRUSHED BY ÄS NÖDT?
HE'S PRETTY DAMN TOUGH.
THAT BASTARD.
WAIT?
WHERE THE HELL IS PEPE?
THIS BATTLE WOULD BE A BIT MORE INTERESTING IF WE HAD HIS ABILITY!
HE'S REALLY CREEPY SO I DON'T MIND THAT HE'S NOT HERE...
HE COULD BE VOMIT OR A PIG, IT'S STILL BETTER TO HAVE HIM HERE!
ZSH

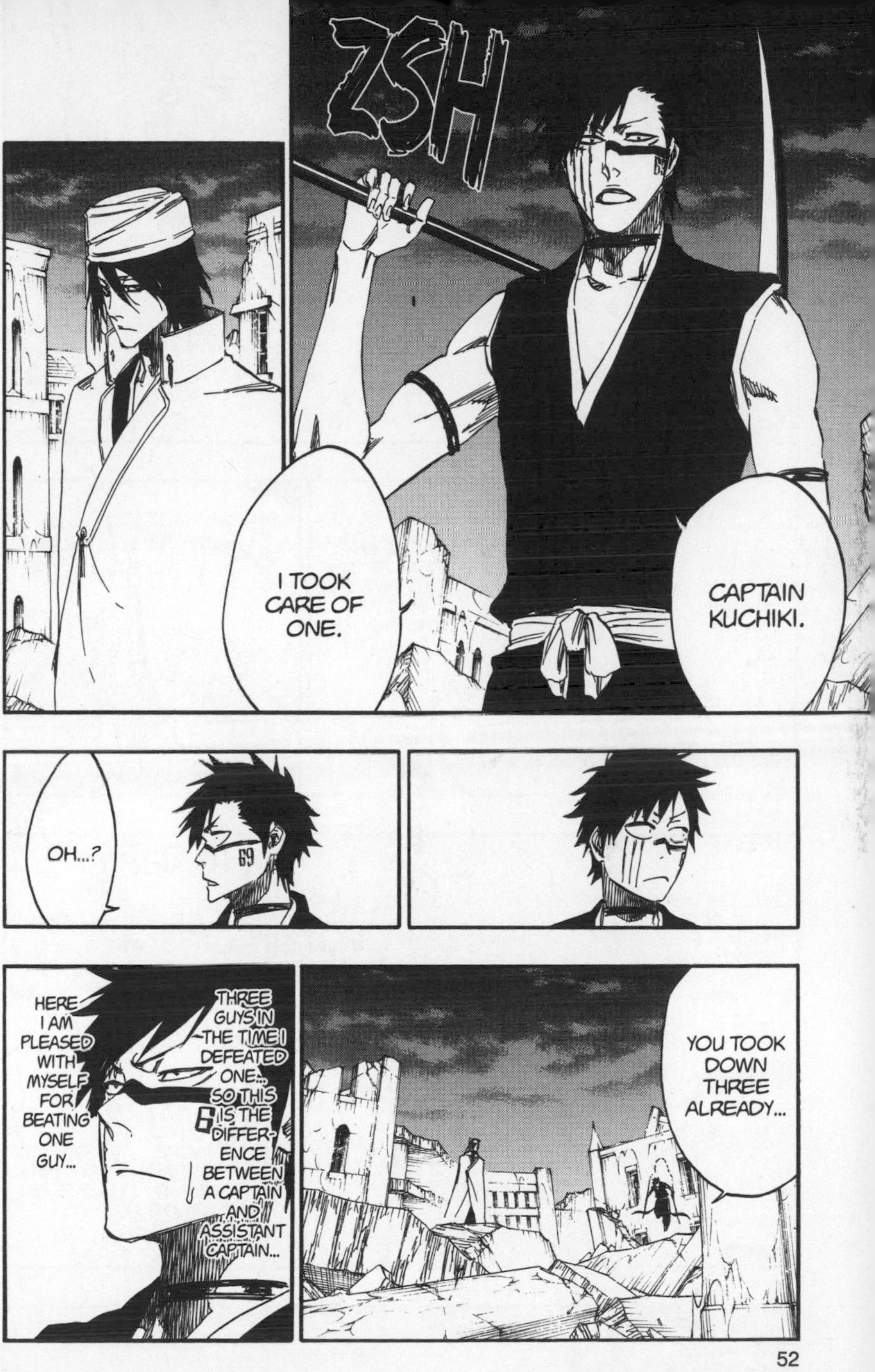
ZSH
CAPTAIN KUCHIKI.
I TOOK CARE OF ONE.
OH...?
YOU TOOK DOWN THREE ALREADY...
THREE GUYS IN THE TIME I DEFEATED ONE... SO THIS IS THE DIFFERENCE BETWEEN A CAPTAIN AND ASSISTANT CAPTAIN...
HERE I AM PLEASED WITH MYSELF FOR BEATING ONE GUY...

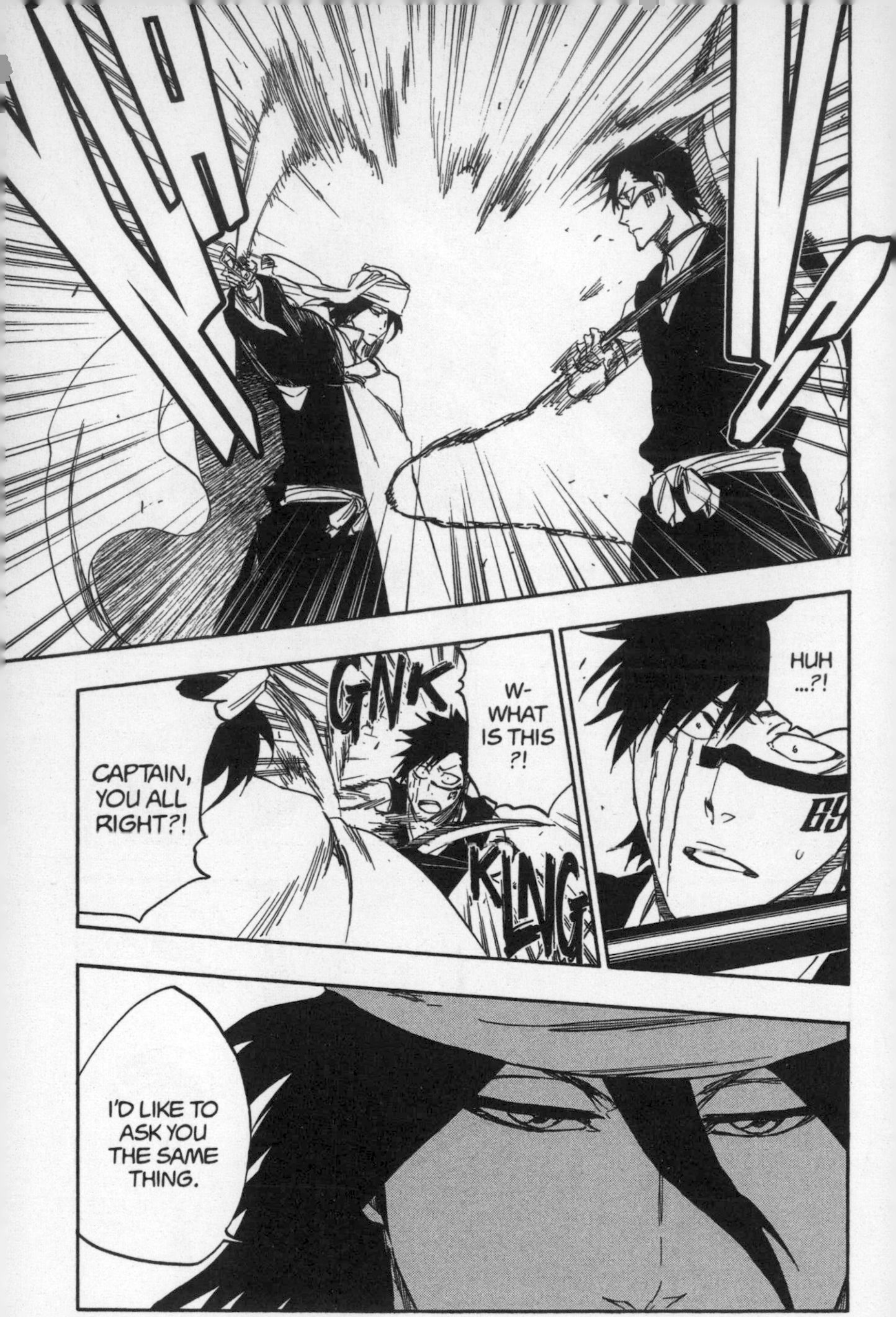
HUH ...?!
W- WHAT IS THIS ?!
GNK
CAPTAIN, YOU ALL RIGHT?!
KLING
I'D LIKE TO ASK YOU THE SAME THING.

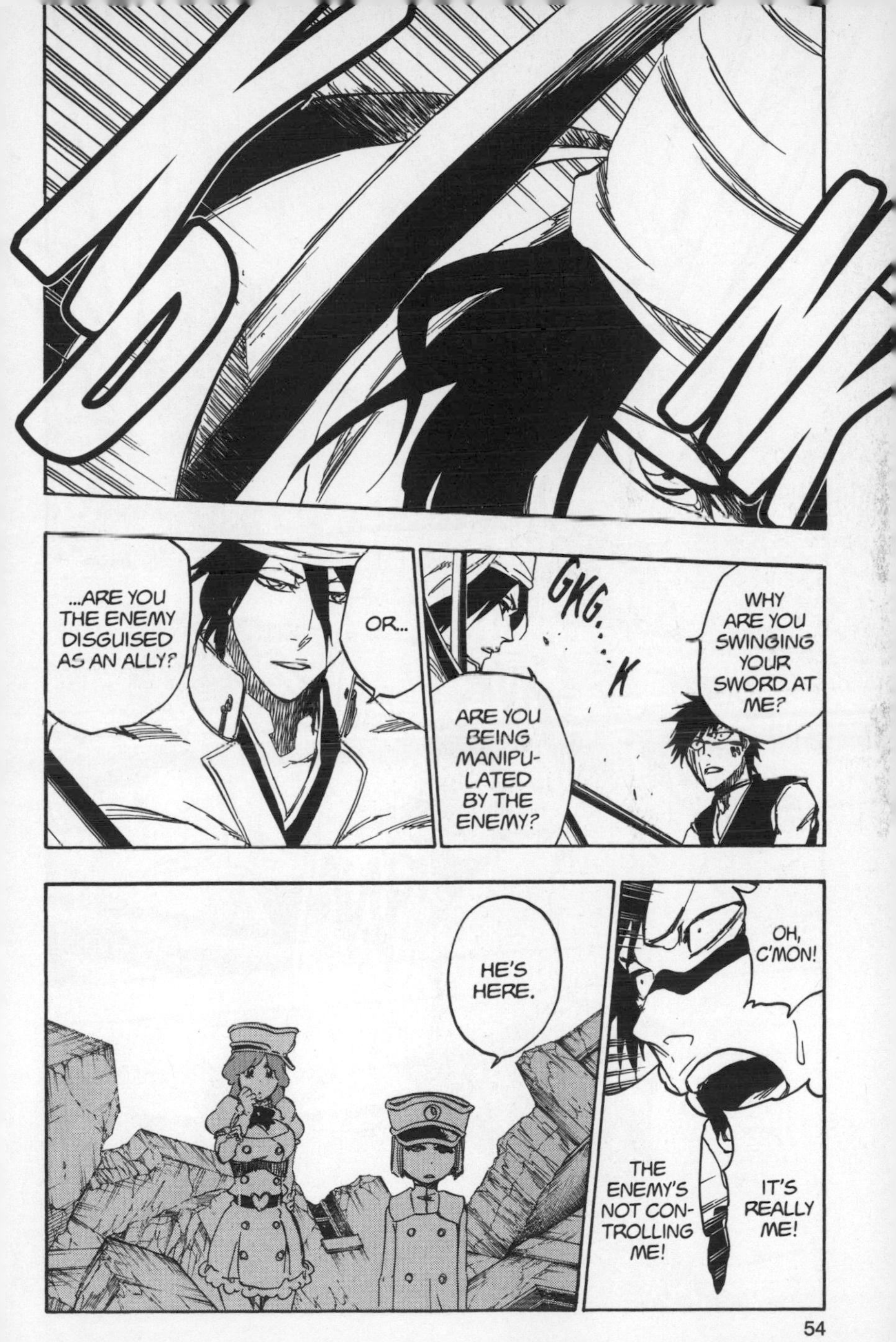
WHY ARE YOU SWINGING YOUR SWORD AT ME?
GKG...K
ARE YOU BEING MANIPU-LATED BY THE ENEMY?
OR...
...ARE YOU THE ENEMY DISGUISED AS AN ALLY?
OH, C'MON!
IT'S REALLY ME!
THE ENEMY'S NOT CON-TROLLING ME!
HE'S HERE.

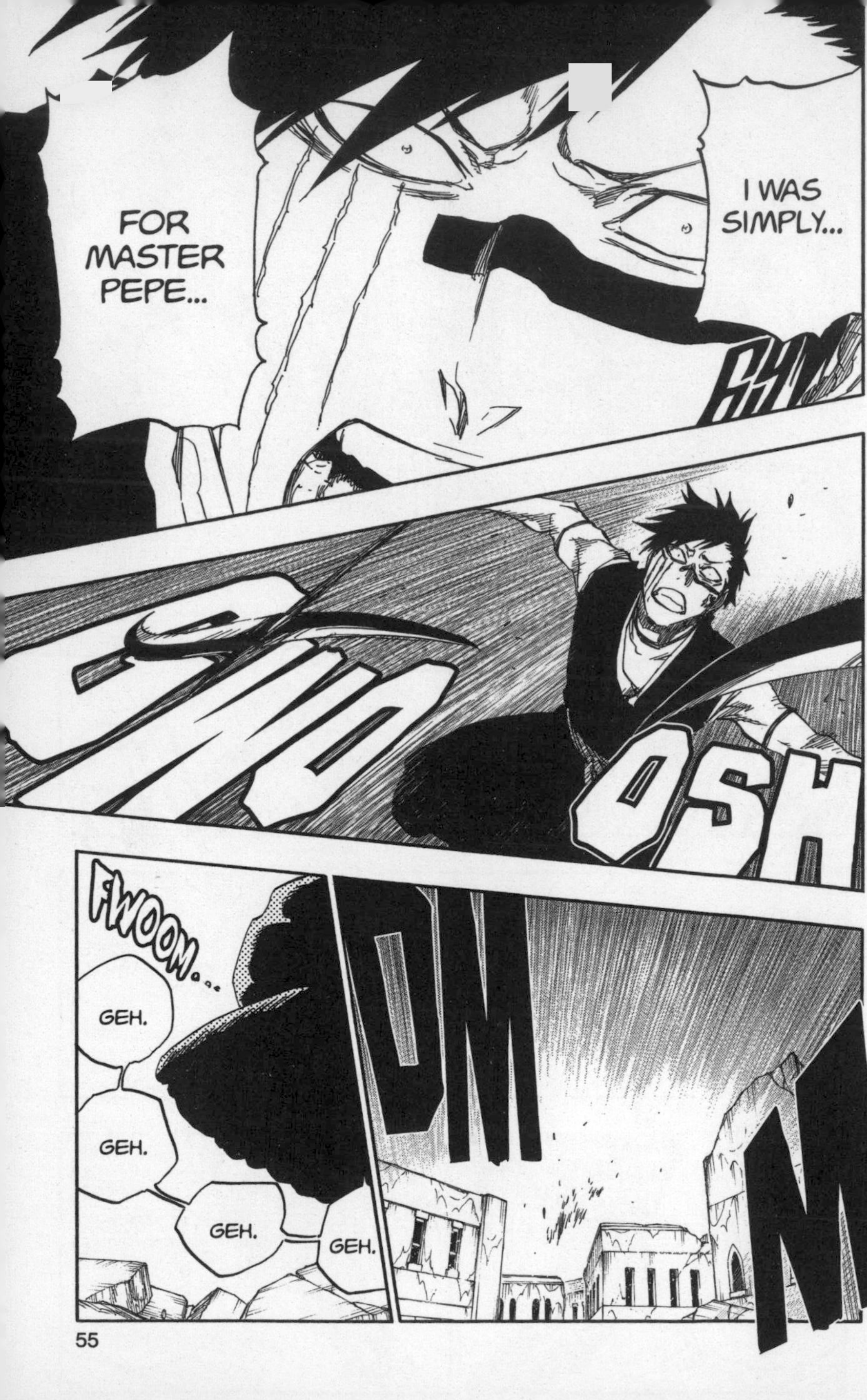
I WAS SIMPLY...
FOR MASTER PEPE...
FWOOM...
GEH.
GEH.
GEH.
GEH.

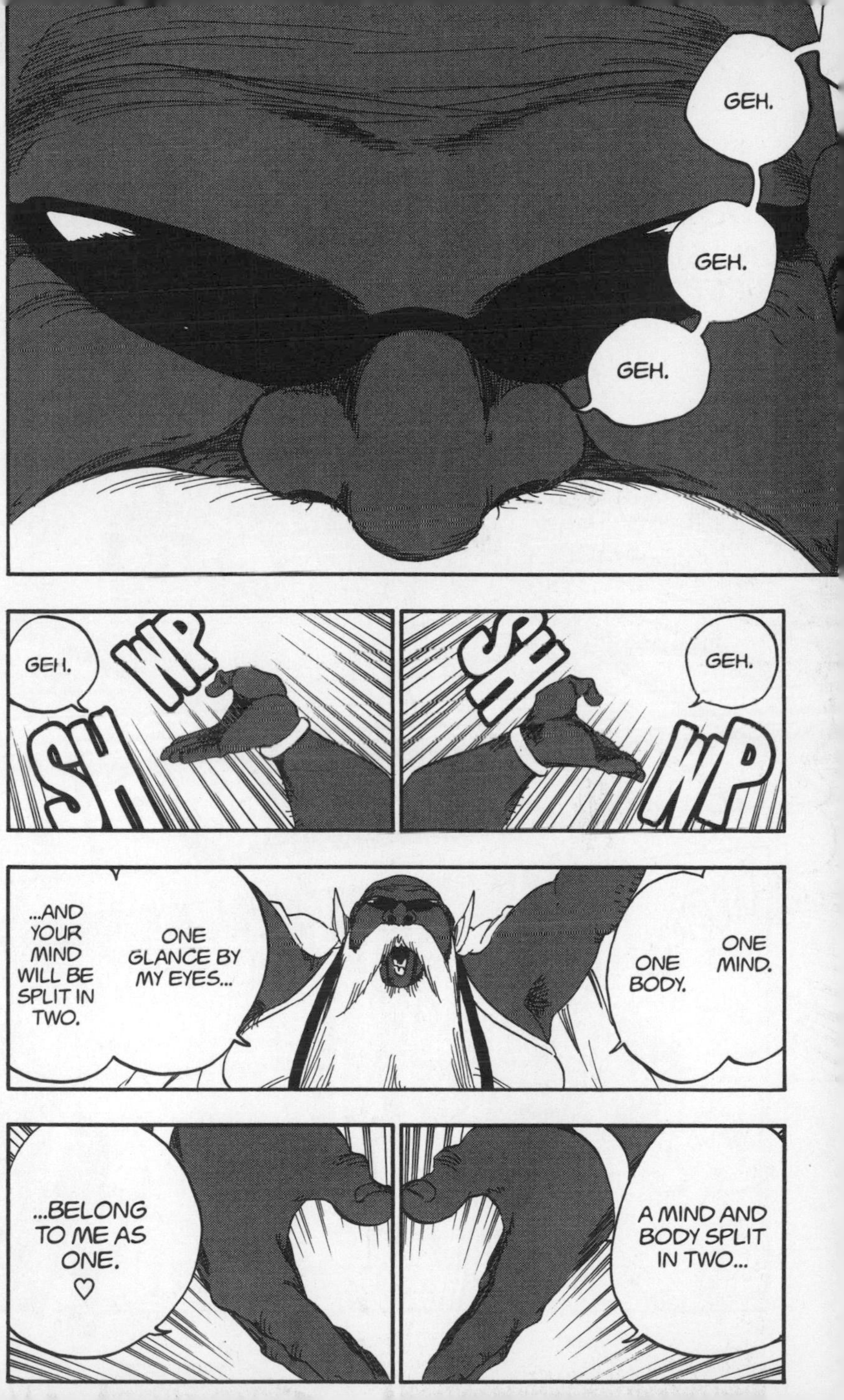
GEH.
GEH.
GEH.
GEH.
SHWP
GEH.
SHWP
ONE MIND.
ONE BODY.
ONE GLANCE BY MY EYES...
...AND YOUR MIND WILL BE SPLIT IN TWO.
A MIND AND BODY SPLIT IN TWO...
...BELONG TO ME AS ONE. ♡

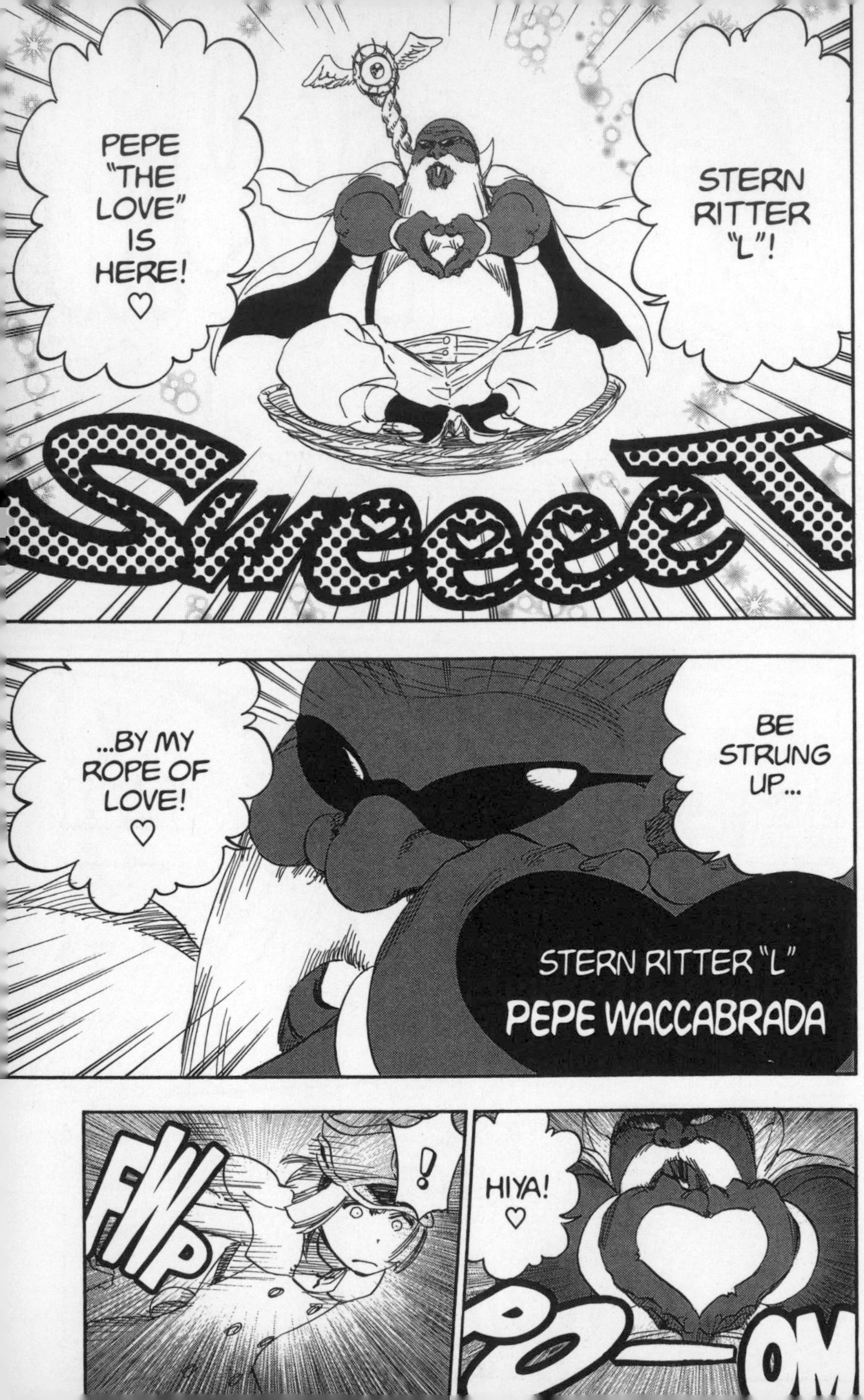
STERN RITTER "L"!
PEPE "THE LOVE" IS HERE! ♡
SWEEET
BE STRUNG UP...
...BY MY ROPE OF LOVE! ♡
STERN RITTER "L"
PEPE WACCABRADA
HIYA! ♡
PO-OM
!
FWP

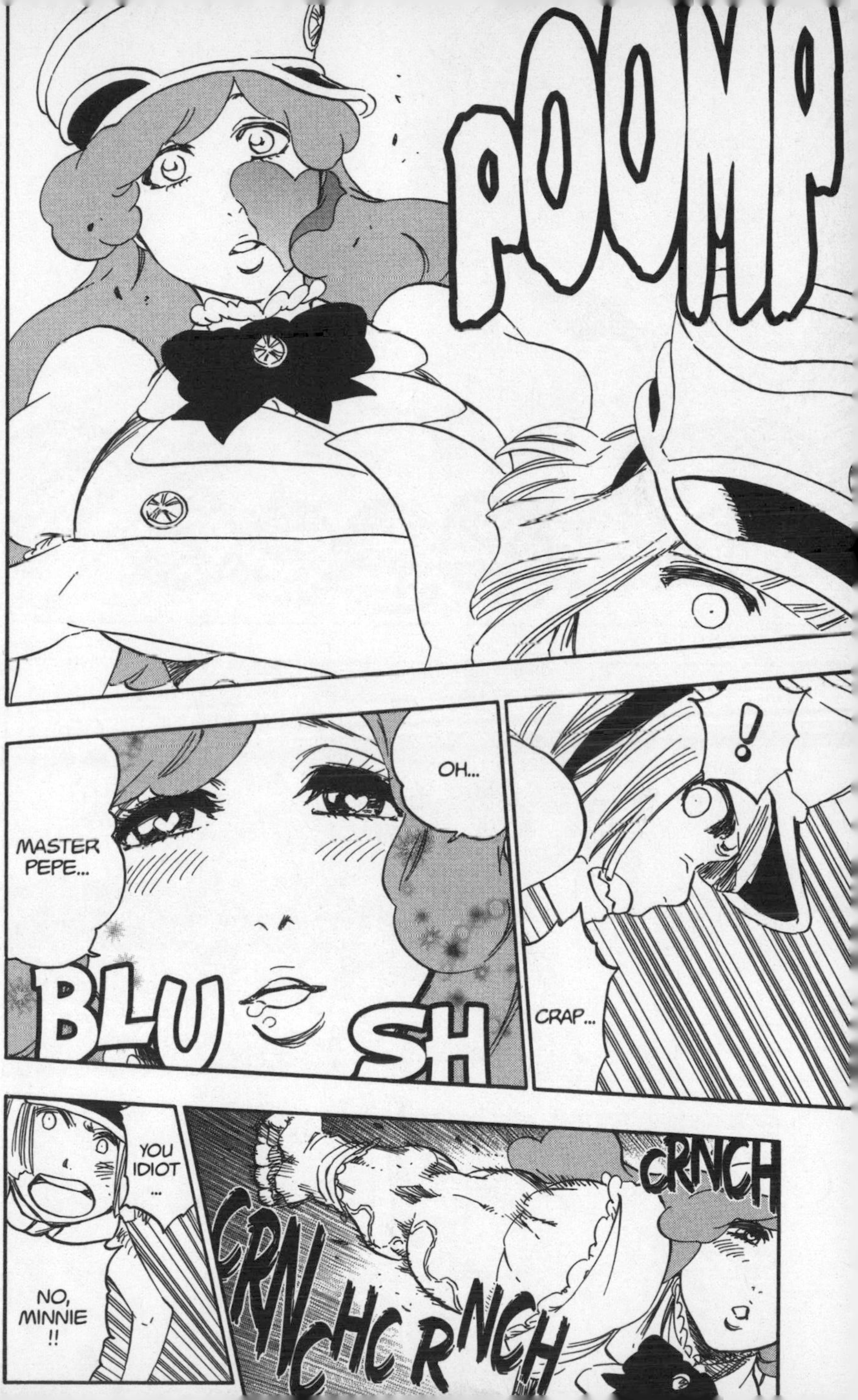
POOMP
!
CRAP...
OH...
MASTER PEPE...
BLUSH
CRNCH
CRNCH CRNCH
YOU IDIOT ...
NO, MINNIE !!

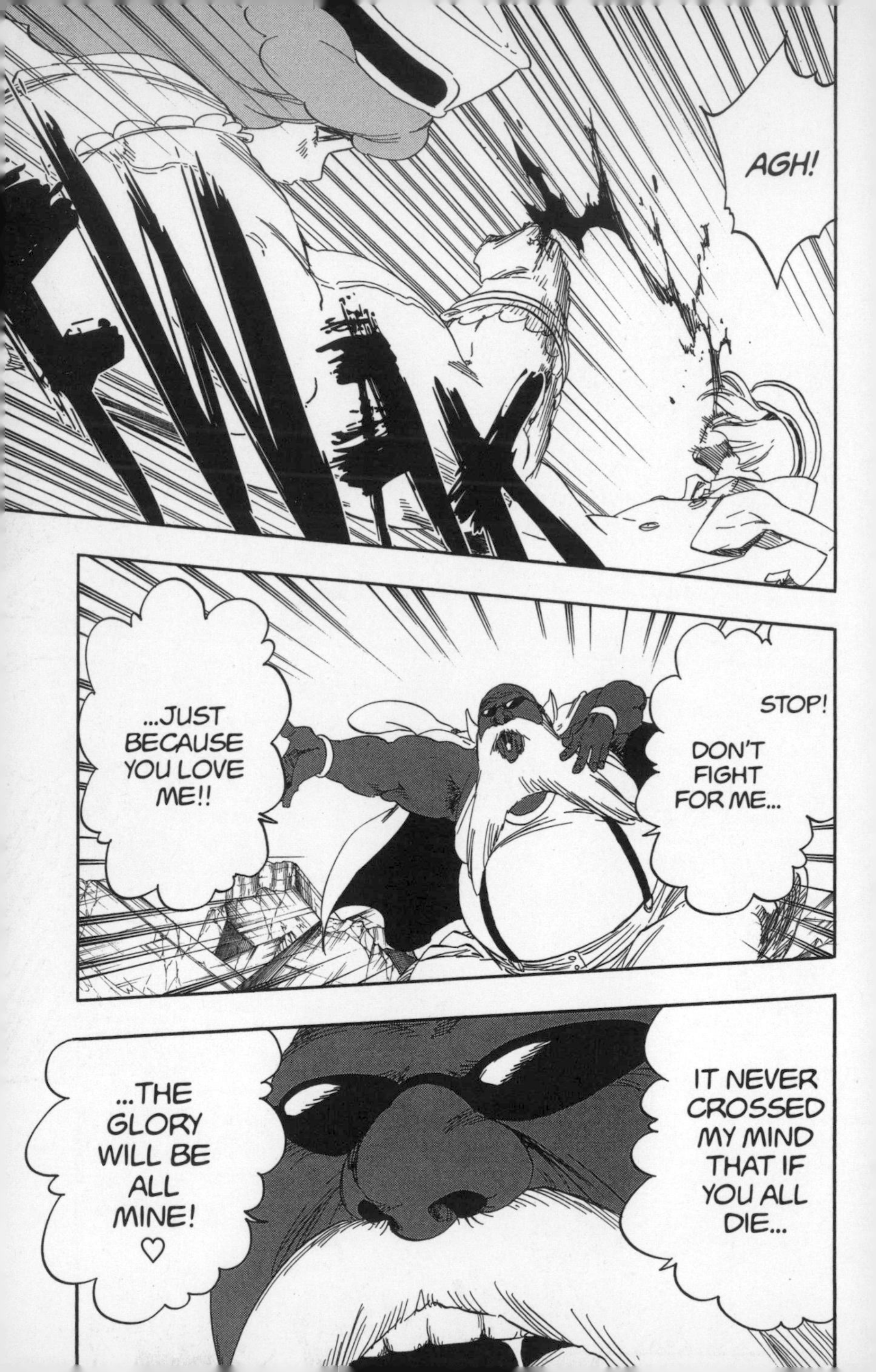
AGH!
STOP!
DON'T FIGHT FOR ME...
...JUST BECAUSE YOU LOVE ME!!
IT NEVER CROSSED MY MIND THAT IF YOU ALL DIE...
...THE GLORY WILL BE ALL MINE! ♡

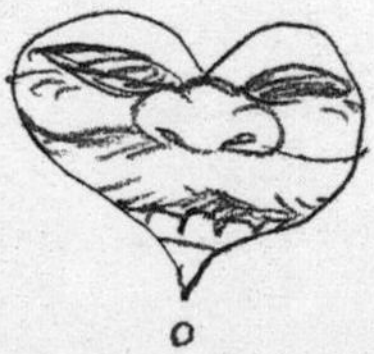

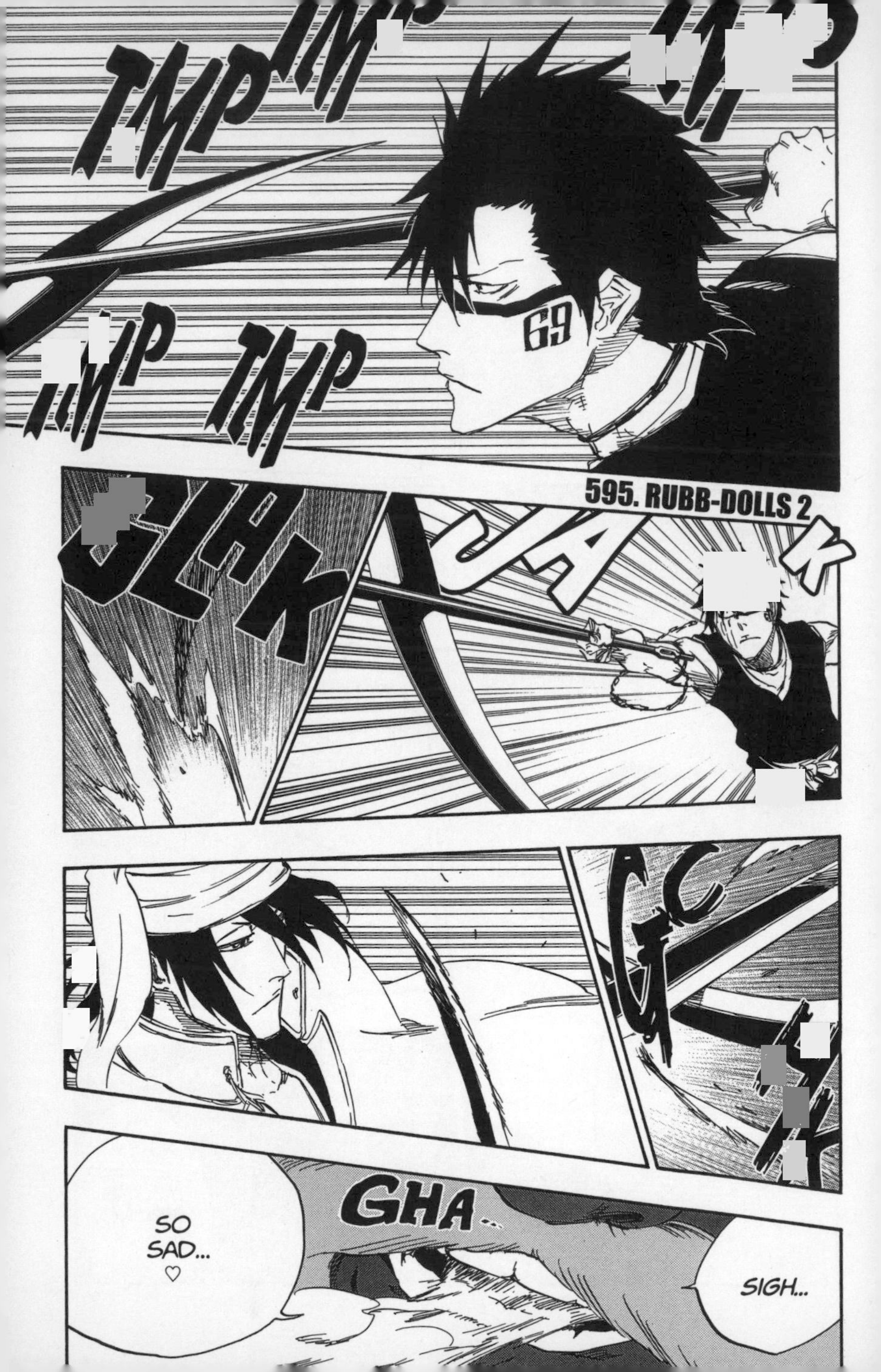
TMP
TMP
TMP
595. RUBB-DOLLS 2
SIGH...
GHA..
SO SAD... ♡

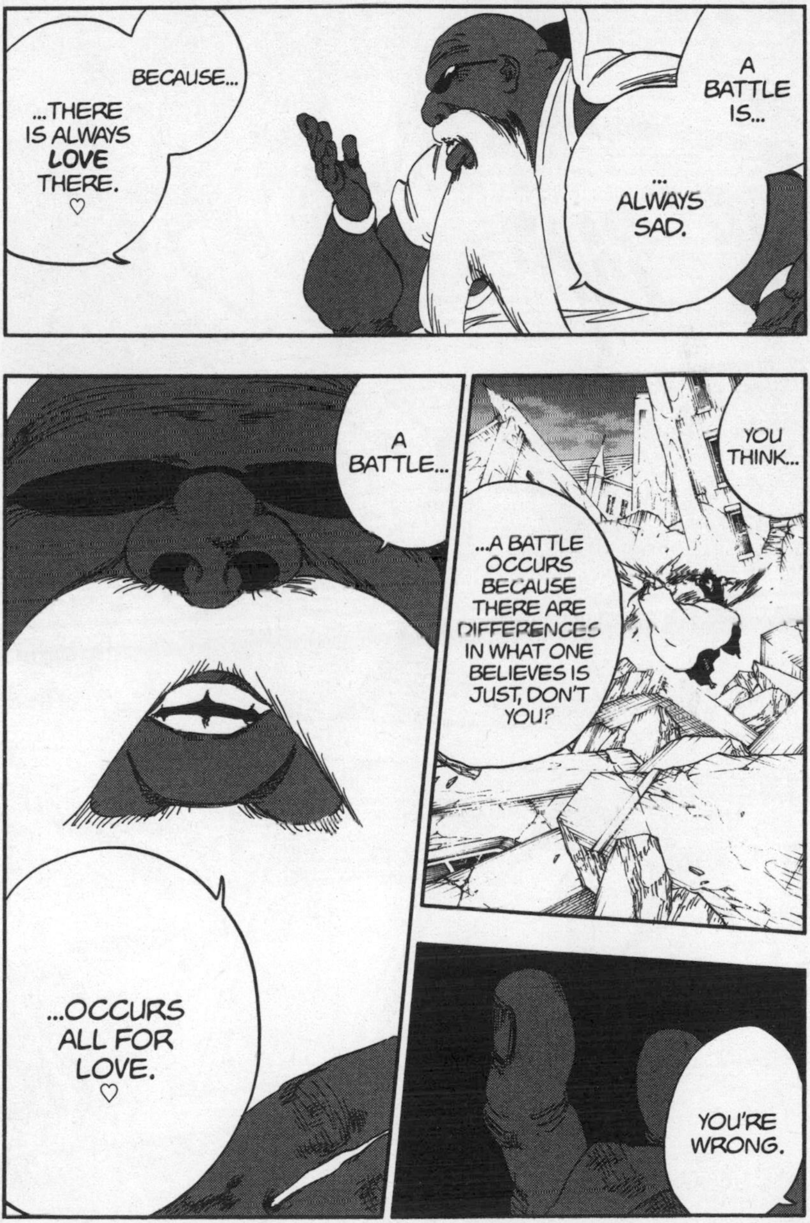
A BATTLE IS...
...ALWAYS SAD.
BECAUSE...
...THERE IS ALWAYS LOVE THERE. ♡
YOU THINK...
...A BATTLE OCCURS BECAUSE THERE ARE DIFFERENCES IN WHAT ONE BELIEVES IS JUST, DON'T YOU?
YOU'RE WRONG.
A BATTLE...
...OCCURS ALL FOR LOVE. ♡

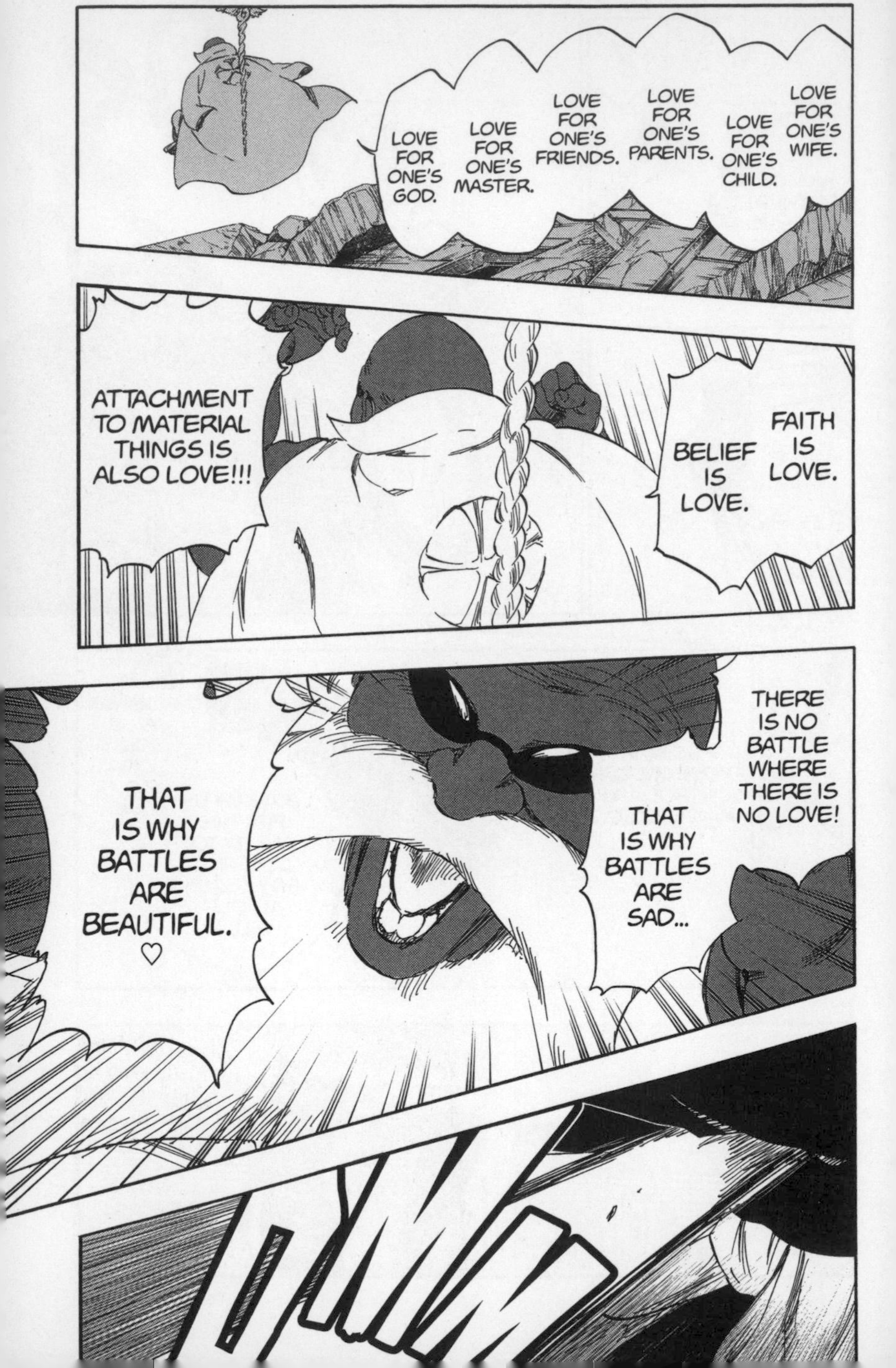
LOVE FOR ONE'S WIFE.
LOVE FOR ONE'S CHILD.
LOVE FOR ONE'S PARENTS.
LOVE FOR ONE'S FRIENDS.
LOVE FOR ONE'S MASTER.
LOVE FOR ONE'S GOD.
FAITH IS LOVE.
BELIEF IS LOVE.
ATTACHMENT TO MATERIAL THINGS IS ALSO LOVE!!!
THERE IS NO BATTLE WHERE THERE IS NO LOVE!
THAT IS WHY BATTLES ARE SAD...
THAT IS WHY BATTLES ARE BEAUTIFUL. ♡

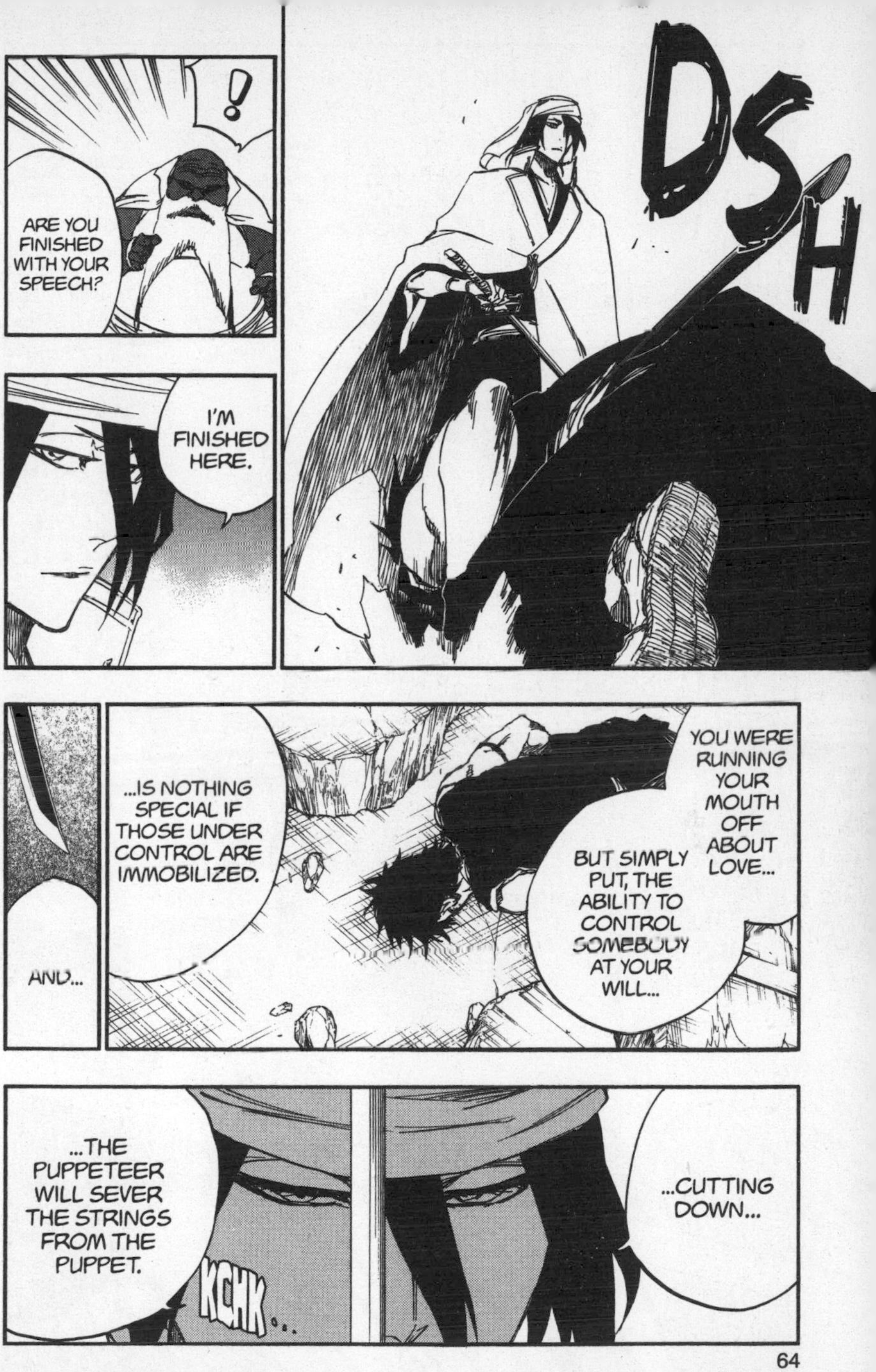
DSH
!
ARE YOU FINISHED WITH YOUR SPEECH?
I'M FINISHED HERE.
YOU WERE RUNNING YOUR MOUTH OFF ABOUT LOVE...
BUT SIMPLY PUT, THE ABILITY TO CONTROL SOMEBODY AT YOUR WILL...
...IS NOTHING SPECIAL IF THOSE UNDER CONTROL ARE IMMOBILIZED.
AND...
...CUTTING DOWN...
KCHK...
...THE PUPPETEER WILL SEVER THE STRINGS FROM THE PUPPET.

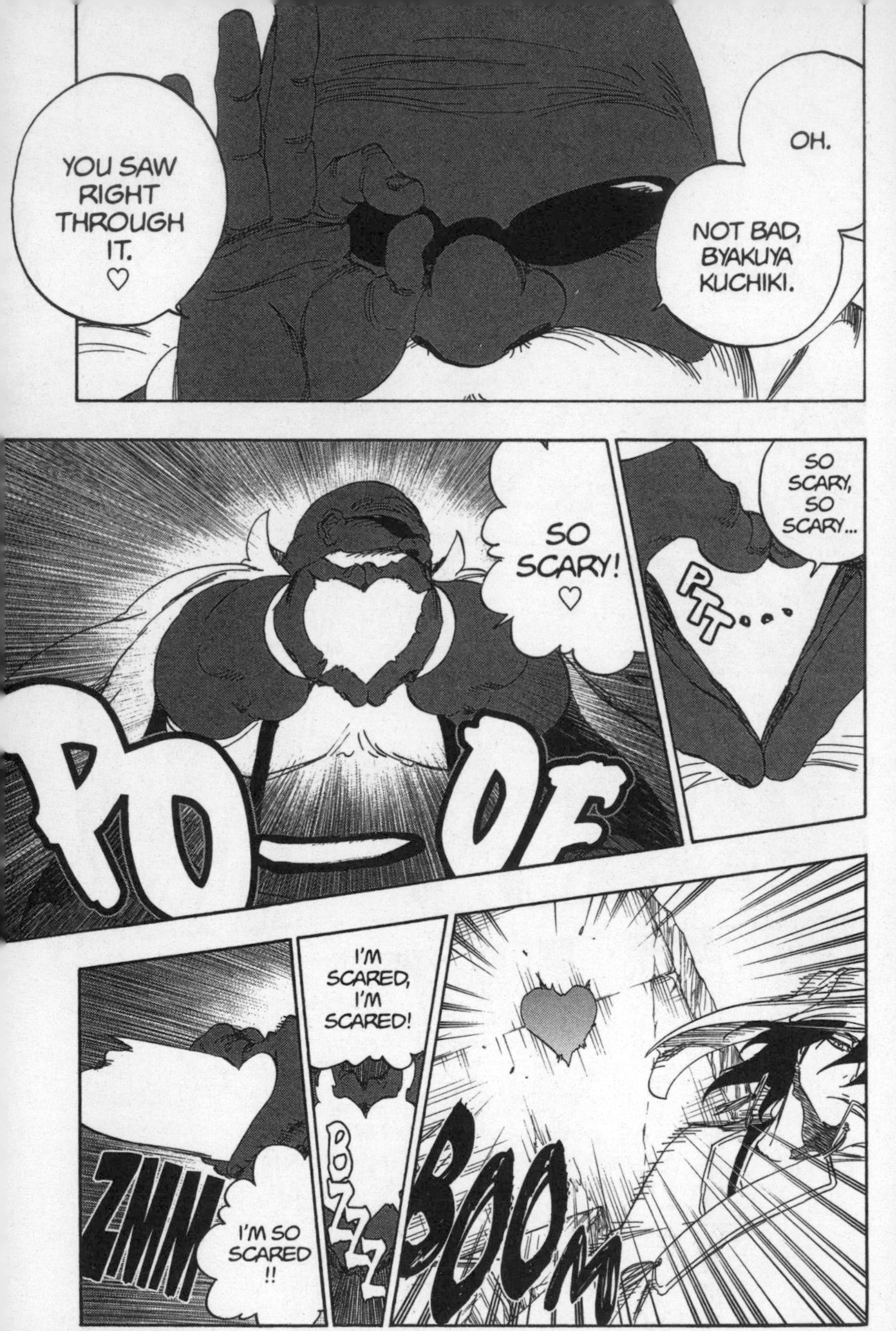
OH.
NOT BAD, BYAKUYA KUCHIKI.
YOU SAW RIGHT THROUGH IT. ♡
SO SCARY, SO SCARY...
PTT...
SO SCARY! ♡
PO—OF
BOOM
I'M SCARED, I'M SCARED!
BZZZ
ZMM
I'M SO SCARED !!

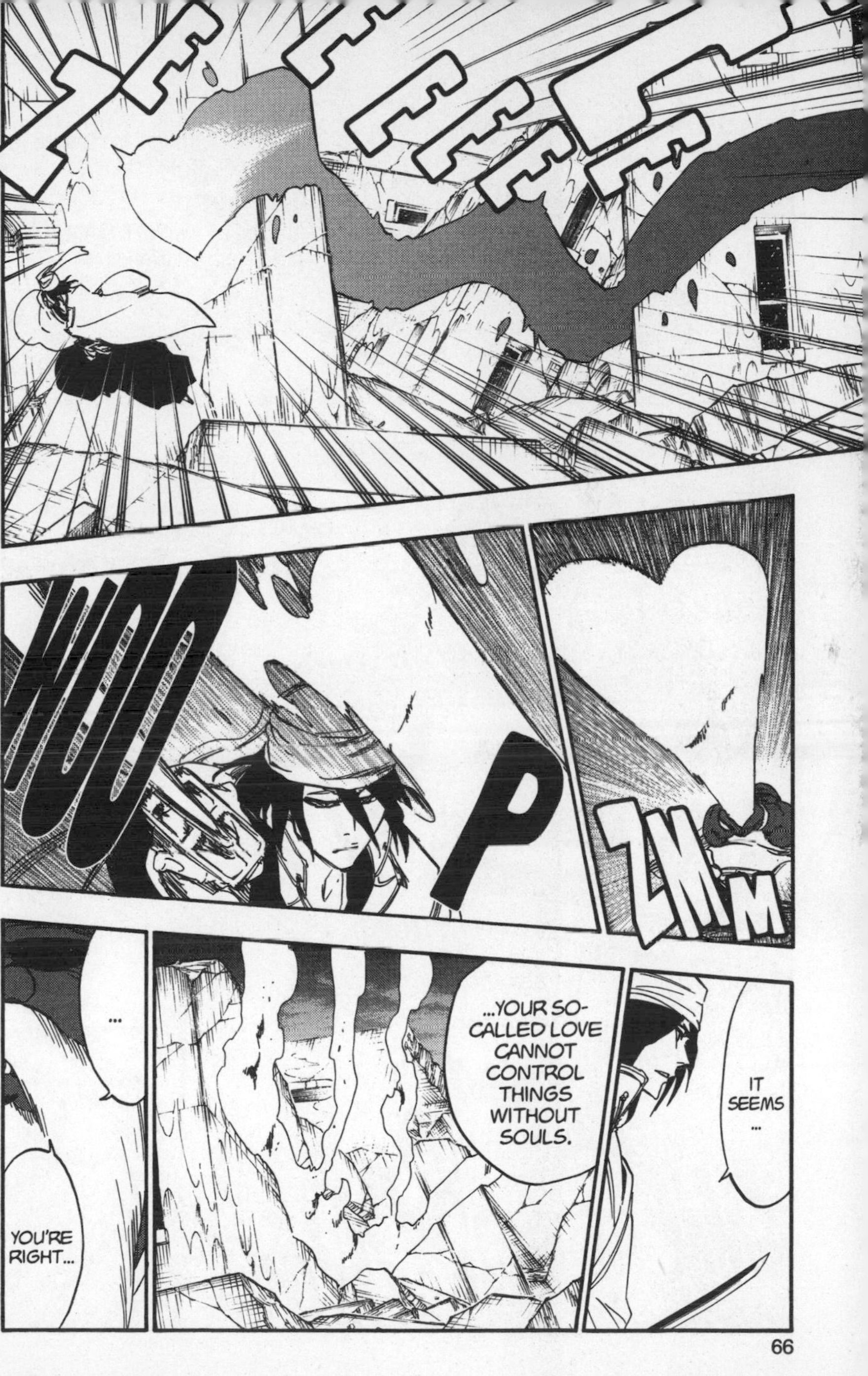
ZMMM
IT SEEMS ...
...YOUR SO-CALLED LOVE CANNOT CONTROL THINGS WITHOUT SOULS.
...
YOU'RE RIGHT...

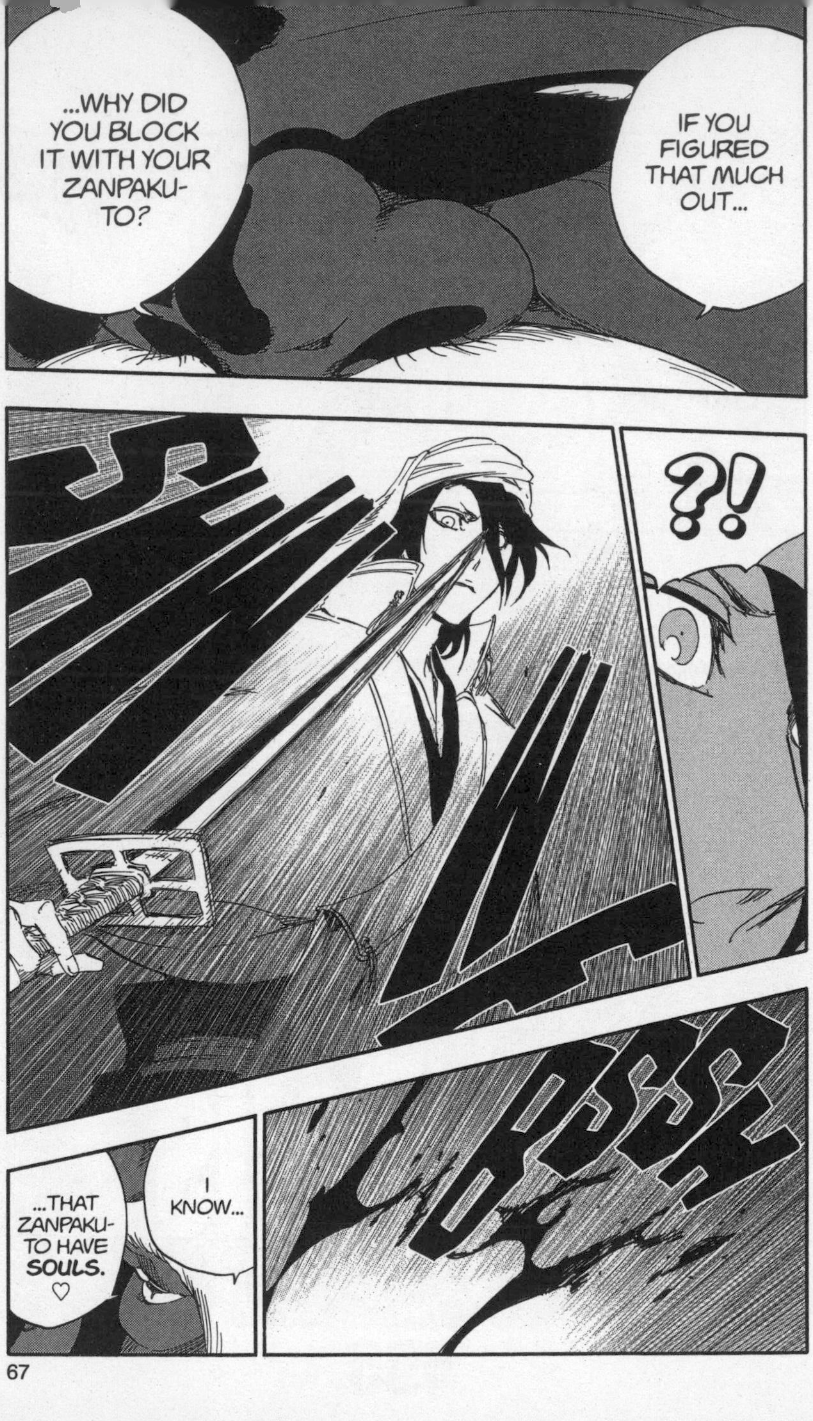
IF YOU FIGURED THAT MUCH OUT...
...WHY DID YOU BLOCK IT WITH YOUR ZANPAKU-TO?
?!
I KNOW...
...THAT ZANPAKU-TO HAVE **SOULS.** ♡

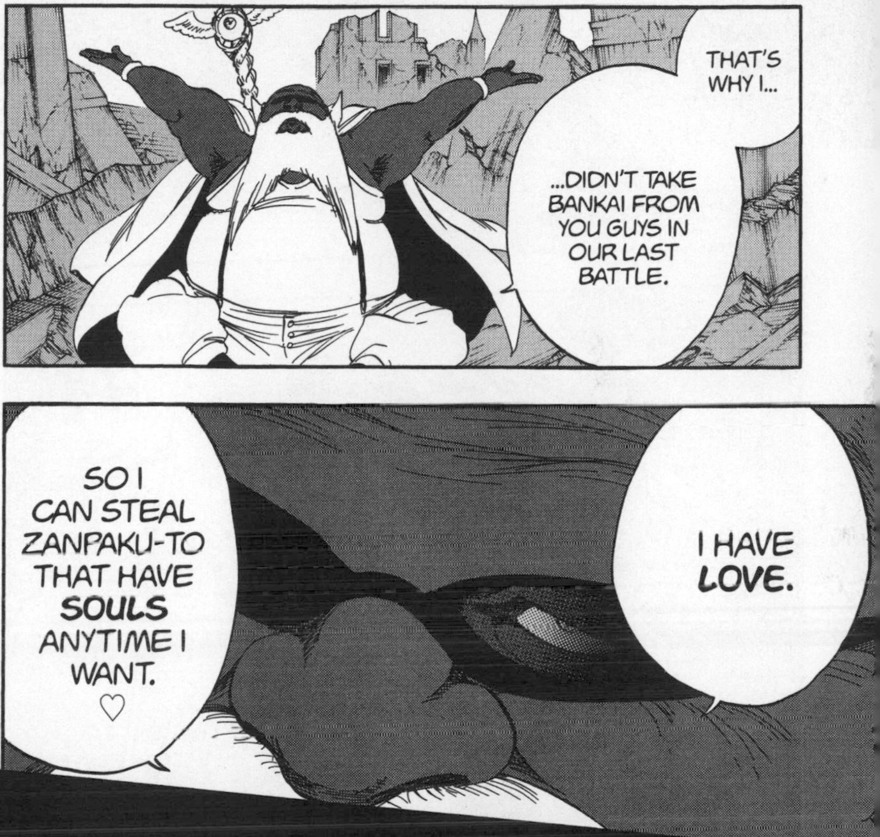
THAT'S WHY I...
...DIDN'T TAKE BANKAI FROM YOU GUYS IN OUR LAST BATTLE.
I HAVE **LOVE.**
SO I CAN STEAL ZANPAKU-TO THAT HAVE **SOULS** ANYTIME I WANT. ♡

Rubb-Dolls 2

595.

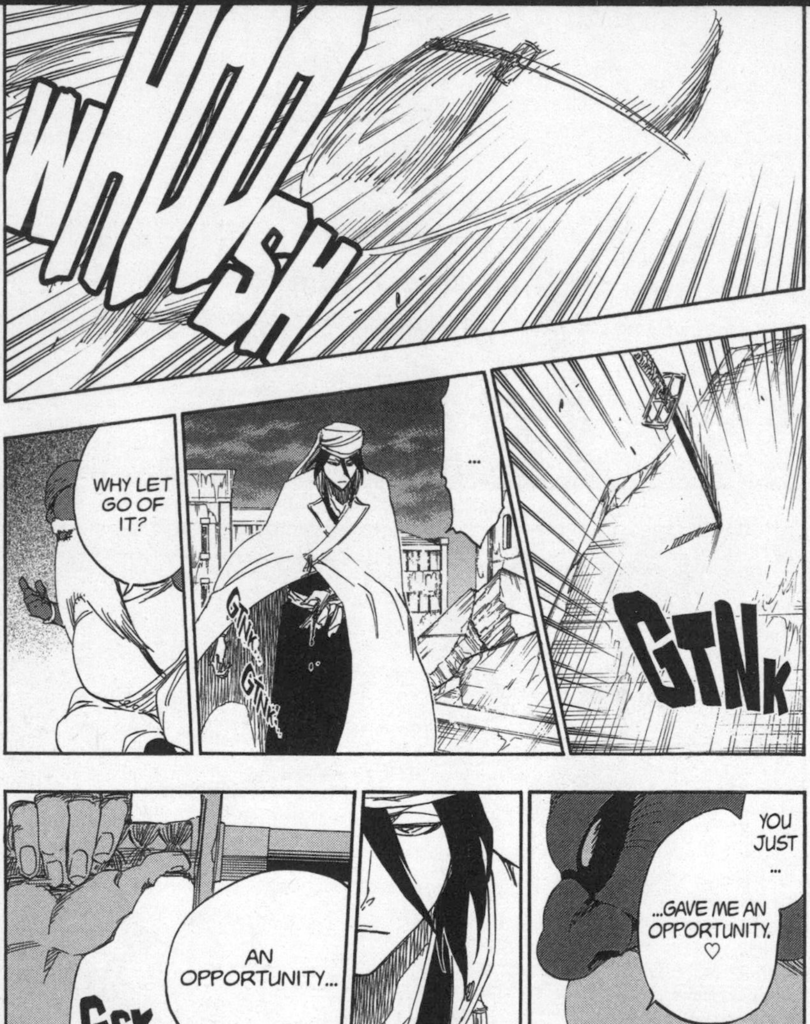
WHOOSH
GTNK
...
GTNK... GTNK... GTNK...
WHY LET GO OF IT?
YOU JUST ...
...GAVE ME AN OPPORTUNITY. ♡
AN OPPORTUNITY...
GCK

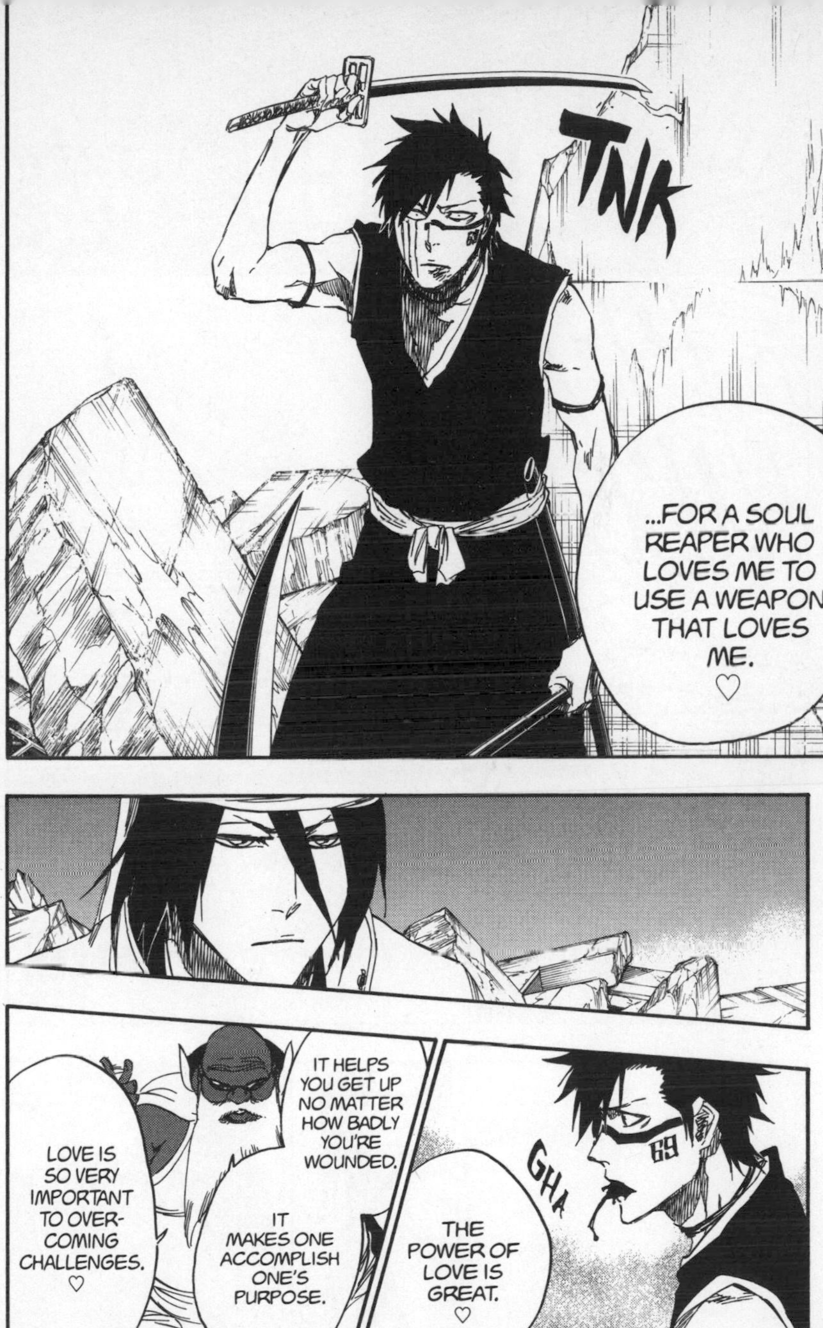
TNK
...FOR A SOUL REAPER WHO LOVES ME TO USE A WEAPON THAT LOVES ME. ♡
GHA
THE POWER OF LOVE IS GREAT. ♡
IT HELPS YOU GET UP NO MATTER HOW BADLY YOU'RE WOUNDED.
IT MAKES ONE ACCOMPLISH ONE'S PURPOSE.
LOVE IS SO VERY IMPORTANT TO OVER-COMING CHALLENGES. ♡

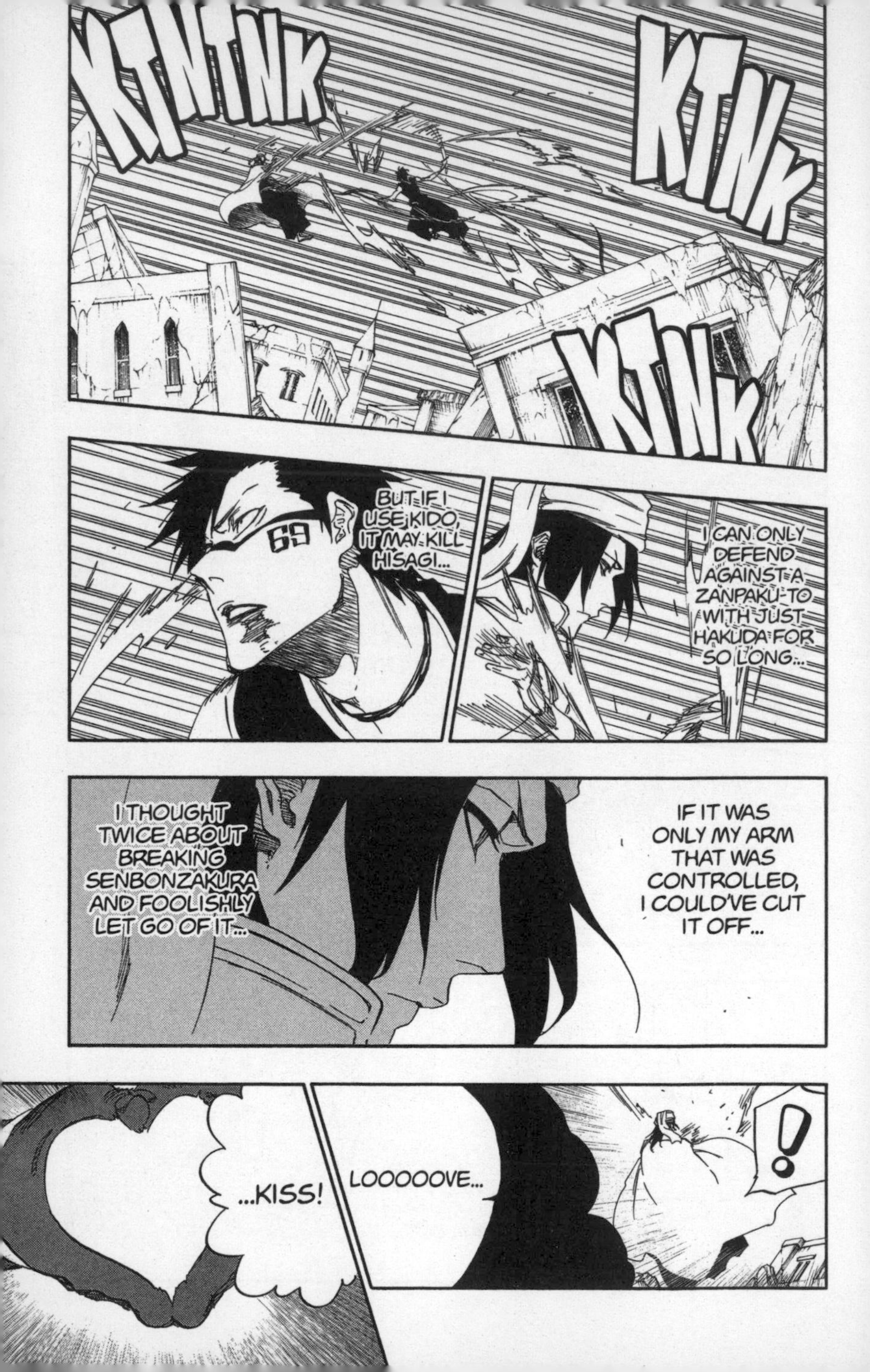
KTINK
KTINTINK
KTINK
I CAN ONLY DEFEND AGAINST A ZANPAKU-TO WITH JUST HAKUDA FOR SO LONG...
BUT IF I USE KIDO, IT MAY KILL HISAGI...
IF IT WAS ONLY MY ARM THAT WAS CONTROLLED, I COULD'VE CUT IT OFF...
I THOUGHT TWICE ABOUT BREAKING SENBONZAKURA AND FOOLISHLY LET GO OF IT...
!
LOOOOOVE...
...KISS!

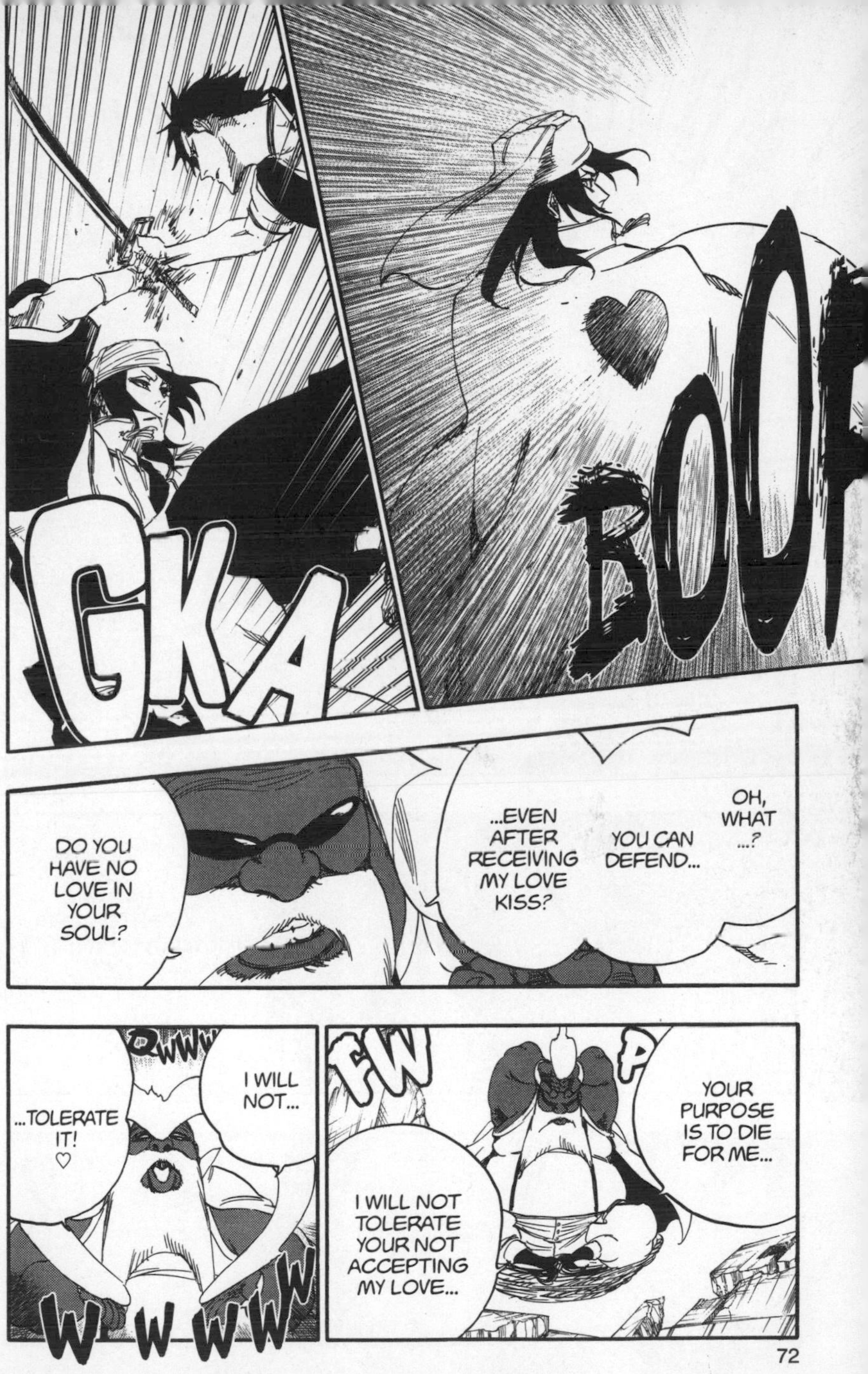
BOOF
GKA
OH, WHAT ...?
YOU CAN DEFEND...
...EVEN AFTER RECEIVING MY LOVE KISS?
DO YOU HAVE NO LOVE IN YOUR SOUL?
FW
P
YOUR PURPOSE IS TO DIE FOR ME...
I WILL NOT TOLERATE YOUR NOT ACCEPTING MY LOVE...
QWWW
I WILL NOT...
...TOLERATE IT! ♡
WWWWW

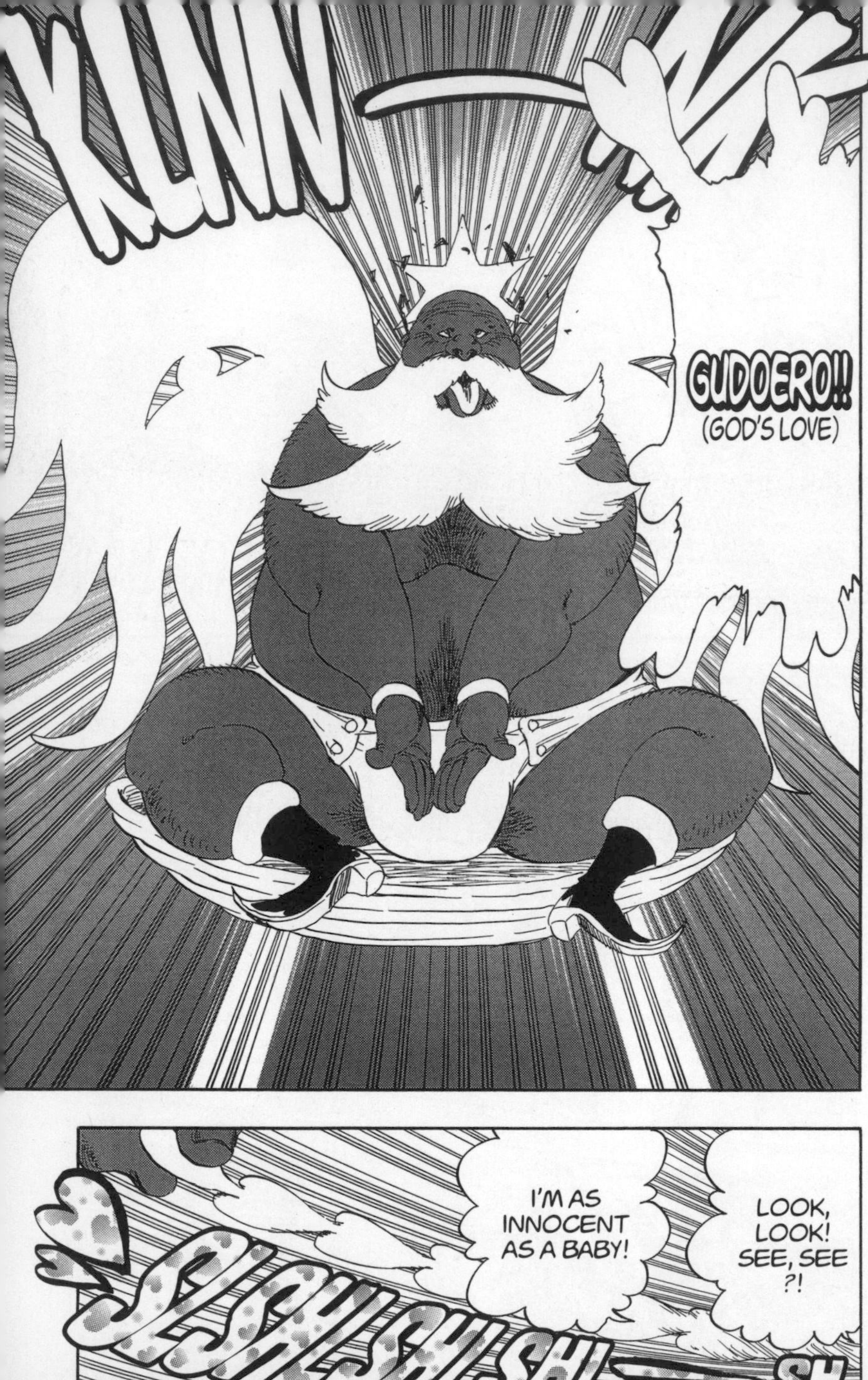
KLINN—
GUDOERO!!
(GOD'S LOVE)
LOOK, LOOK! SEE, SEE ?!
I'M AS INNOCENT AS A BABY!
SHLSHLSHL—SH

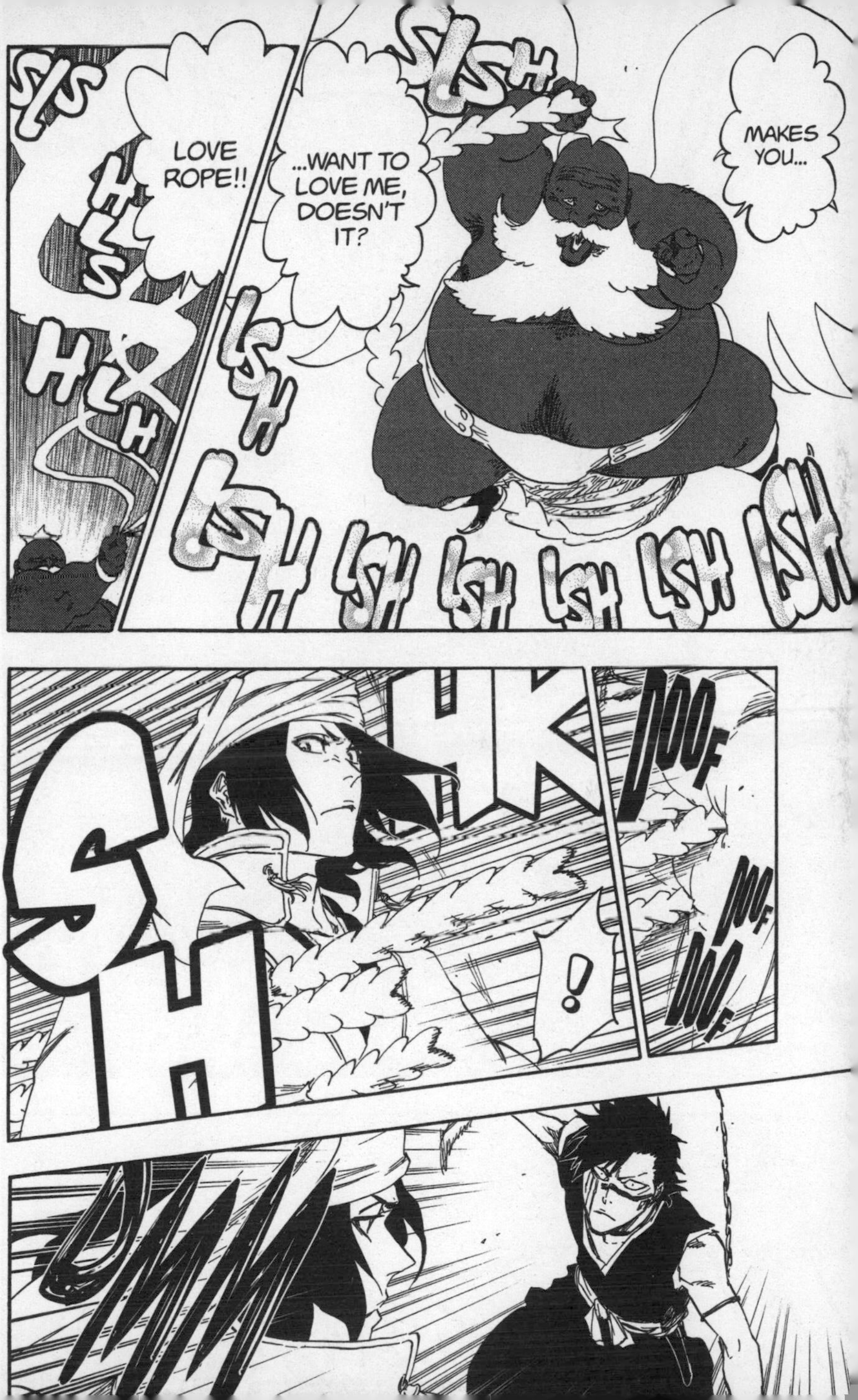
MAKES YOU...
...WANT TO LOVE ME, DOESN'T IT?
LOVE ROPE!!
DOOF
DOOF
DOOF
!
SHK

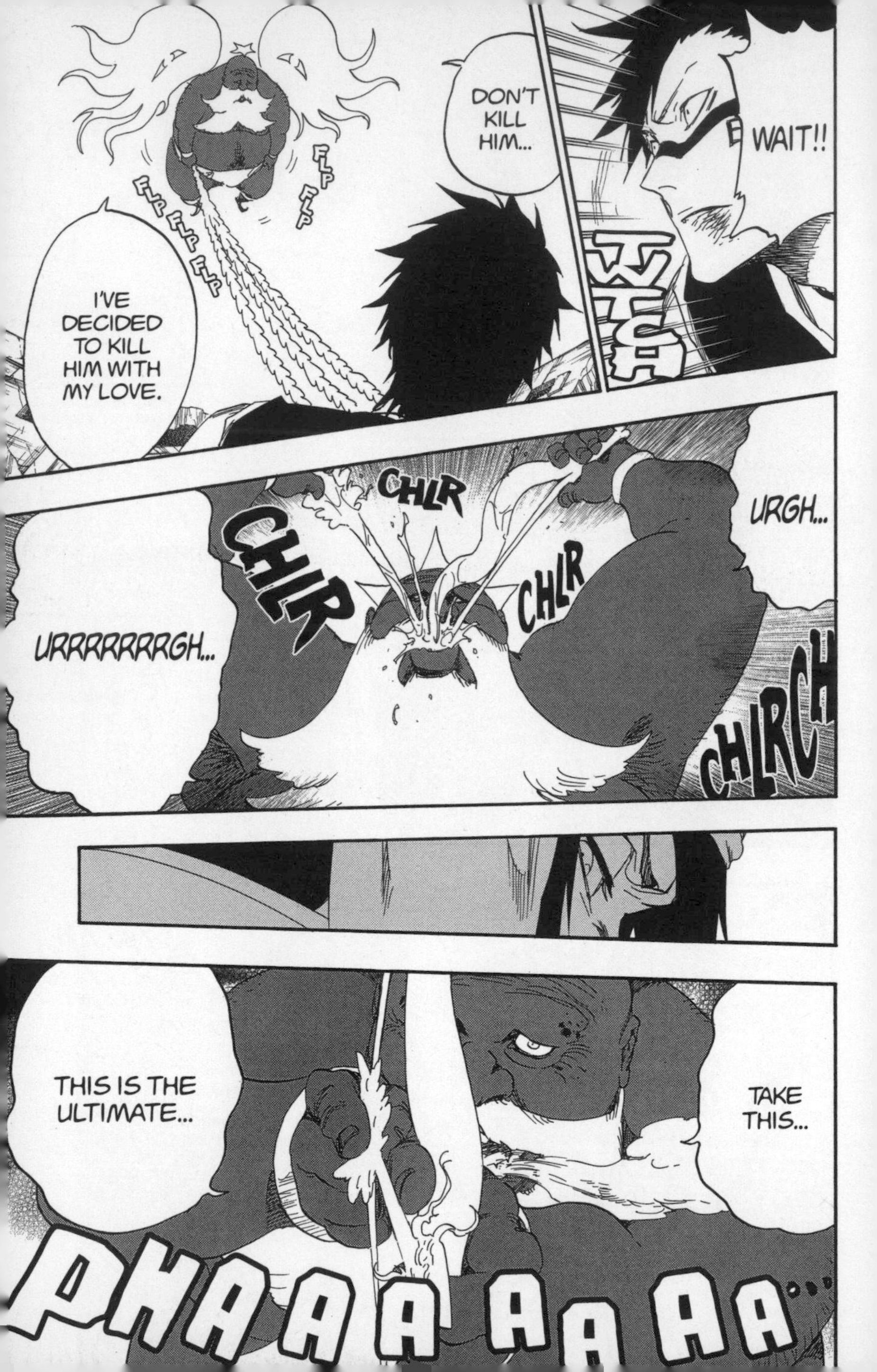
WAIT!!
TWTCH
DON'T KILL HIM...
FLP FLP
FLP FLP FLP FLP
I'VE DECIDED TO KILL HIM WITH MY LOVE.
URGH...
CHLR
CHLR
CHLR
URRRRRRRGH...
CHLRCH
TAKE THIS...
THIS IS THE ULTIMATE...
PHAAAAAAA...

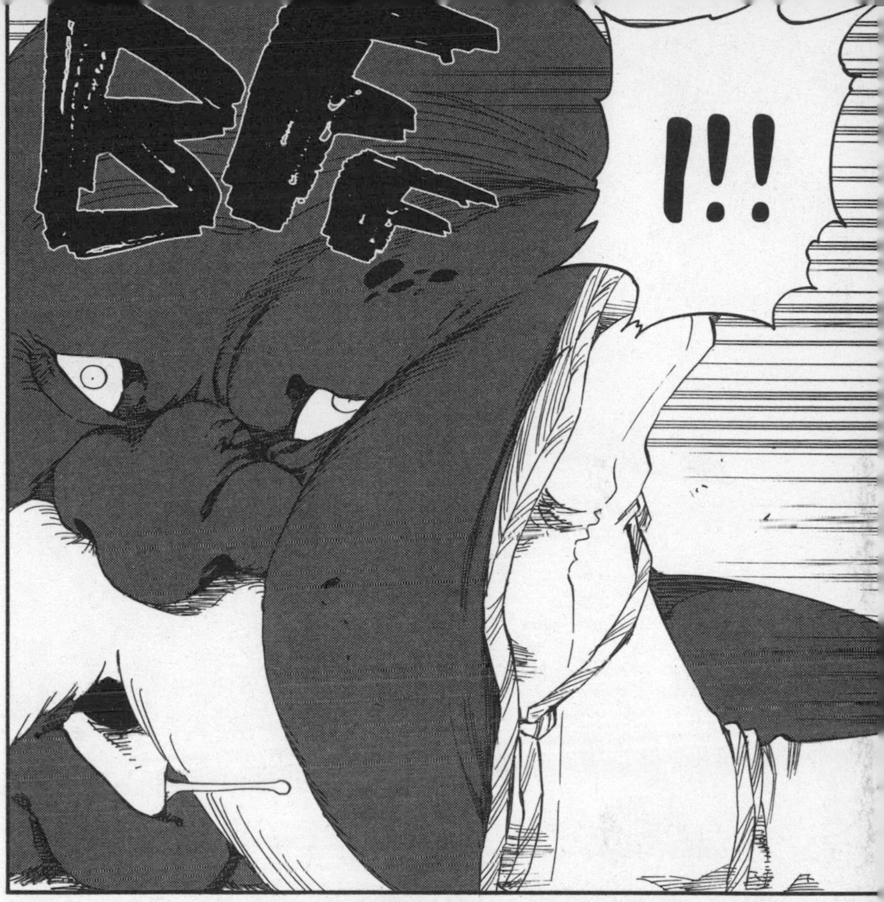
BFF
!!!
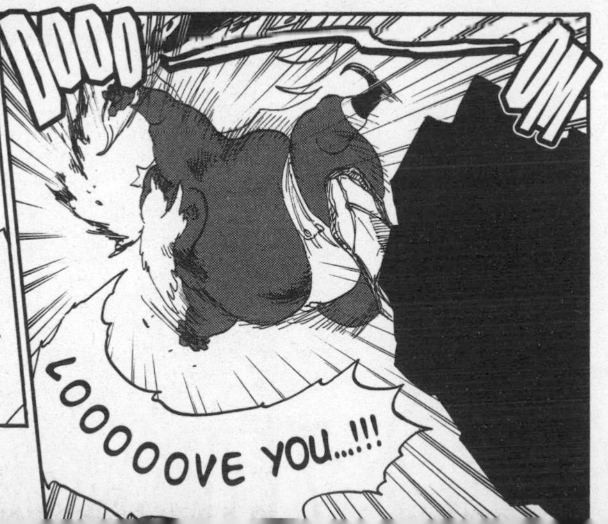
DOOO
OM
LOOOOOVE YOU...!!!
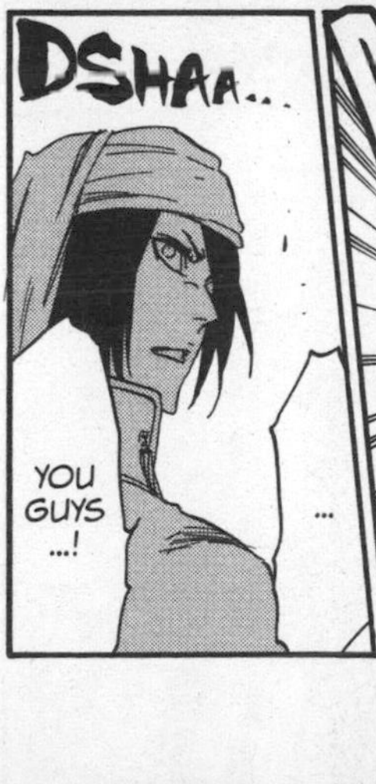
DSHAA...
YOU GUYS ...!
...

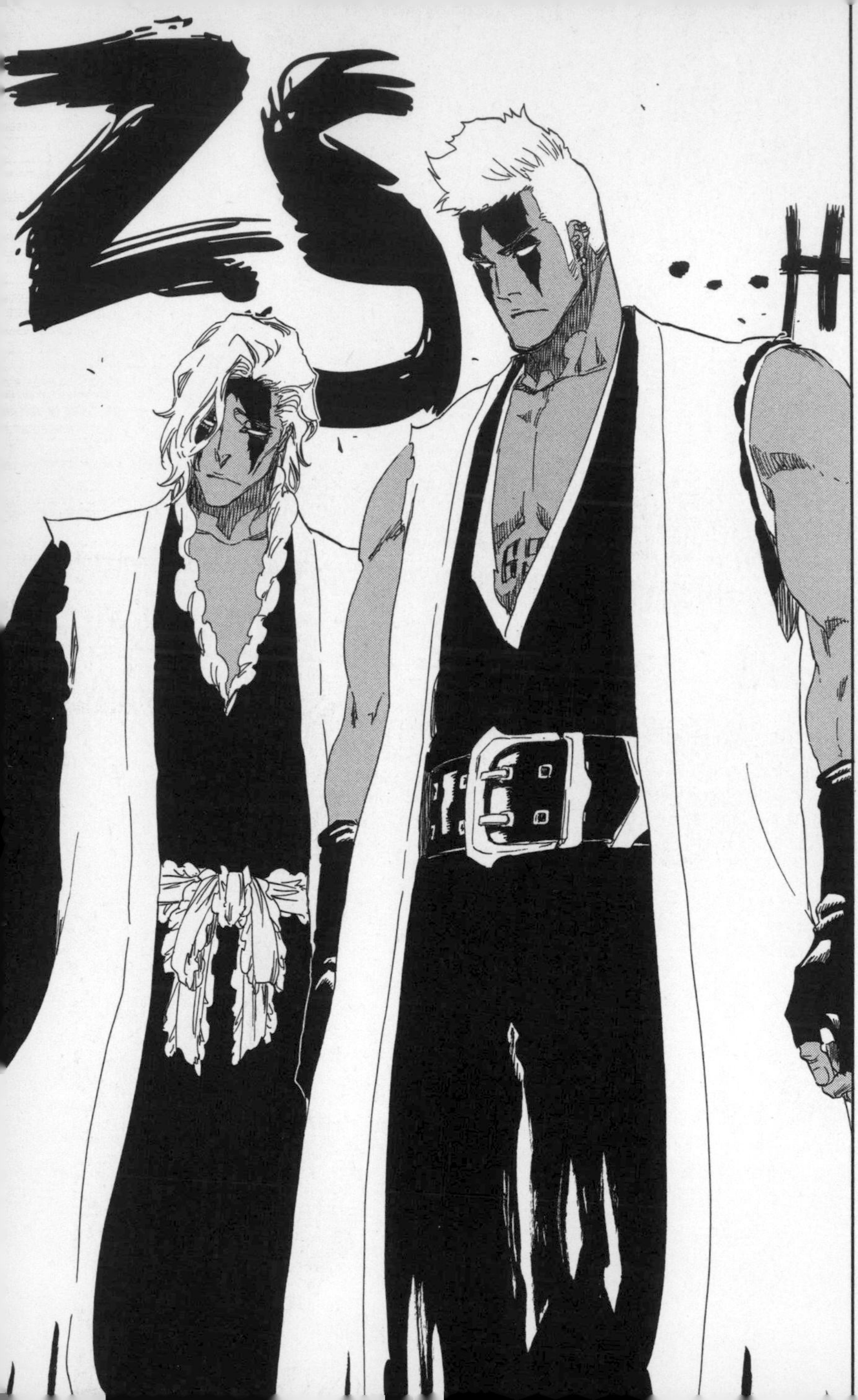
ZS...H

THE QUINCY CROSS IS HERE.

LOVE STICK BESHANUL

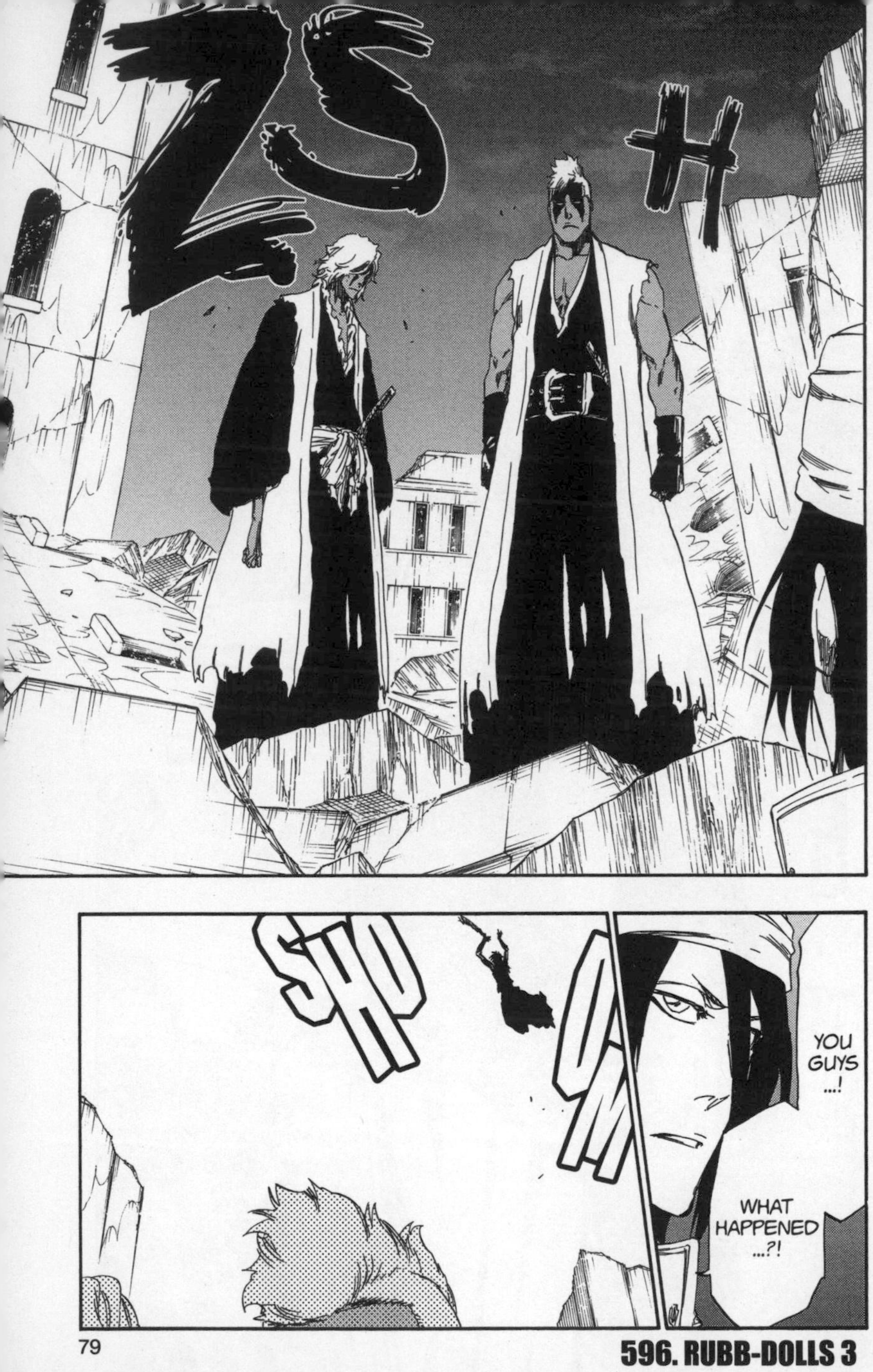
ZS
H
YOU GUYS ...!
WHAT HAPPENED ...?!
SHO
OM

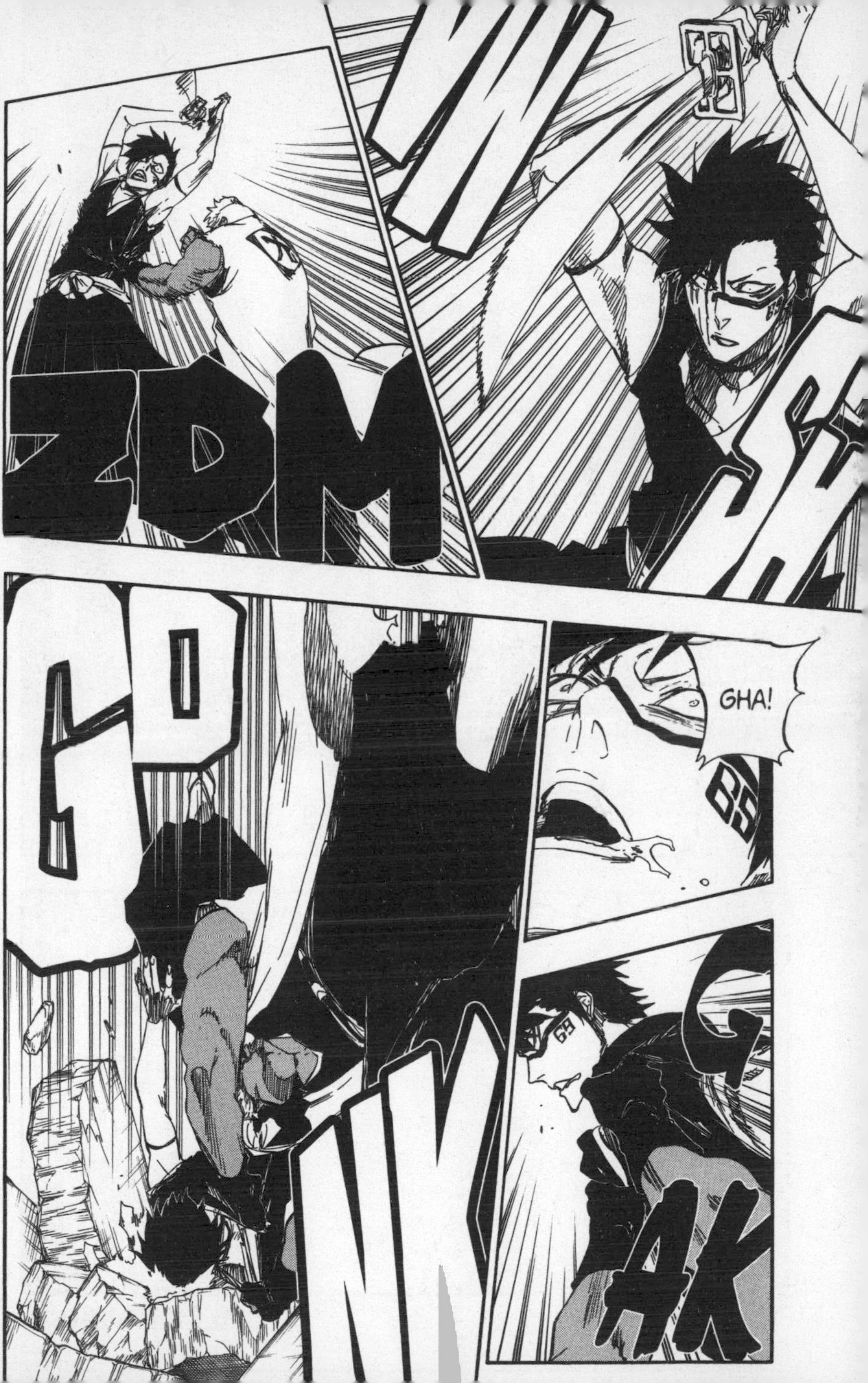
GHA!

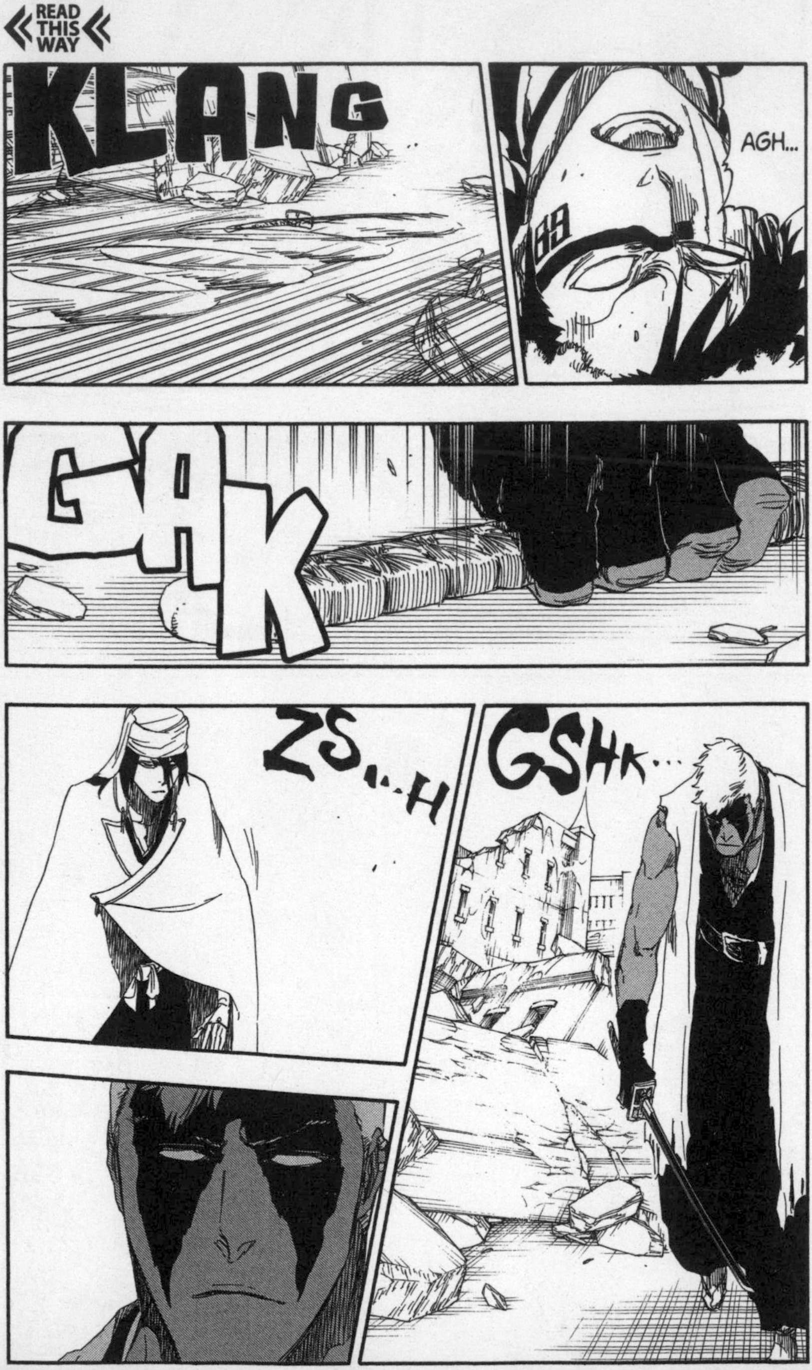
READ THIS WAY
AGH...
KLANG
GAK
GSHK...
ZS...H

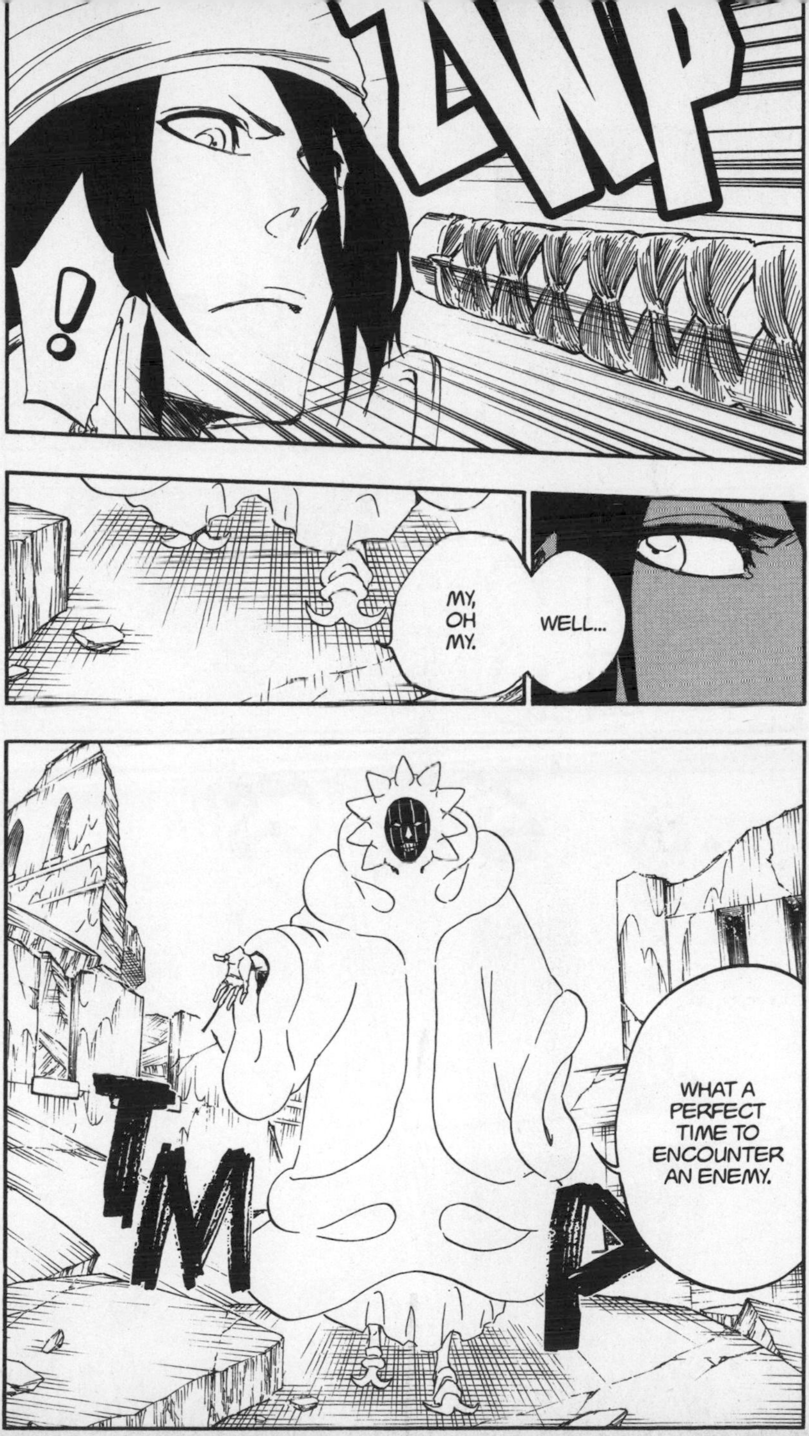
!
WELL...
MY, OH MY.
TMP
WHAT A PERFECT TIME TO ENCOUNTER AN ENEMY.

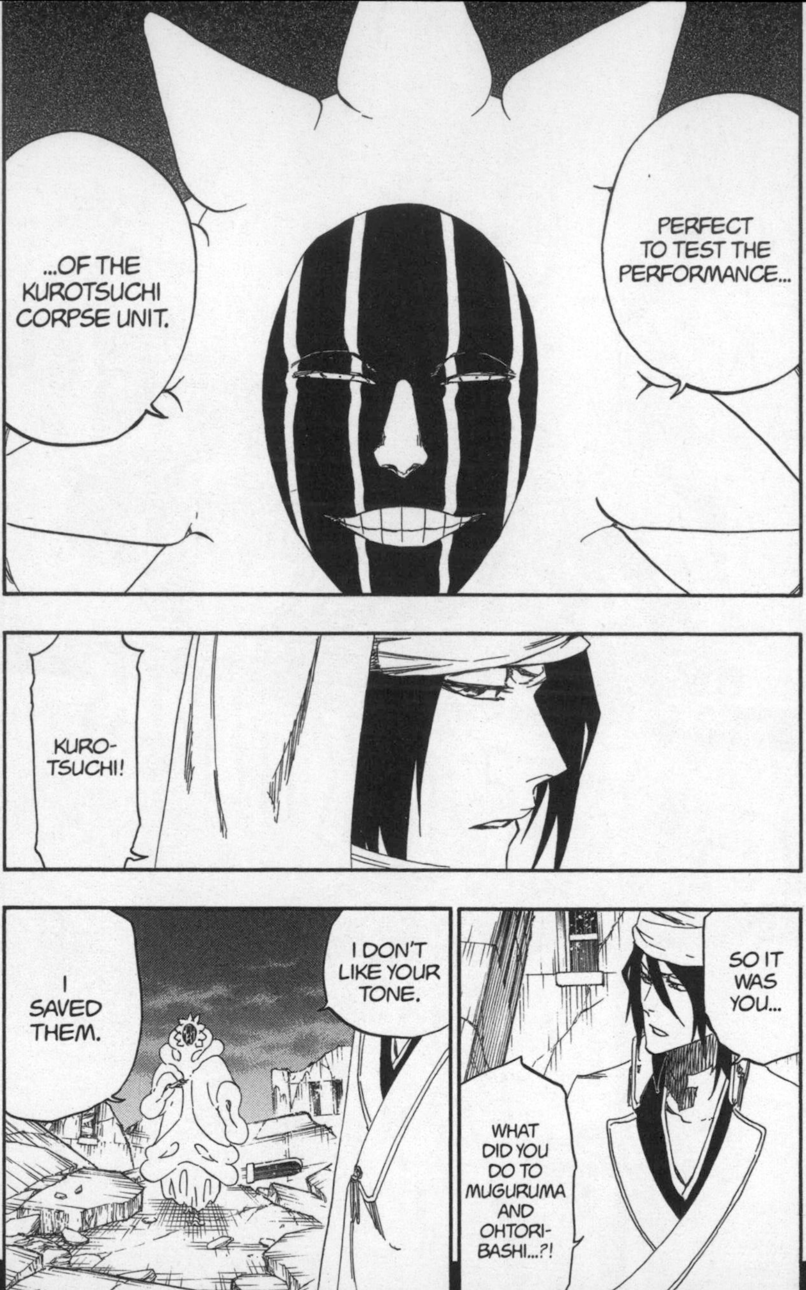
PERFECT TO TEST THE PERFORMANCE...
...OF THE KUROTSUCHI CORPSE UNIT.
KURO-TSUCHI!
SO IT WAS YOU...
WHAT DID YOU DO TO MUGURUMA AND OHTORI-BASHI...?!
I DON'T LIKE YOUR TONE.
I SAVED THEM.

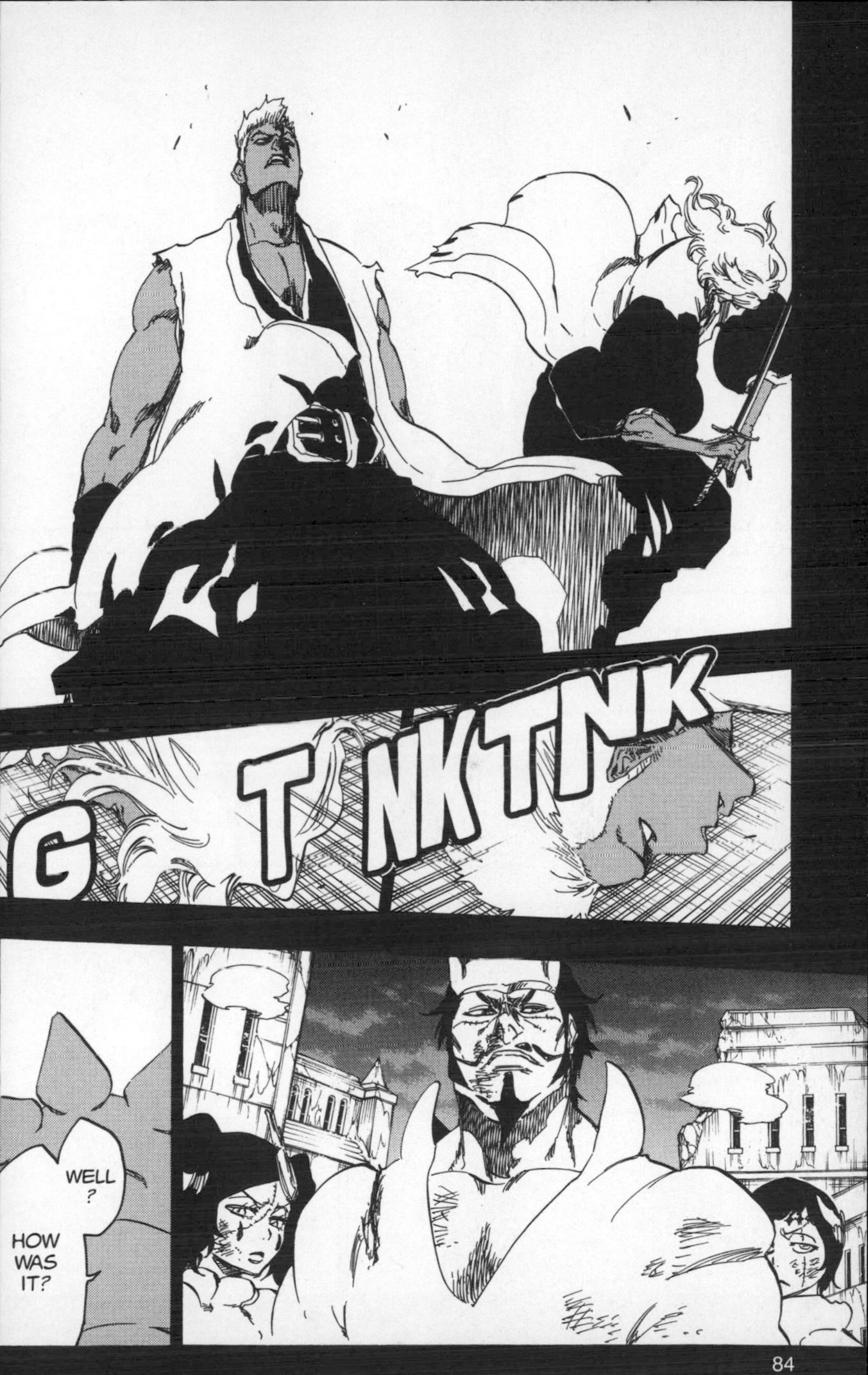
G
TNKTNK
WELL?
HOW WAS IT?

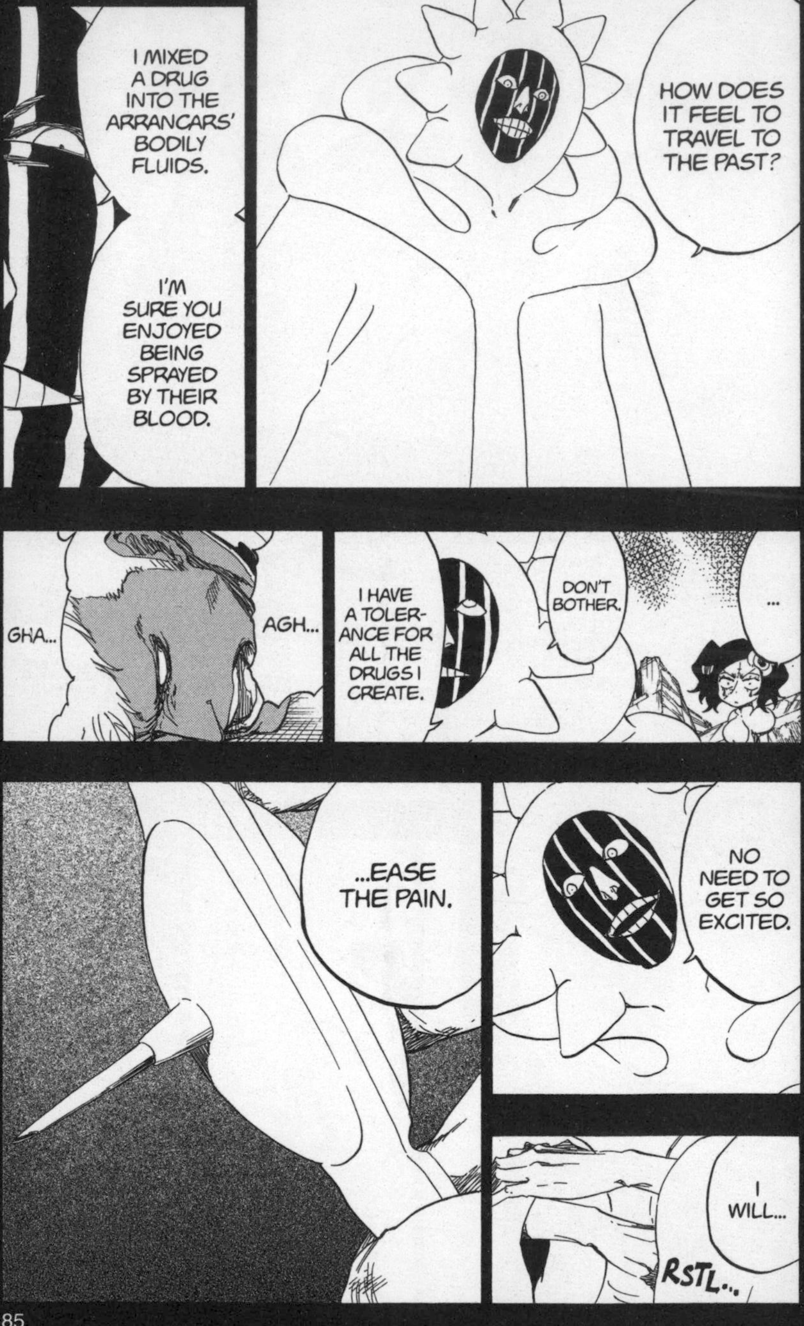
HOW DOES IT FEEL TO TRAVEL TO THE PAST?
I MIXED A DRUG INTO THE ARRANCARS' BODILY FLUIDS.
I'M SURE YOU ENJOYED BEING SPRAYED BY THEIR BLOOD.
...
DON'T BOTHER.
I HAVE A TOLER-ANCE FOR ALL THE DRUGS I CREATE.
AGH...
GHA...
NO NEED TO GET SO EXCITED.
I WILL...
RSTL...
...EASE THE PAIN.

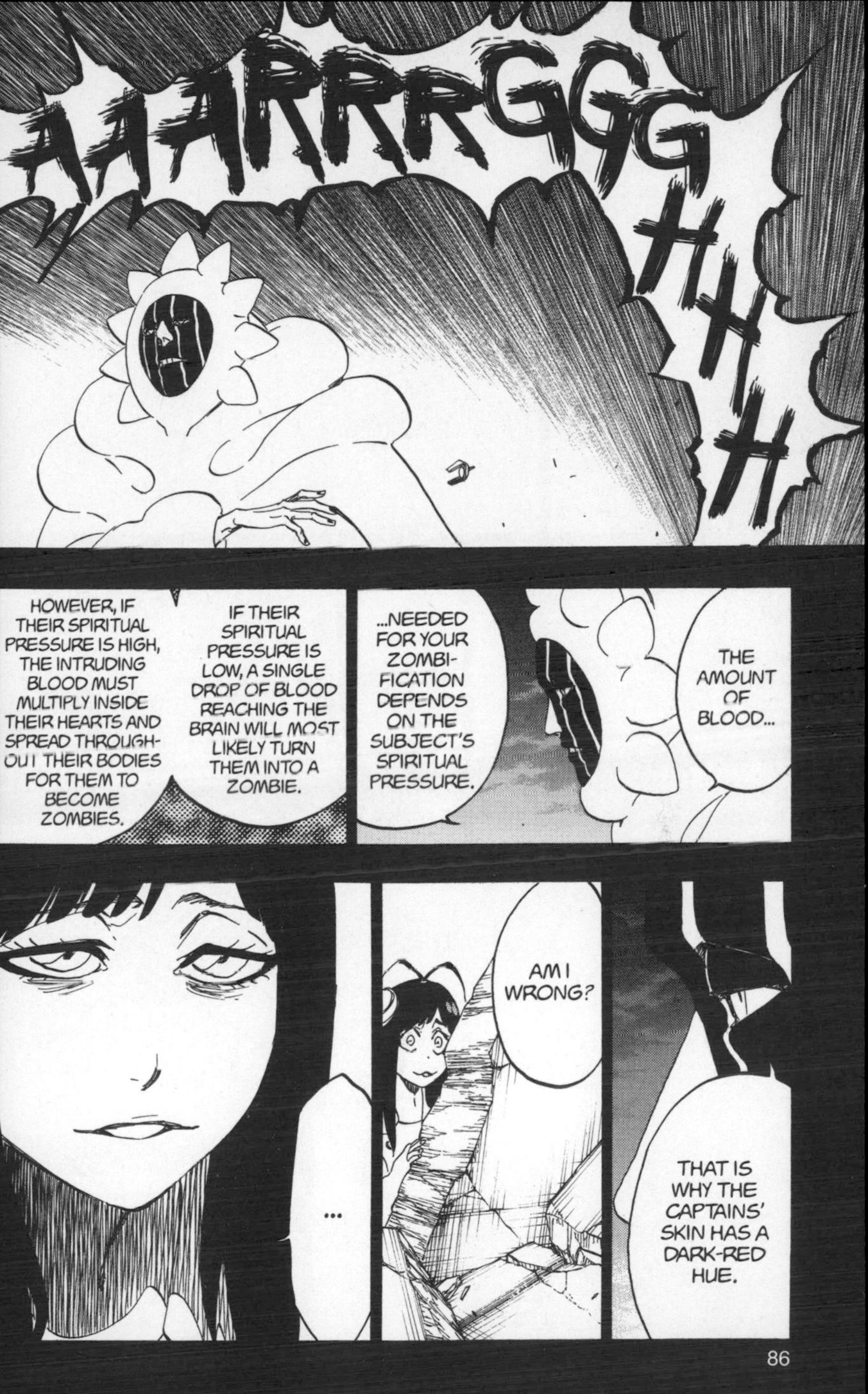
AAARRRGGHHHH
THE AMOUNT OF BLOOD...
...NEEDED FOR YOUR ZOMBIFICATION DEPENDS ON THE SUBJECT'S SPIRITUAL PRESSURE.
IF THEIR SPIRITUAL PRESSURE IS LOW, A SINGLE DROP OF BLOOD REACHING THE BRAIN WILL MOST LIKELY TURN THEM INTO A ZOMBIE.
HOWEVER, IF THEIR SPIRITUAL PRESSURE IS HIGH, THE INTRUDING BLOOD MUST MULTIPLY INSIDE THEIR HEARTS AND SPREAD THROUGHOUT THEIR BODIES FOR THEM TO BECOME ZOMBIES.
THAT IS WHY THE CAPTAINS' SKIN HAS A DARK-RED HUE.
AM I WRONG?
...

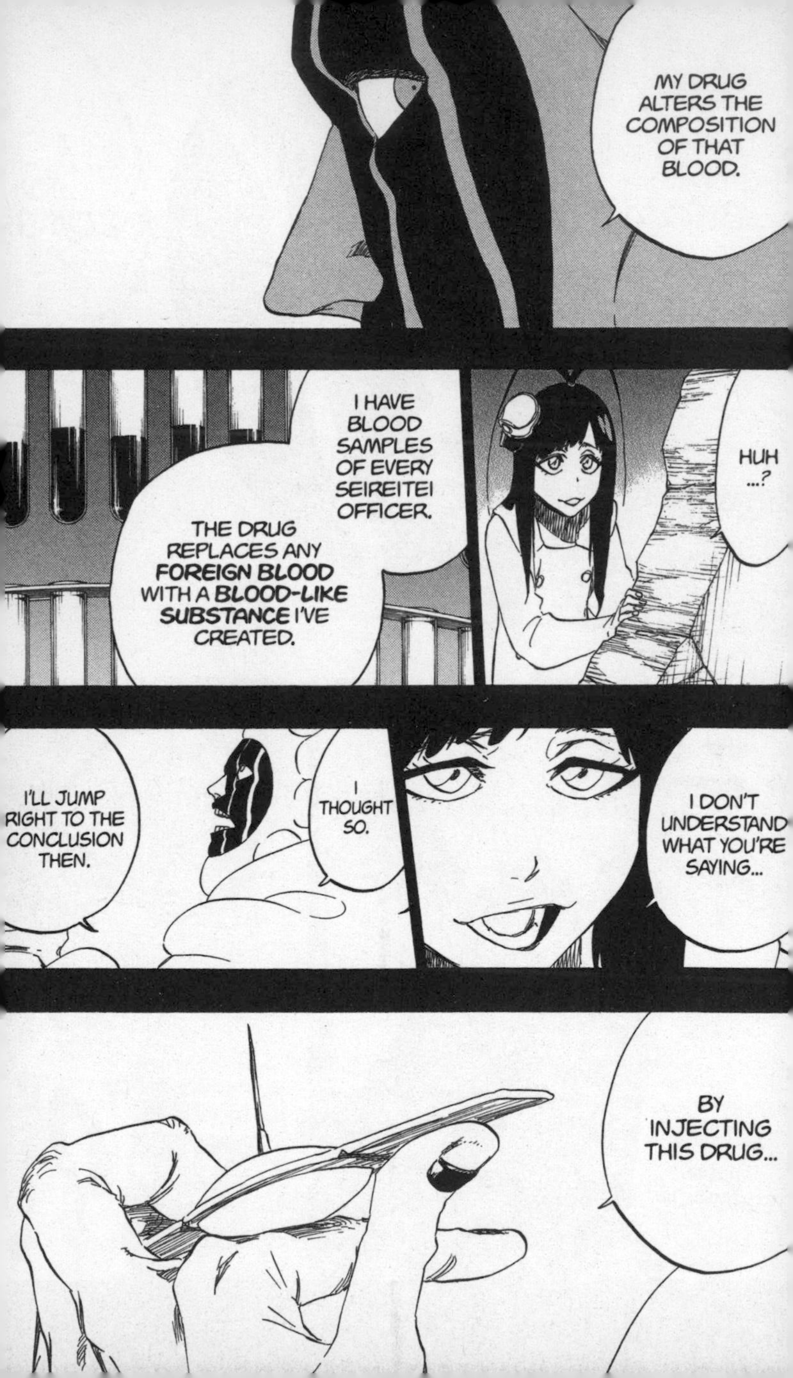

MY DRUG ALTERS THE COMPOSITION OF THAT BLOOD.
HUH ...?
I HAVE BLOOD SAMPLES OF EVERY SEIREITEI OFFICER.
THE DRUG REPLACES ANY **FOREIGN BLOOD** WITH A **BLOOD-LIKE SUBSTANCE** I'VE CREATED.
I DON'T UNDERSTAND WHAT YOU'RE SAYING...
I THOUGHT SO.
I'LL JUMP RIGHT TO THE CONCLUSION THEN.
BY INJECTING THIS DRUG...

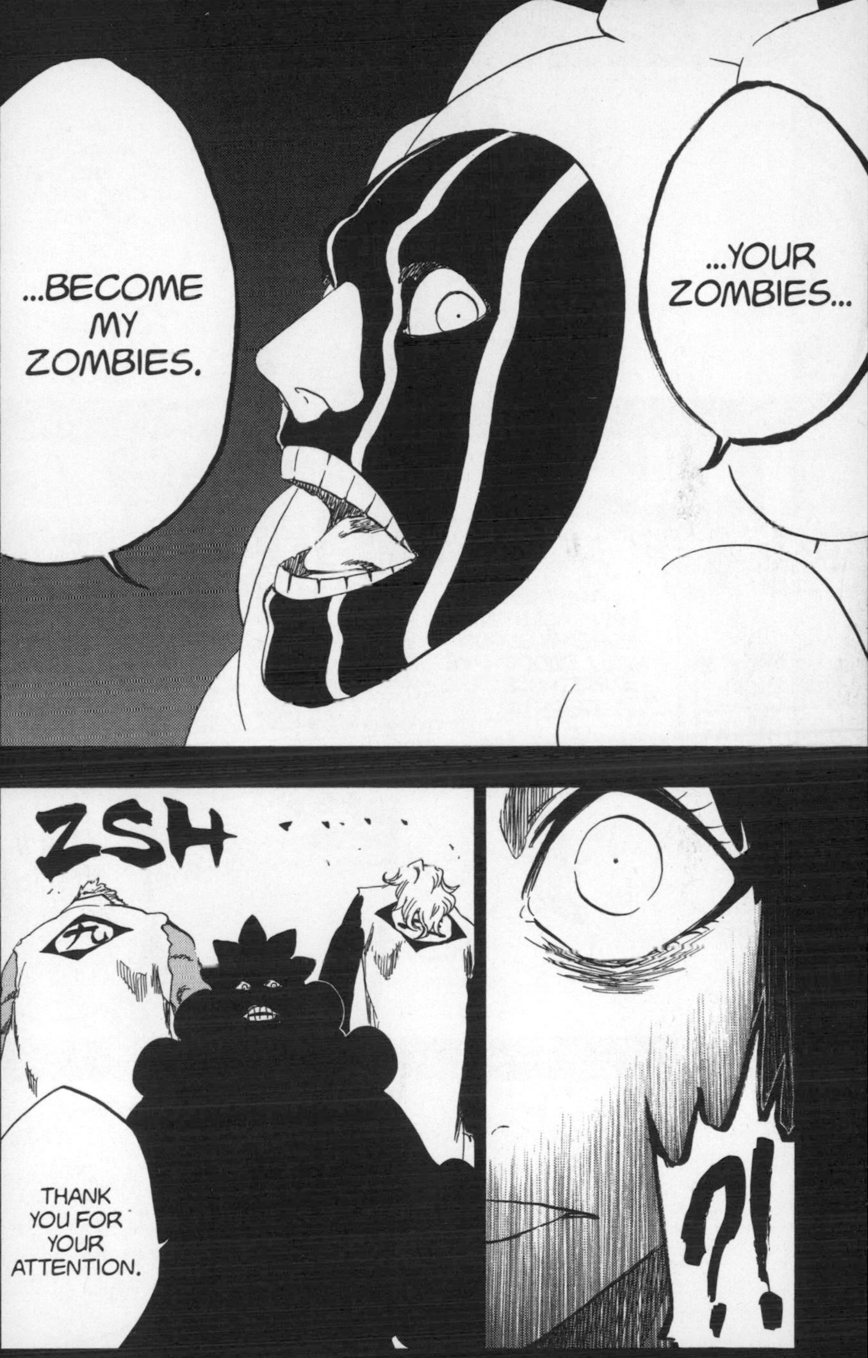
...YOUR ZOMBIES...
...BECOME MY ZOMBIES.
?!
ZSH
THANK YOU FOR YOUR ATTENTION.

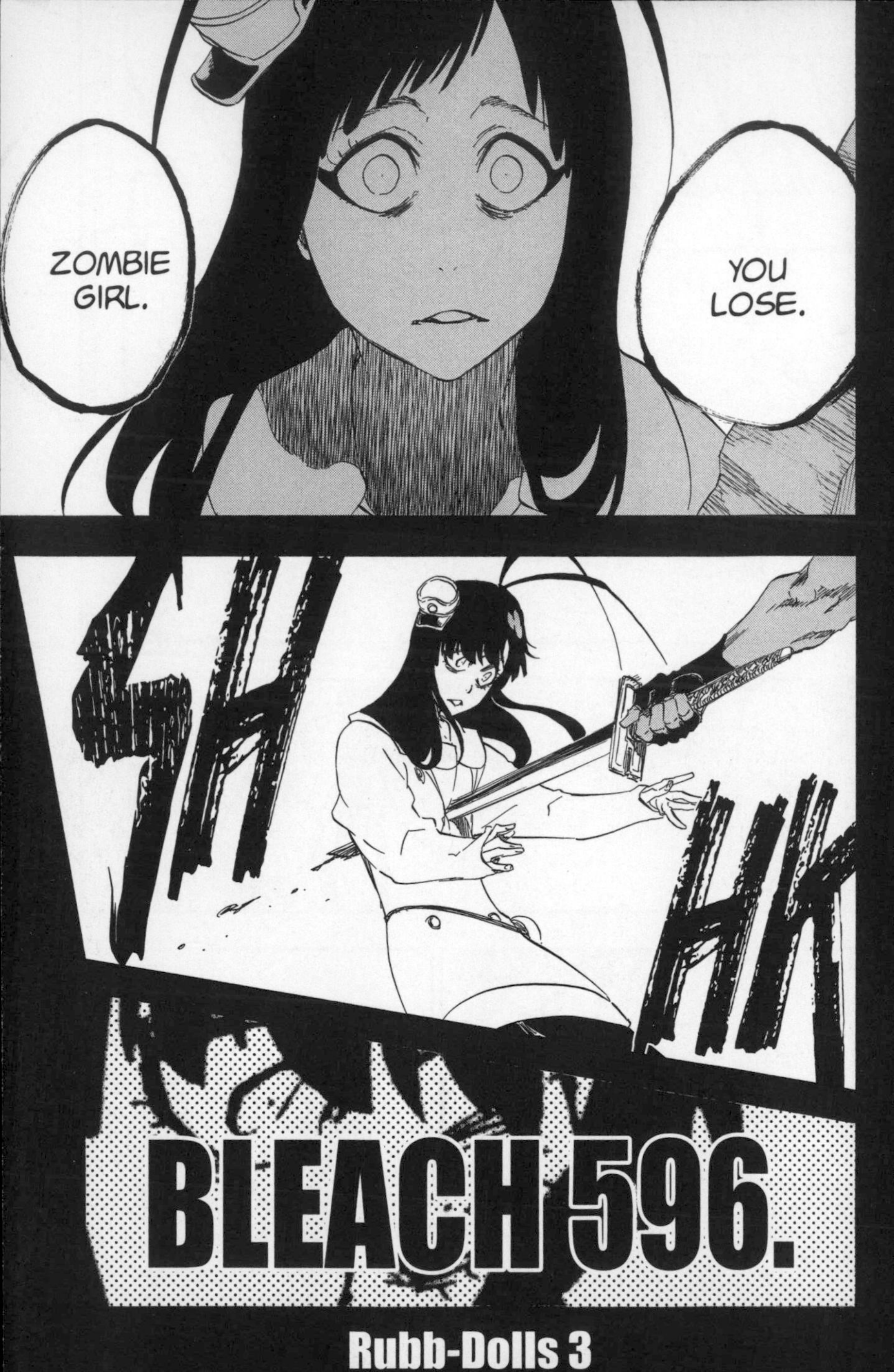
YOU LOSE.
ZOMBIE GIRL.
SHHK
BLEACH 596.
Rubb-Dolls 3

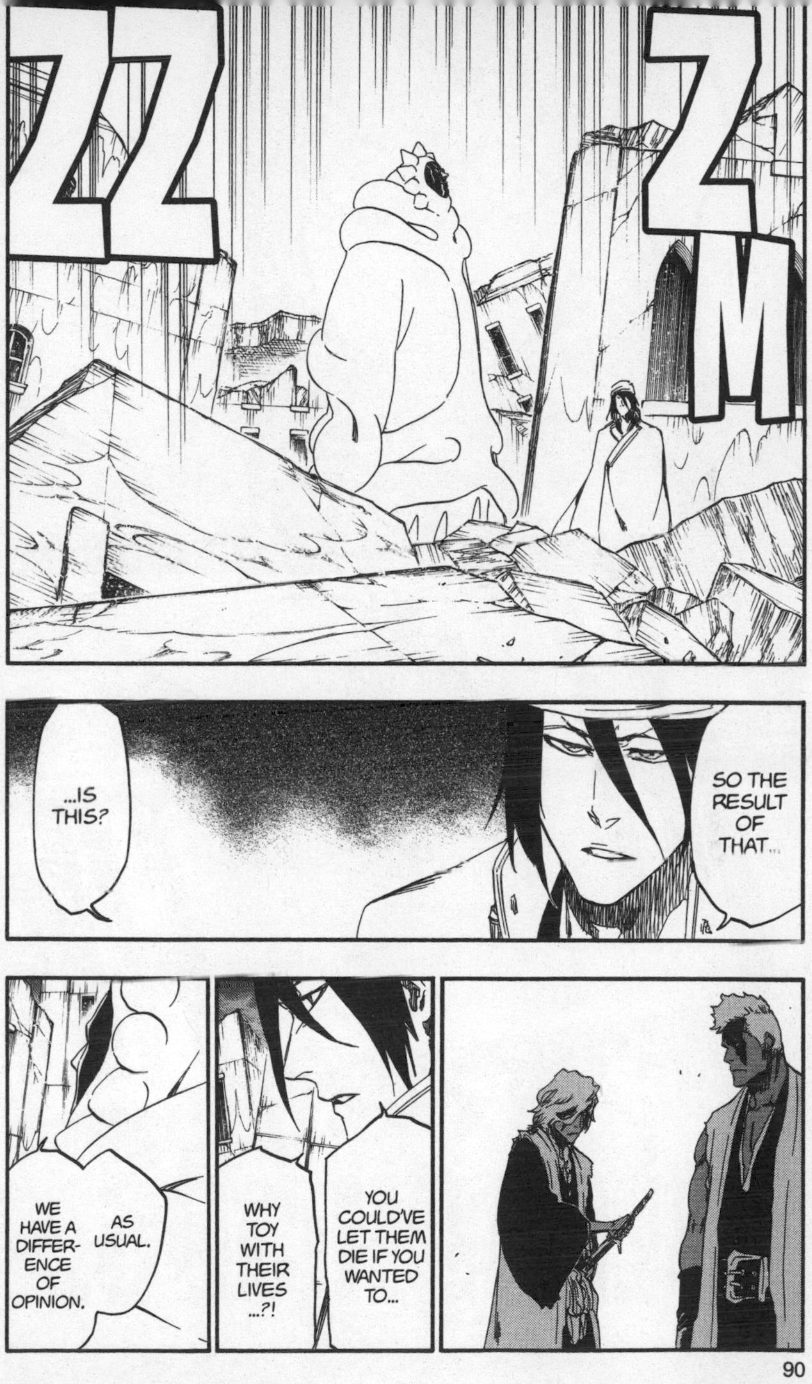
Z M
ZZ
SO THE RESULT OF THAT...
...IS THIS?
YOU COULD'VE LET THEM DIE IF YOU WANTED TO...
WHY TOY WITH THEIR LIVES ...?!
AS USUAL.
WE HAVE A DIFFER-ENCE OF OPINION.

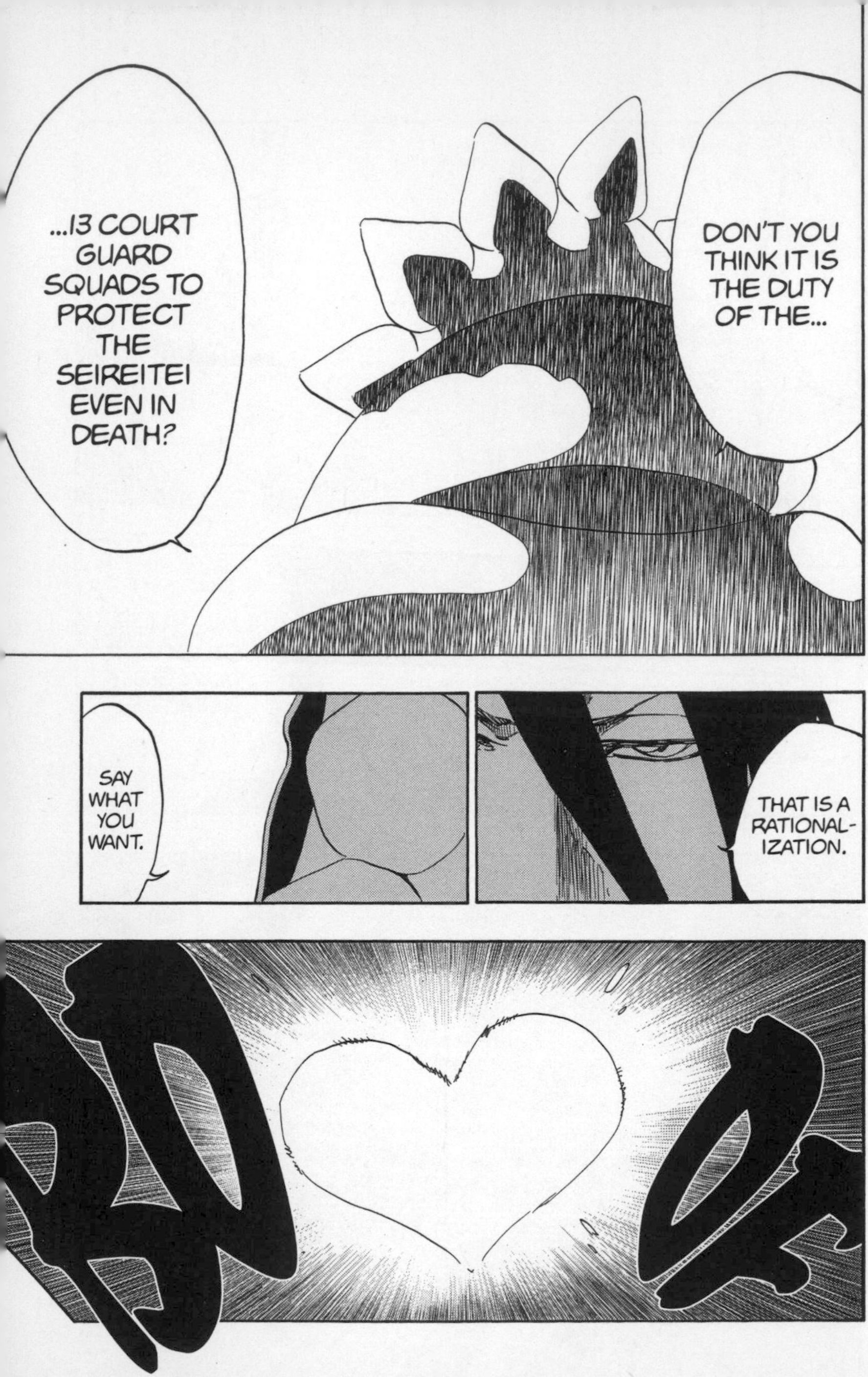
DON'T YOU THINK IT IS THE DUTY OF THE...
...13 COURT GUARD SQUADS TO PROTECT THE SEIREITEI EVEN IN DEATH?
THAT IS A RATIONAL-IZATION.
SAY WHAT YOU WANT.

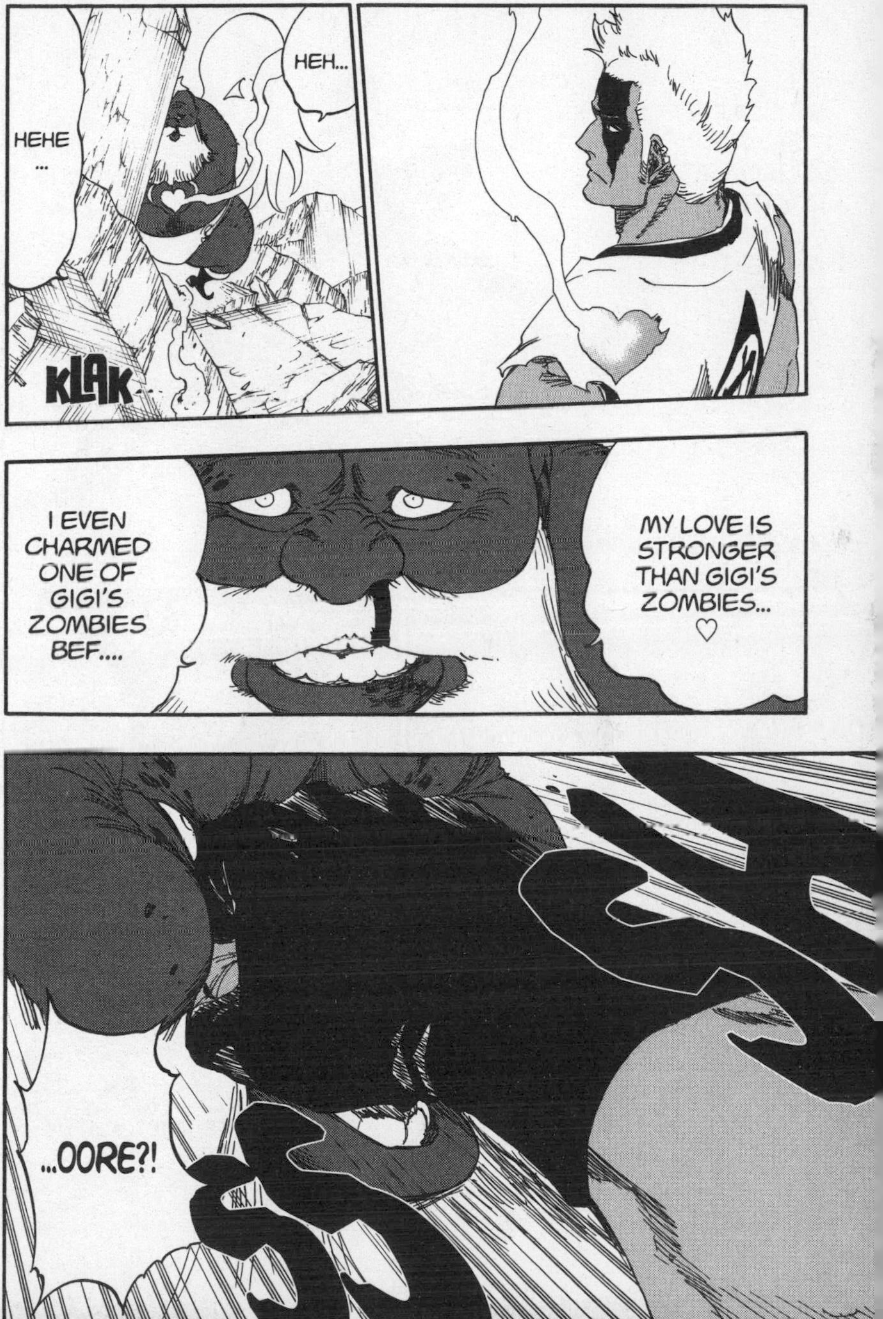
HEH...
HEHE ...
KLAK
MY LOVE IS STRONGER THAN GIGI'S ZOMBIES... ♡
I EVEN CHARMED ONE OF GIGI'S ZOMBIES BEF....
...OORE?!

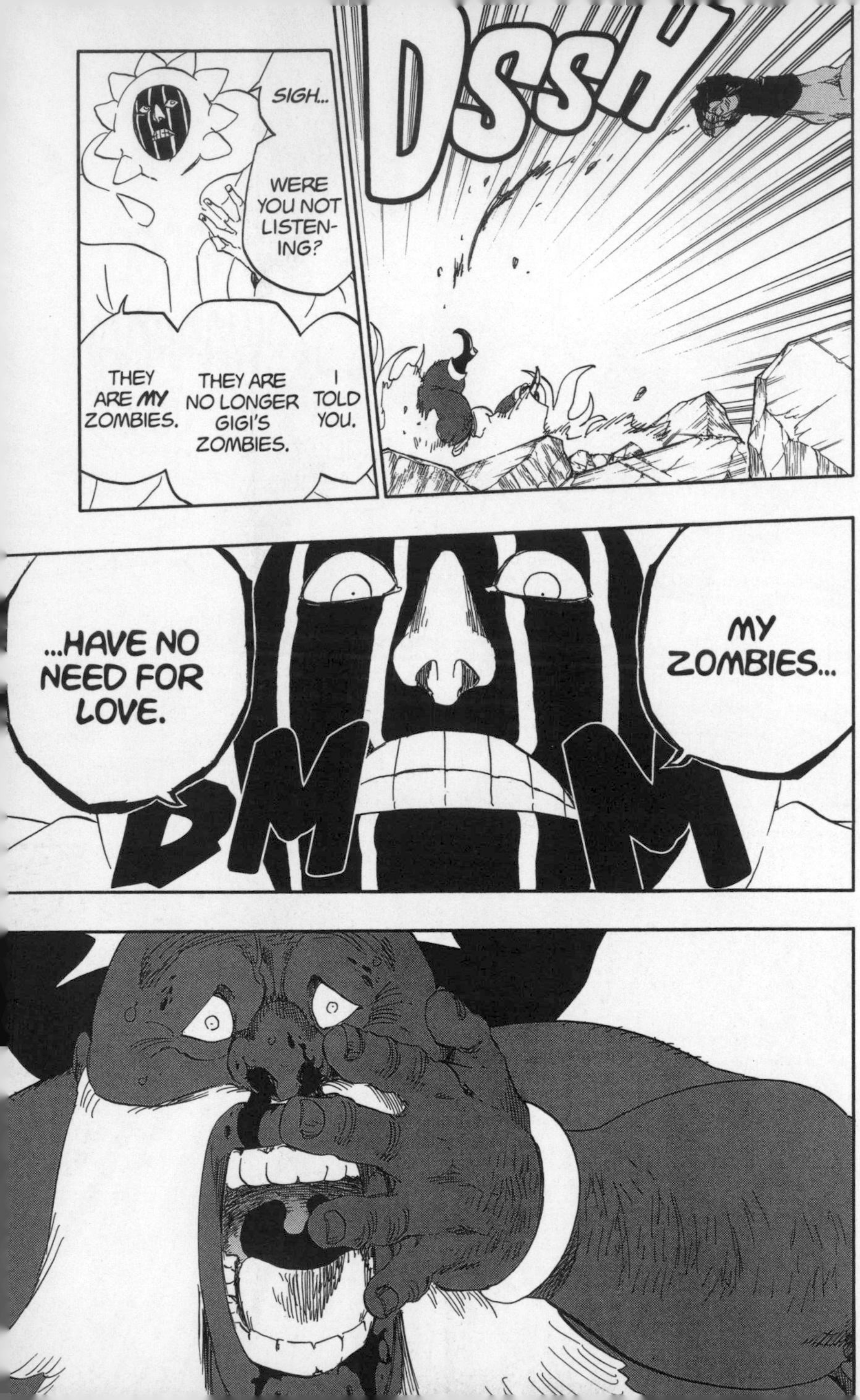
DSSH
SIGH...
WERE YOU NOT LISTEN-ING?
I TOLD YOU.
THEY ARE NO LONGER GIGI'S ZOMBIES.
THEY ARE MY ZOMBIES.
MY ZOMBIES...
...HAVE NO NEED FOR LOVE.
DMM

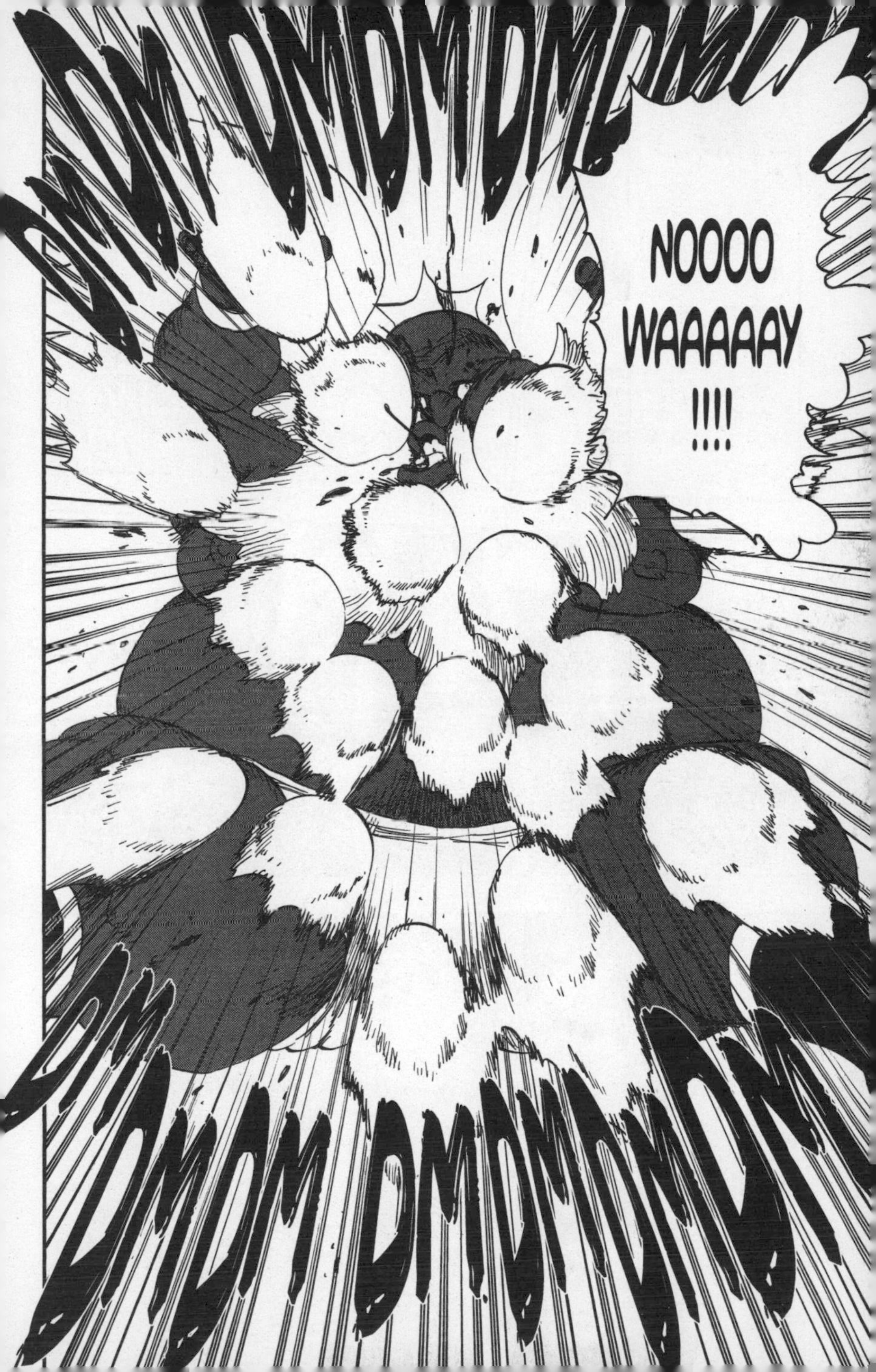
NOOOO WAAAAAY !!!!

READ THIS WAY

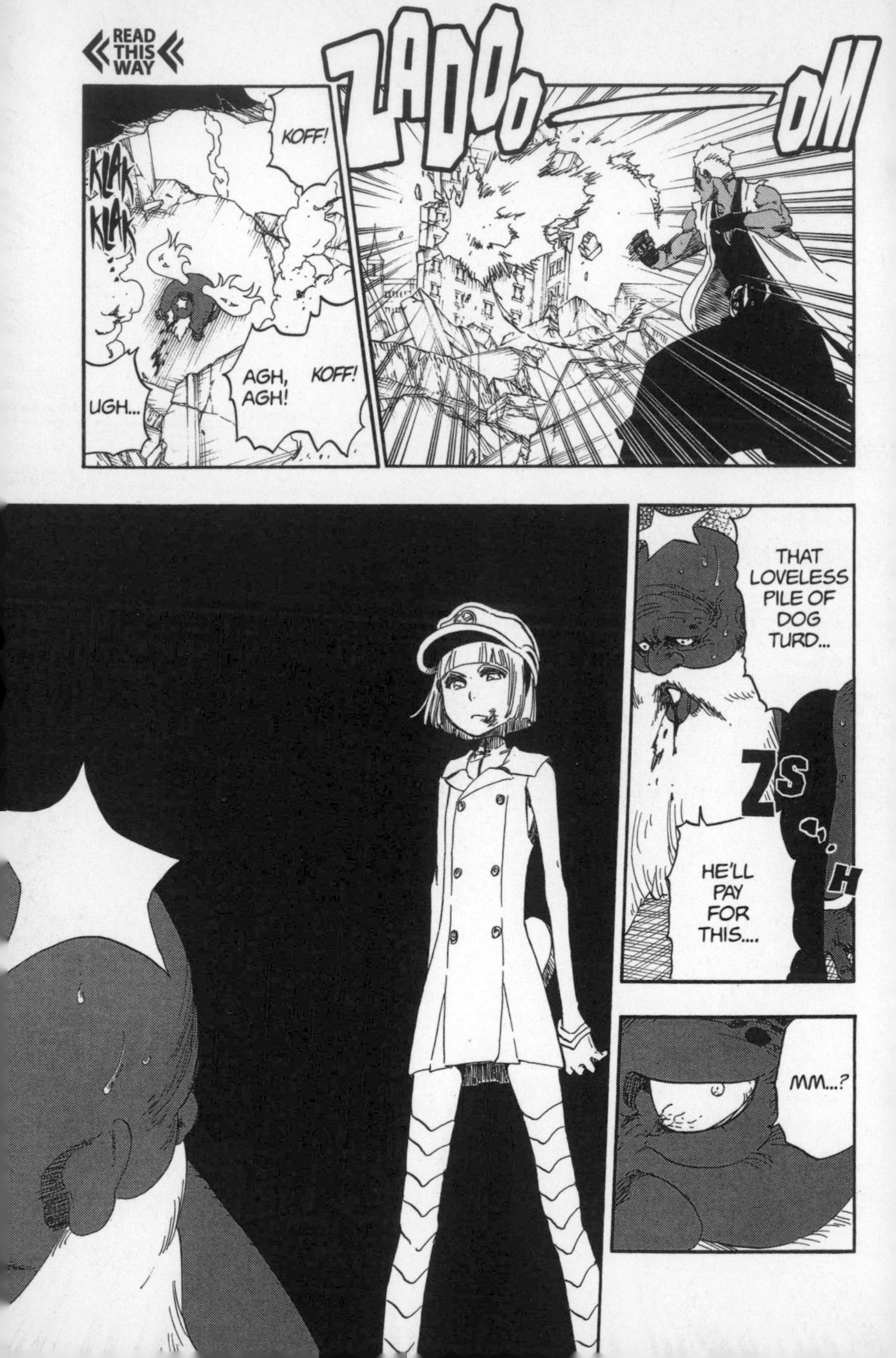
ZADOOO—OM
KOFF!
KLAK KLAK
KOFF!
AGH, AGH!
UGH...
THAT LOVELESS PILE OF DOG TURD...
ZSH
HE'LL PAY FOR THIS....
MM...?

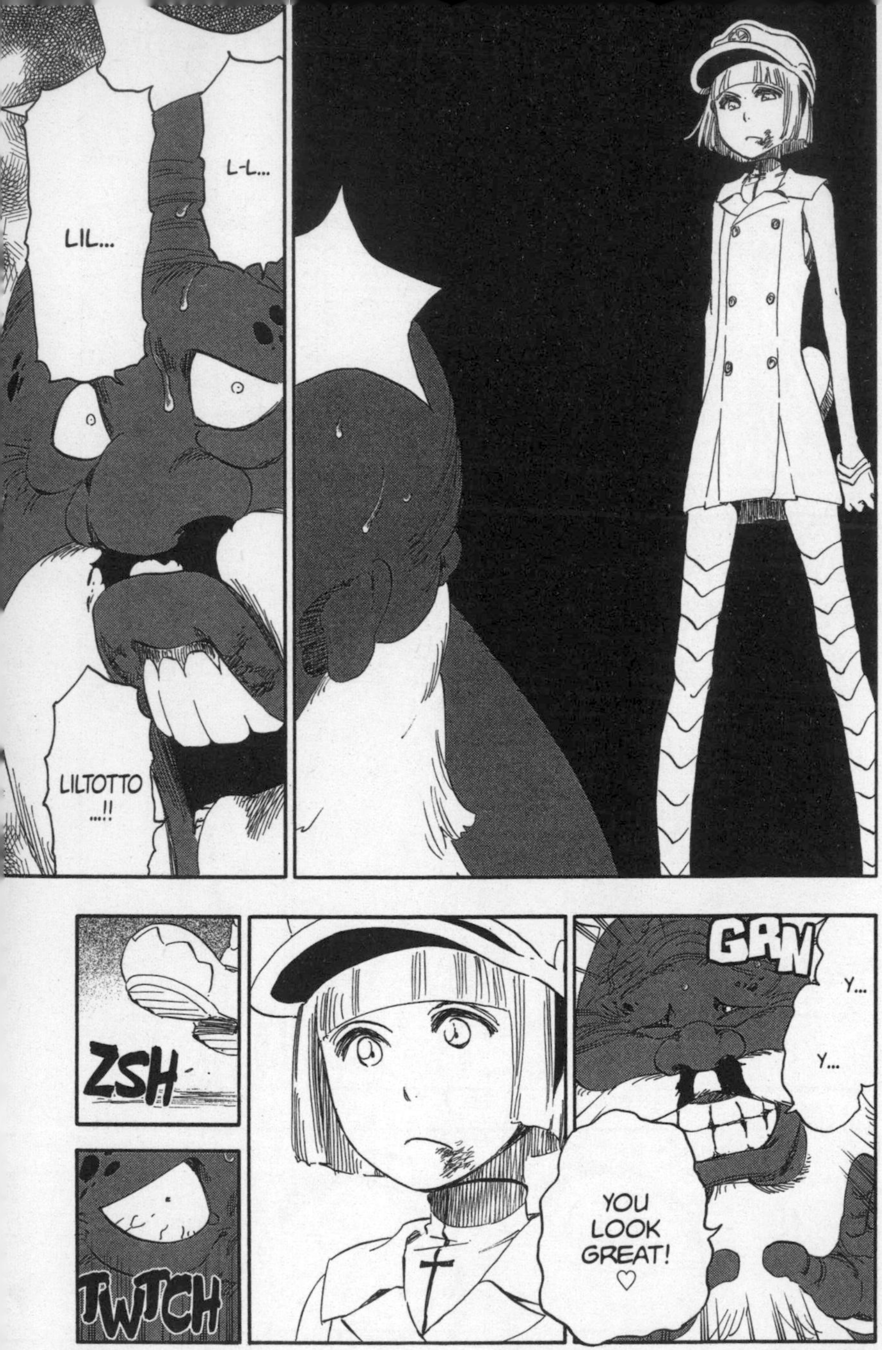
L-L...
LIL...
LILTOTTO ...!!
GRN
Y...
Y...
YOU LOOK GREAT! ♡
ZSH
TWITCH

597. WINDED BY THE SHADOW

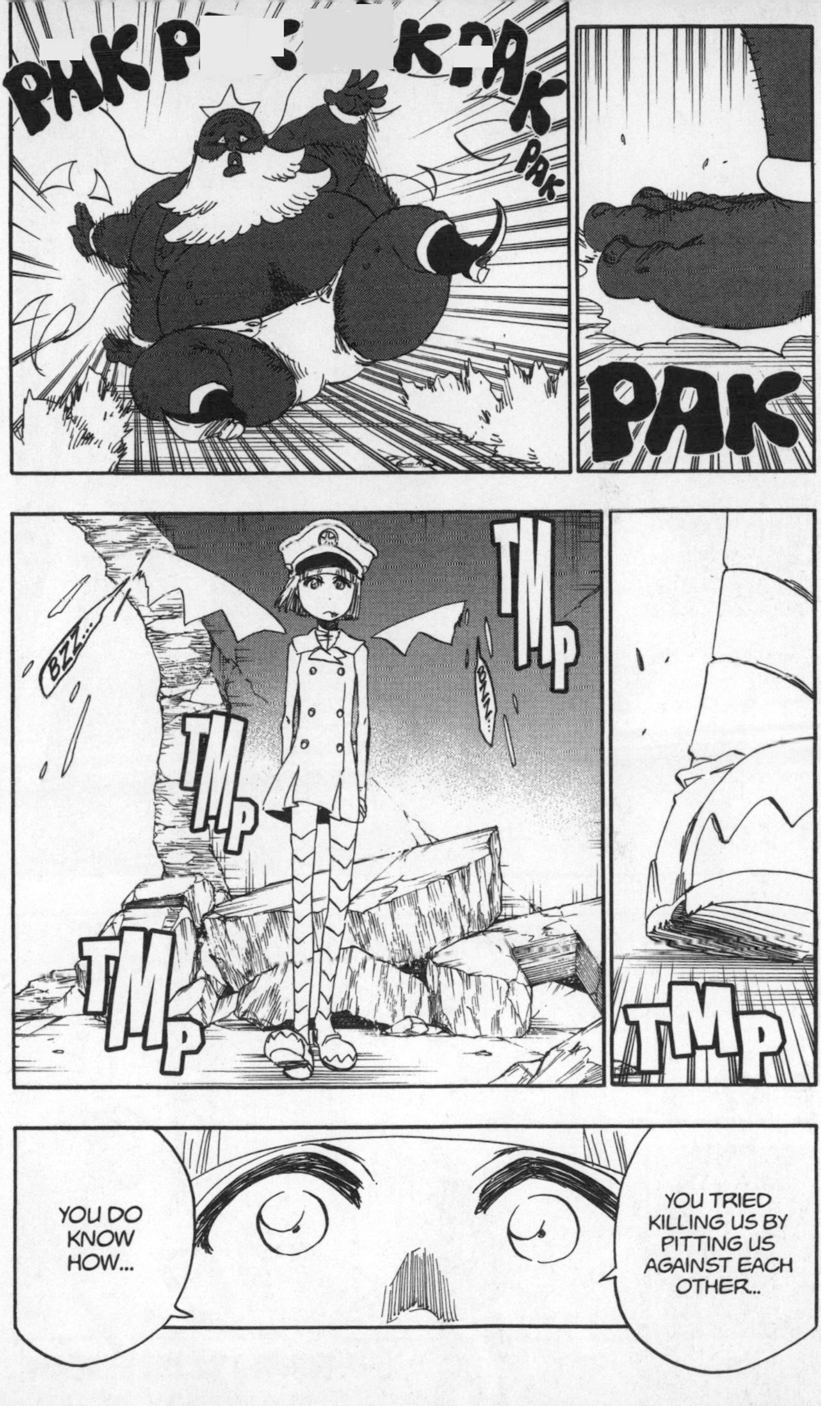

PAK
PAK
PAK
PAK
TMP
TMP
BZZ...
BZZ...
TMP
TMP
YOU TRIED KILLING US BY PITTING US AGAINST EACH OTHER...
YOU DO KNOW HOW...

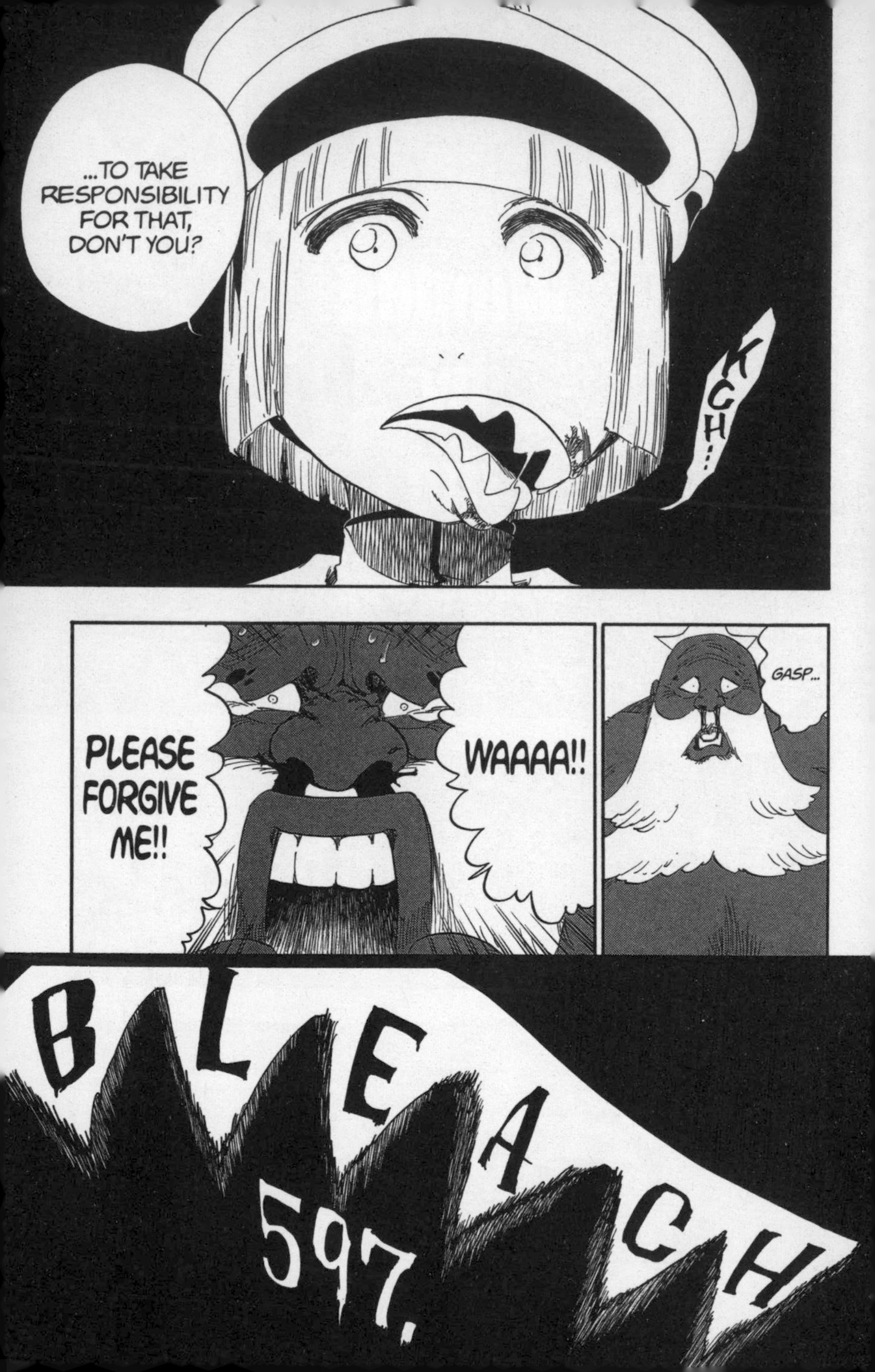
...TO TAKE RESPONSIBILITY FOR THAT, DON'T YOU?
KCH...
GASP...
WAAAA!!
PLEASE FORGIVE ME!!
BLEACH
597.

BLEACH 597.

Winded by the Shadow

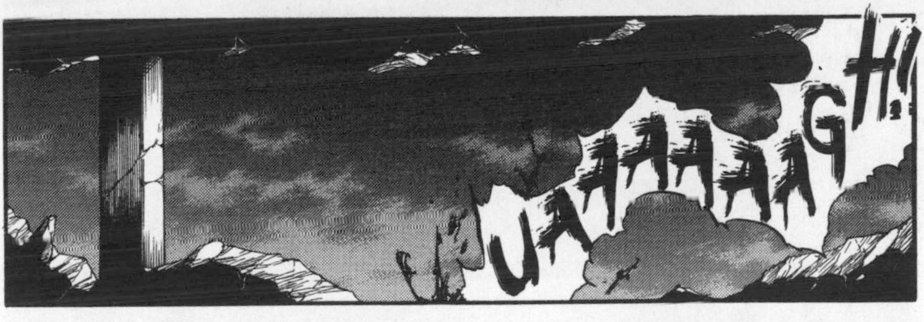
UAAAAAAAGH!!

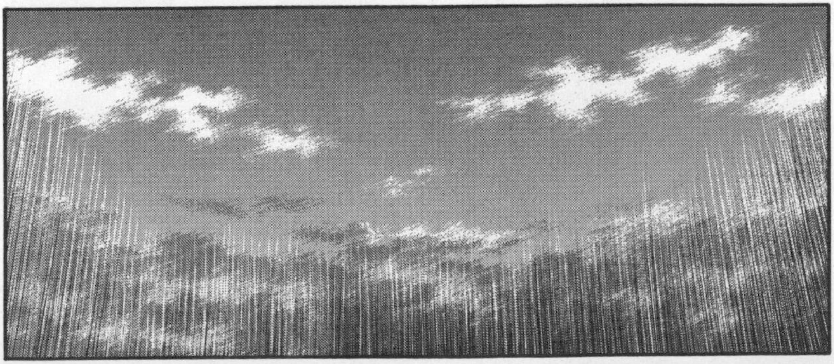

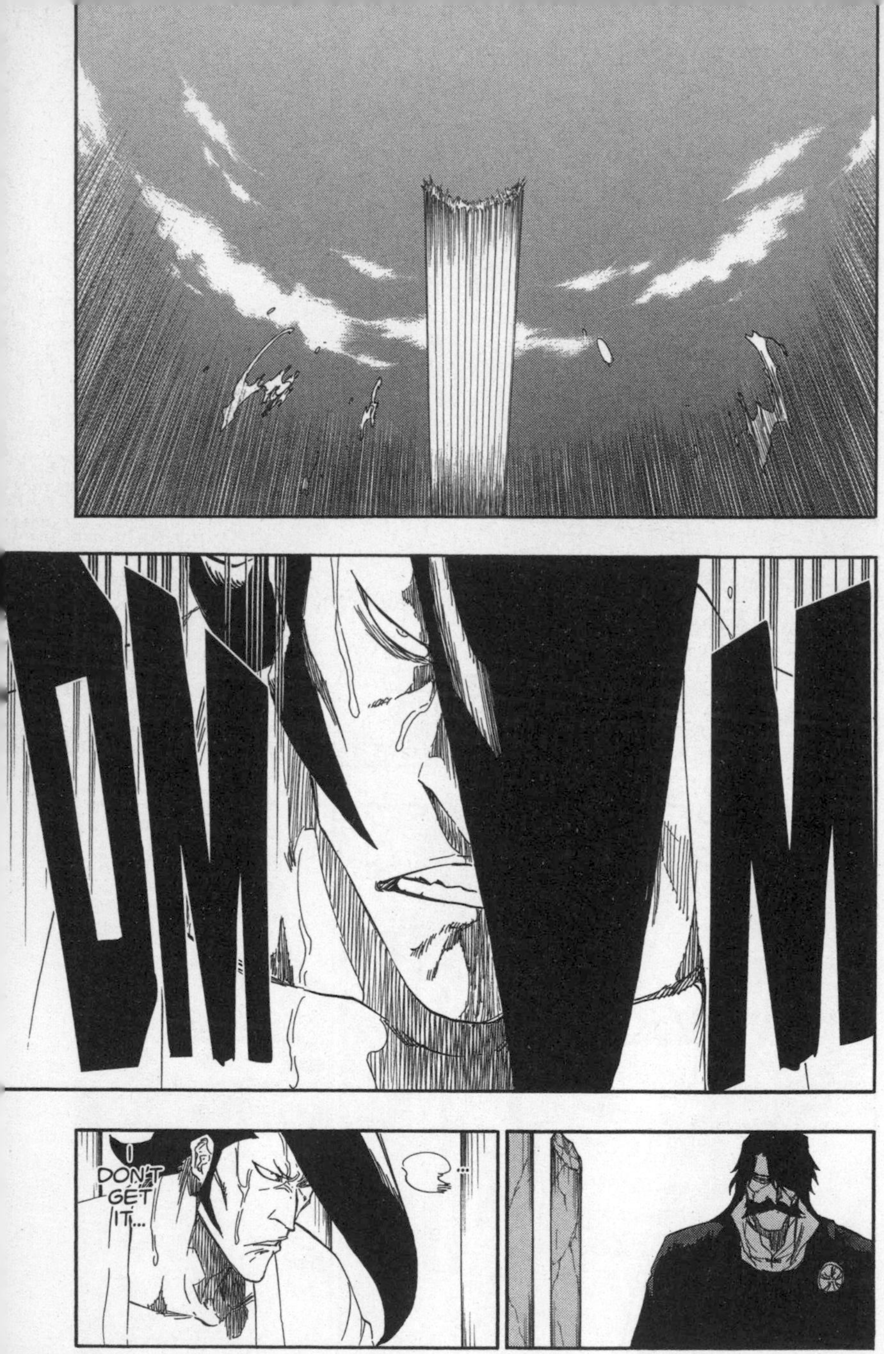
DMM
...
I DON'T GET IT...

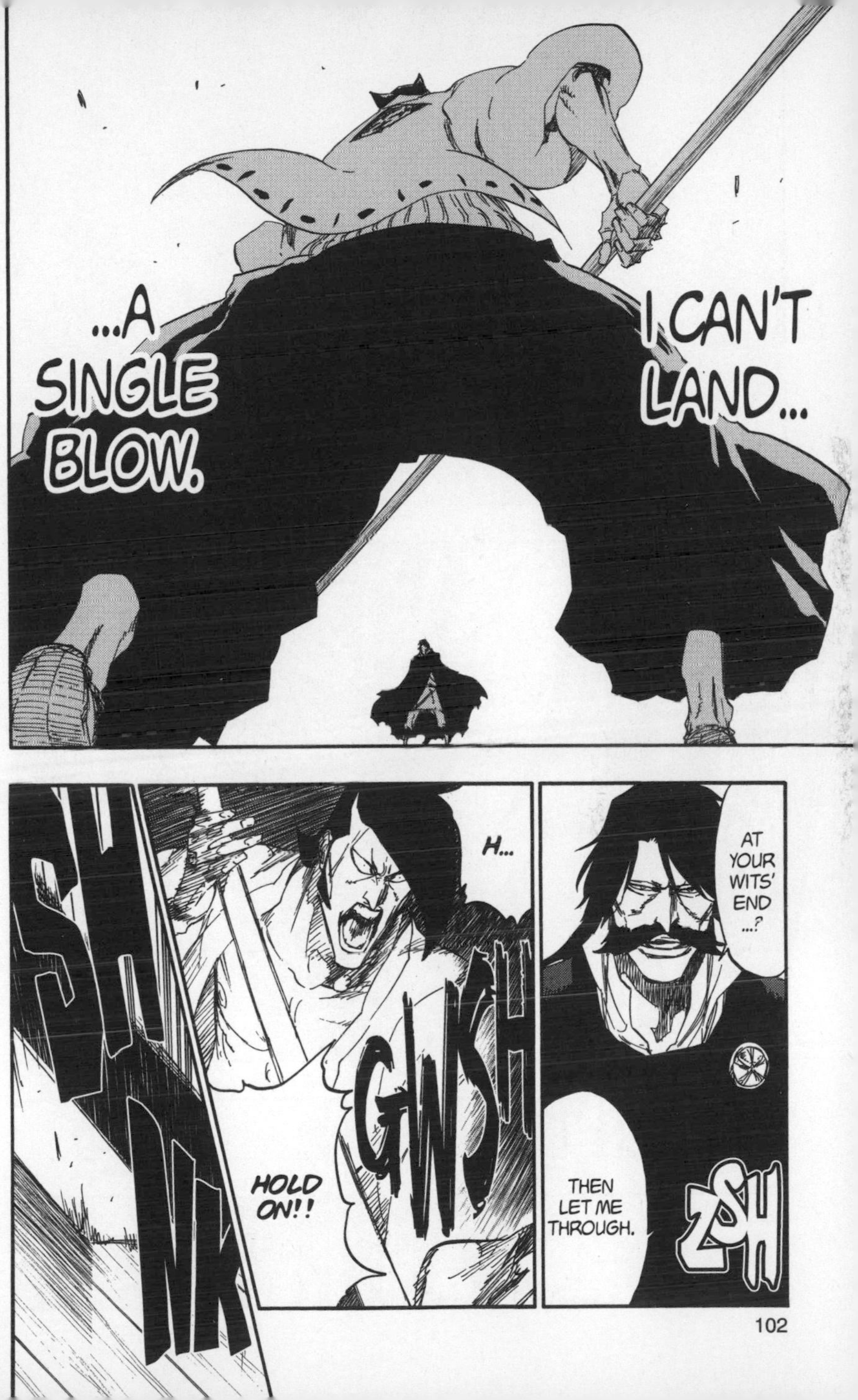
I CAN'T LAND...
...A SINGLE BLOW.
AT YOUR WITS' END ...?
THEN LET ME THROUGH.
ZSH
H...
HOLD ON!!
GWSH
SHNK

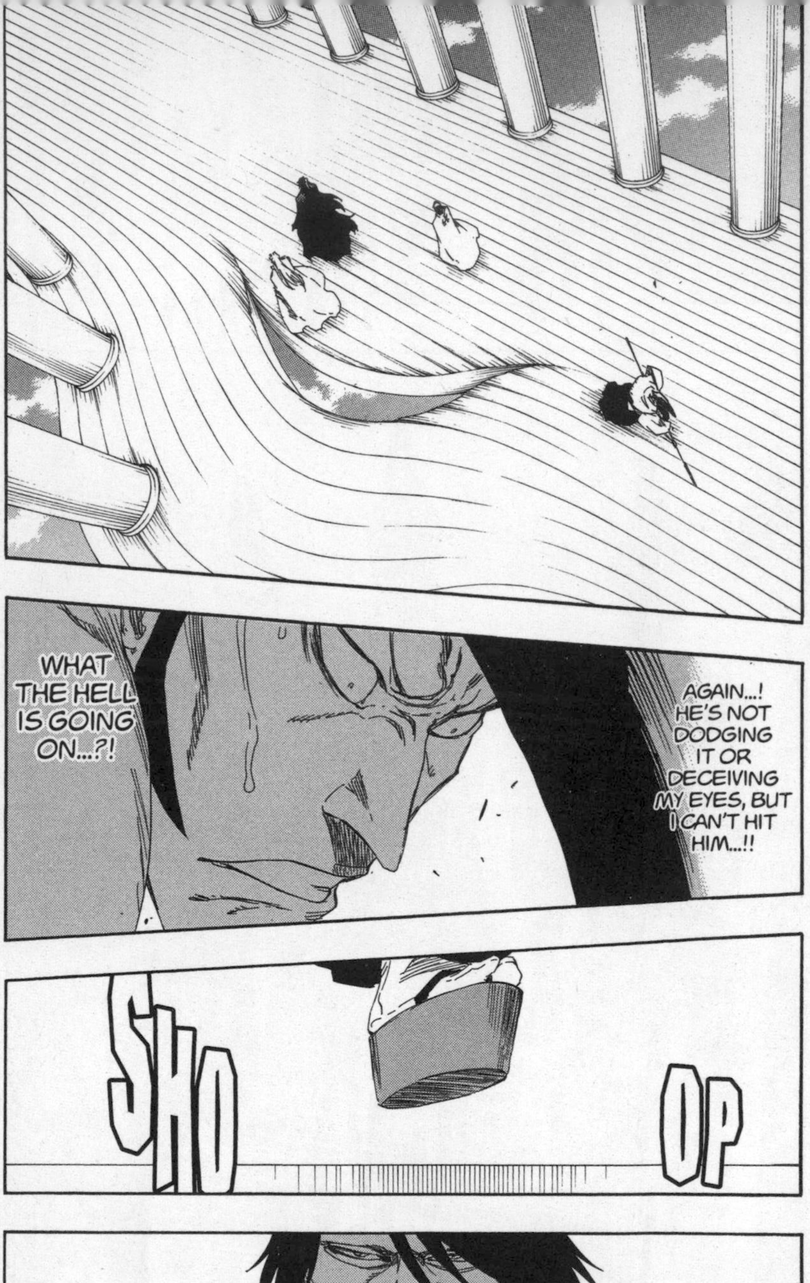
AGAIN...! HE'S NOT DODGING IT OR DECEIVING MY EYES, BUT I CAN'T HIT HIM...!!
WHAT THE HELL IS GOING ON...?!
SHO OP

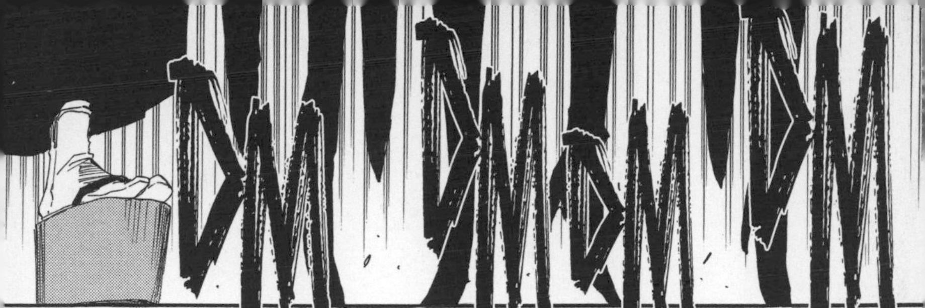
DM DM DM DM

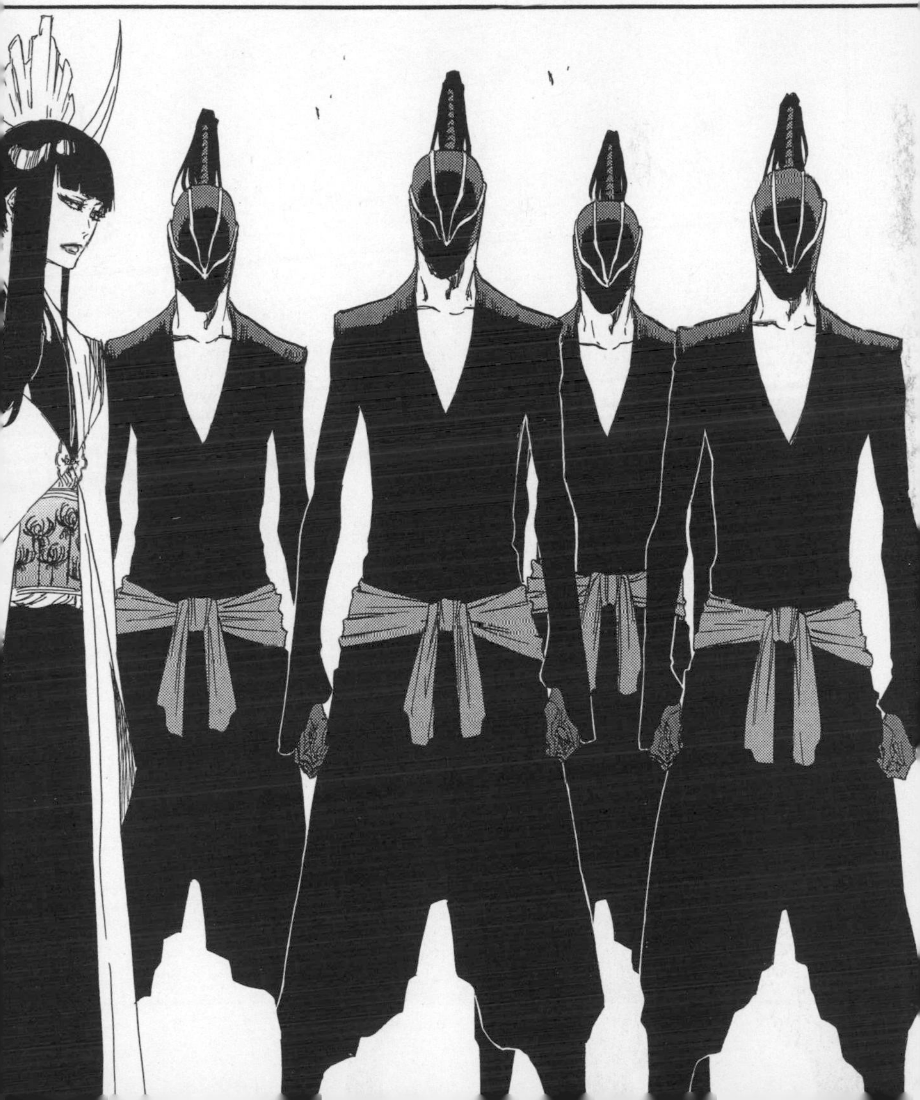

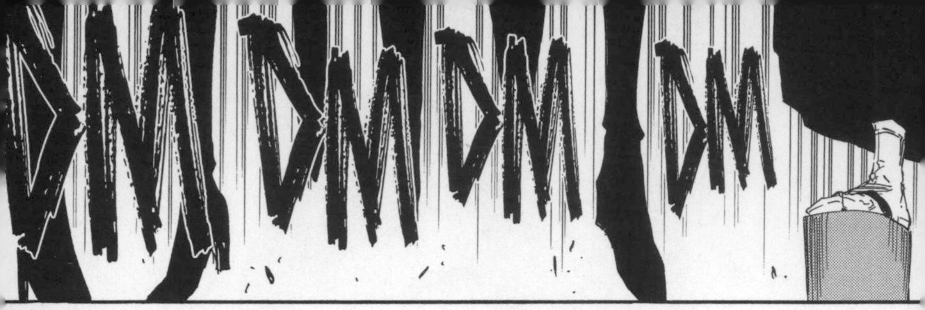
DM DM DM DM

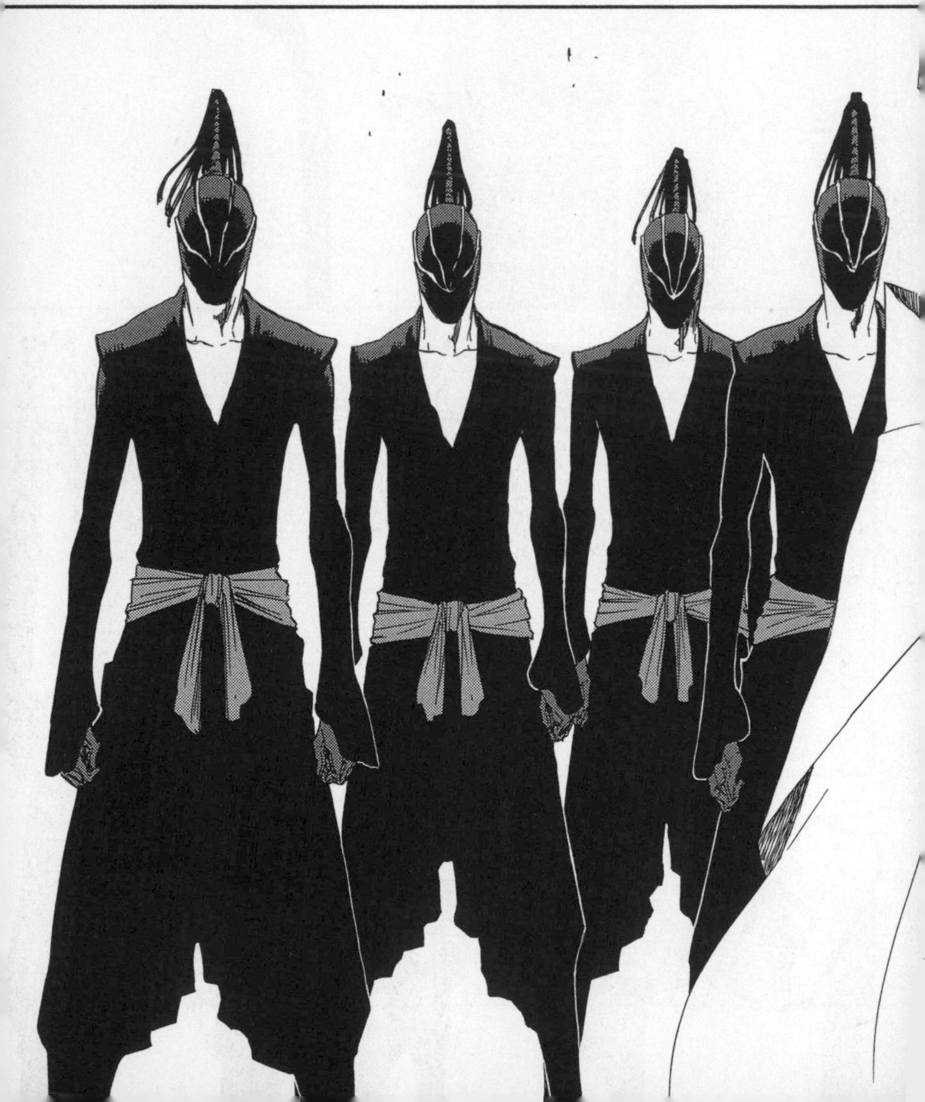

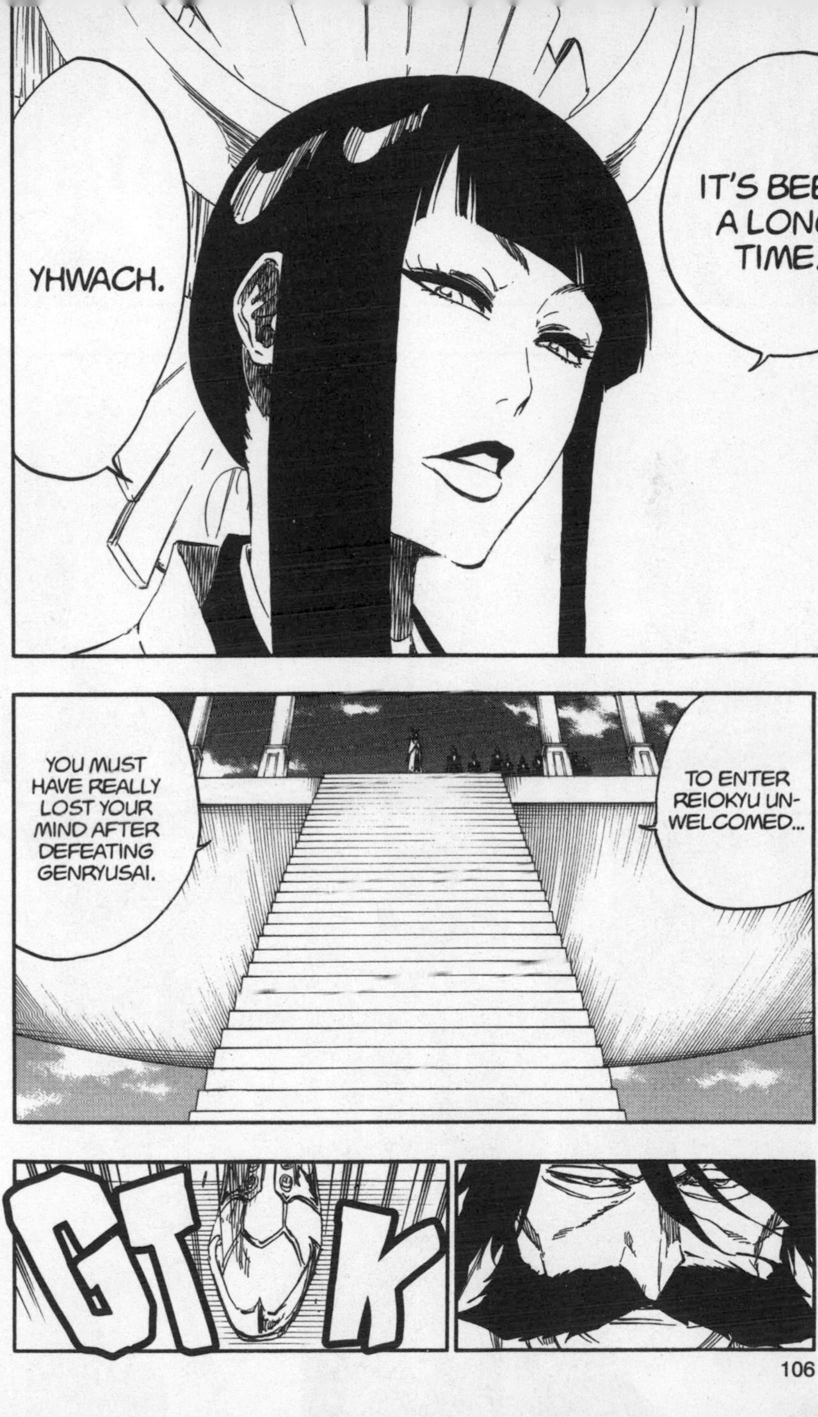
IT'S BEEN A LONG TIME.
YHWACH.
TO ENTER REIOKYU UN-WELCOMED...
YOU MUST HAVE REALLY LOST YOUR MIND AFTER DEFEATING GENRYUSAI.
GTK

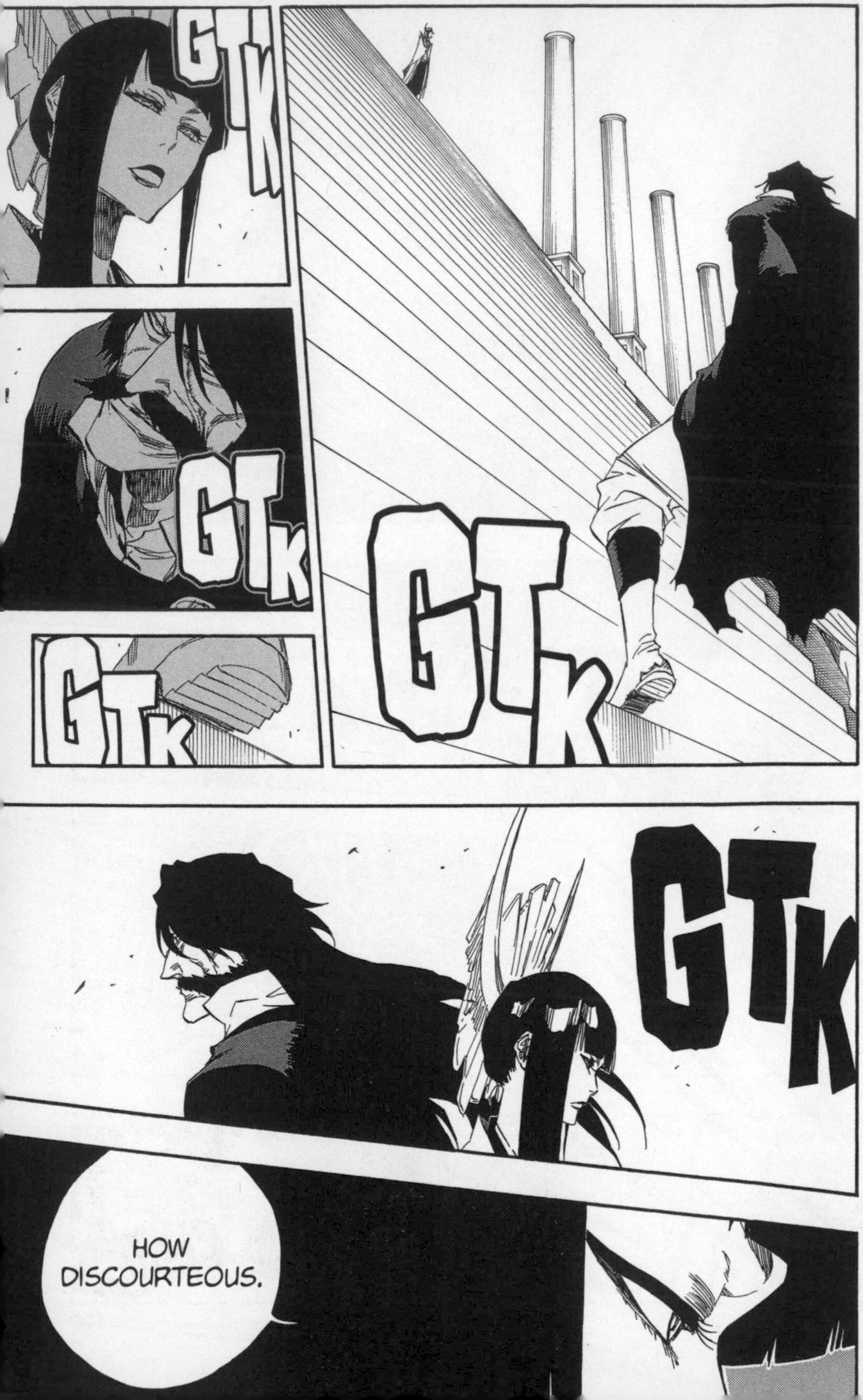
GTK
GTK
GTK
GTK
GTK
HOW DISCOURTEOUS.

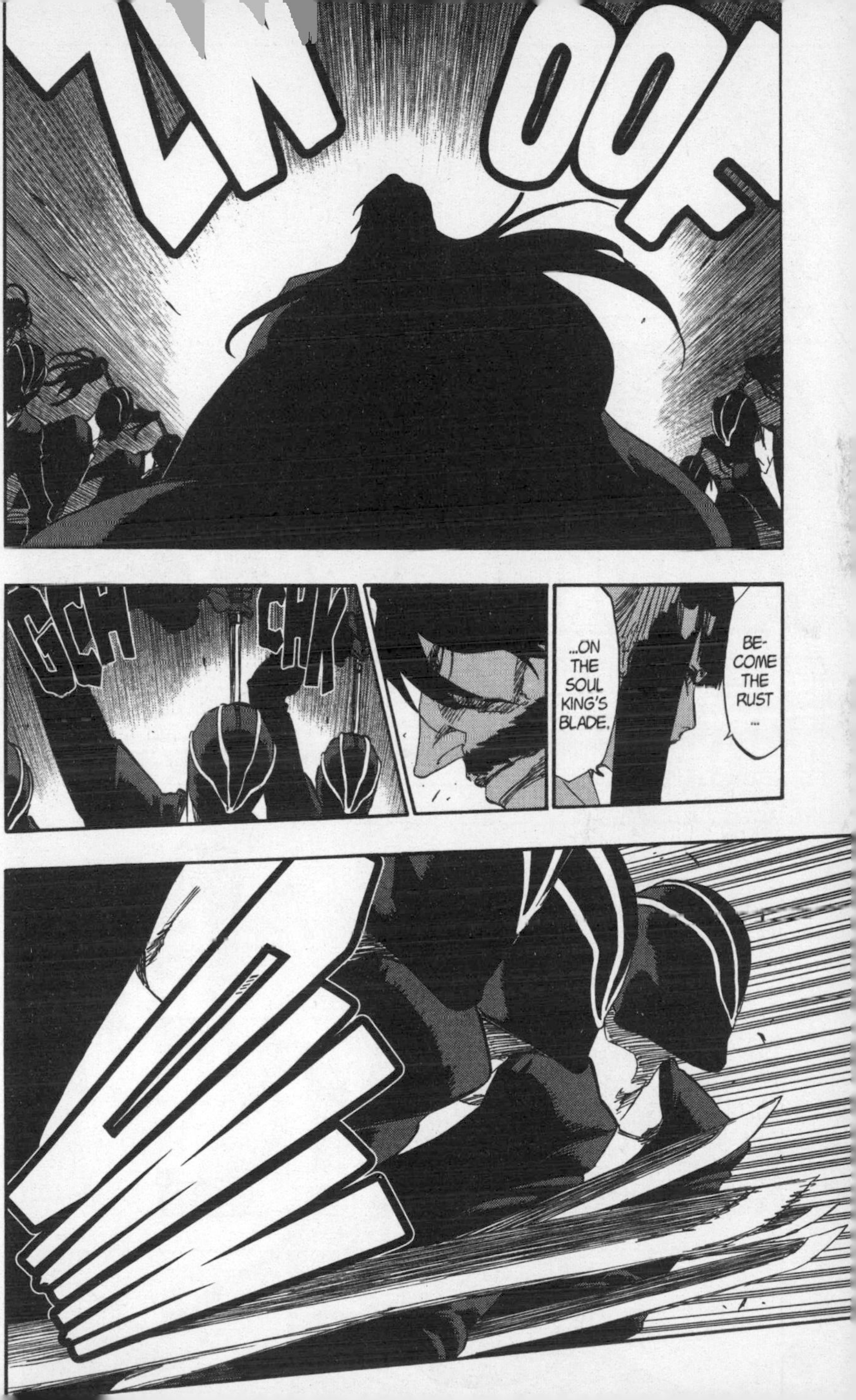
BE-COME THE RUST ...
...ON THE SOUL KING'S BLADE.

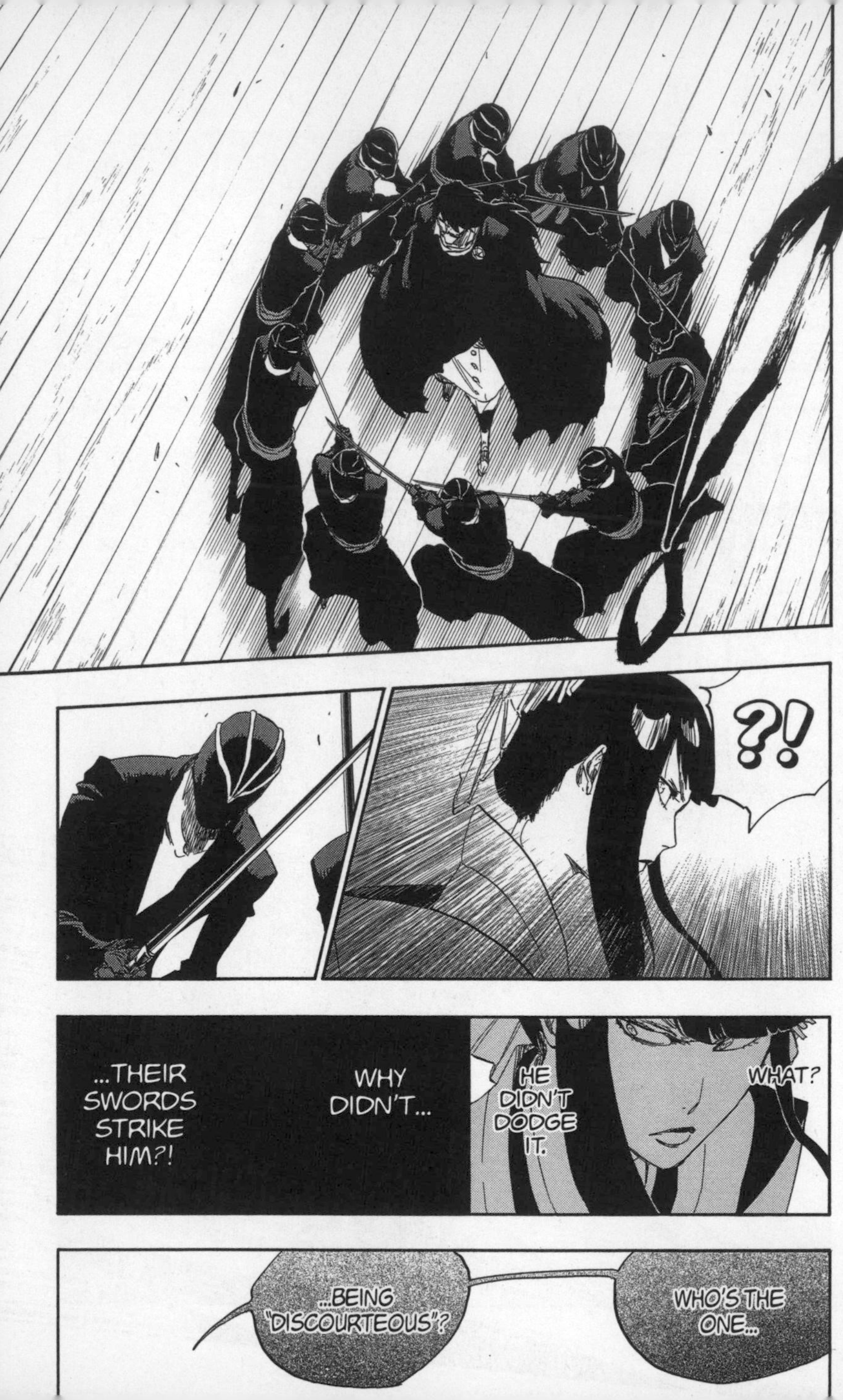
?!
WHAT?
HE DIDN'T DODGE IT.
WHY DIDN'T...
...THEIR SWORDS STRIKE HIM?!
WHO'S THE ONE...
...BEING "DISCOURTEOUS"?

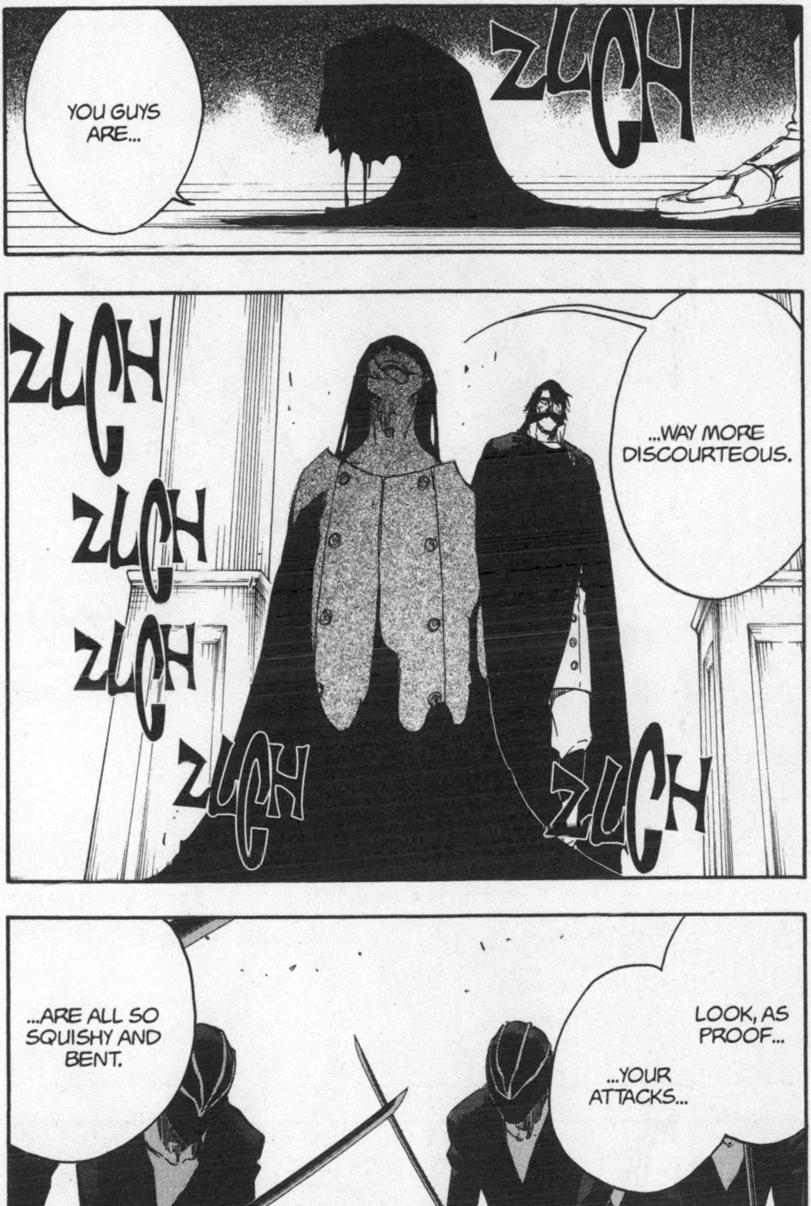
ZUCH
YOU GUYS ARE...
...WAY MORE DISCOURTEOUS.
ZUCH
ZUCH
ZUCH
ZUCH
ZUCH
LOOK, AS PROOF...
...YOUR ATTACKS...
...ARE ALL SO SQUISHY AND BENT.

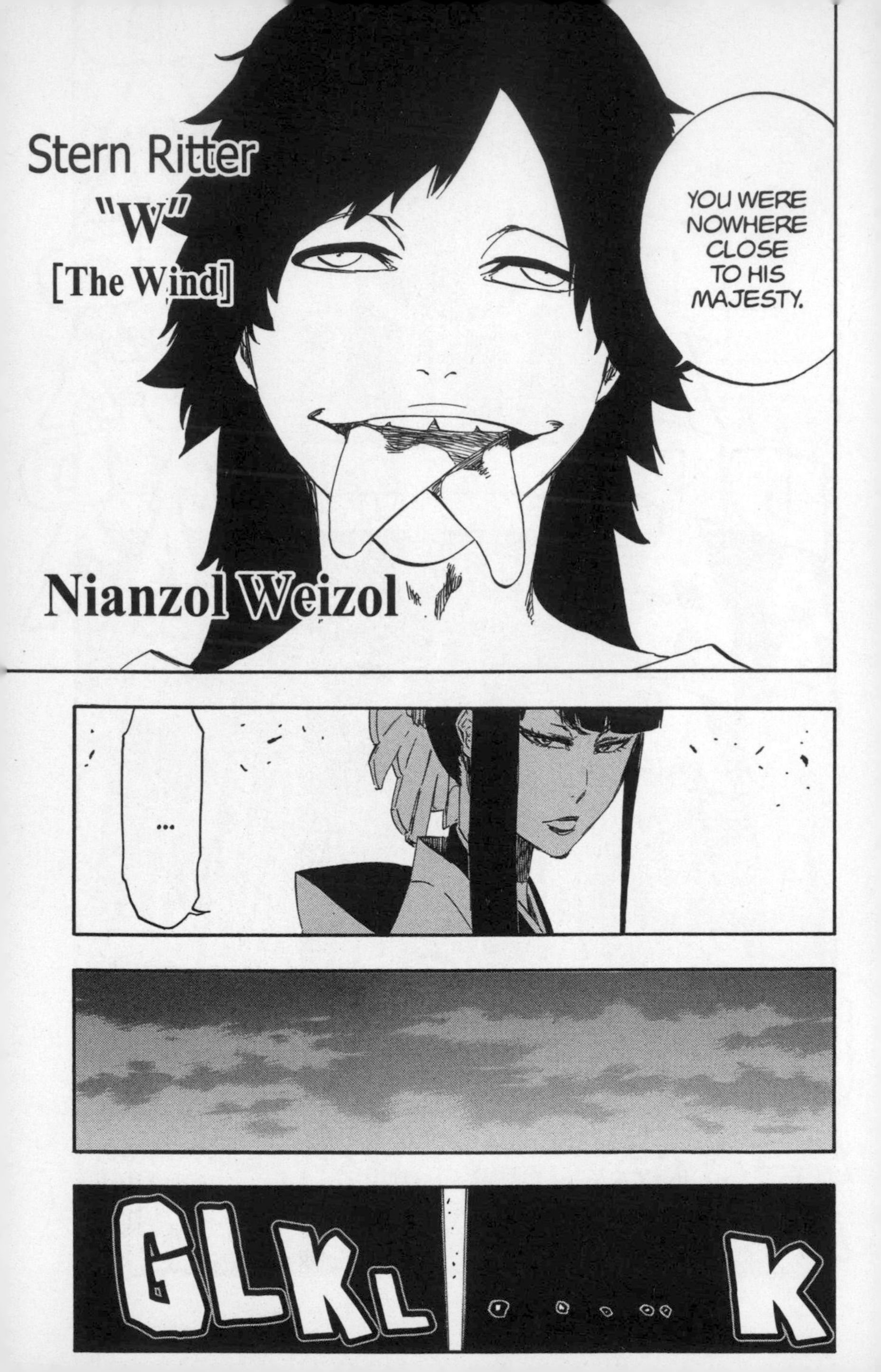
YOU WERE NOWHERE CLOSE TO HIS MAJESTY.
Stern Ritter "W" [The Wind]
Nianzol Weizol
...
GLKL... K

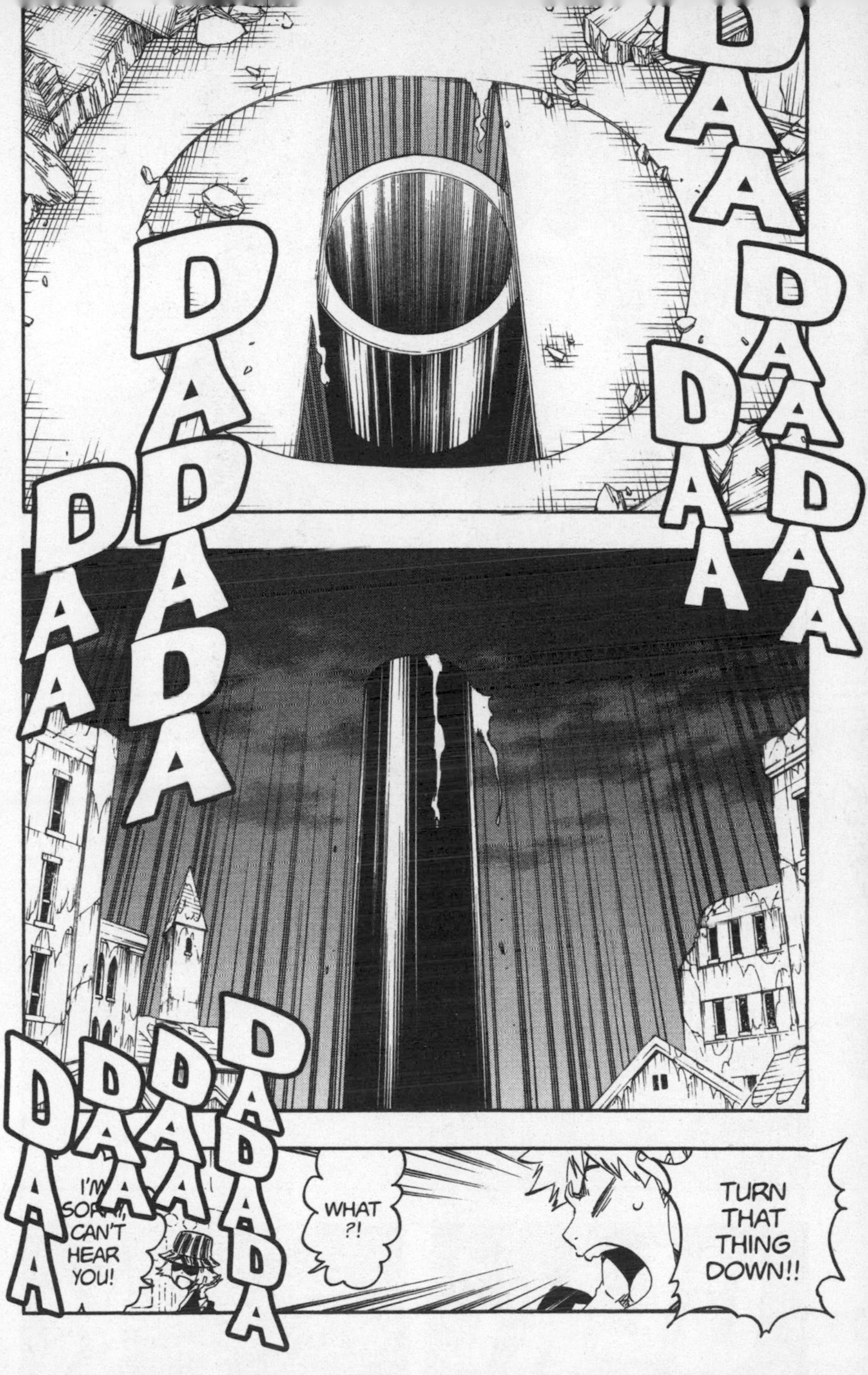
DAAADADADAA
DADAA
DADADA
DADA
DAAA
DADAA
DADADADA
TURN THAT THING DOWN!!
WHAT ?!
I'M
CAN'T HEAR YOU!

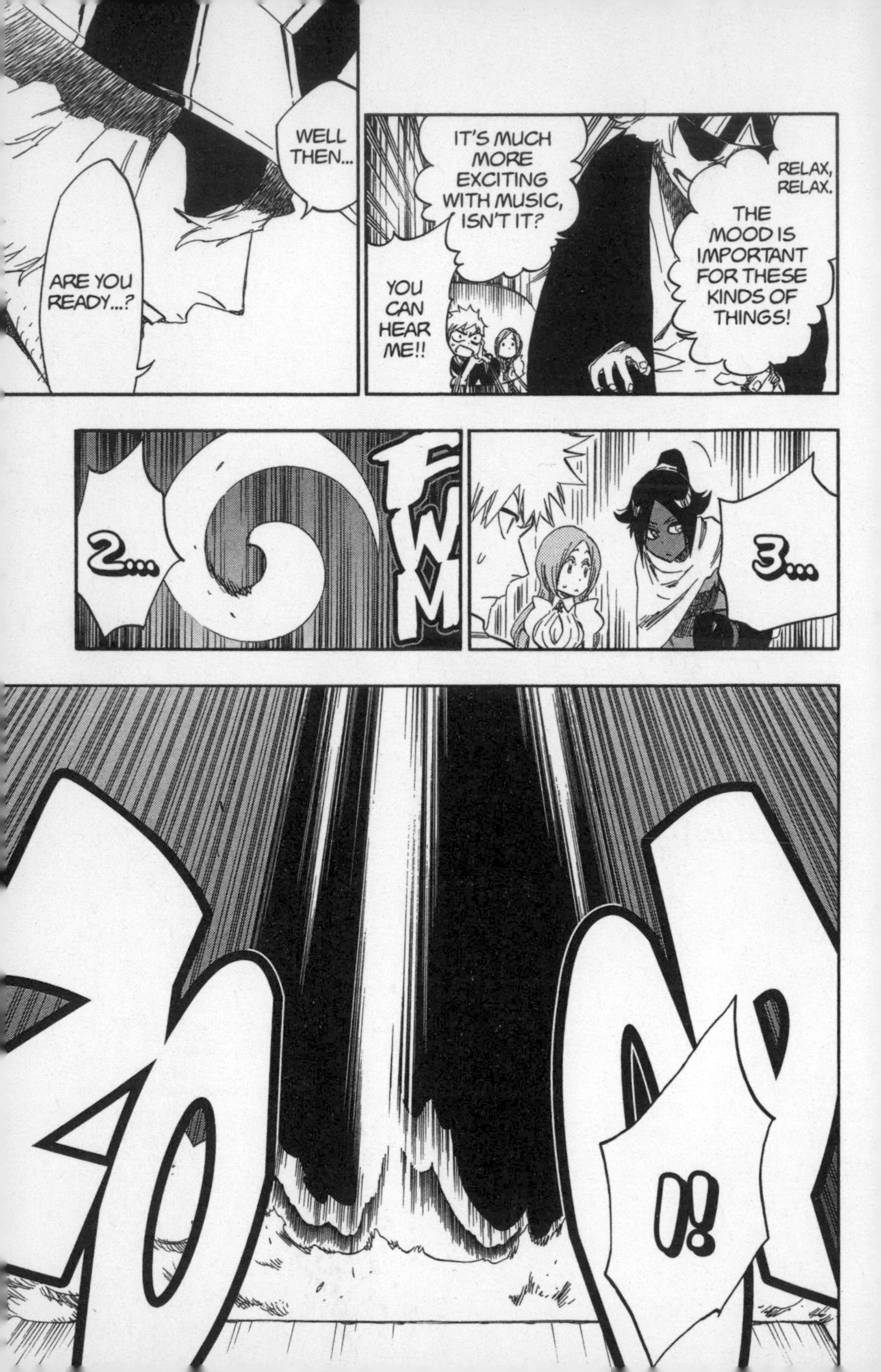
RELAX, RELAX.
THE MOOD IS IMPORTANT FOR THESE KINDS OF THINGS!
IT'S MUCH MORE EXCITING WITH MUSIC, ISN'T IT?
YOU CAN HEAR ME!!
WELL THEN...
ARE YOU READY...?
3...
FWM
2...
!!

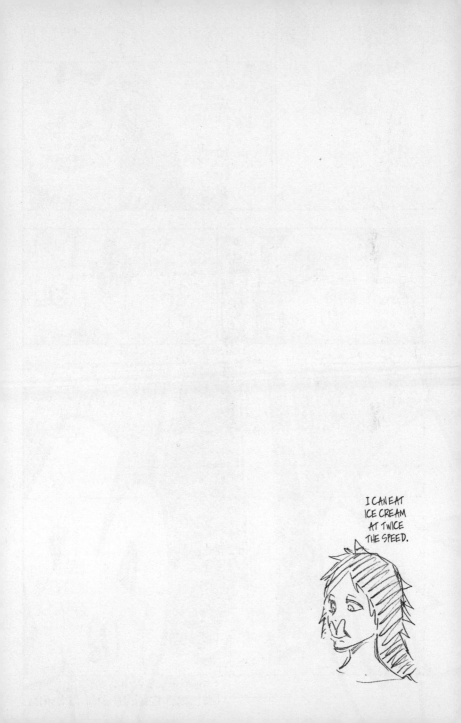

I CAN EAT
ICE CREAM
AT TWICE
THE SPEED.

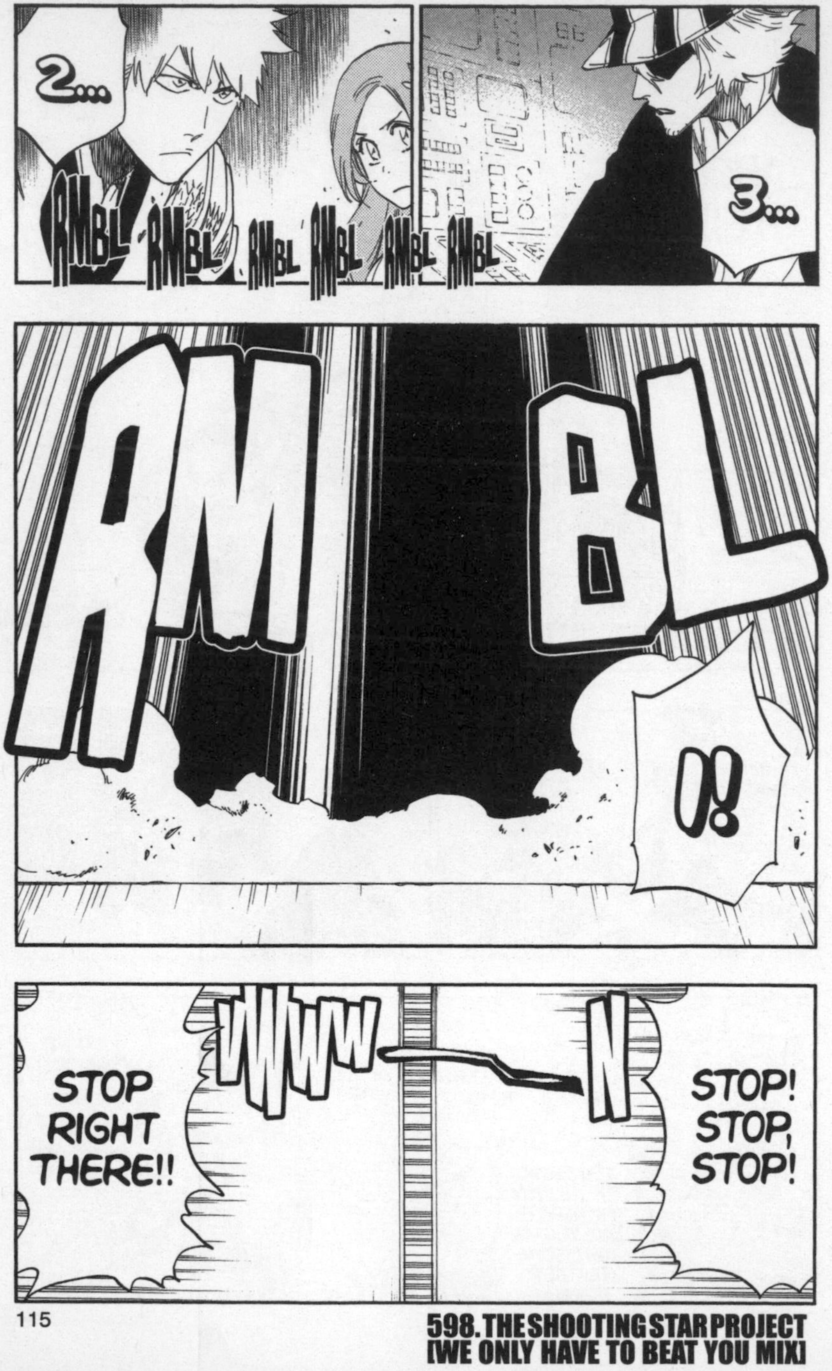
3...
2...
RMBL RMBL RMBL RMBL RMBL RMBL
RAMBL
0!!
STOP! STOP, STOP!
VWWW—N
STOP RIGHT THERE!!

598. THE SHOOTING STAR PROJECT [WE ONLY HAVE TO BEAT YOU MIX]

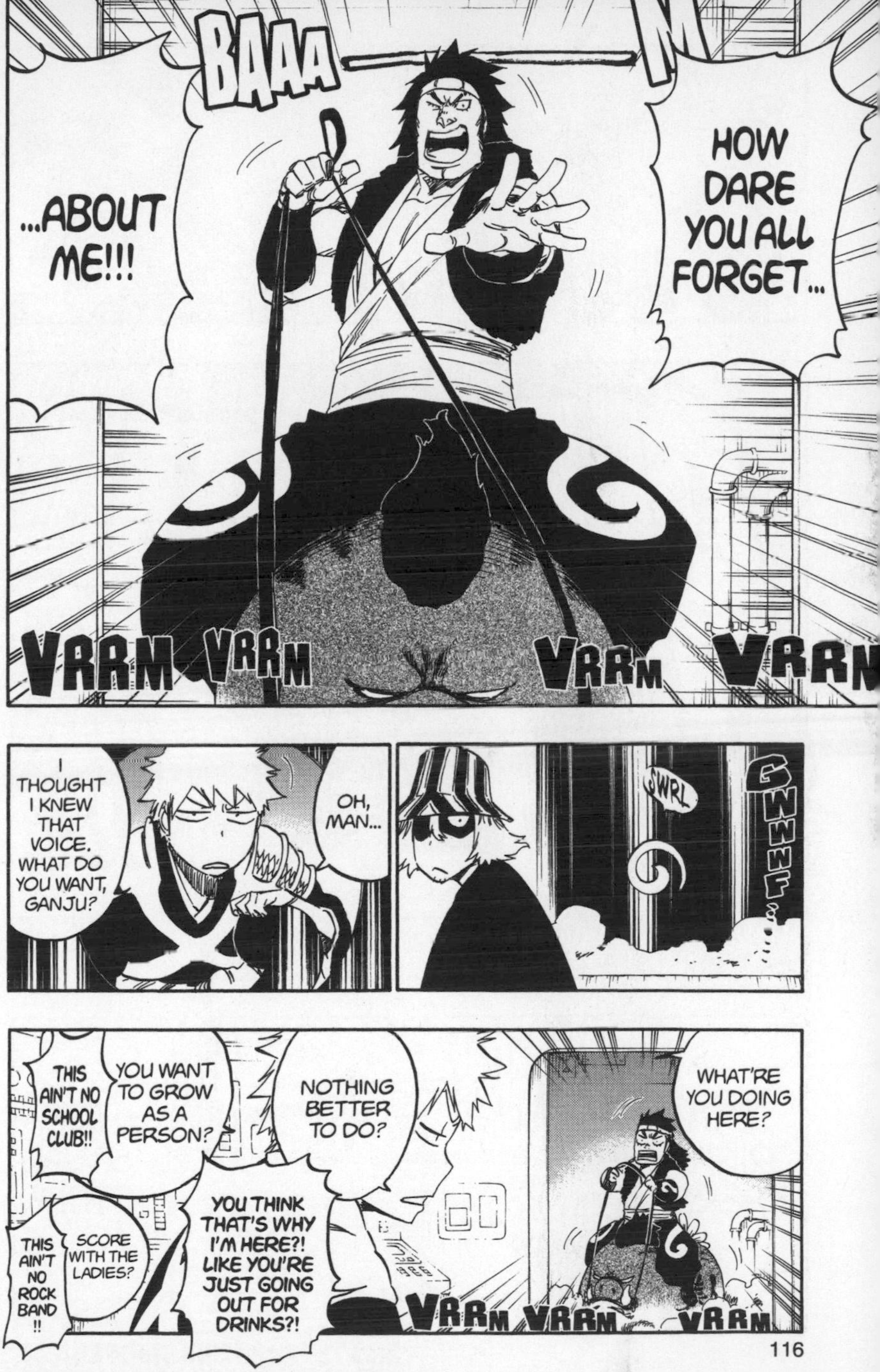
BAAA—M
HOW DARE YOU ALL FORGET...
...ABOUT ME!!!
VRRM VRRM VRRM VRRM
SWRL
GWWWF
OH, MAN...
I THOUGHT I KNEW THAT VOICE. WHAT DO YOU WANT, GANJU?
WHAT'RE YOU DOING HERE?
NOTHING BETTER TO DO?
YOU WANT TO GROW AS A PERSON?
THIS AIN'T NO SCHOOL CLUB!!
YOU THINK THAT'S WHY I'M HERE?! LIKE YOU'RE JUST GOING OUT FOR DRINKS?!
SCORE WITH THE LADIES?
THIS AIN'T NO ROCK BAND!!
VRRM VRRM VRRM

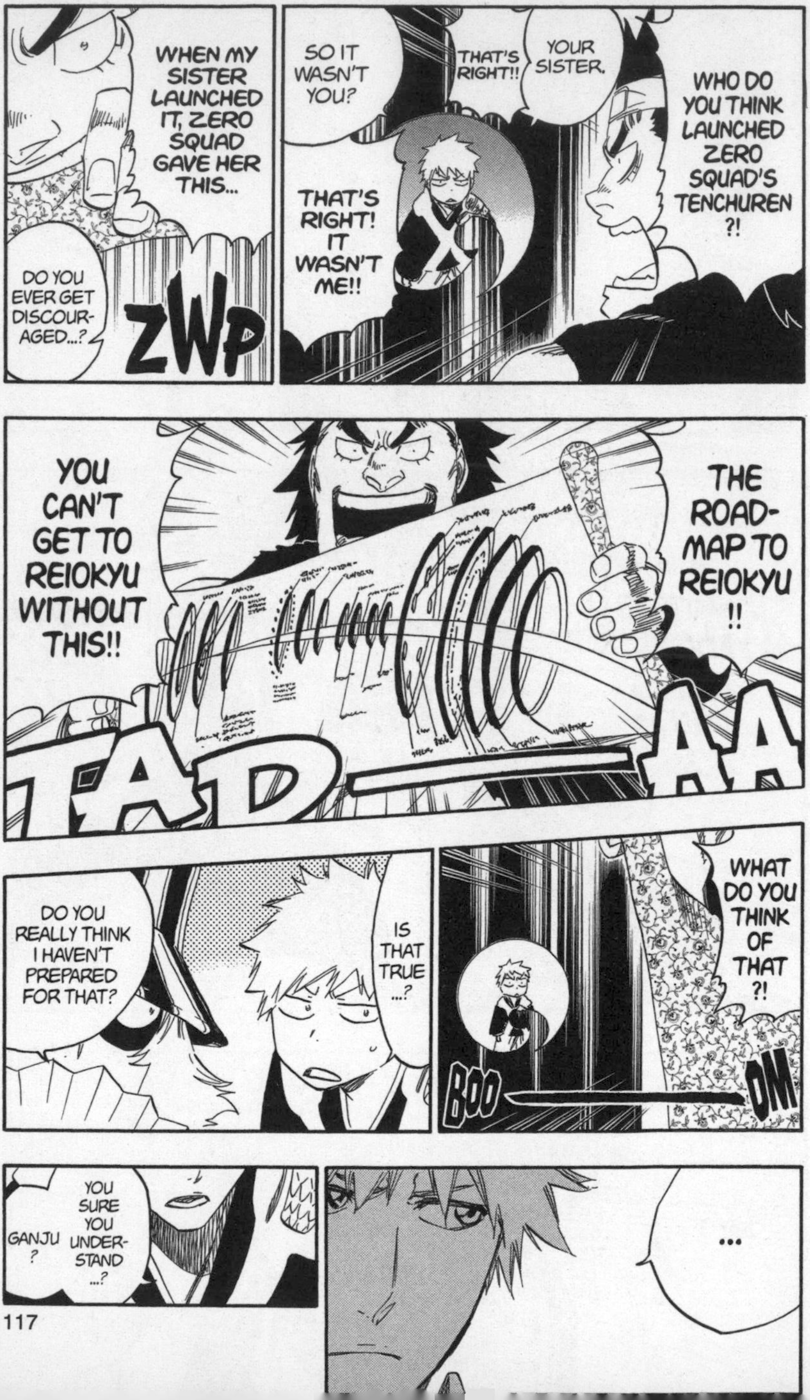
WHO DO YOU THINK LAUNCHED ZERO SQUAD'S TENCHUREN ?!
YOUR SISTER.
THAT'S RIGHT!!
SO IT WASN'T YOU?
THAT'S RIGHT! IT WASN'T ME!!
WHEN MY SISTER LAUNCHED IT, ZERO SQUAD GAVE HER THIS...
DO YOU EVER GET DISCOUR-AGED...?
ZWP
THE ROAD-MAP TO REIOKYU !!
YOU CAN'T GET TO REIOKYU WITHOUT THIS!!
TAD——AA
WHAT DO YOU THINK OF THAT ?!
BOO——OM
IS THAT TRUE ...?
DO YOU REALLY THINK I HAVEN'T PREPARED FOR THAT?
...
YOU SURE YOU UNDER-STAND ...?
GANJU ?

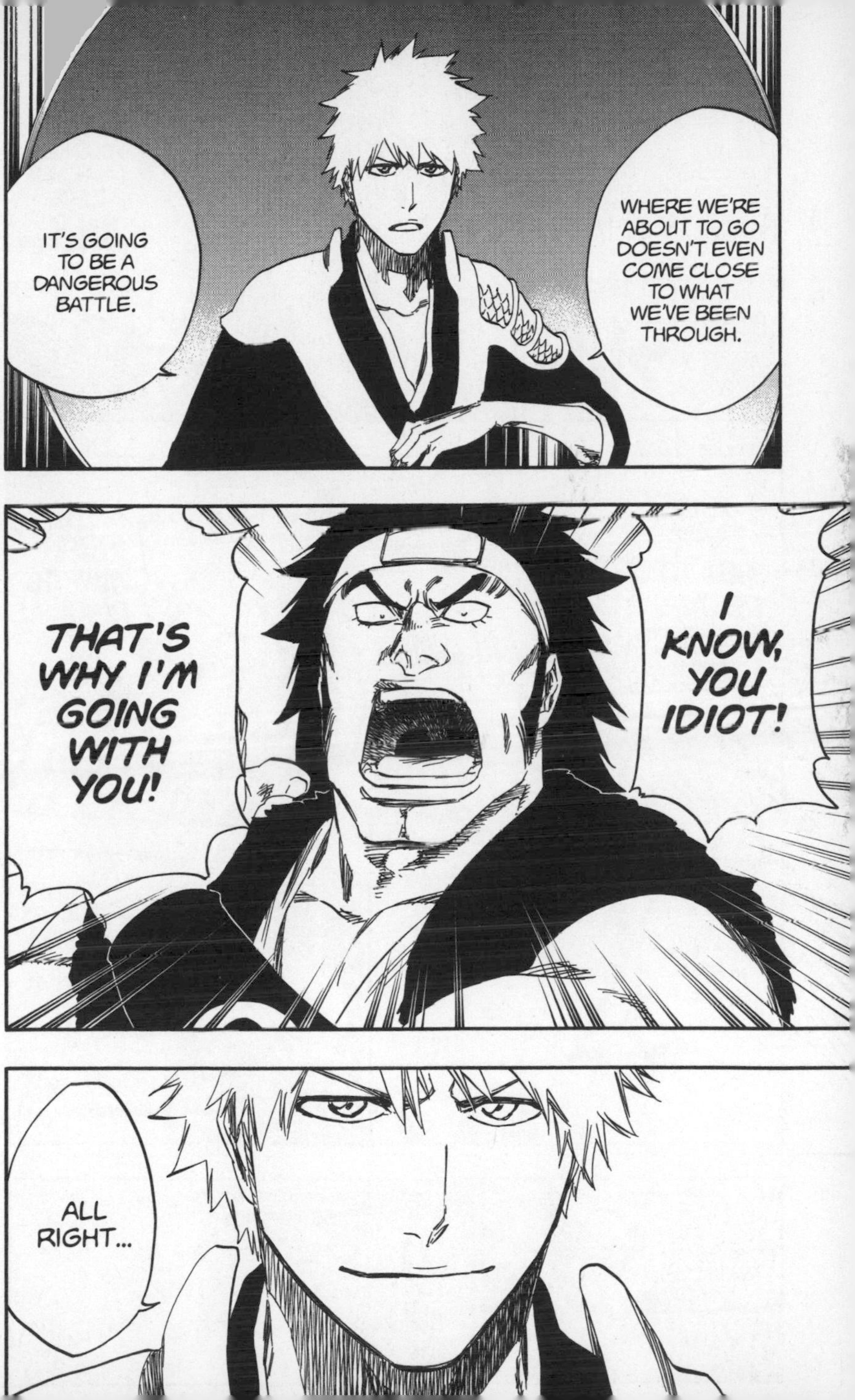
WHERE WE'RE ABOUT TO GO DOESN'T EVEN COME CLOSE TO WHAT WE'VE BEEN THROUGH.
IT'S GOING TO BE A DANGEROUS BATTLE.
I KNOW, YOU IDIOT!
THAT'S WHY I'M GOING WITH YOU!
ALL RIGHT...

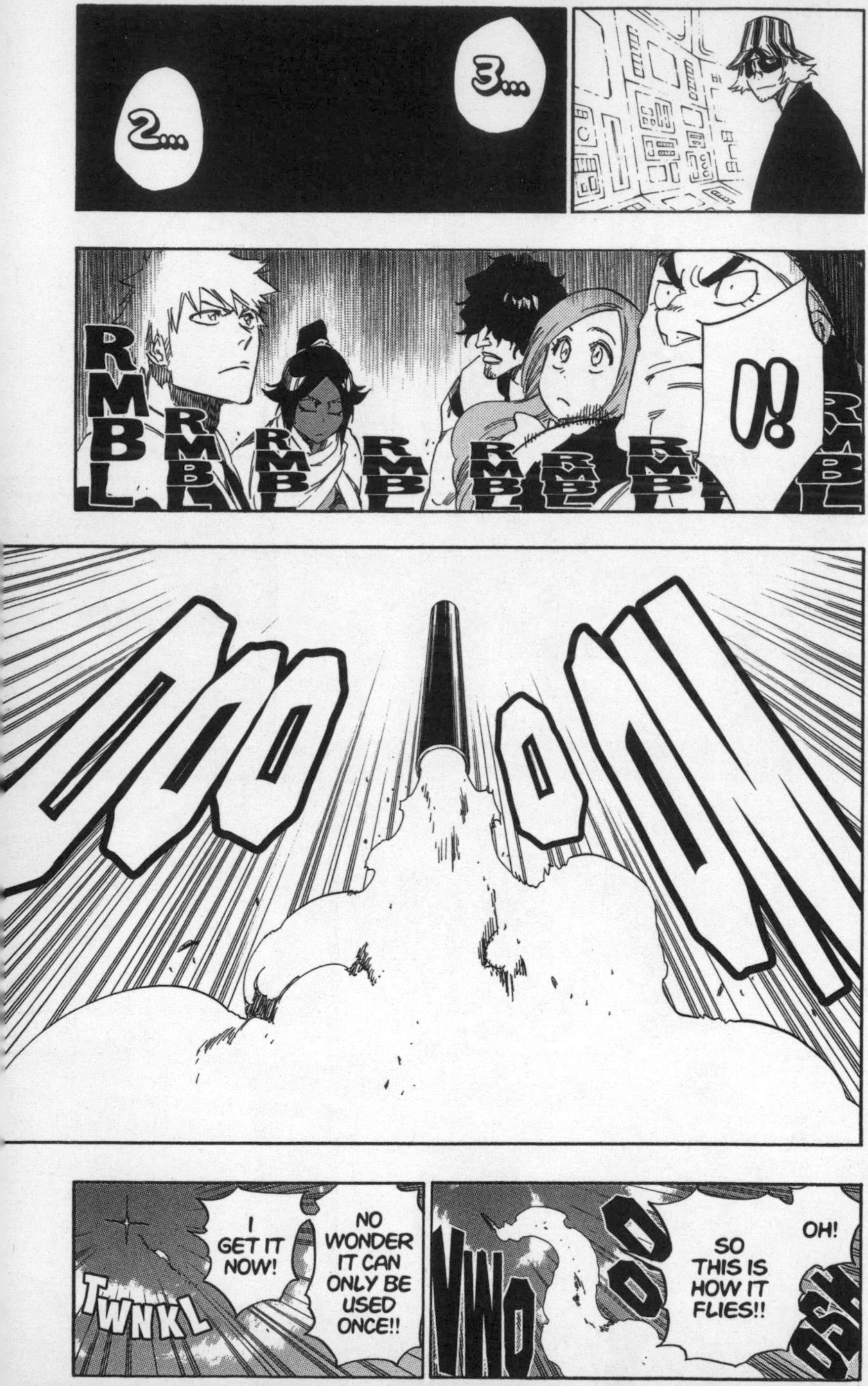
3...
2...
O!
RMBL
OH!
SO THIS IS HOW IT FLIES!!
NO WONDER IT CAN ONLY BE USED ONCE!!
I GET IT NOW!
TWNKL

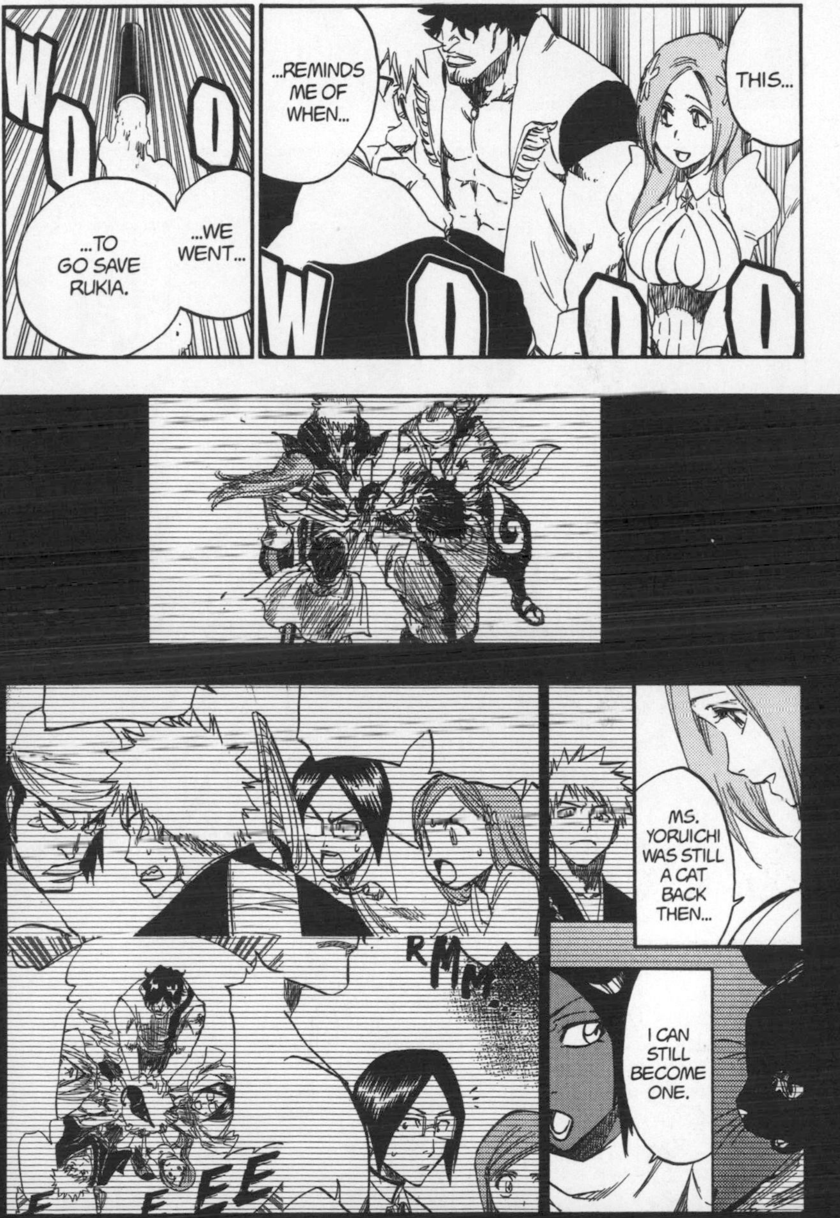
THIS...
...REMINDS ME OF WHEN...
WOOOO
...WE WENT...
...TO GO SAVE RUKIA.
WOO
MS. YORUICHI WAS STILL A CAT BACK THEN...
I CAN STILL BECOME ONE.
RMM
EEEEE

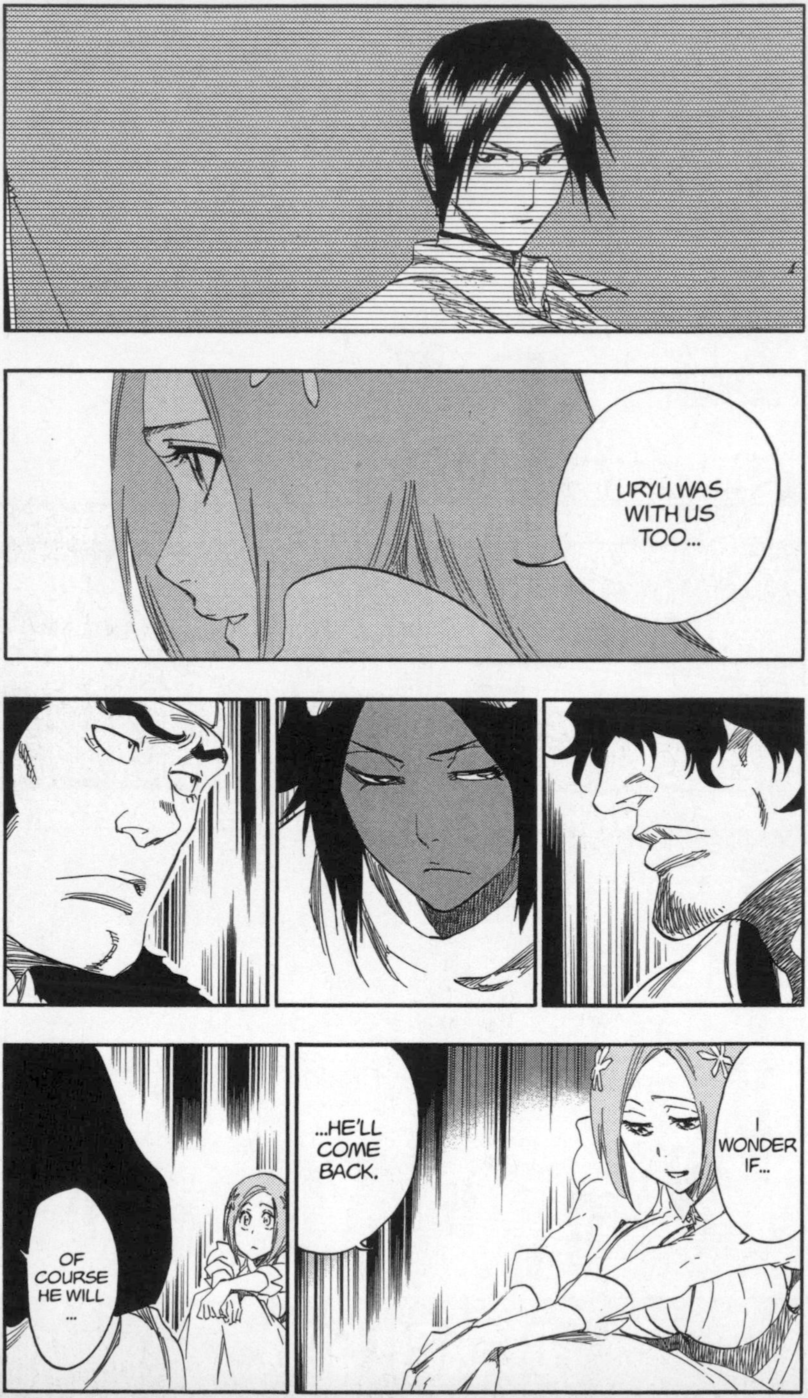
URYU WAS WITH US TOO...
I WONDER IF...
...HE'LL COME BACK.
OF COURSE HE WILL ...

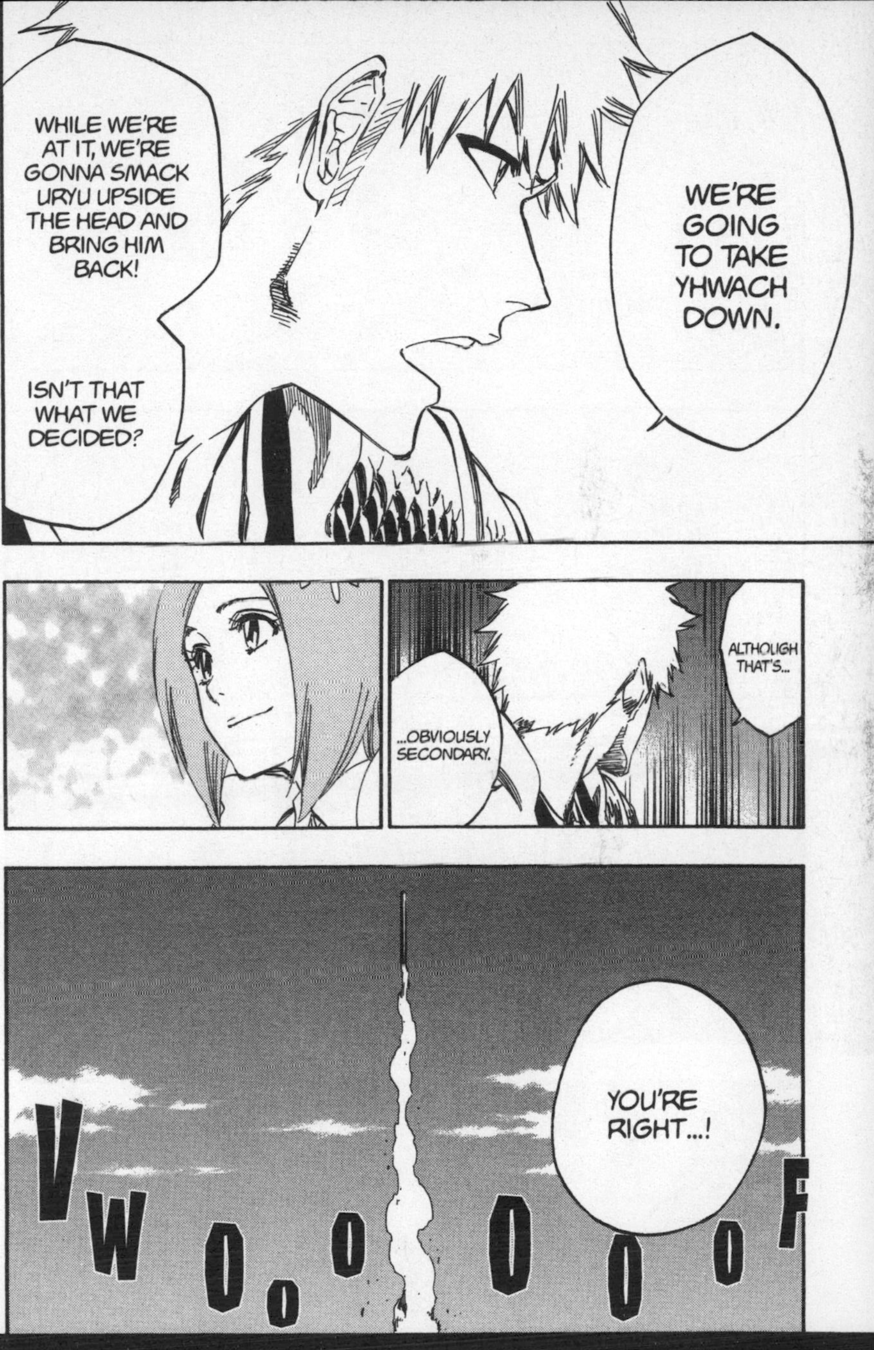
WE'RE GOING TO TAKE YHWACH DOWN.
WHILE WE'RE AT IT, WE'RE GONNA SMACK URYU UPSIDE THE HEAD AND BRING HIM BACK!
ISN'T THAT WHAT WE DECIDED?
ALTHOUGH THAT'S...
...OBVIOUSLY SECONDARY.
YOU'RE RIGHT...!
VWOOOOOOF

BLEACH 598.

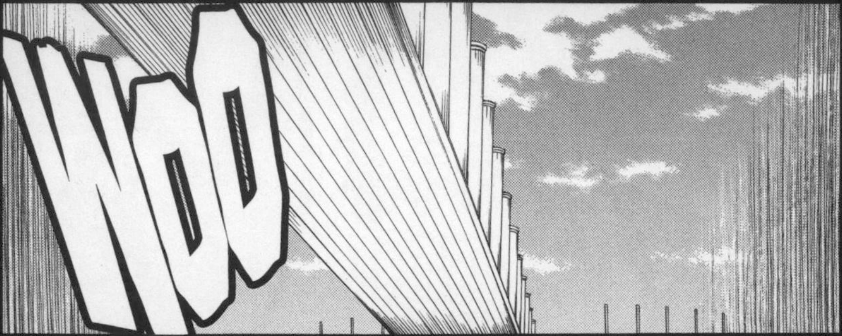
WHOO

The Shooting Star Project

[We Only Have to Beat You Mix]

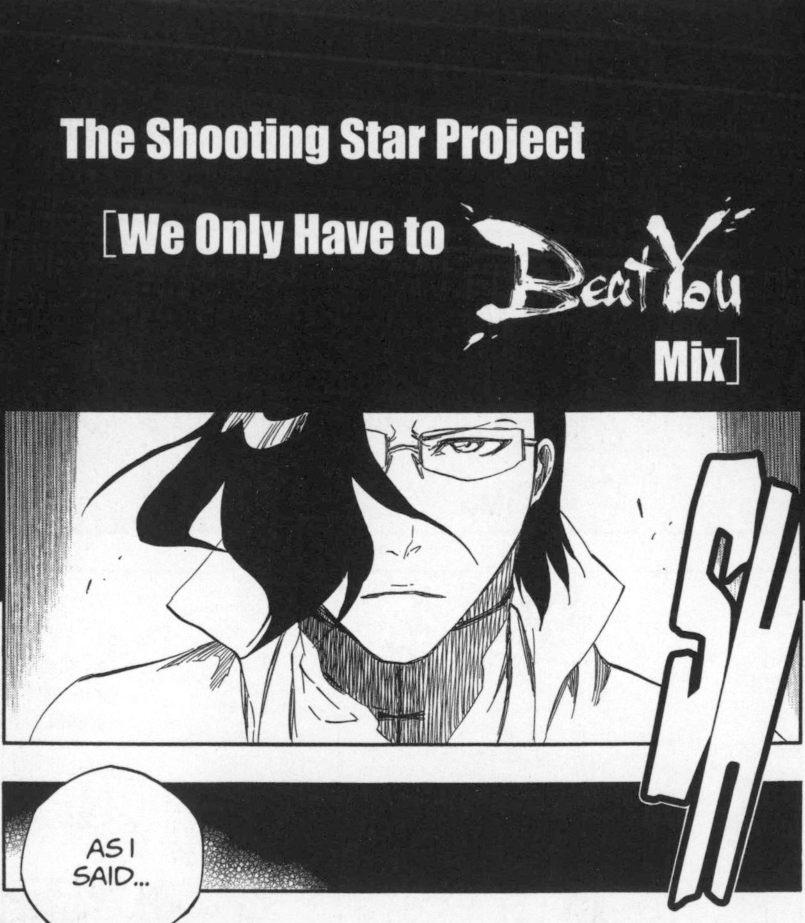
SH
AS I SAID...

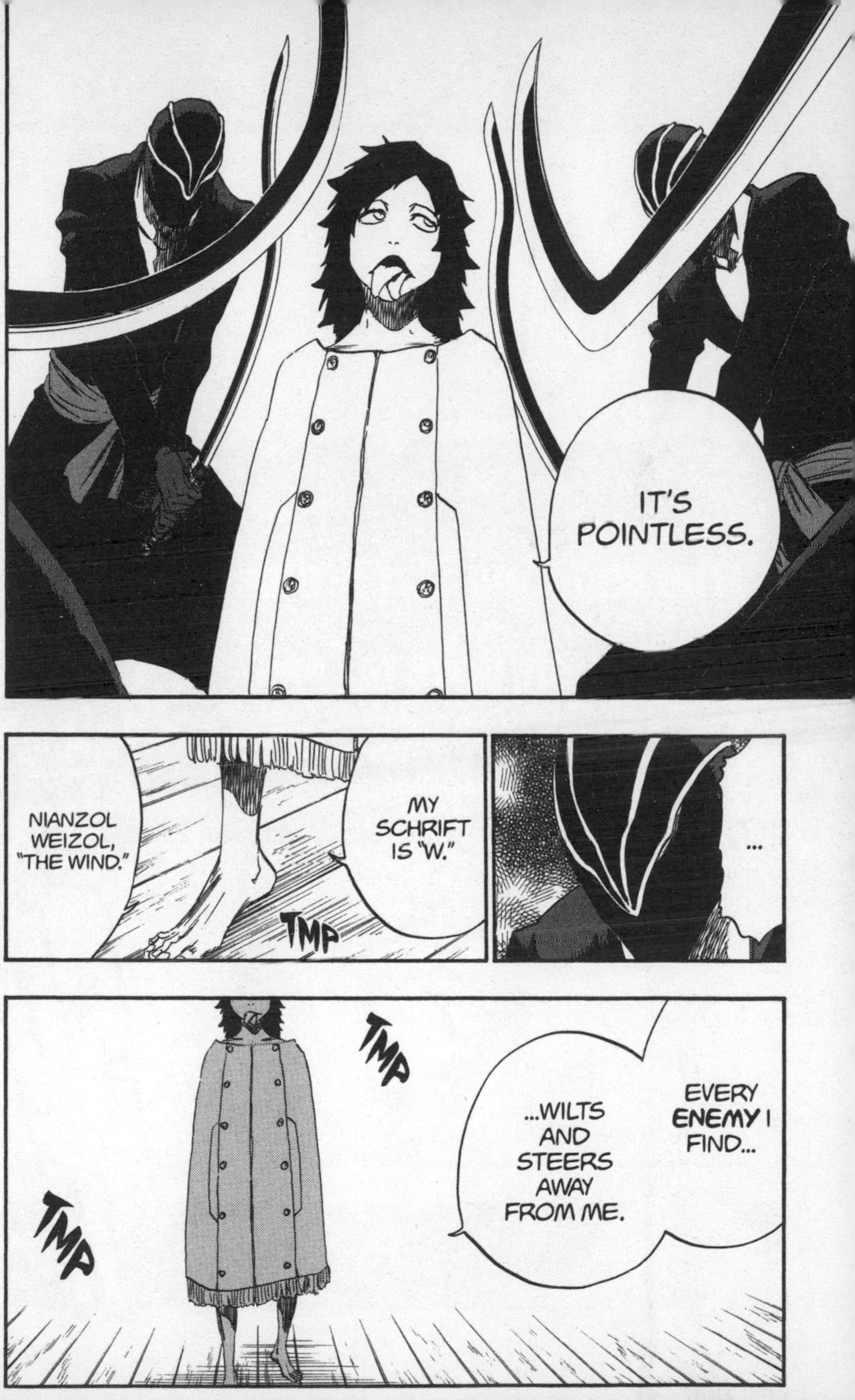
IT'S POINTLESS.
...
MY SCHRIFT IS "W."
NIANZOL WEIZOL, "THE WIND."
TMP
EVERY ENEMY I FIND...
...WILTS AND STEERS AWAY FROM ME.
TMP
TMP

READ THIS WAY

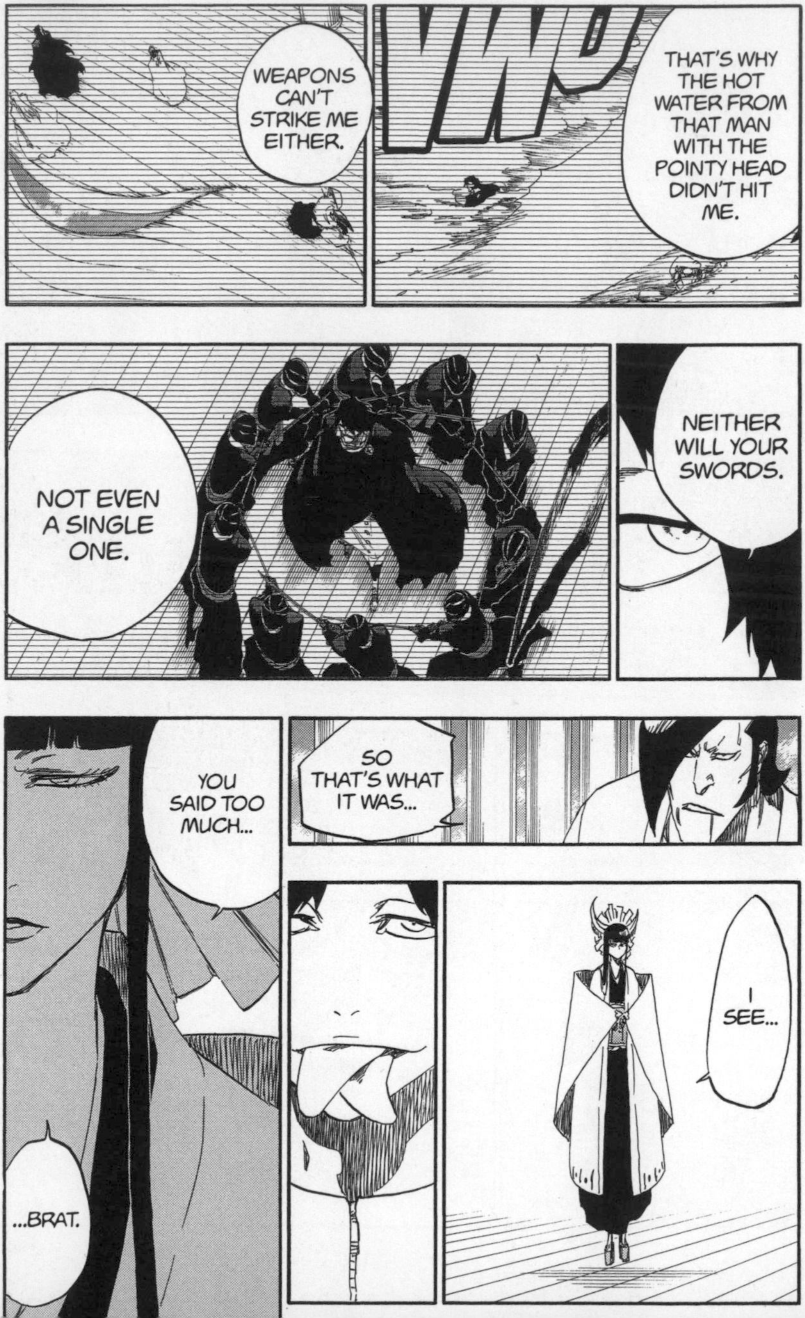
VWP
THAT'S WHY THE HOT WATER FROM THAT MAN WITH THE POINTY HEAD DIDN'T HIT ME.
WEAPONS CAN'T STRIKE ME EITHER.
NEITHER WILL YOUR SWORDS.
NOT EVEN A SINGLE ONE.
SO THAT'S WHAT IT WAS...
I SEE...
YOU SAID TOO MUCH...
...BRAT.

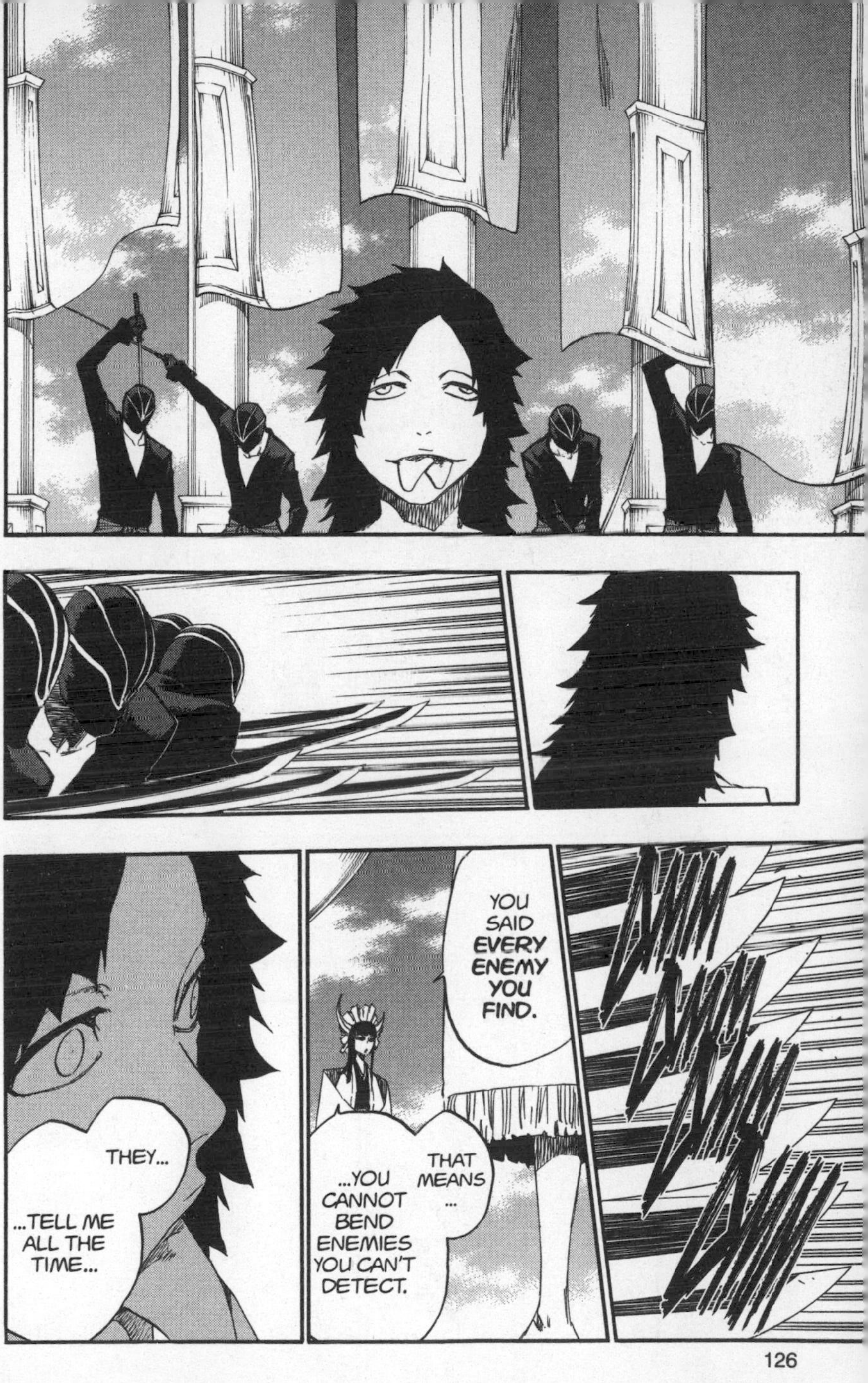
YOU SAID EVERY ENEMY YOU FIND.
THAT MEANS...
...YOU CANNOT BEND ENEMIES YOU CAN'T DETECT.
THEY...
...TELL ME ALL THE TIME...

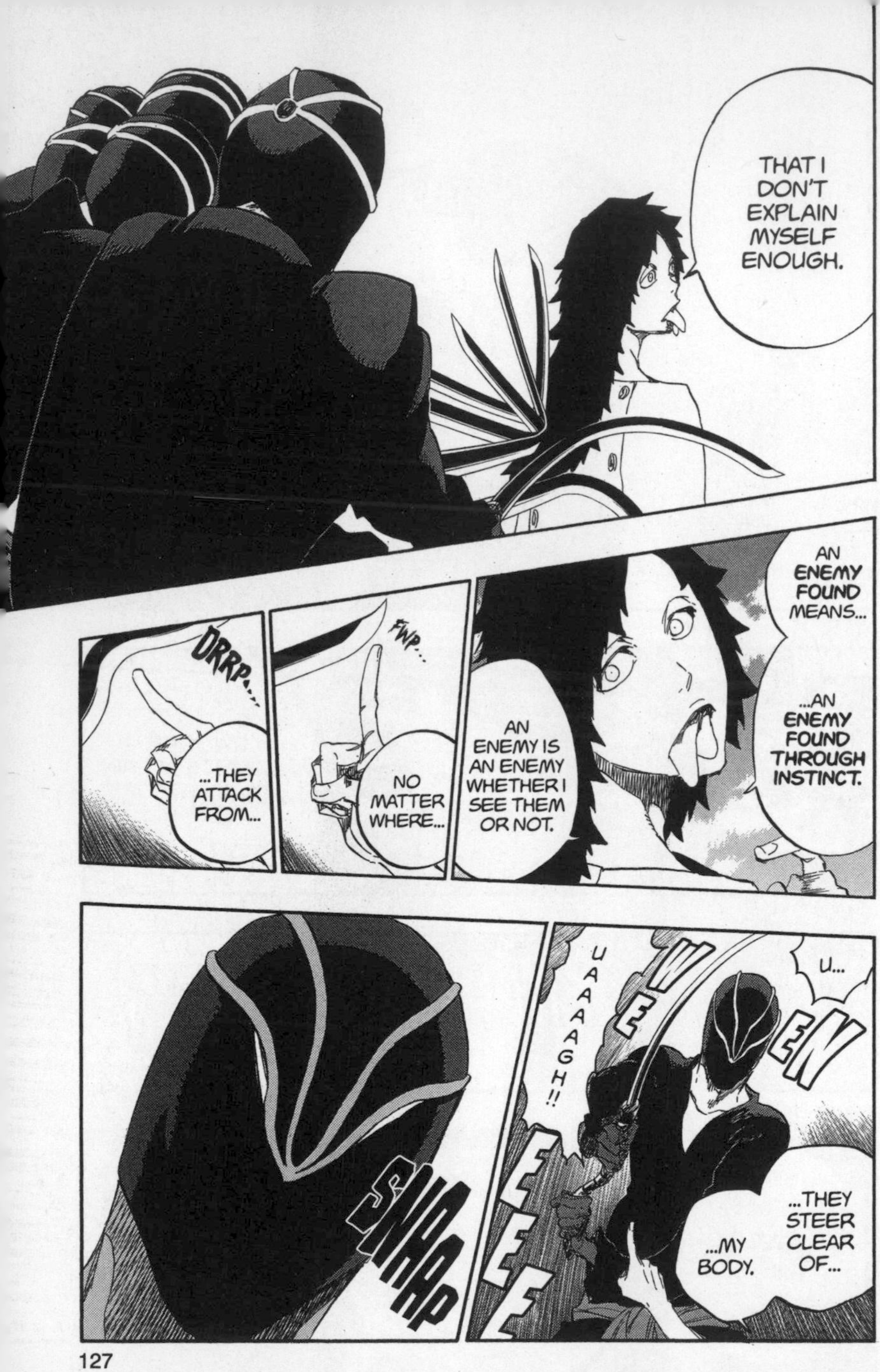
THAT I DON'T EXPLAIN MYSELF ENOUGH.
AN ENEMY FOUND MEANS...
...AN ENEMY FOUND THROUGH INSTINCT.
AN ENEMY IS AN ENEMY WHETHER I SEE THEM OR NOT.
FWP...
NO MATTER WHERE...
DRRP...
...THEY ATTACK FROM...
U...
UAAAAAGH!!
WEEEEEEN
...THEY STEER CLEAR OF...
...MY BODY.
SNAP

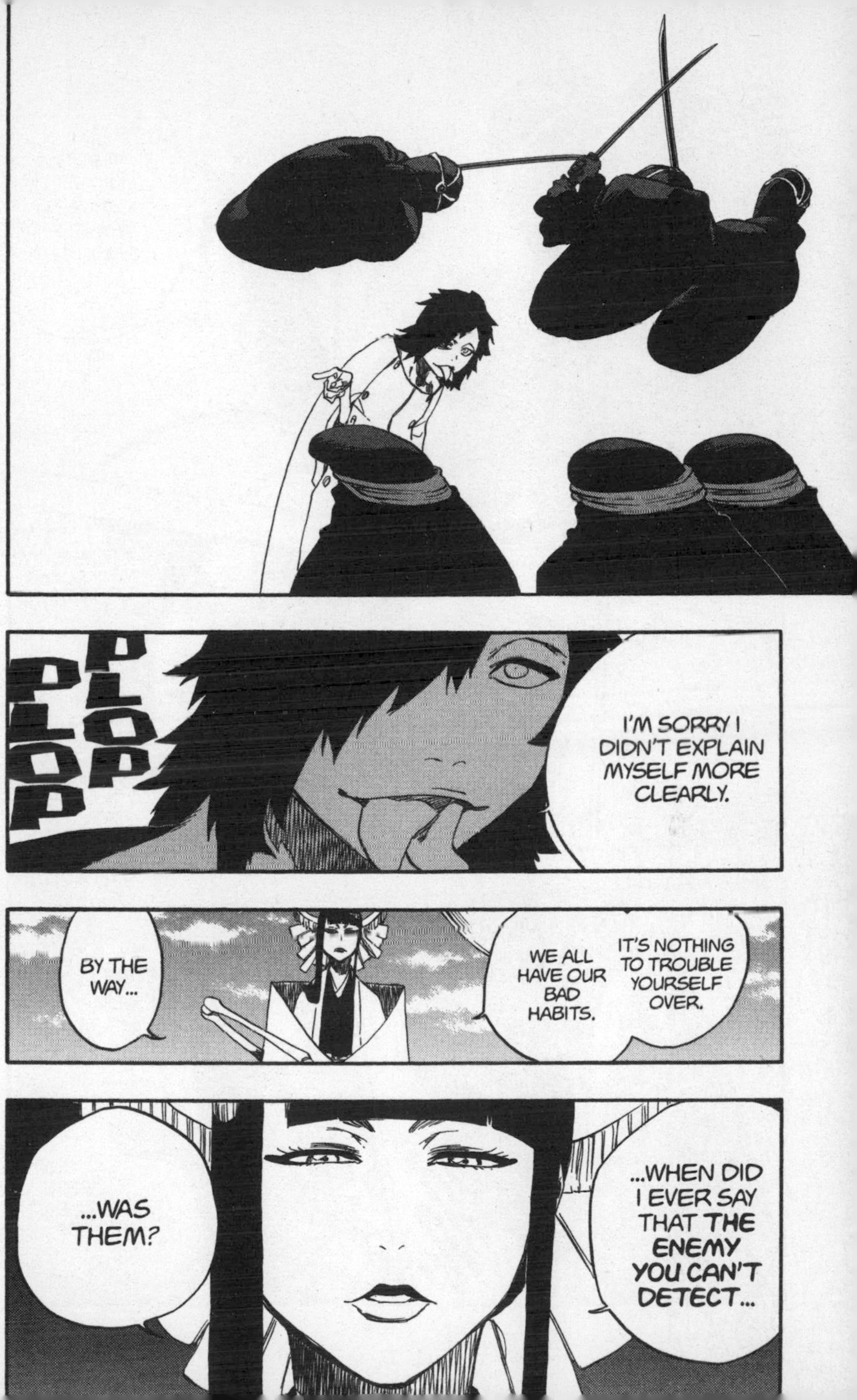
I'M SORRY I DIDN'T EXPLAIN MYSELF MORE CLEARLY.
PLOP
PLOP
IT'S NOTHING TO TROUBLE YOURSELF OVER.
WE ALL HAVE OUR BAD HABITS.
BY THE WAY...
...WHEN DID I EVER SAY THAT THE ENEMY YOU CAN'T DETECT...
...WAS THEM?

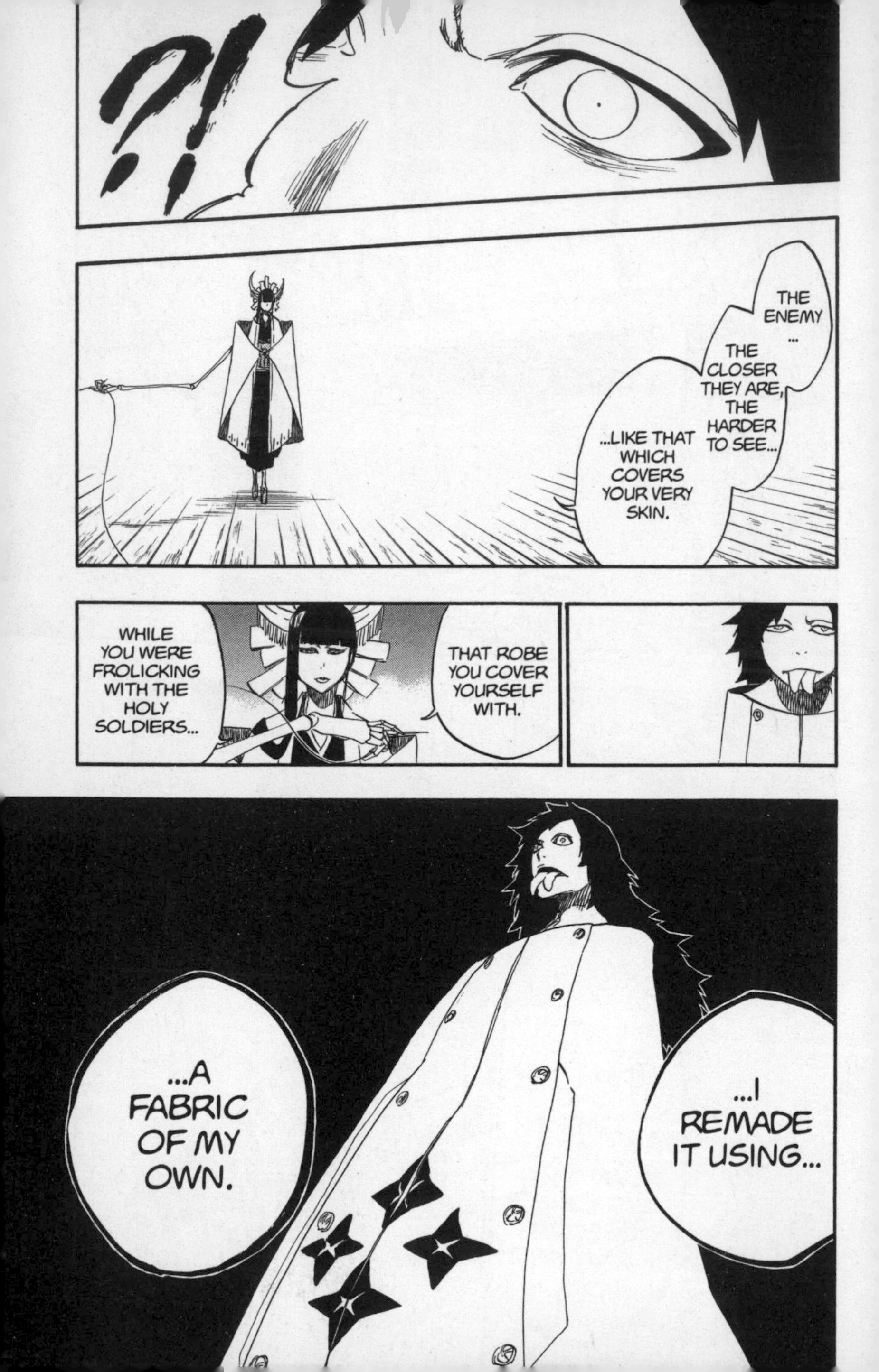
?!
THE ENEMY ... THE CLOSER THEY ARE, THE HARDER TO SEE...
...LIKE THAT WHICH COVERS YOUR VERY SKIN.
THAT ROBE YOU COVER YOURSELF WITH.
WHILE YOU WERE FROLICKING WITH THE HOLY SOLDIERS...
...I REMADE IT USING...
...A FABRIC OF MY OWN.

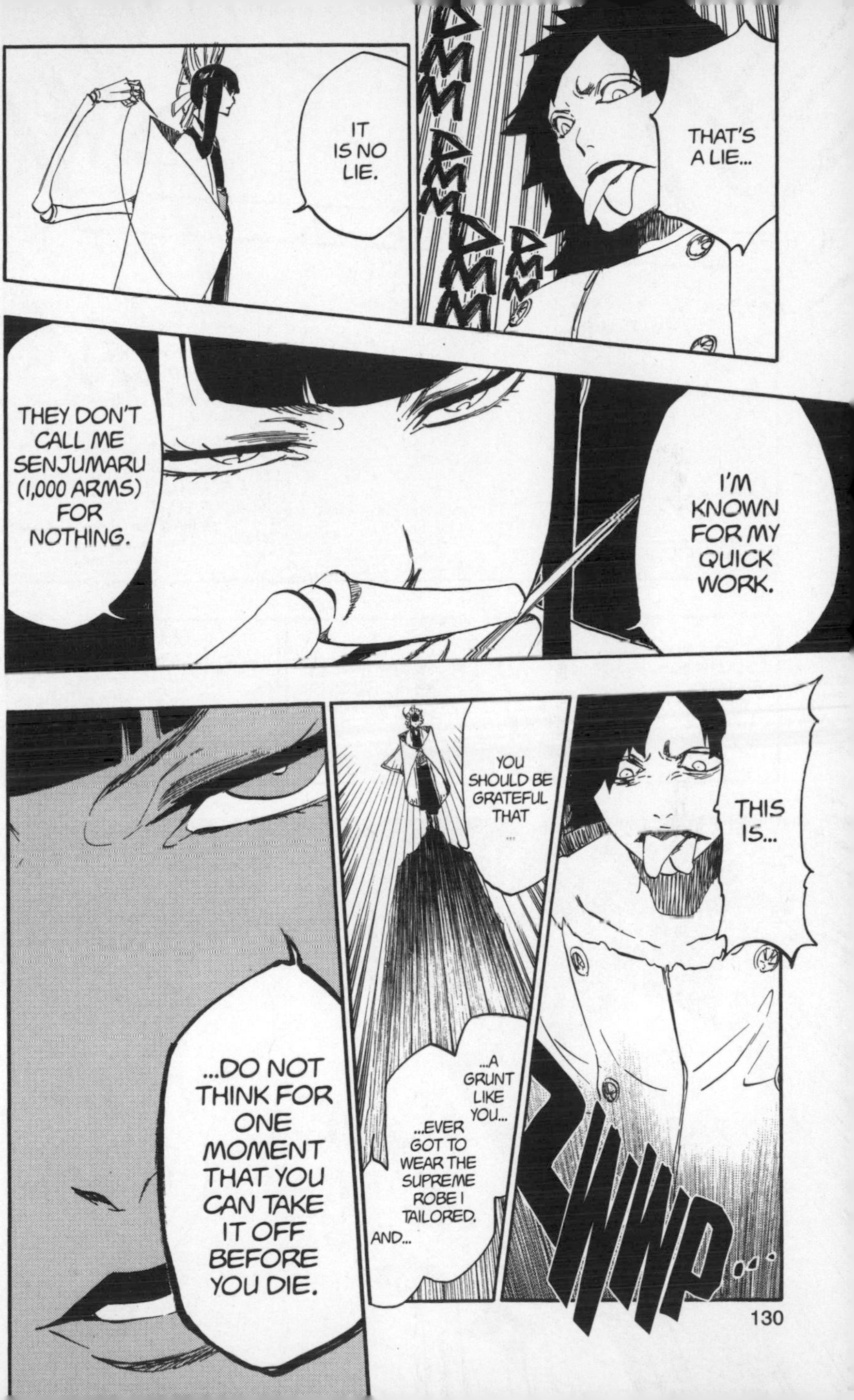
THAT'S A LIE...
IT IS NO LIE.
I'M KNOWN FOR MY QUICK WORK.
THEY DON'T CALL ME SENJUMARU (1,000 ARMS) FOR NOTHING.
THIS IS...
YOU SHOULD BE GRATEFUL THAT ...
...A GRUNT LIKE YOU...
...EVER GOT TO WEAR THE SUPREME ROBE I TAILORED.
AND...
...DO NOT THINK FOR ONE MOMENT THAT YOU CAN TAKE IT OFF BEFORE YOU DIE.

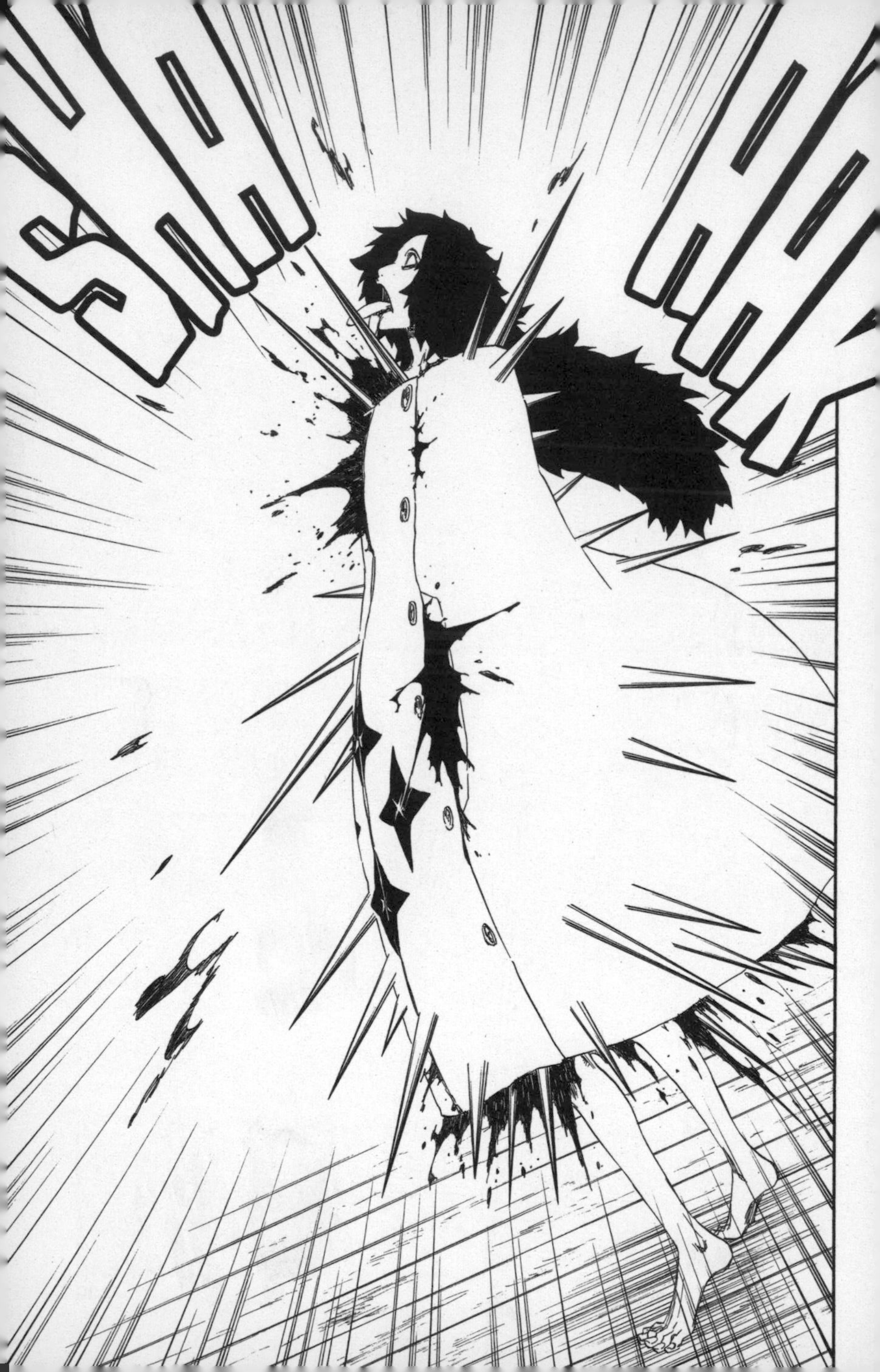

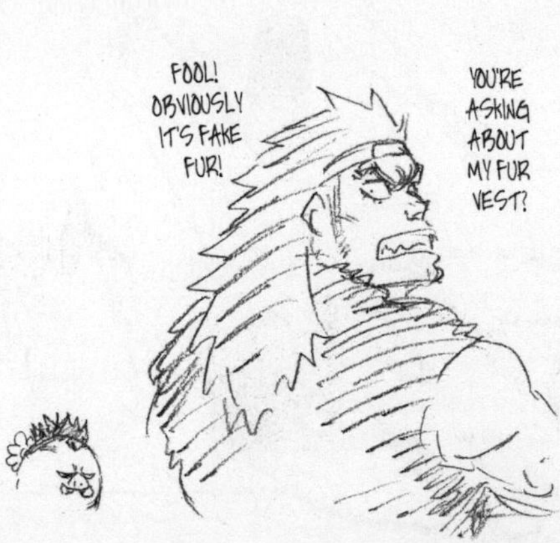
YOU'RE ASKING ABOUT MY FUR VEST?
FOOL! OBVIOUSLY IT'S FAKE FUR!

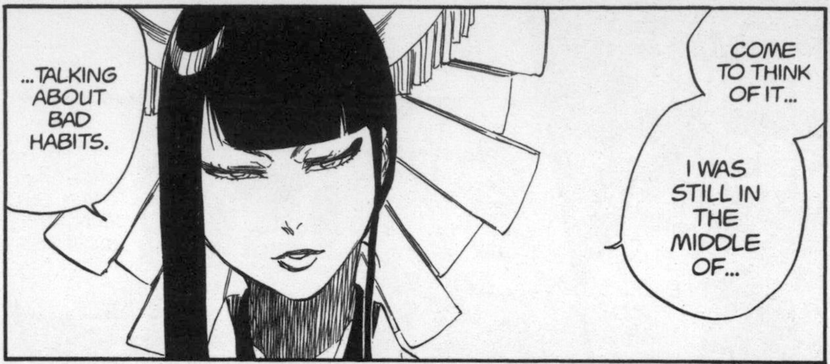
COME TO THINK OF IT...
I WAS STILL IN THE MIDDLE OF...
...TALKING ABOUT BAD HABITS.

599. TOO EARLY TO WIN TOO LATE TO KNOW

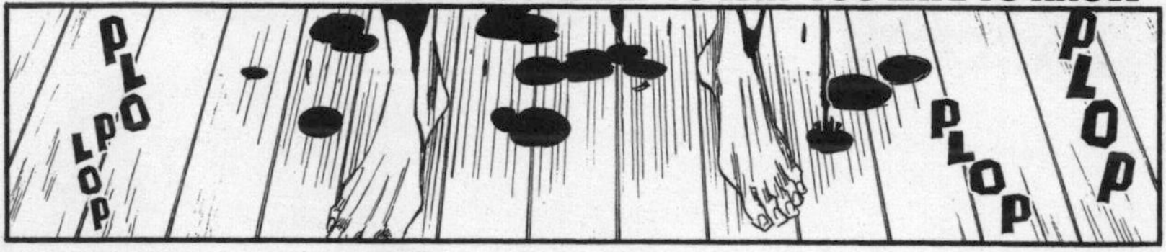
PLOP
PLOP
PLOP
PLOP

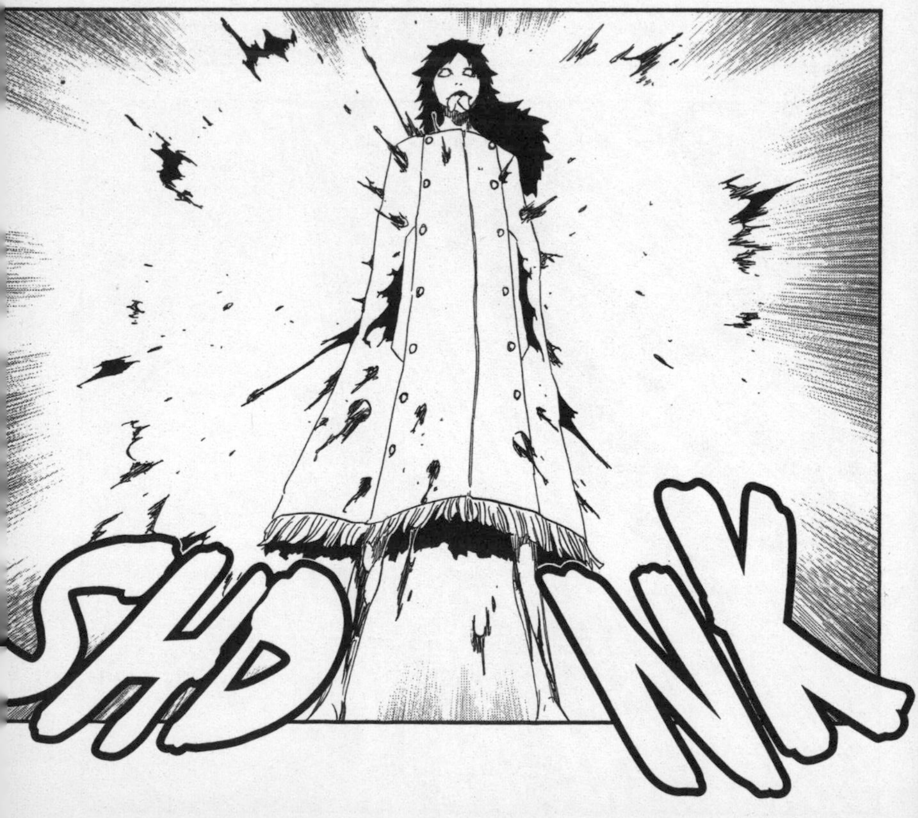

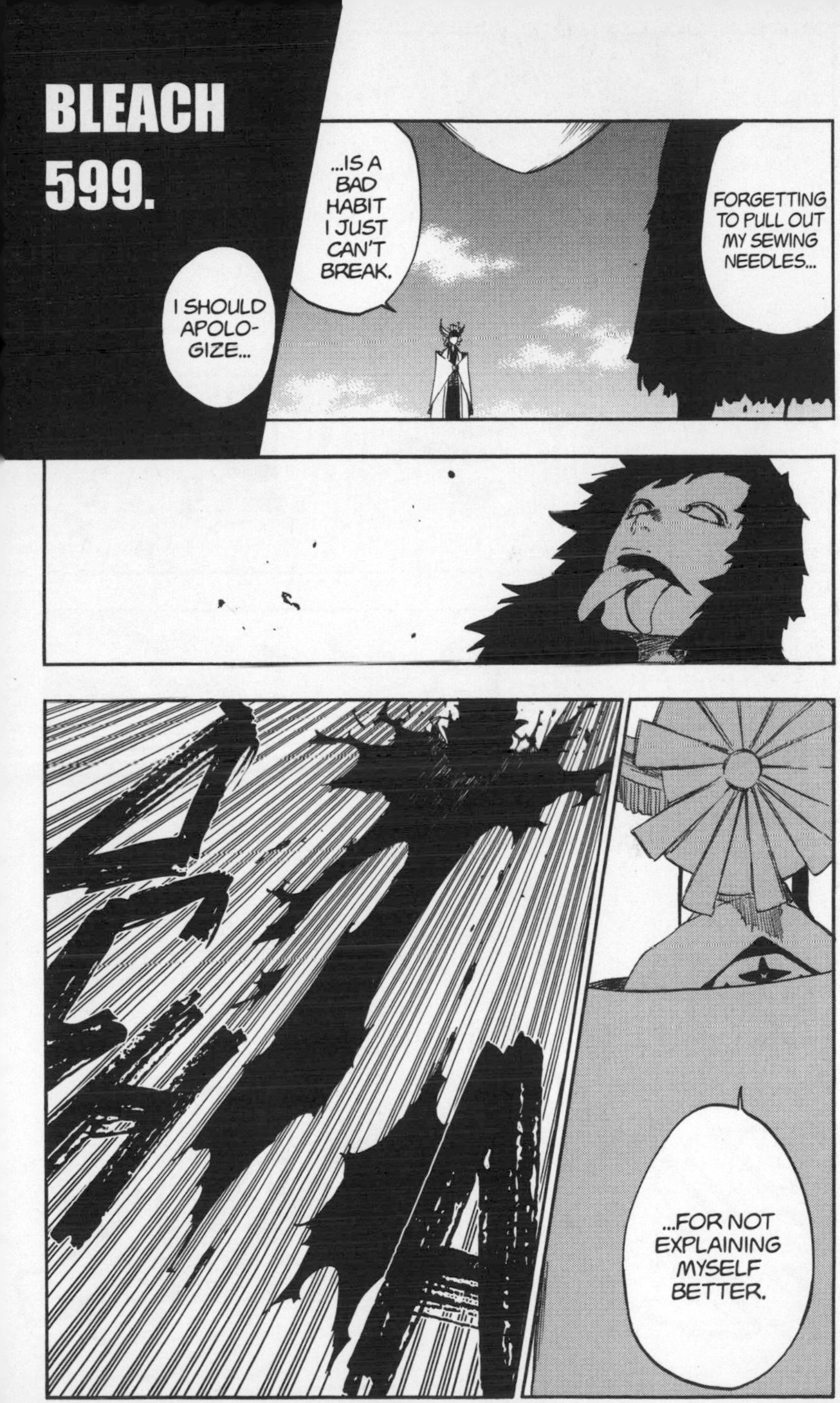
BLEACH 599.
FORGETTING TO PULL OUT MY SEWING NEEDLES...
...IS A BAD HABIT I JUST CAN'T BREAK.
I SHOULD APOLOGIZE...
...FOR NOT EXPLAINING MYSELF BETTER.

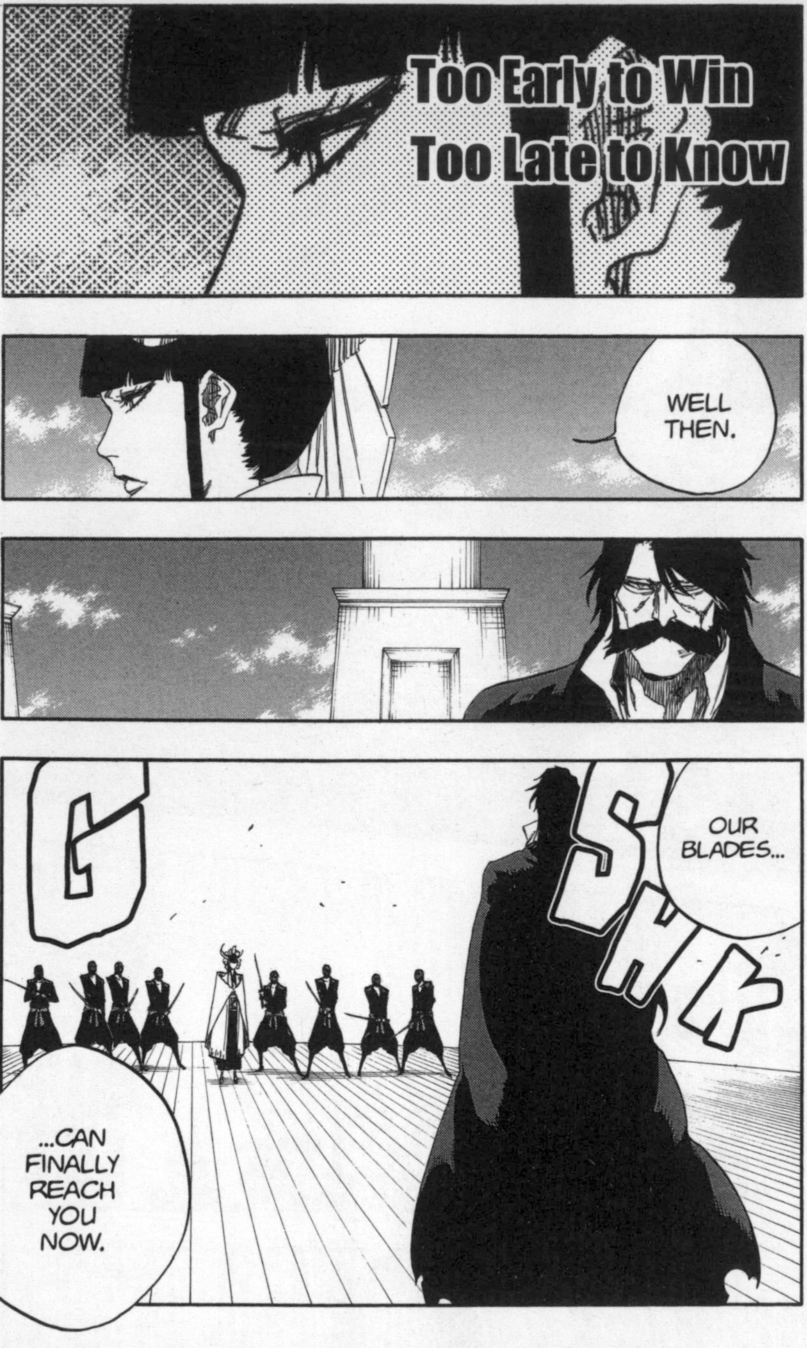
Too Early to Win
Too Late to Know
WELL THEN.
OUR BLADES...
GSHK
...CAN FINALLY REACH YOU NOW.

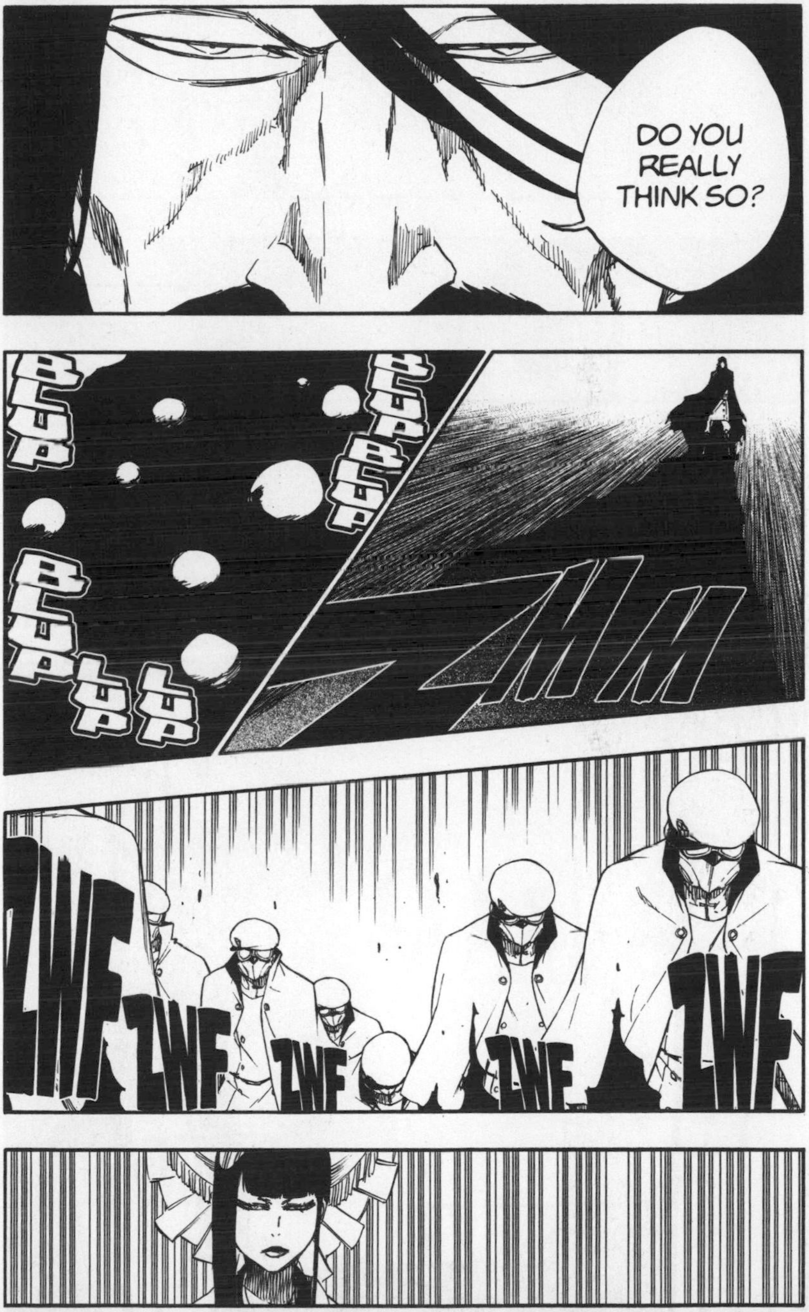
DO YOU REALLY THINK SO?
MM
BLUP BLUP
BLUP
BLUP BLUP BLUP
ZWF
ZWF
ZWF
ZWF
ZWF

READ THIS WAY

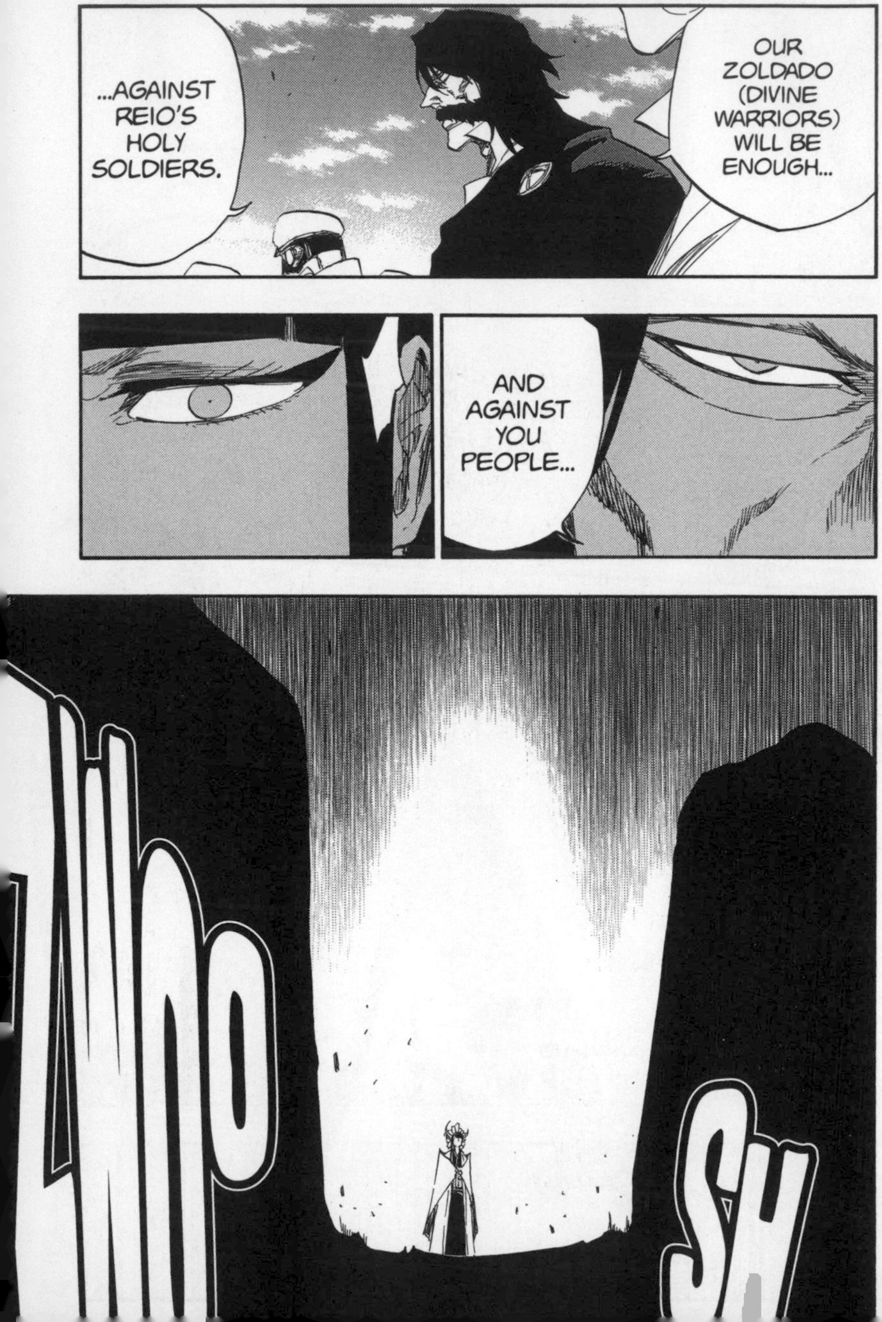
OUR ZOLDADO (DIVINE WARRIORS) WILL BE ENOUGH...
...AGAINST REIO'S HOLY SOLDIERS.
AND AGAINST YOU PEOPLE...
WHOOSH

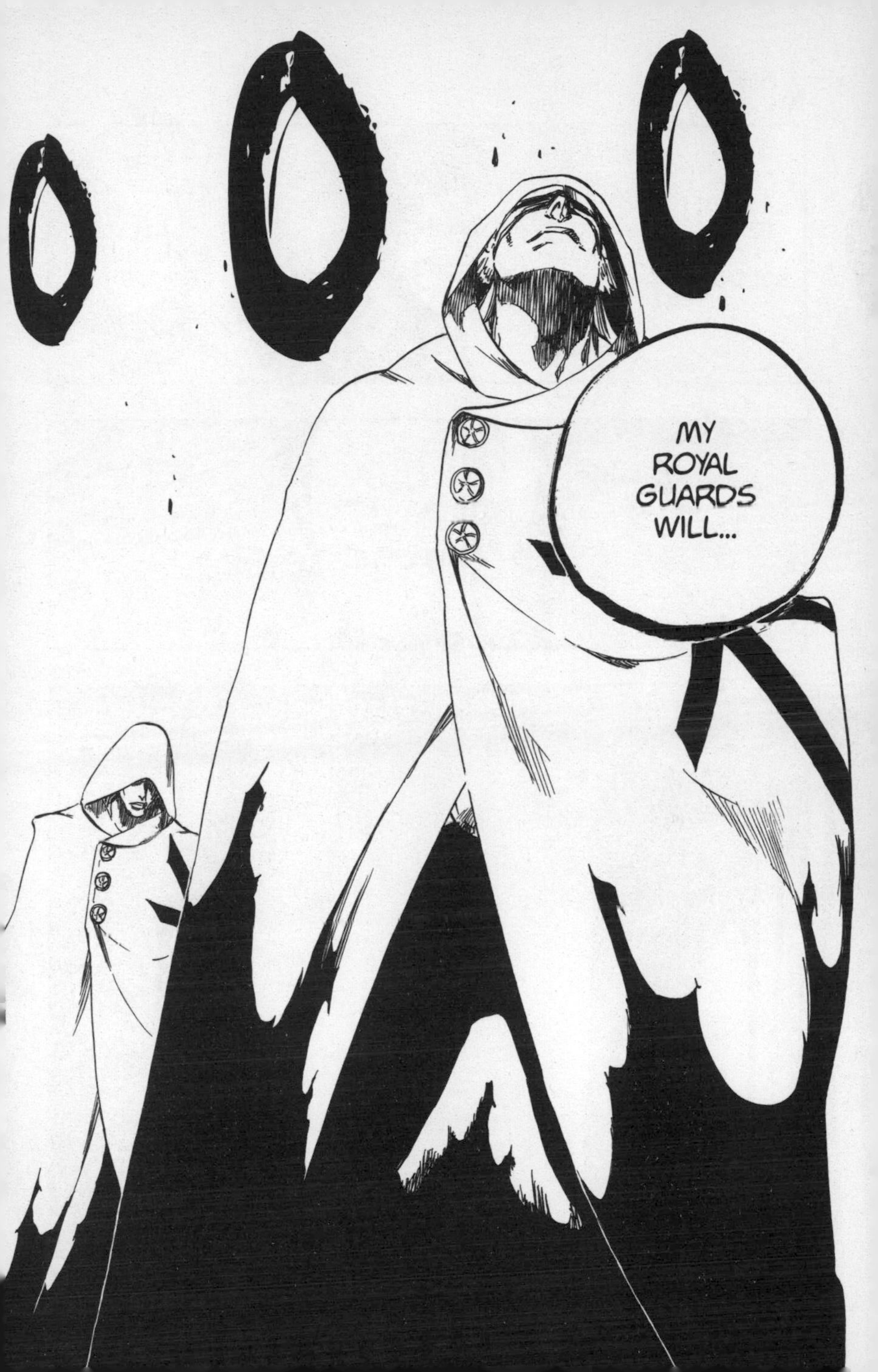
MY ROYAL GUARDS WILL...

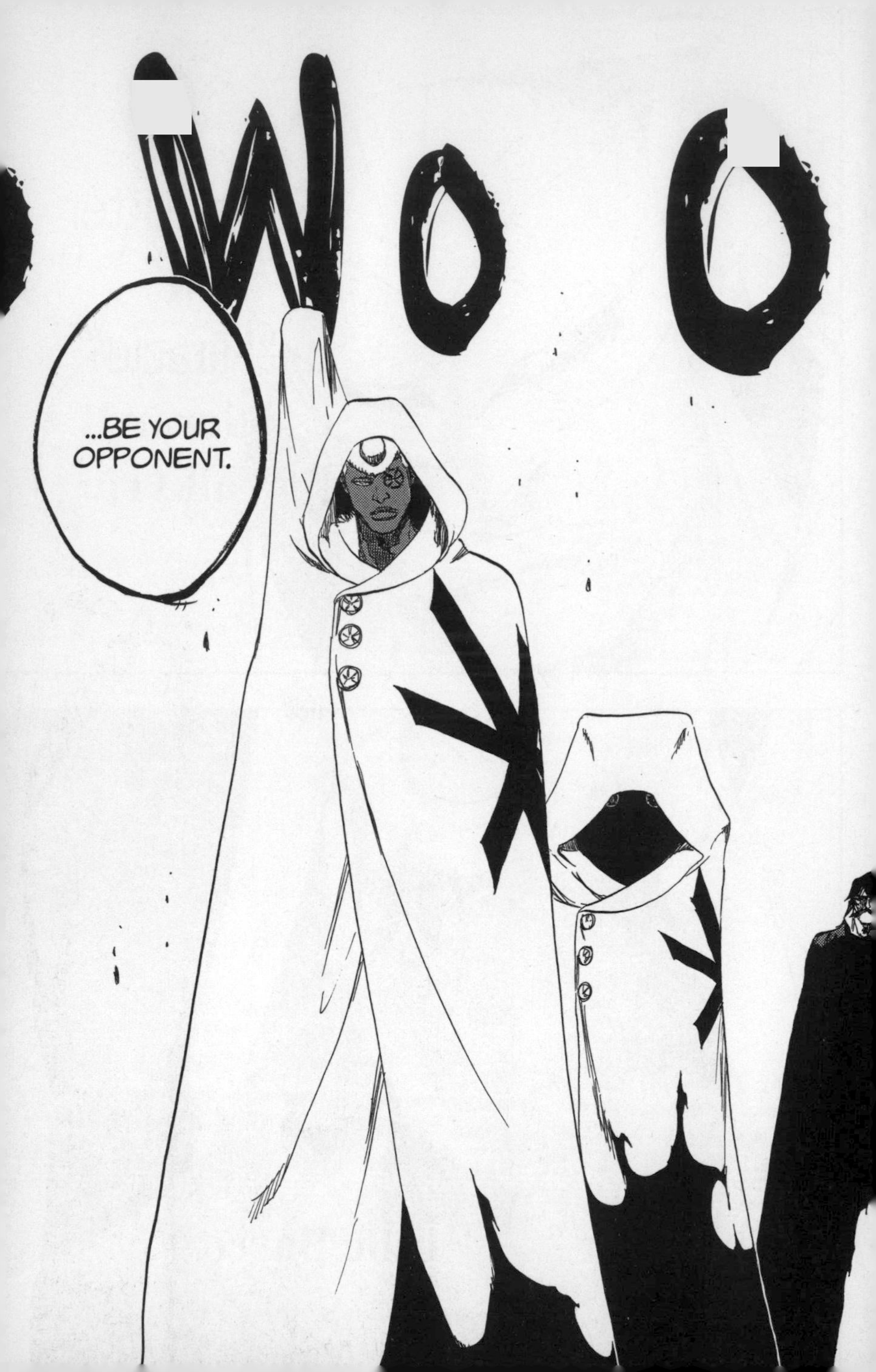
WOO
...BE YOUR OPPONENT.

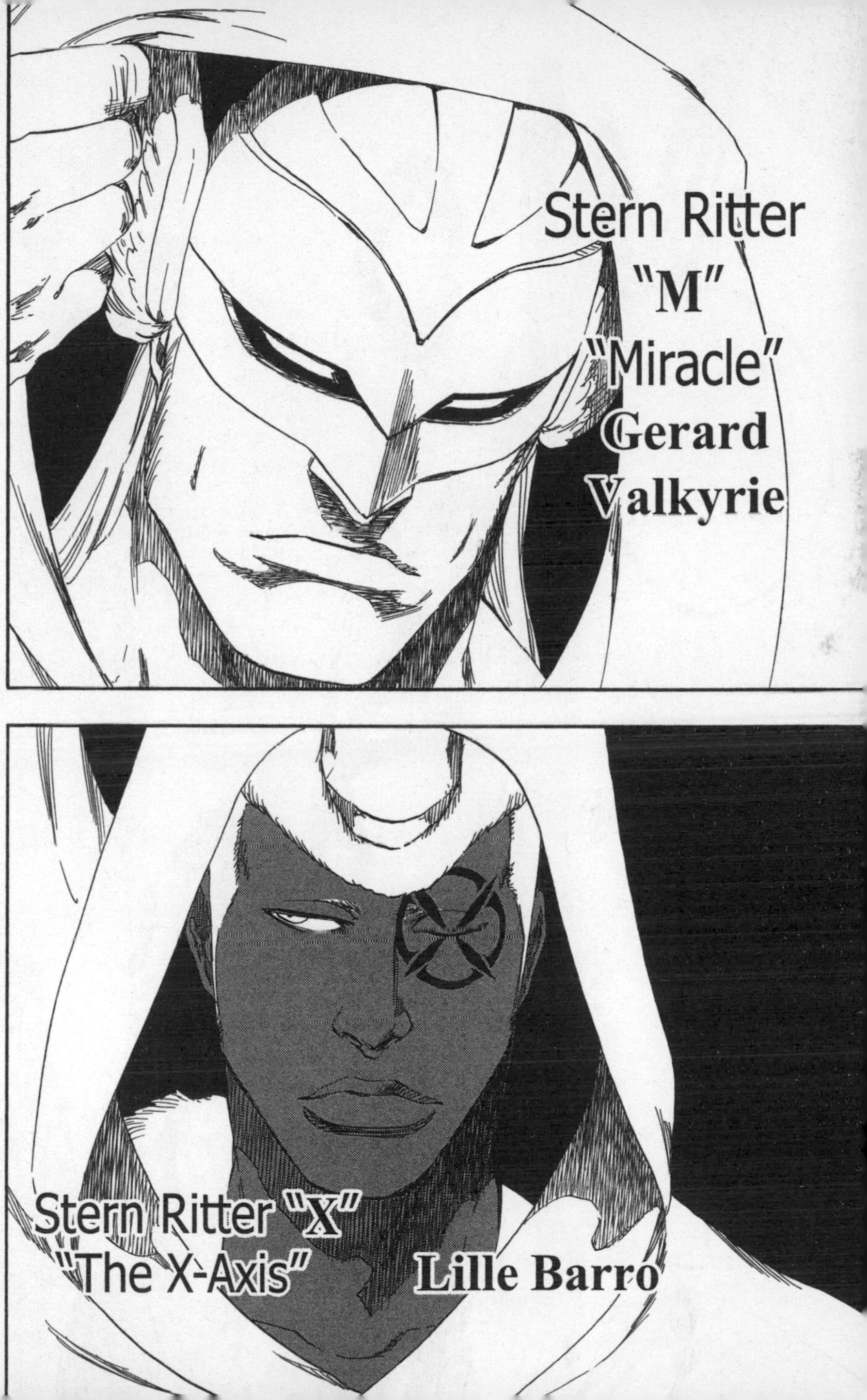
Stern Ritter
"M"
"Miracle"
Gerard
Valkyrie
Stern Ritter "X"
"The X-Axis"
Lille Barro

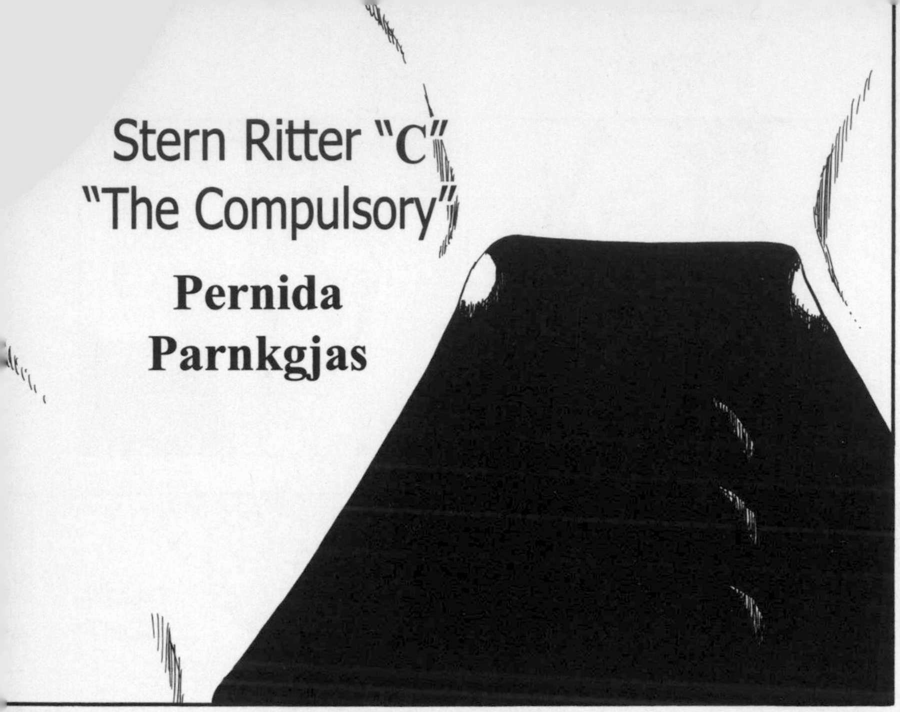
Stern Ritter "C"
"The Compulsory"
Pernida Parnkgjas
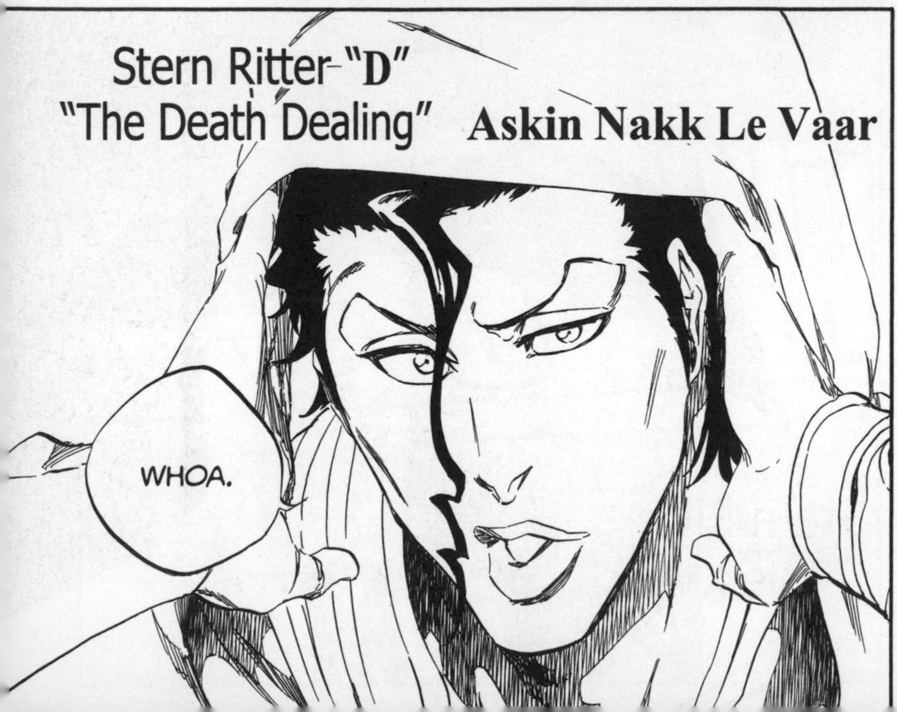
Stern Ritter "D"
"The Death Dealing"
Askin Nakk Le Vaar
WHOA.

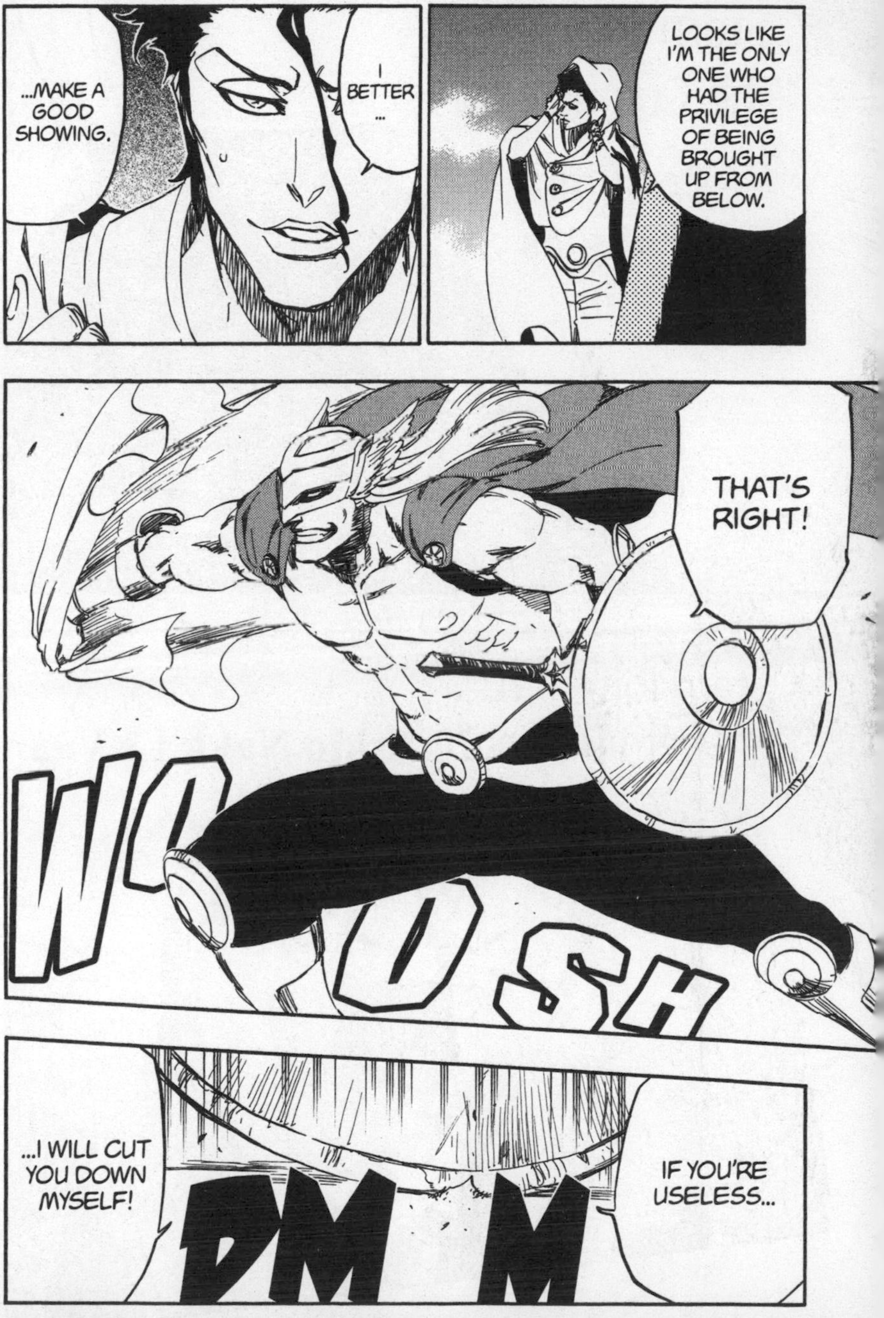
LOOKS LIKE I'M THE ONLY ONE WHO HAD THE PRIVILEGE OF BEING BROUGHT UP FROM BELOW.
I BETTER...
...MAKE A GOOD SHOWING.
THAT'S RIGHT!
WOOSH
IF YOU'RE USELESS...
...I WILL CUT YOU DOWN MYSELF!
DMM

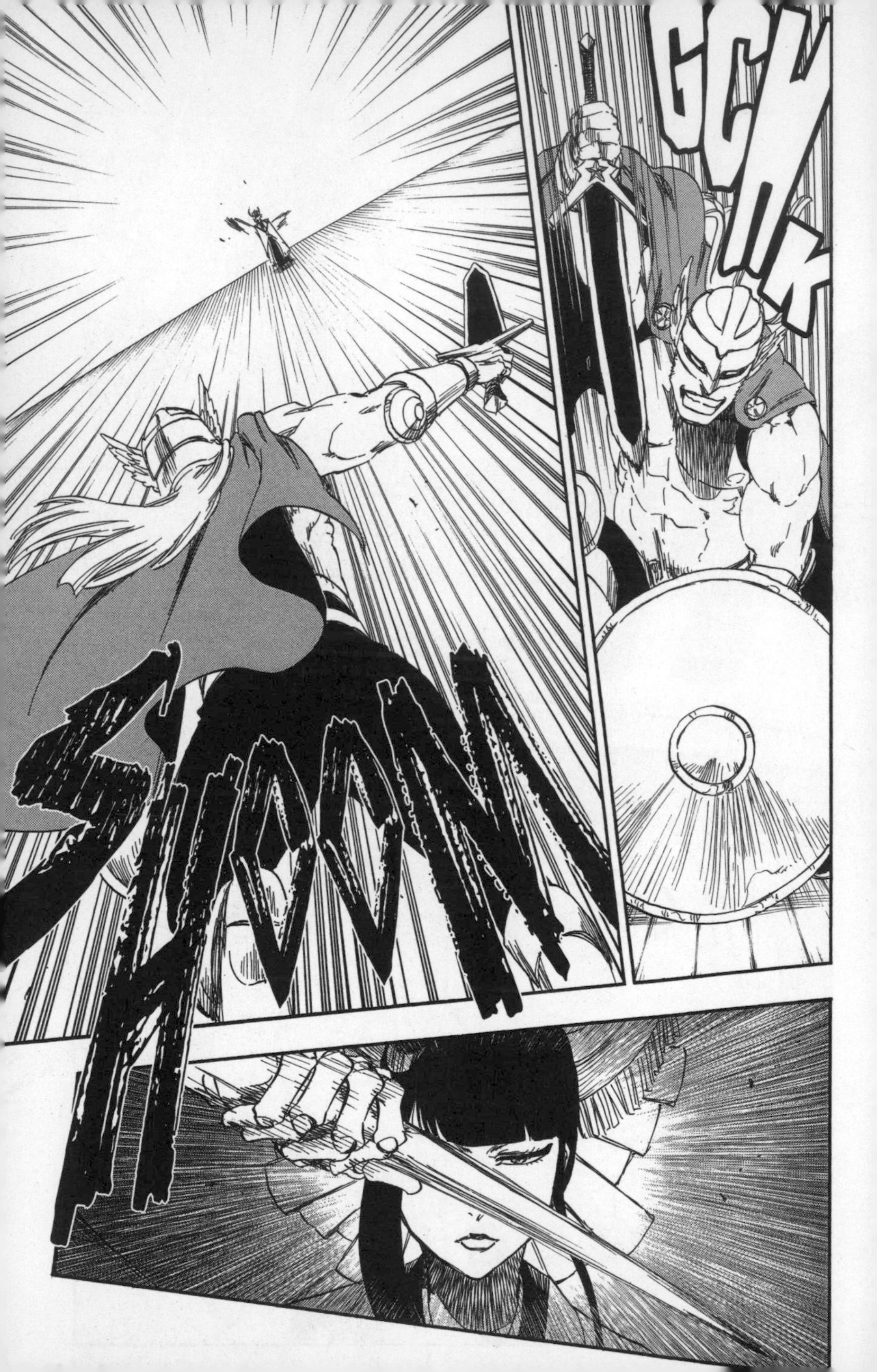
GCHK
SHOOM

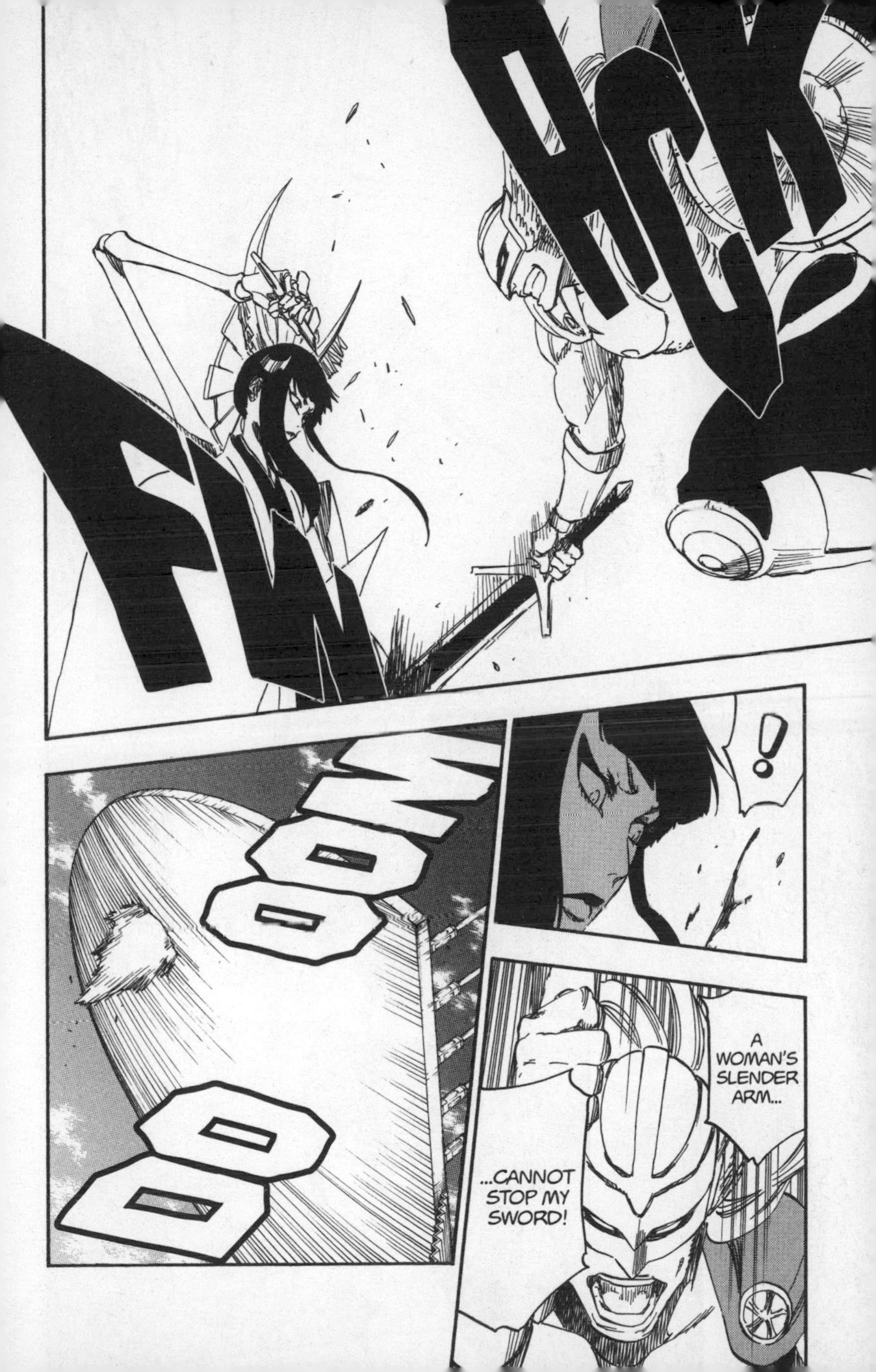
!
A WOMAN'S SLENDER ARM...
...CANNOT STOP MY SWORD!

READ THIS WAY

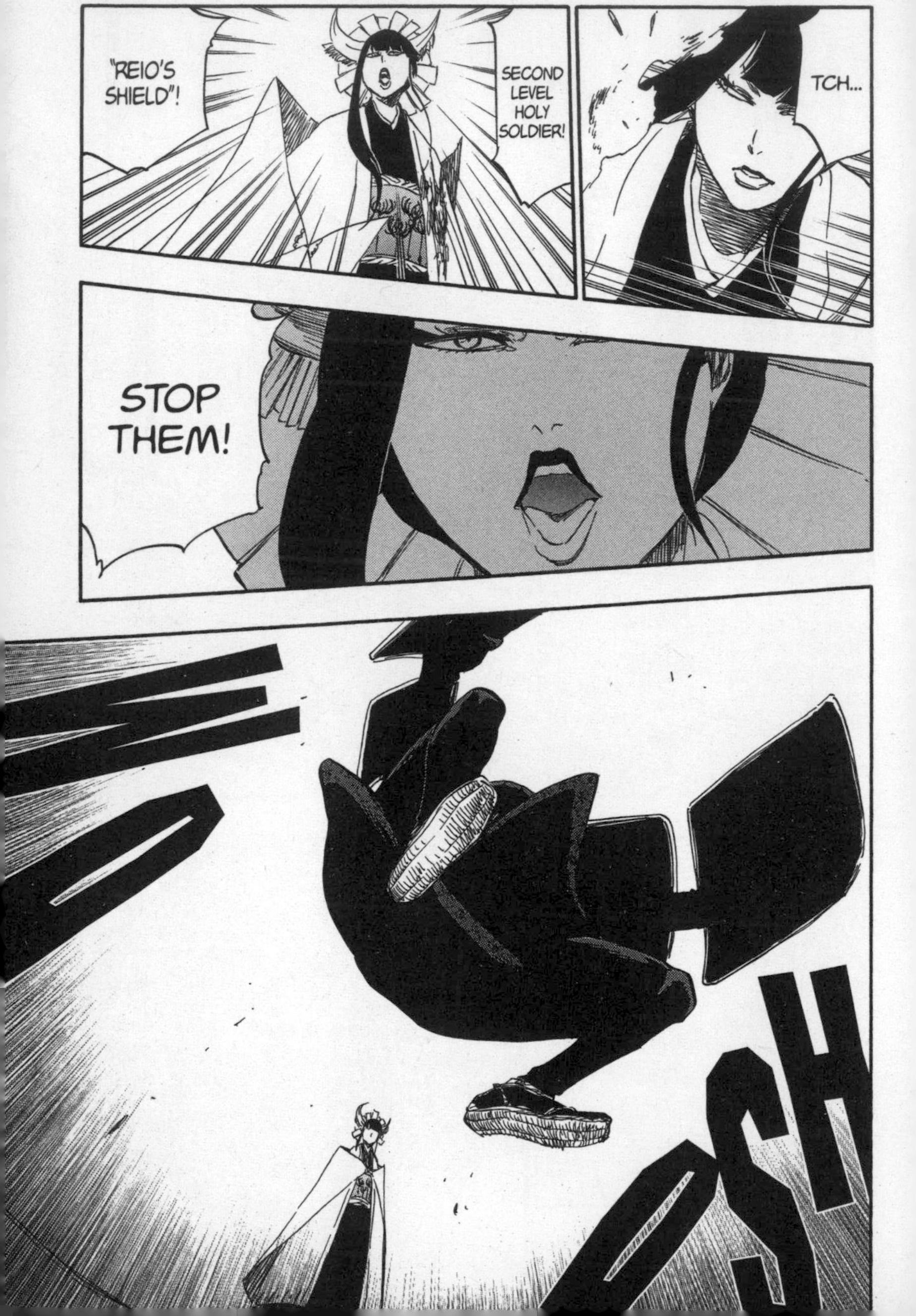
TCH...
SECOND LEVEL HOLY SOLDIER!
"REIO'S SHIELD"!
STOP THEM!

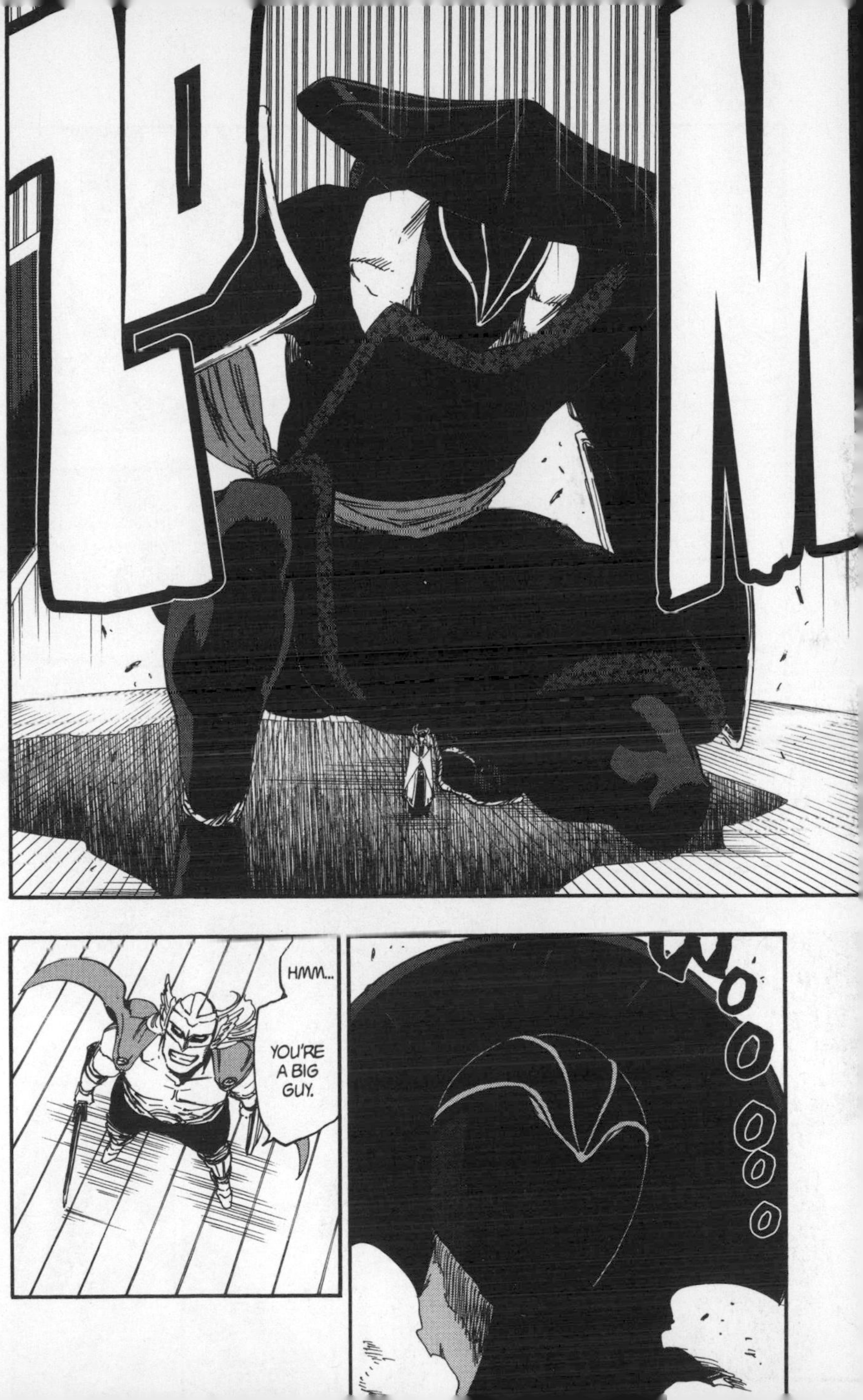
WOOOOOO
HMM...
YOU'RE A BIG GUY.

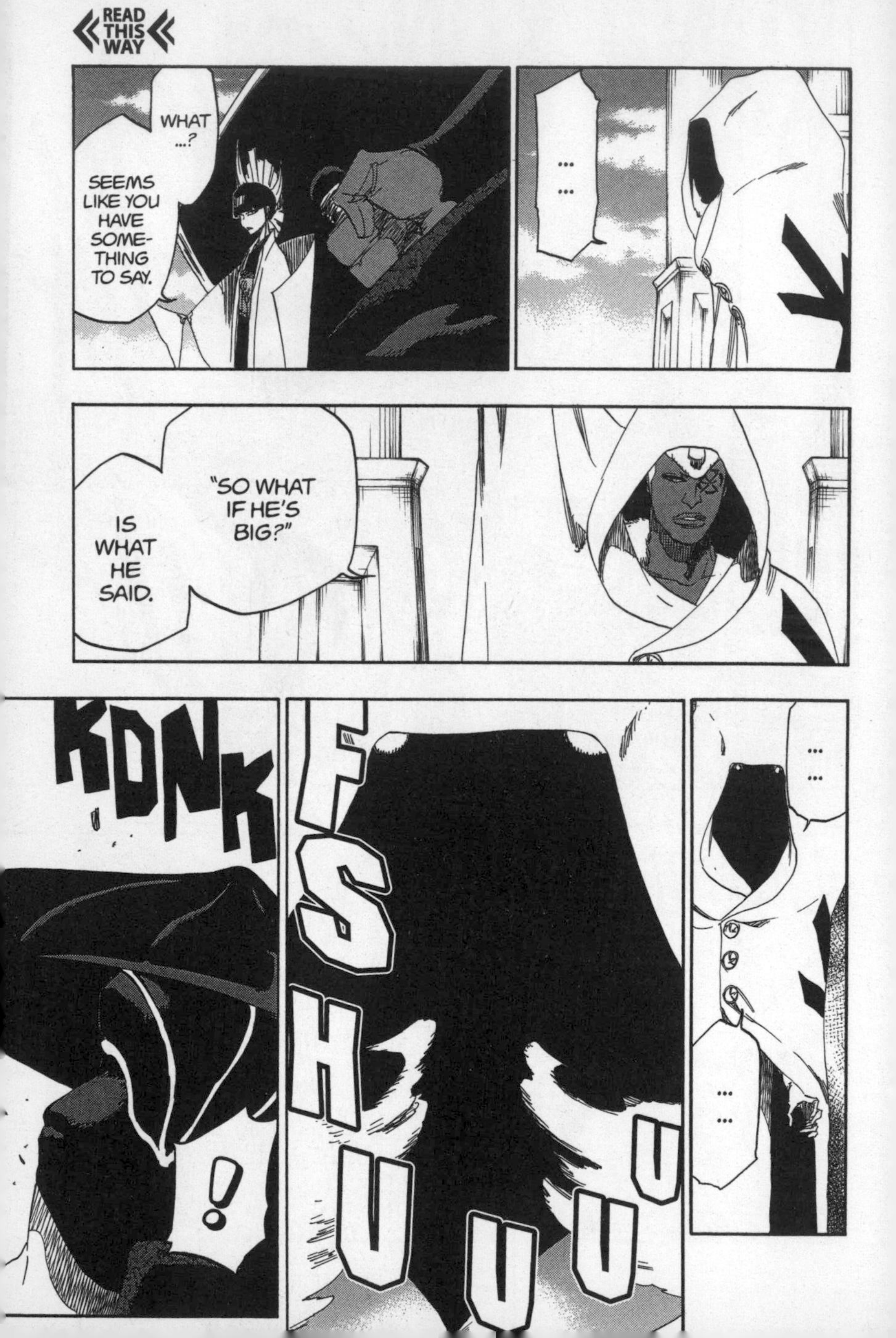
READ THIS WAY
...
...
WHAT ...?
SEEMS LIKE YOU HAVE SOME-THING TO SAY.
"SO WHAT IF HE'S BIG?"
IS WHAT HE SAID.
...
...
...
...
FSHUUUUU
KDNK
!

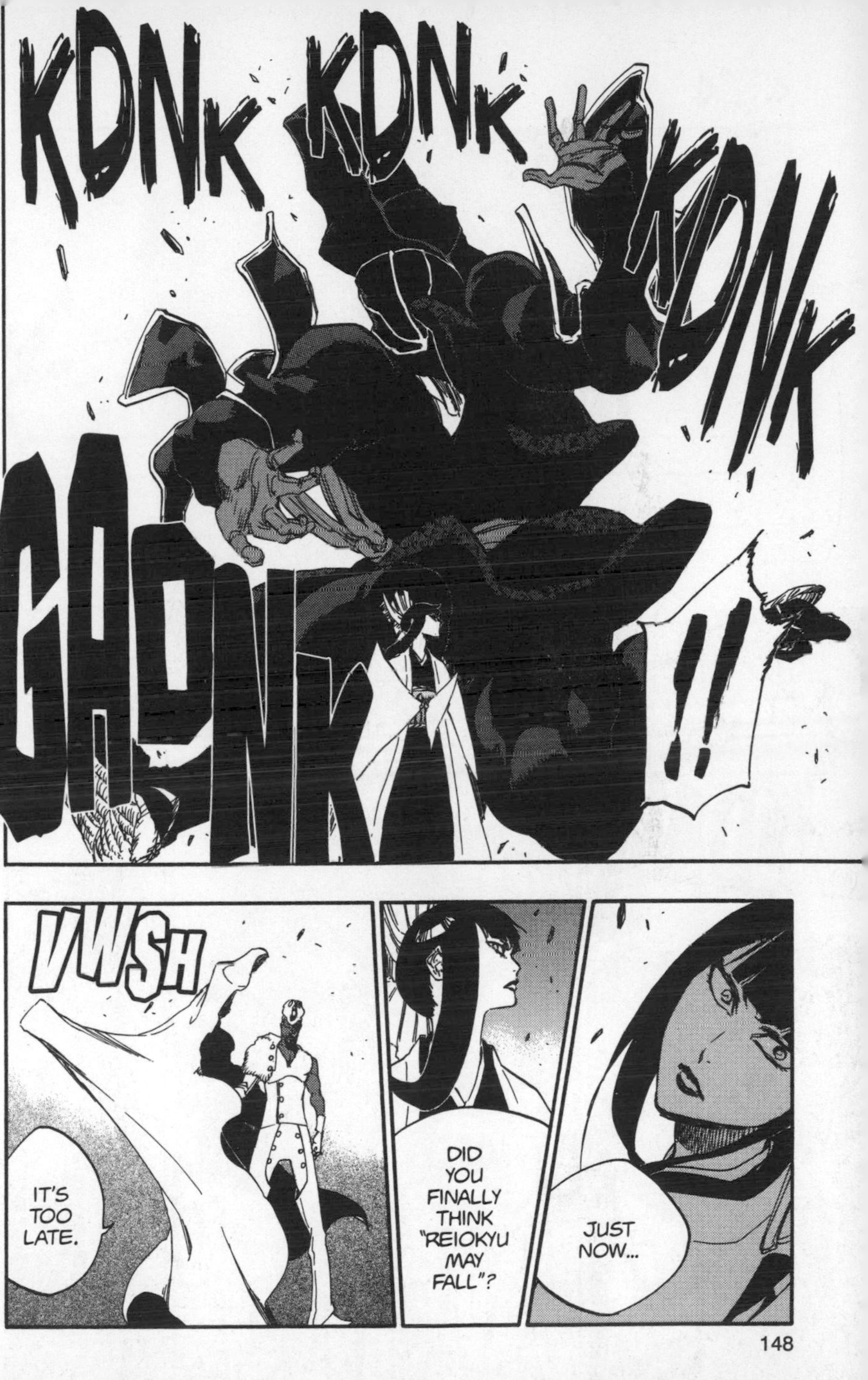
KDNK
KDNK
KDNK
GADNK!!
JUST NOW...
DID YOU FINALLY THINK "REIOKYU MAY FALL"?
VWSH
IT'S TOO LATE.

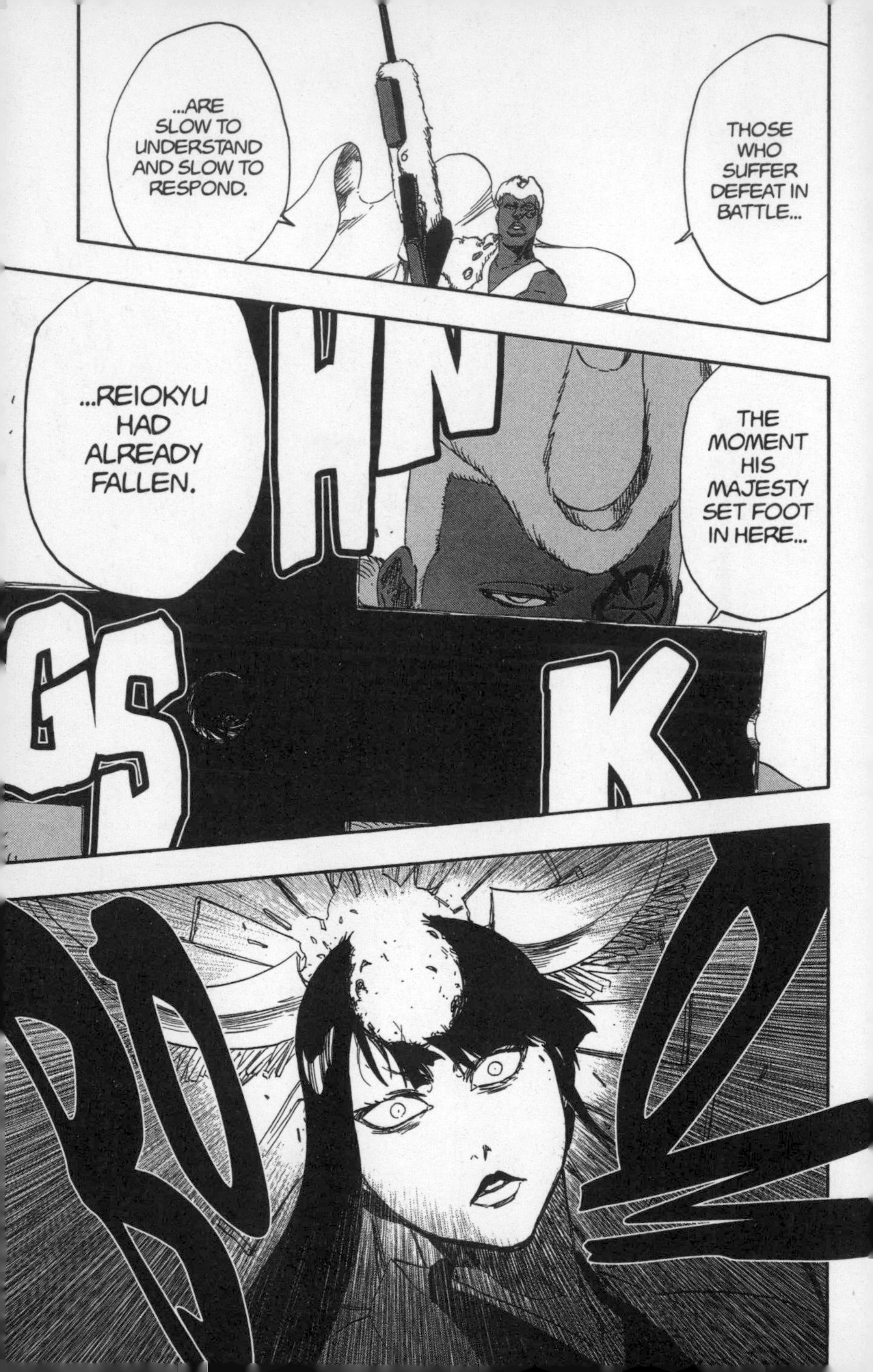
THOSE WHO SUFFER DEFEAT IN BATTLE...
...ARE SLOW TO UNDERSTAND AND SLOW TO RESPOND.
THE MOMENT HIS MAJESTY SET FOOT IN HERE...
...REIOKYU HAD ALREADY FALLEN.

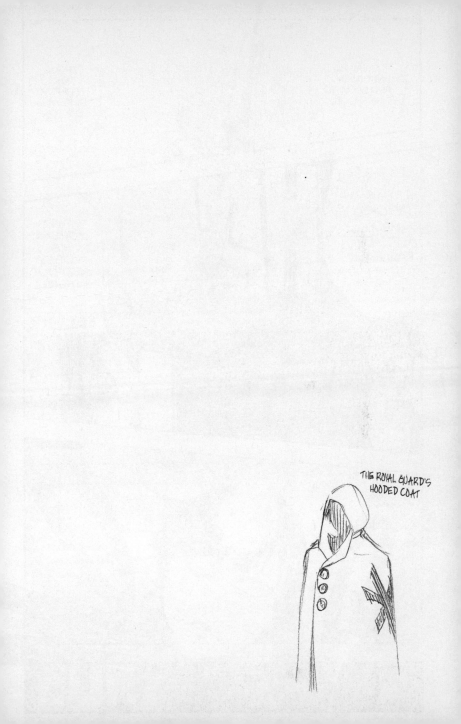

THE ROYAL GUARD'S
HOODED COAT

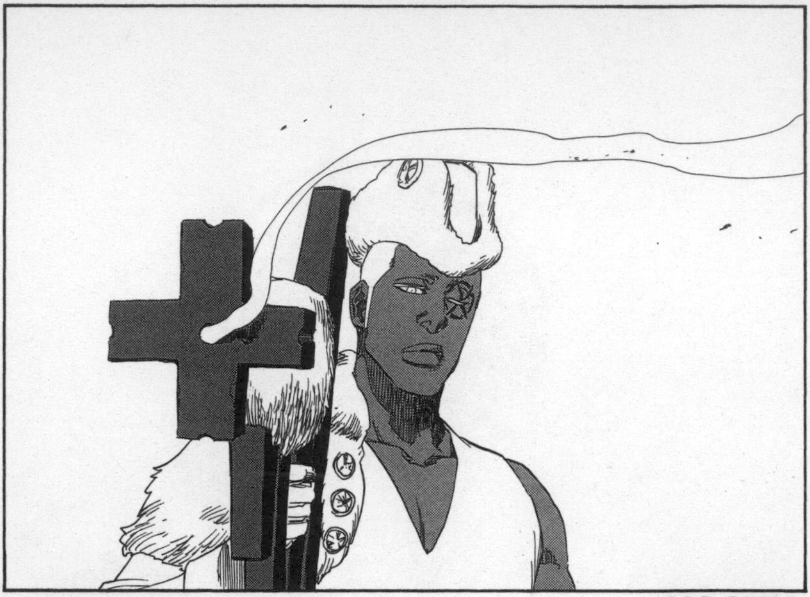

600. SNIPE

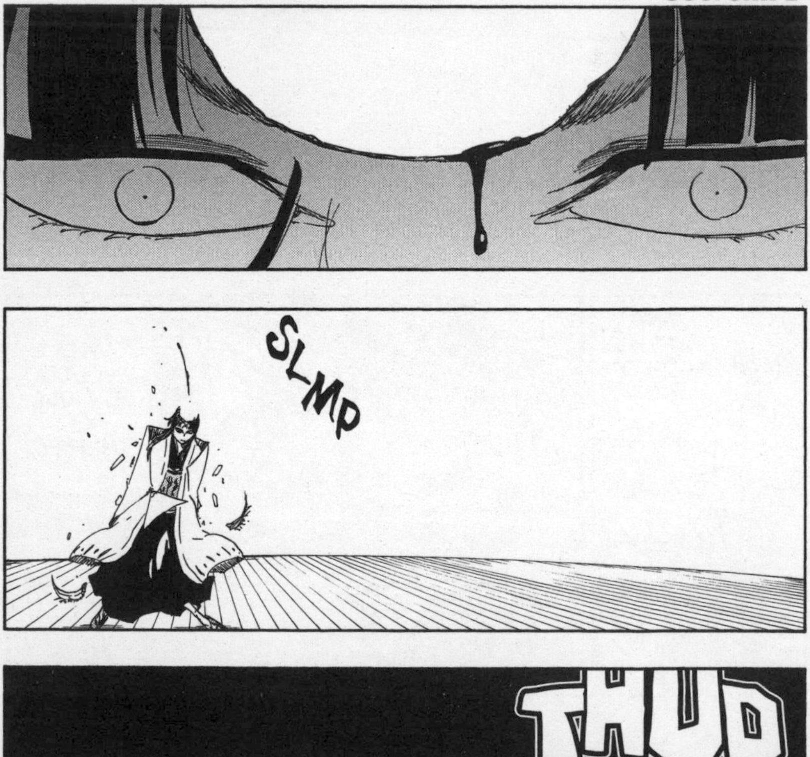
SLMP
THUD

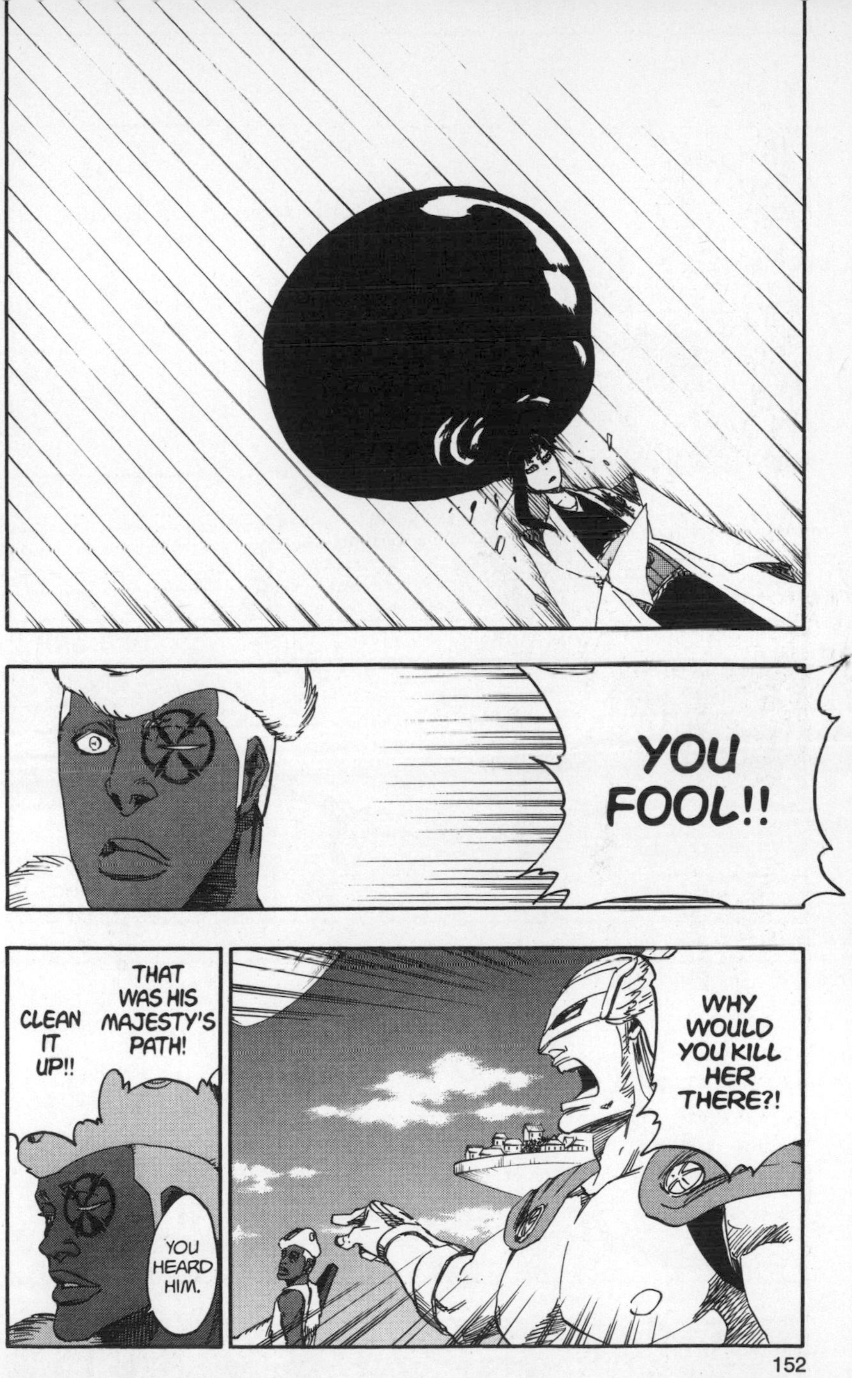
YOU FOOL!!
WHY WOULD YOU KILL HER THERE?!
THAT WAS HIS MAJESTY'S PATH!
CLEAN IT UP!!
YOU HEARD HIM.

READ THIS WAY

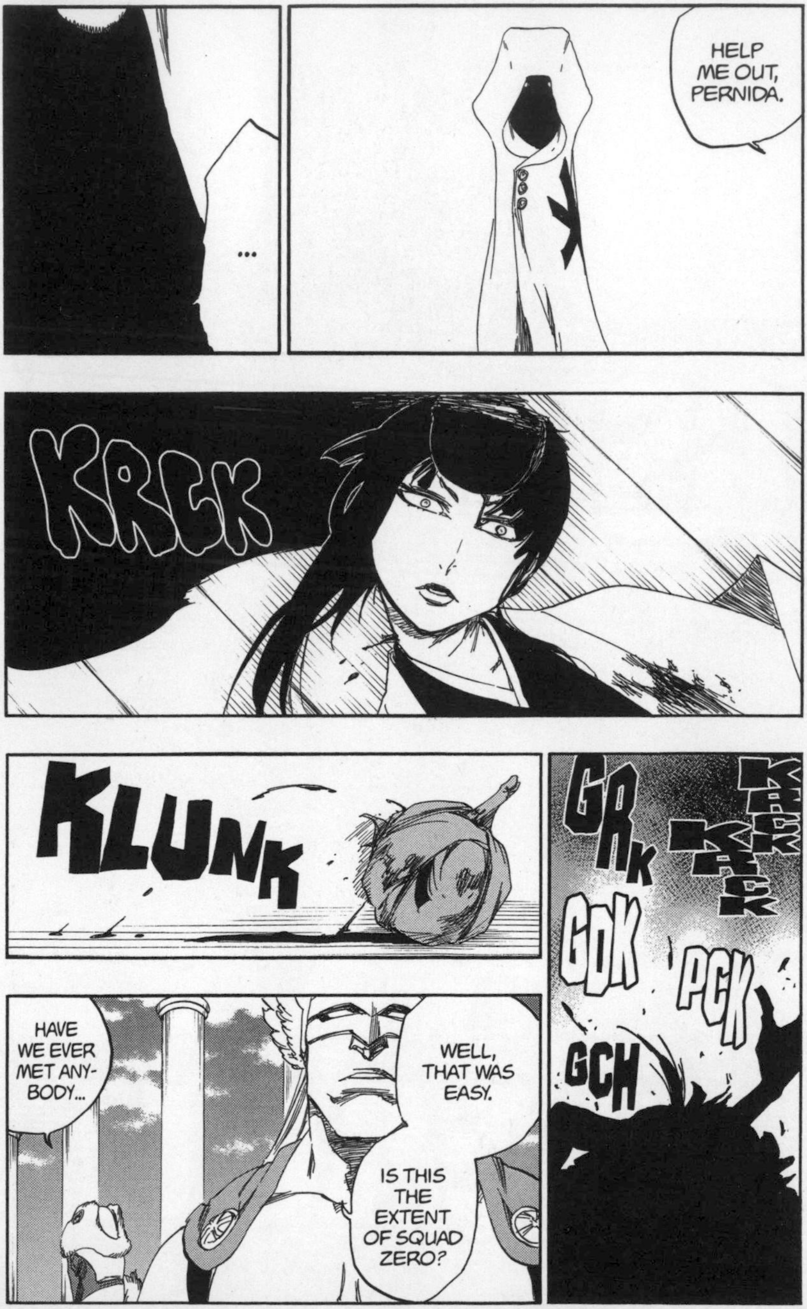
HELP ME OUT, PERNIDA.
...
KRCK
KRCK
KRCK
GRK
GDK
PCK
GCH
KLUNK
WELL, THAT WAS EASY.
IS THIS THE EXTENT OF SQUAD ZERO?
HAVE WE EVER MET ANYBODY...

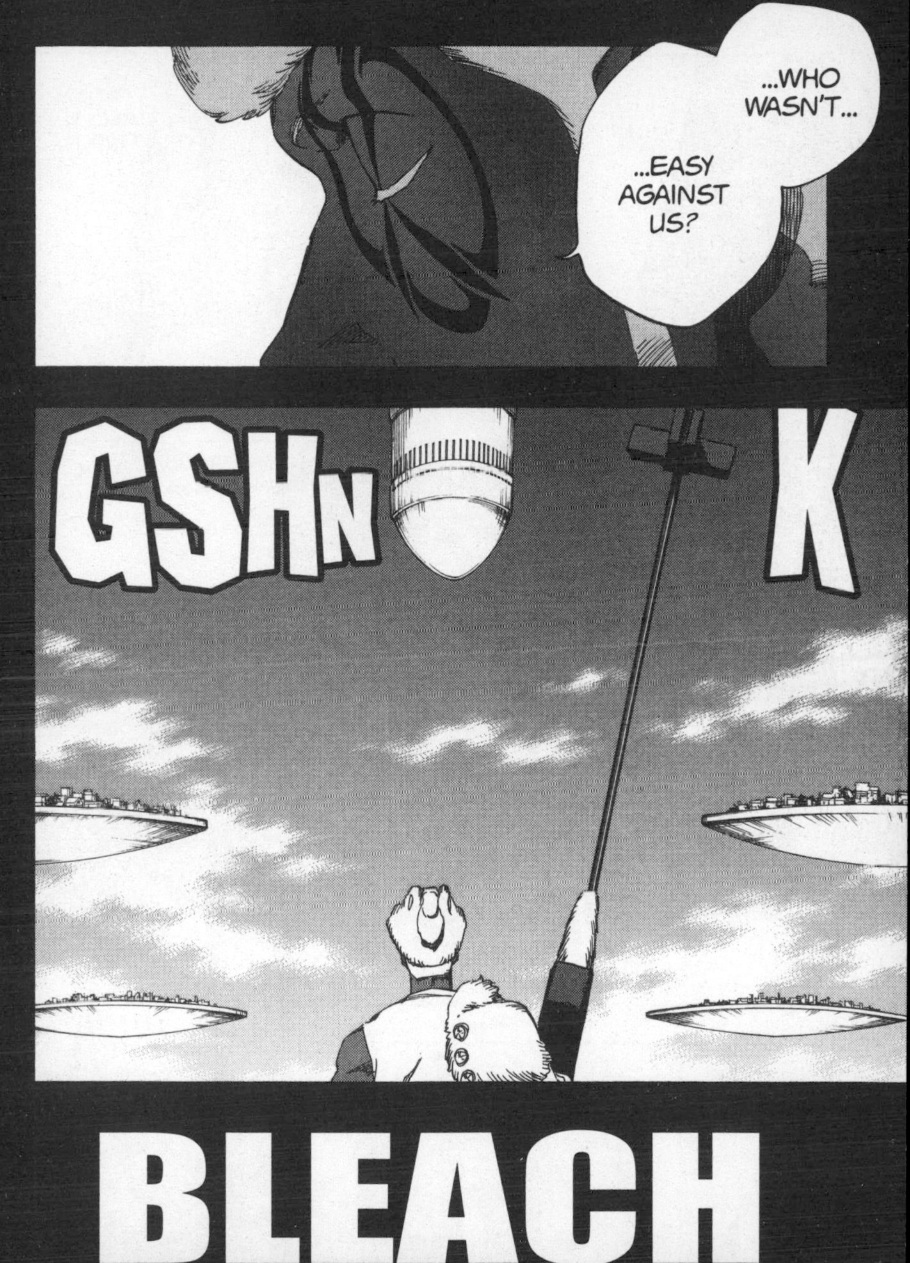
...WHO WASN'T...
...EASY AGAINST US?
GSHNK

BLEACH

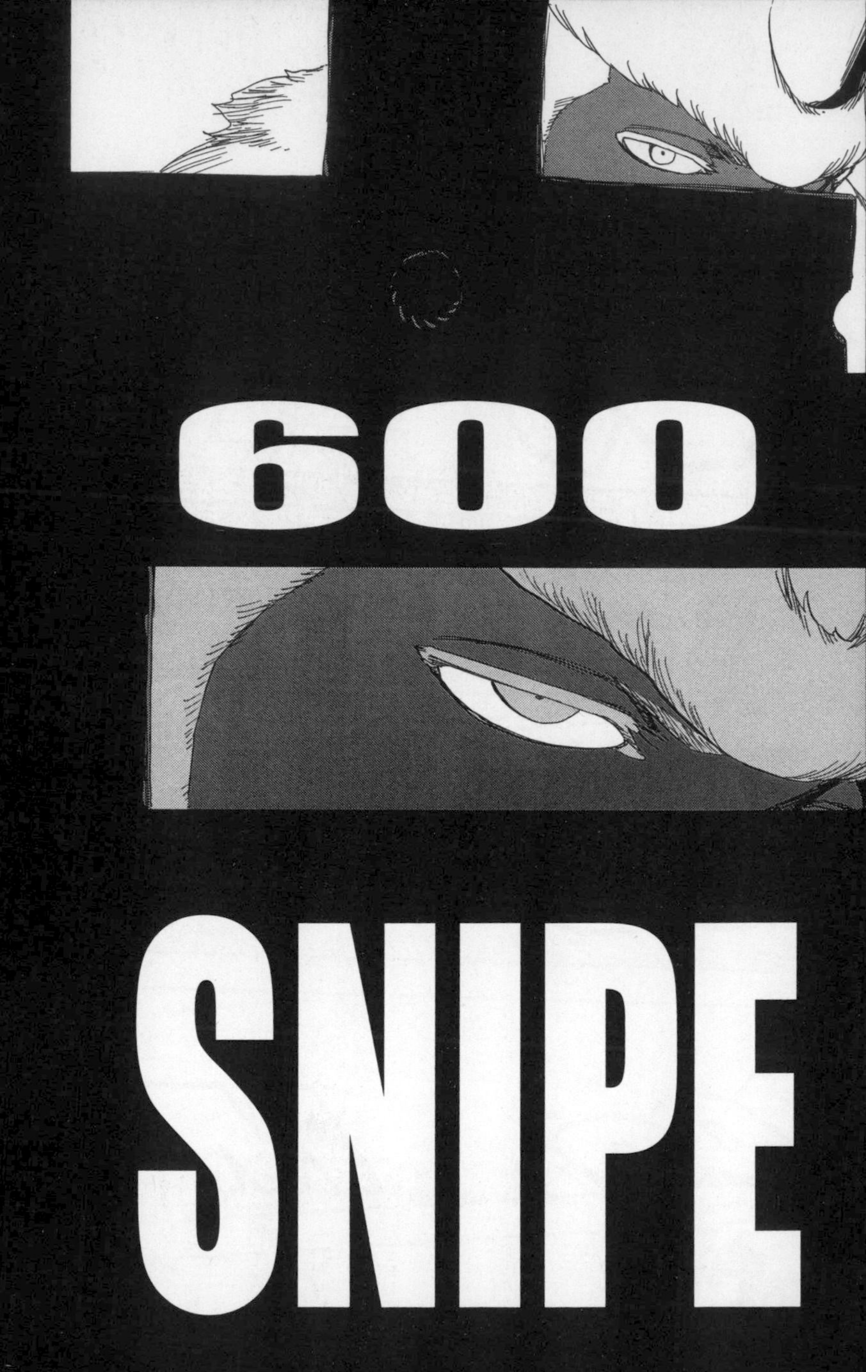
600
SNIPE

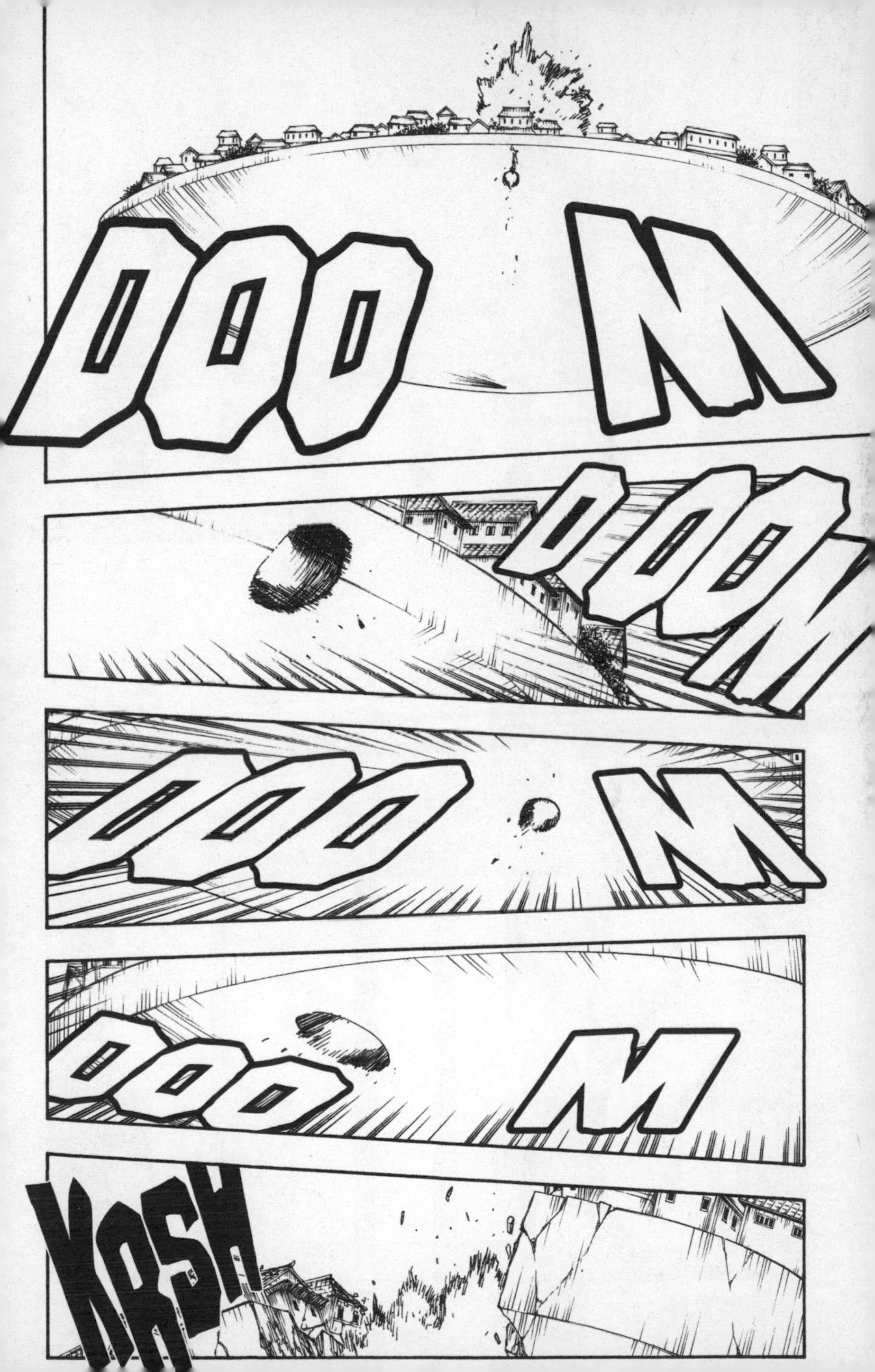
DOOOM
DOOM
DOOOM
DOOOM
KASH

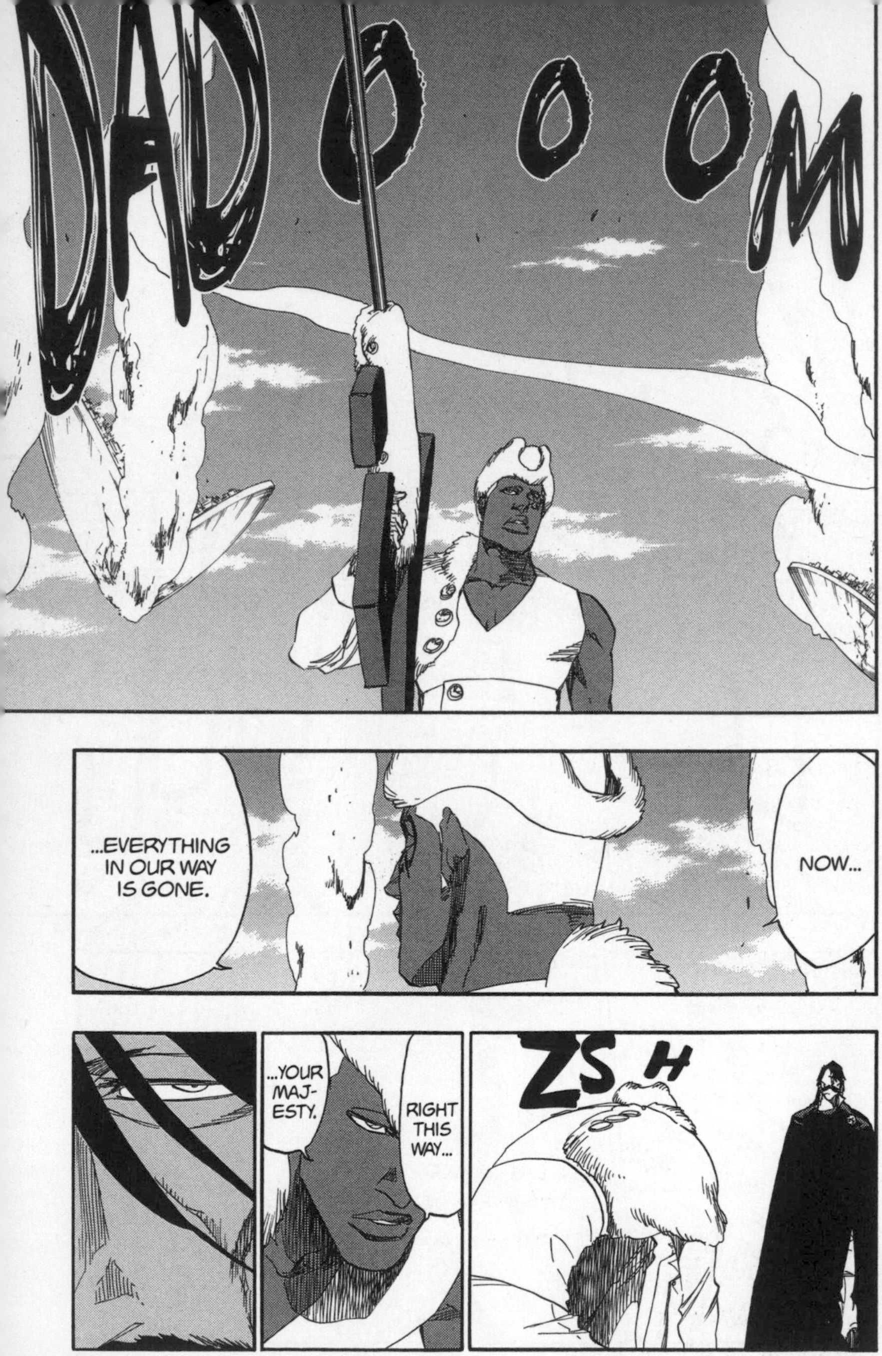
DADOOOM
NOW...
...EVERYTHING IN OUR WAY IS GONE.
ZSH
RIGHT THIS WAY...
...YOUR MAJ-ESTY.

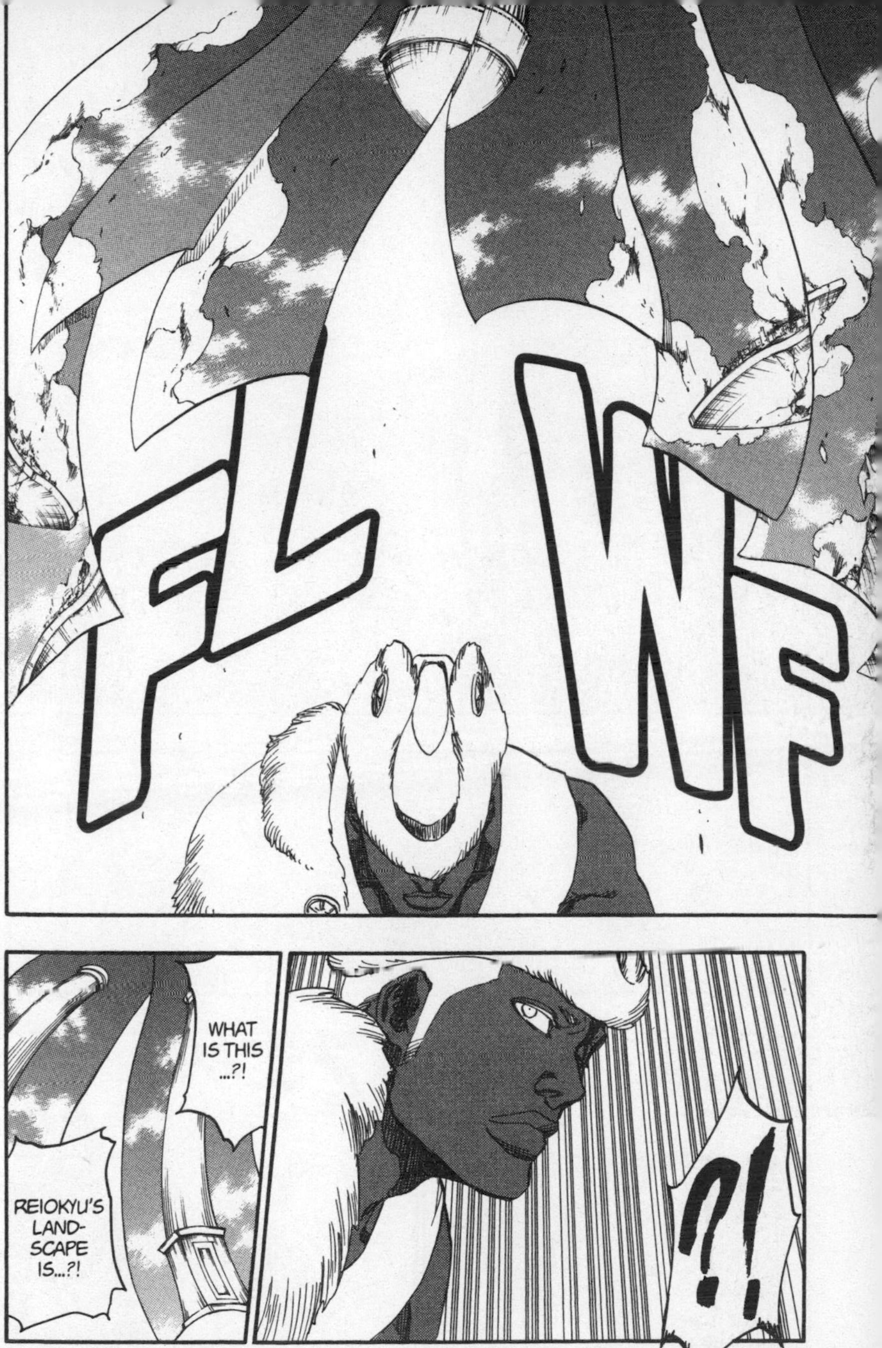
FLWF
?!
WHAT IS THIS ...?!
REIOKYU'S LAND-SCAPE IS...?!

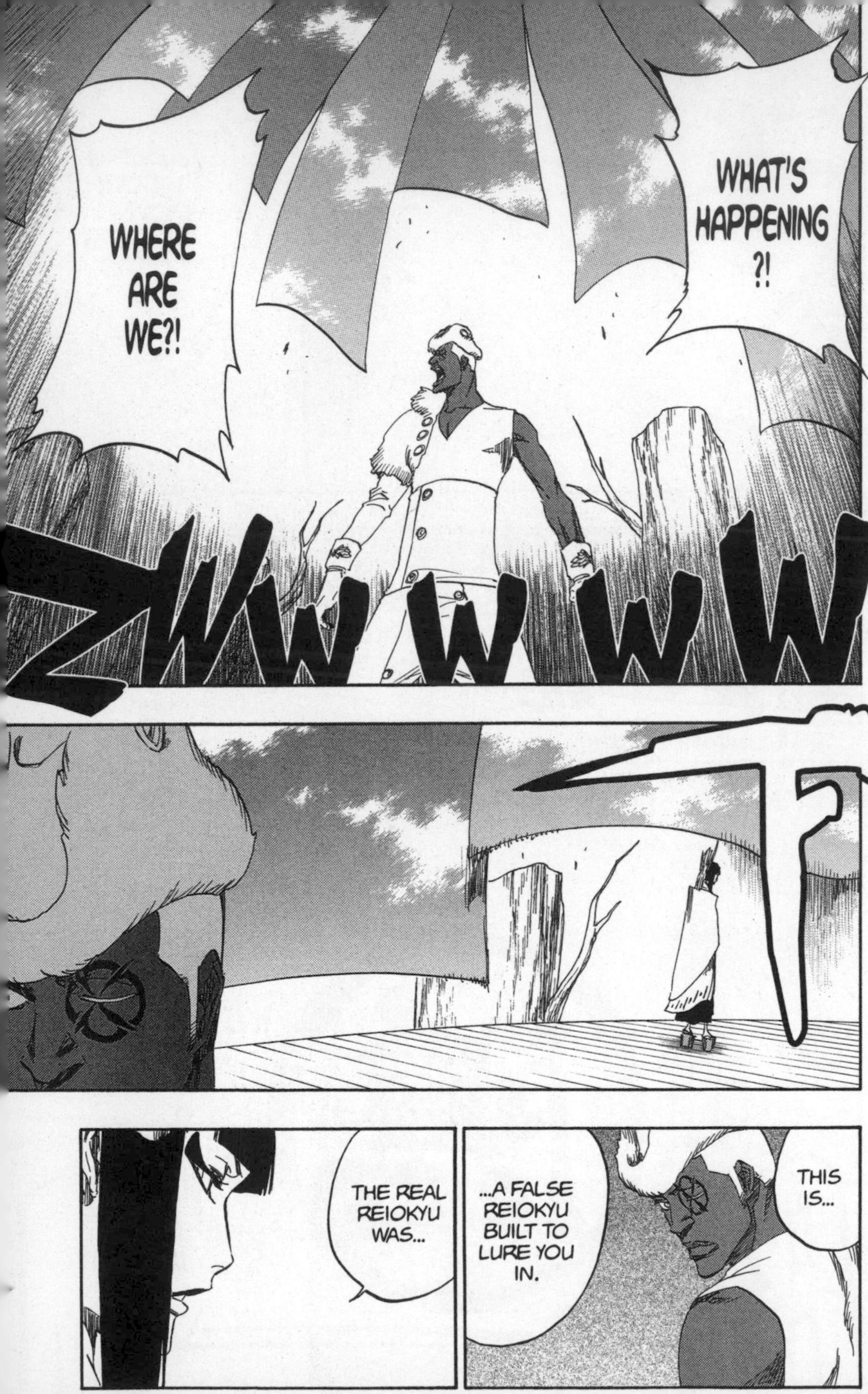
WHAT'S HAPPENING ?!
WHERE ARE WE?!
ZWWWWW
THIS IS...
...A FALSE REIOKYU BUILT TO LURE YOU IN.
THE REAL REIOKYU WAS...

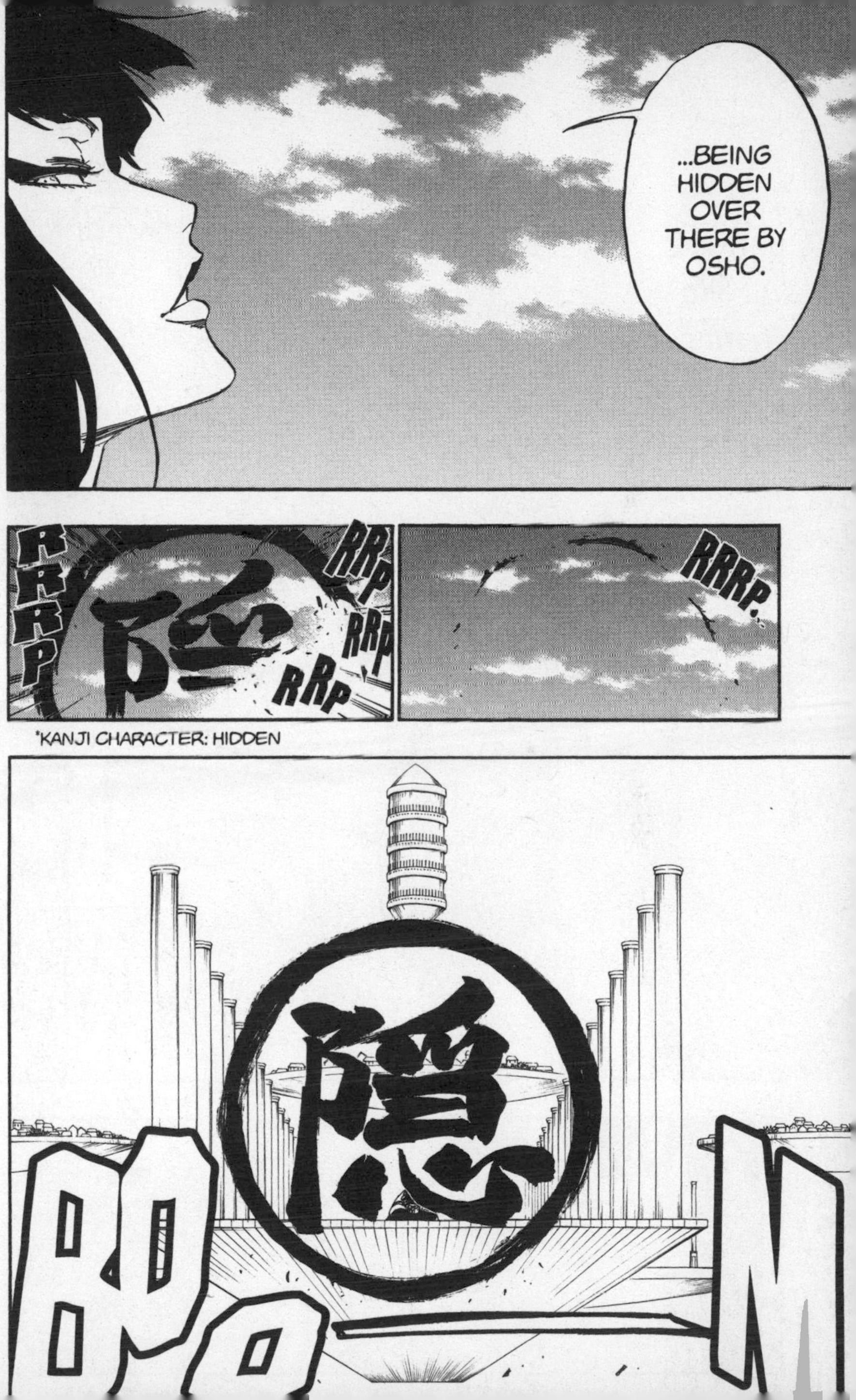
...BEING HIDDEN OVER THERE BY OSHO.
RRRP.
RRP
RRP
RRP
RRRP
隠
隠
BOOM
*KANJI CHARACTER: HIDDEN

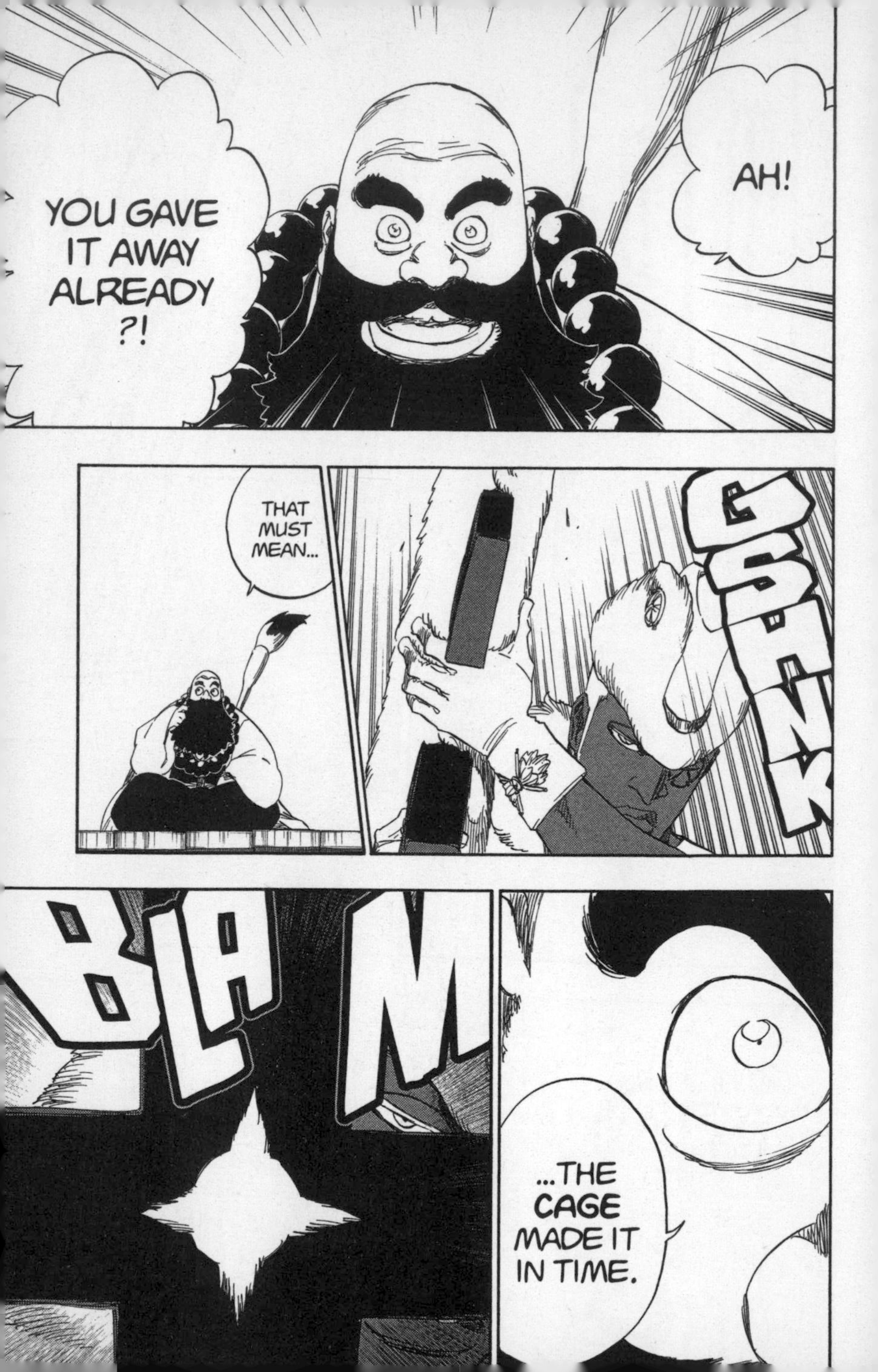
AH!
YOU GAVE IT AWAY ALREADY?!
GSHNK
THAT MUST MEAN...
...THE CAGE MADE IT IN TIME.
BLAM

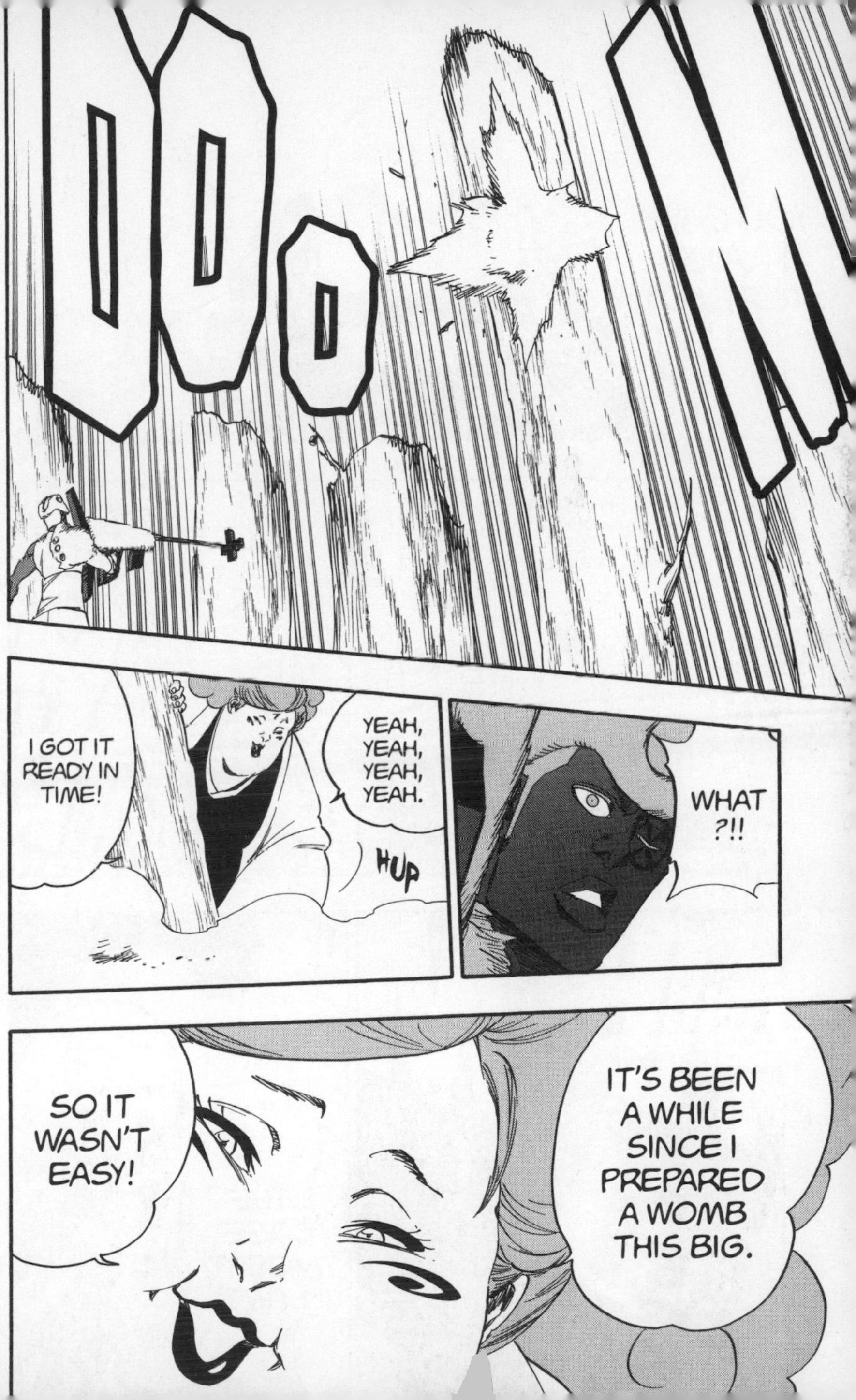
WHAT ?!!
YEAH, YEAH, YEAH, YEAH.
I GOT IT READY IN TIME!
HUP
IT'S BEEN A WHILE SINCE I PREPARED A WOMB THIS BIG.
SO IT WASN'T EASY!

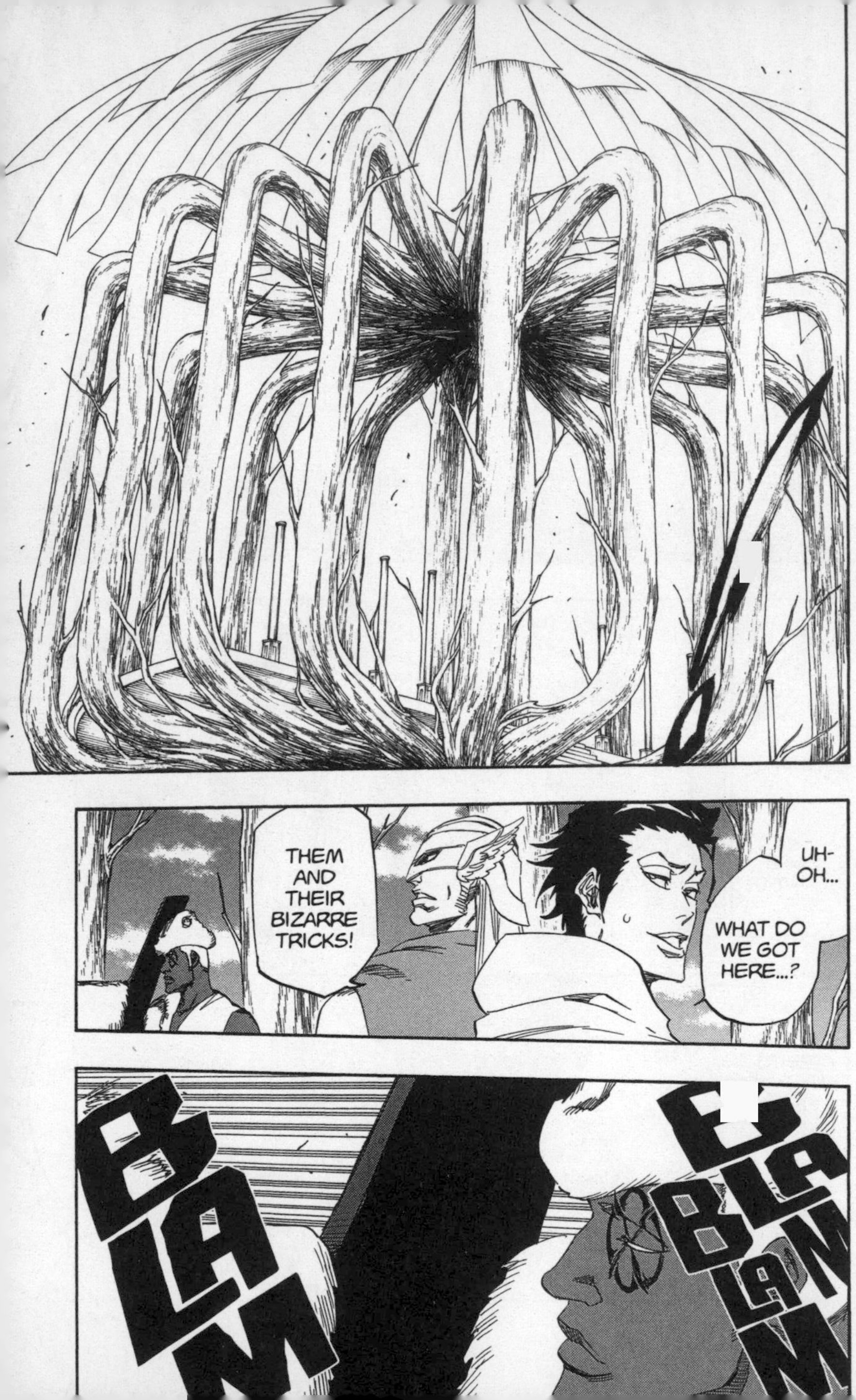
UH-OH...
WHAT DO WE GOT HERE...?
THEM AND THEIR BIZARRE TRICKS!
BLA BLAM
BLAM

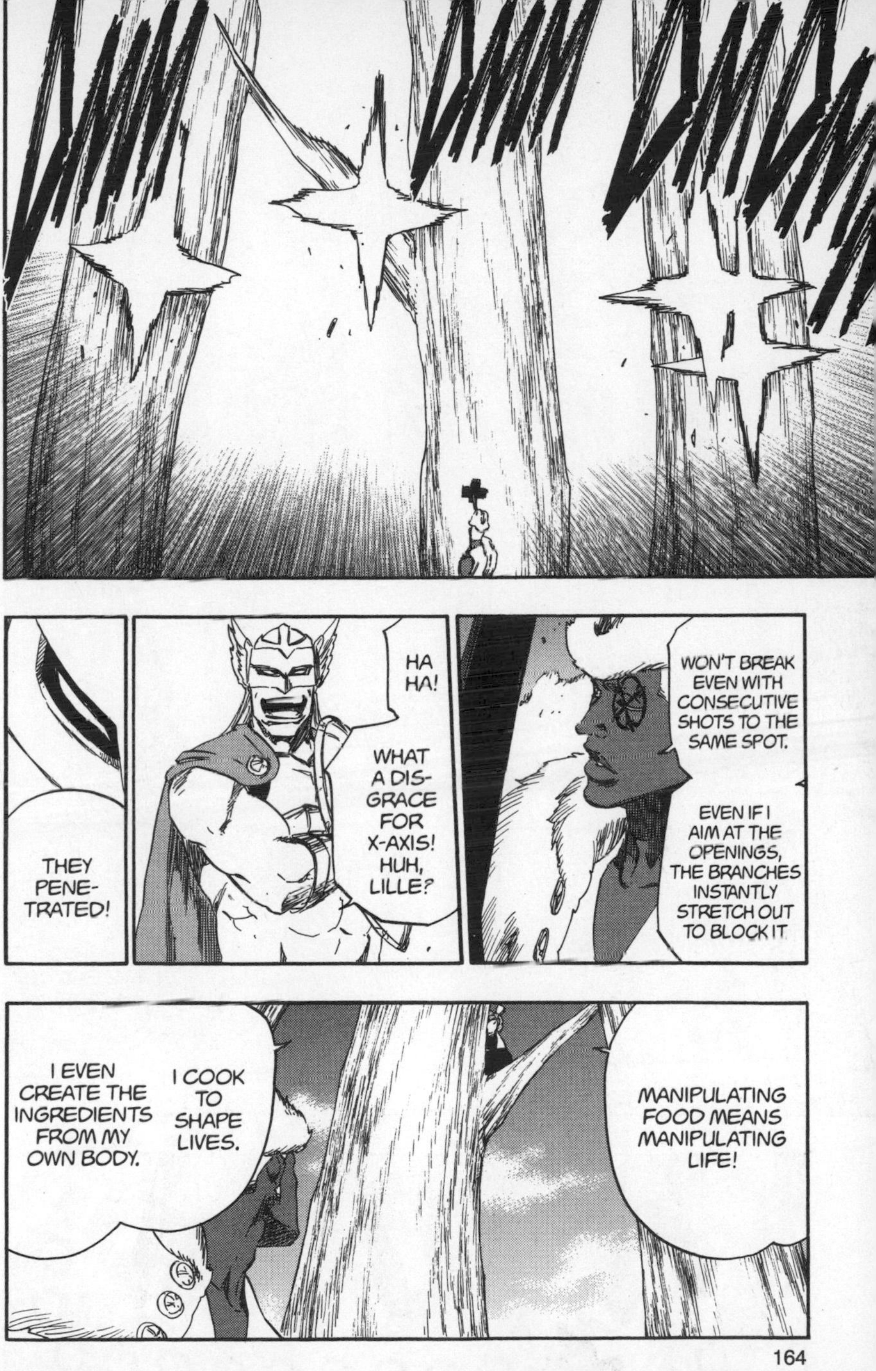
WON'T BREAK EVEN WITH CONSECUTIVE SHOTS TO THE SAME SPOT.
EVEN IF I AIM AT THE OPENINGS, THE BRANCHES INSTANTLY STRETCH OUT TO BLOCK IT.
HA HA!
WHAT A DIS-GRACE FOR X-AXIS! HUH, LILLE?
THEY PENE-TRATED!
MANIPULATING FOOD MEANS MANIPULATING LIFE!
I COOK TO SHAPE LIVES.
I EVEN CREATE THE INGREDIENTS FROM MY OWN BODY.

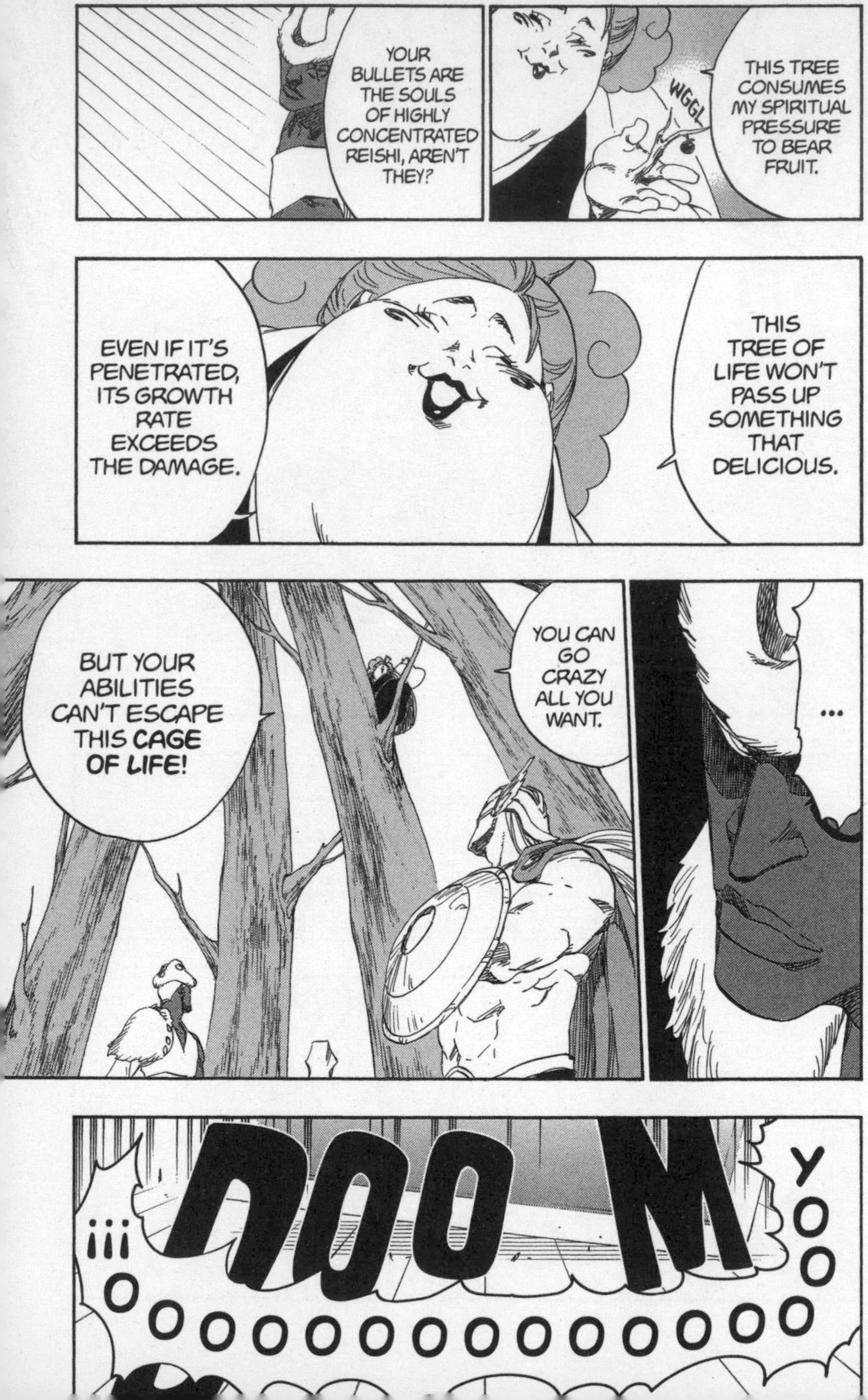
WGGL
THIS TREE CONSUMES MY SPIRITUAL PRESSURE TO BEAR FRUIT.
YOUR BULLETS ARE THE SOULS OF HIGHLY CONCENTRATED REISHI, AREN'T THEY?
THIS TREE OF LIFE WON'T PASS UP SOMETHING THAT DELICIOUS.
EVEN IF IT'S PENETRATED, ITS GROWTH RATE EXCEEDS THE DAMAGE.
...
YOU CAN GO CRAZY ALL YOU WANT.
BUT YOUR ABILITIES CAN'T ESCAPE THIS **CAGE OF LIFE!**
DOOM
YOOOOOOOOOOOOOOOOOOO!!!

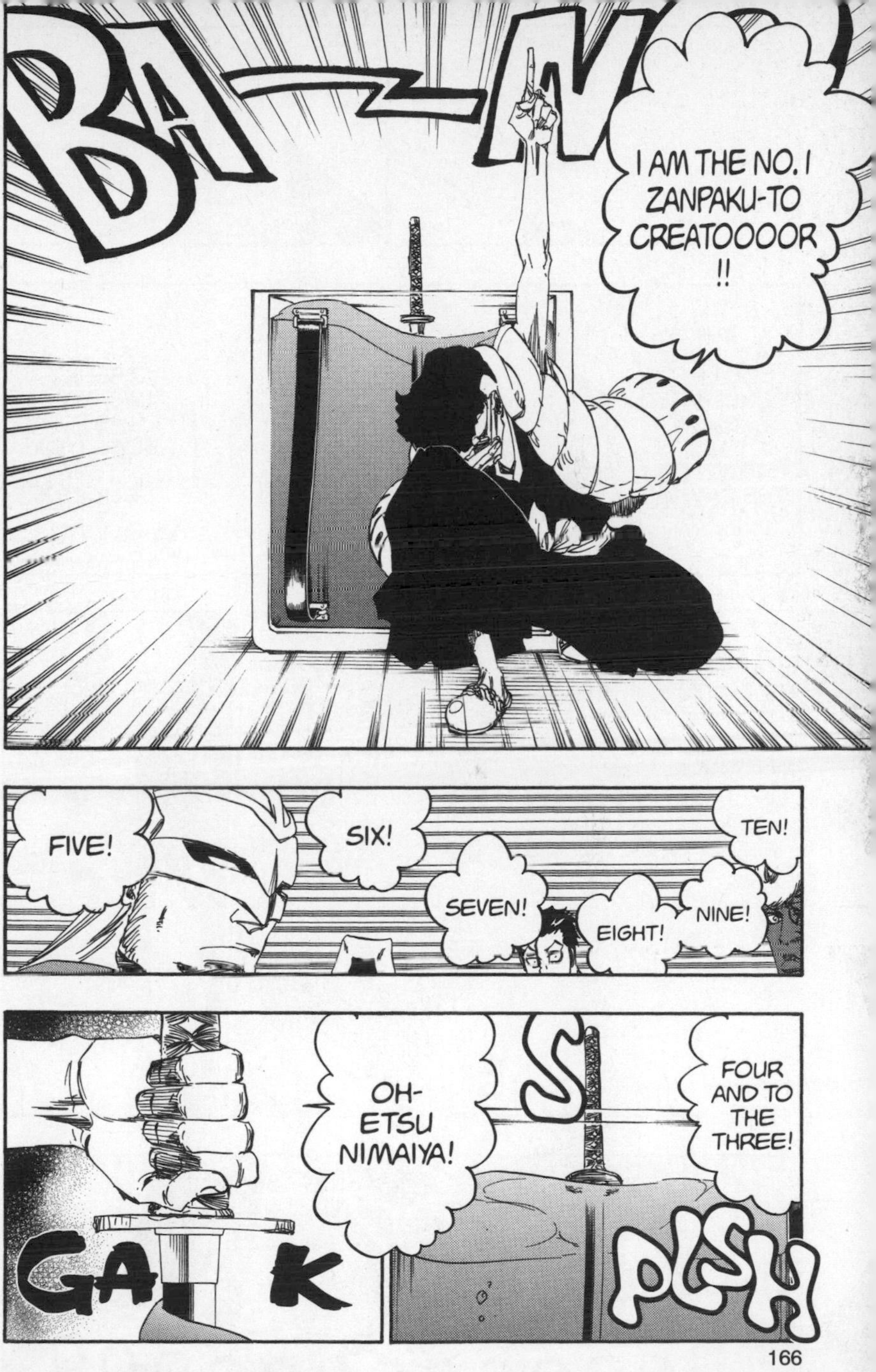
I AM THE NO. 1 ZANPAKU-TO CREATOOOOR!!
BA—M
TEN!
NINE!
EIGHT!
SEVEN!
SIX!
FIVE!
S
FOUR AND TO THE THREE!
PLSH
OH-ETSU NIMAIYA!
GA K

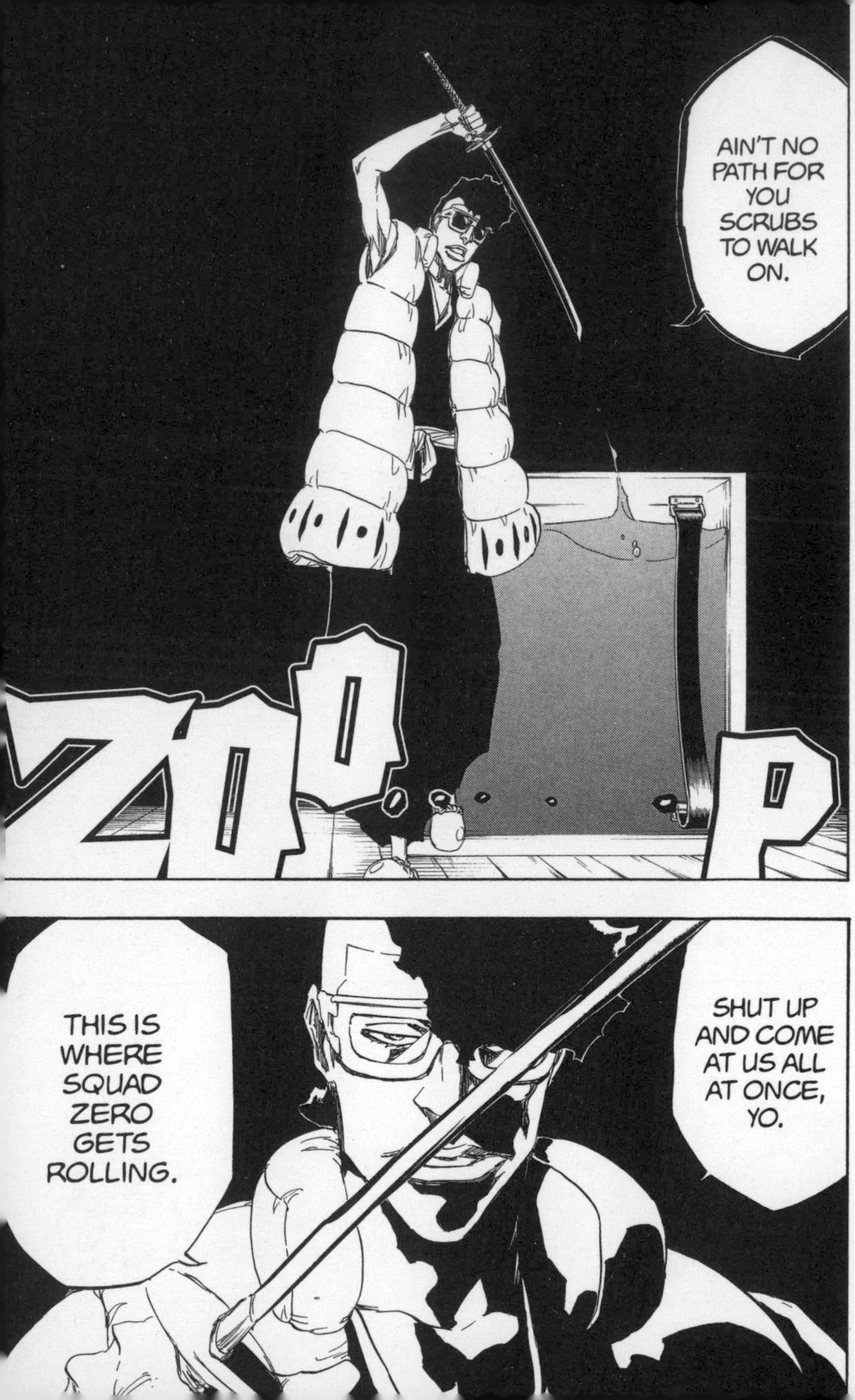
AIN'T NO PATH FOR YOU SCRUBS TO WALK ON.
ZOOP
SHUT UP AND COME AT US ALL AT ONCE, YO.
THIS IS WHERE SQUAD ZERO GETS ROLLING.

LILLE BARRO'S BEAD
EMBROIDERY IS AN
X AND WINGS

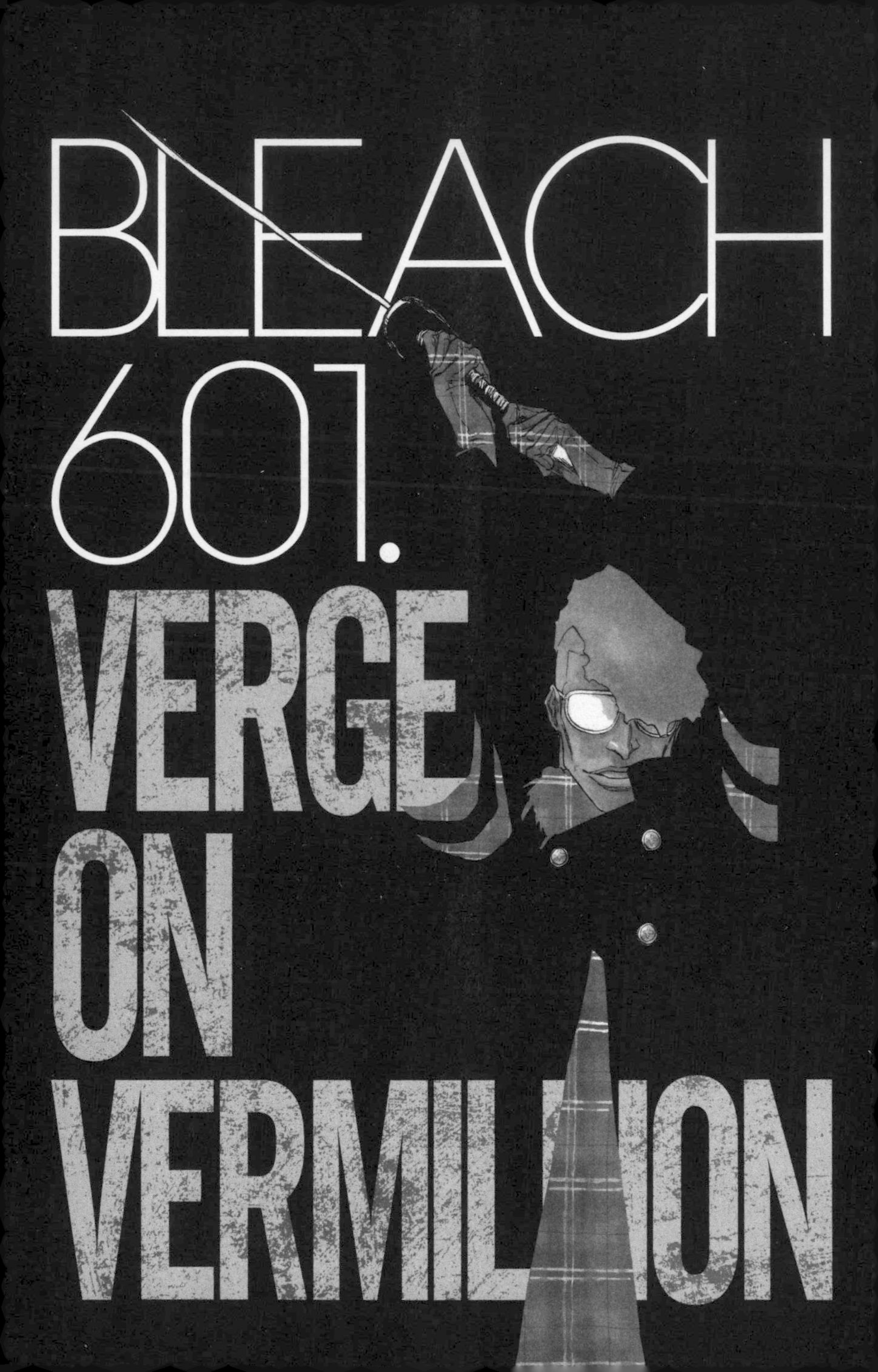
BLEACH
601.
VERGE
ON
VERMILION

BLEACH

ブリーチ

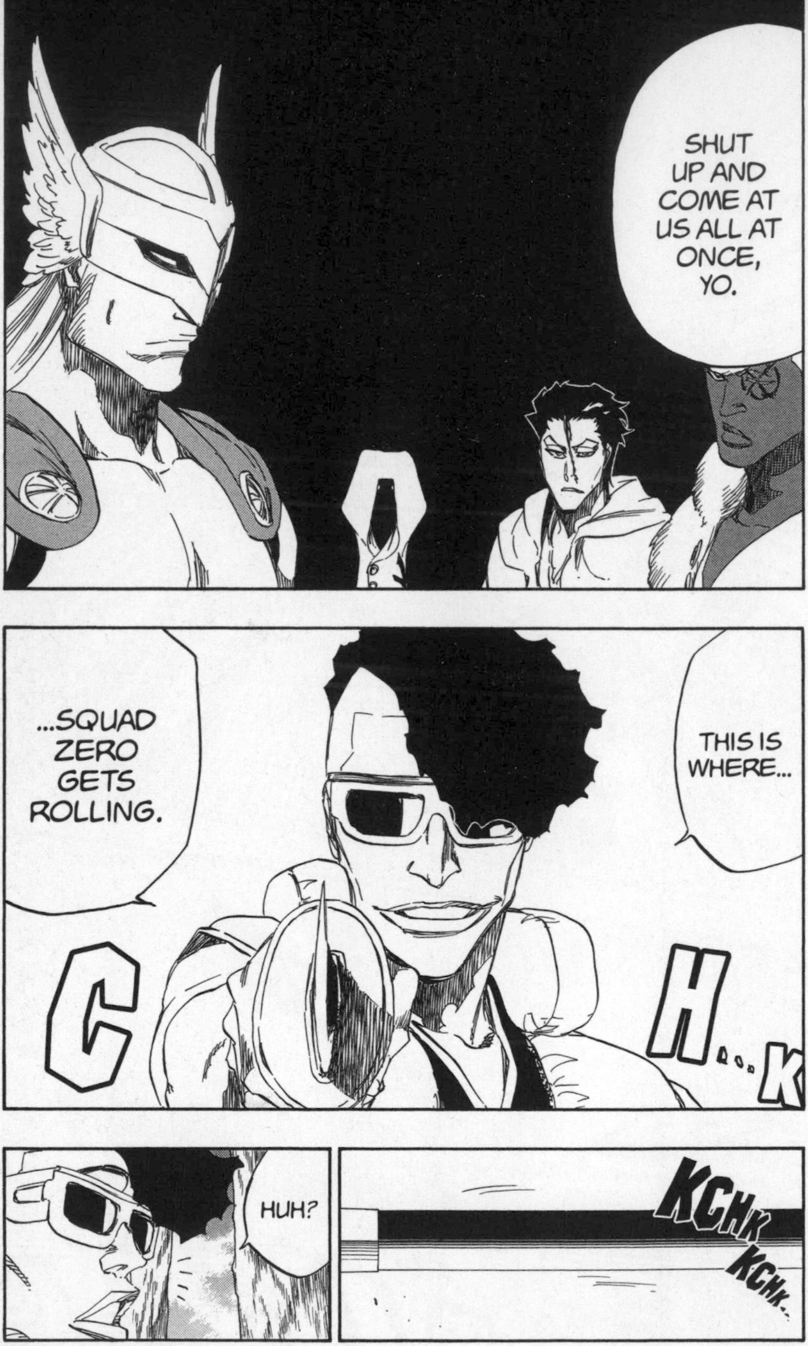
SHUT UP AND COME AT US ALL AT ONCE, YO.
THIS IS WHERE...
...SQUAD ZERO GETS ROLLING.
C
H...K
KCHK
KCHK...
HUH?

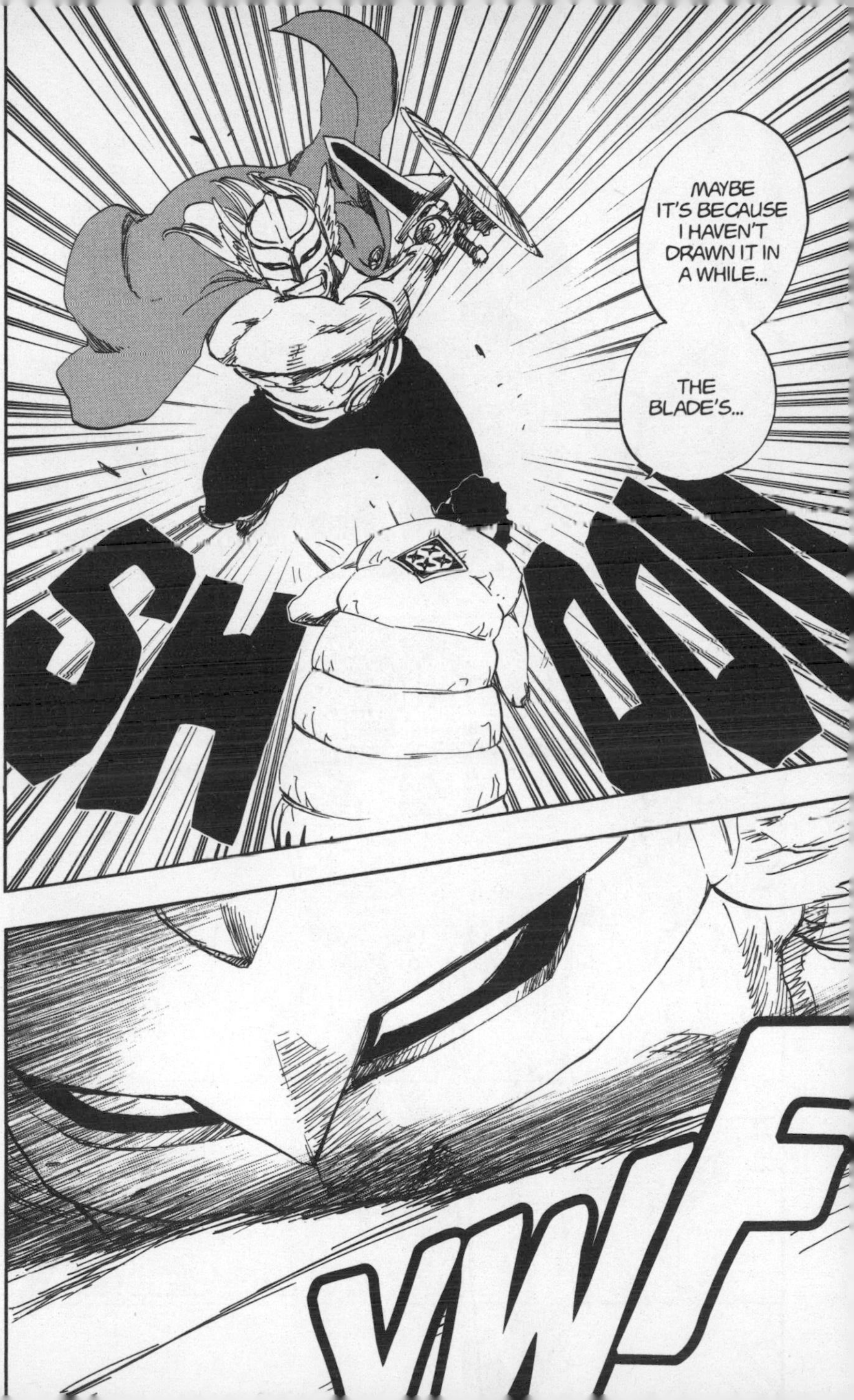
MAYBE IT'S BECAUSE I HAVEN'T DRAWN IT IN A WHILE...
THE BLADE'S...

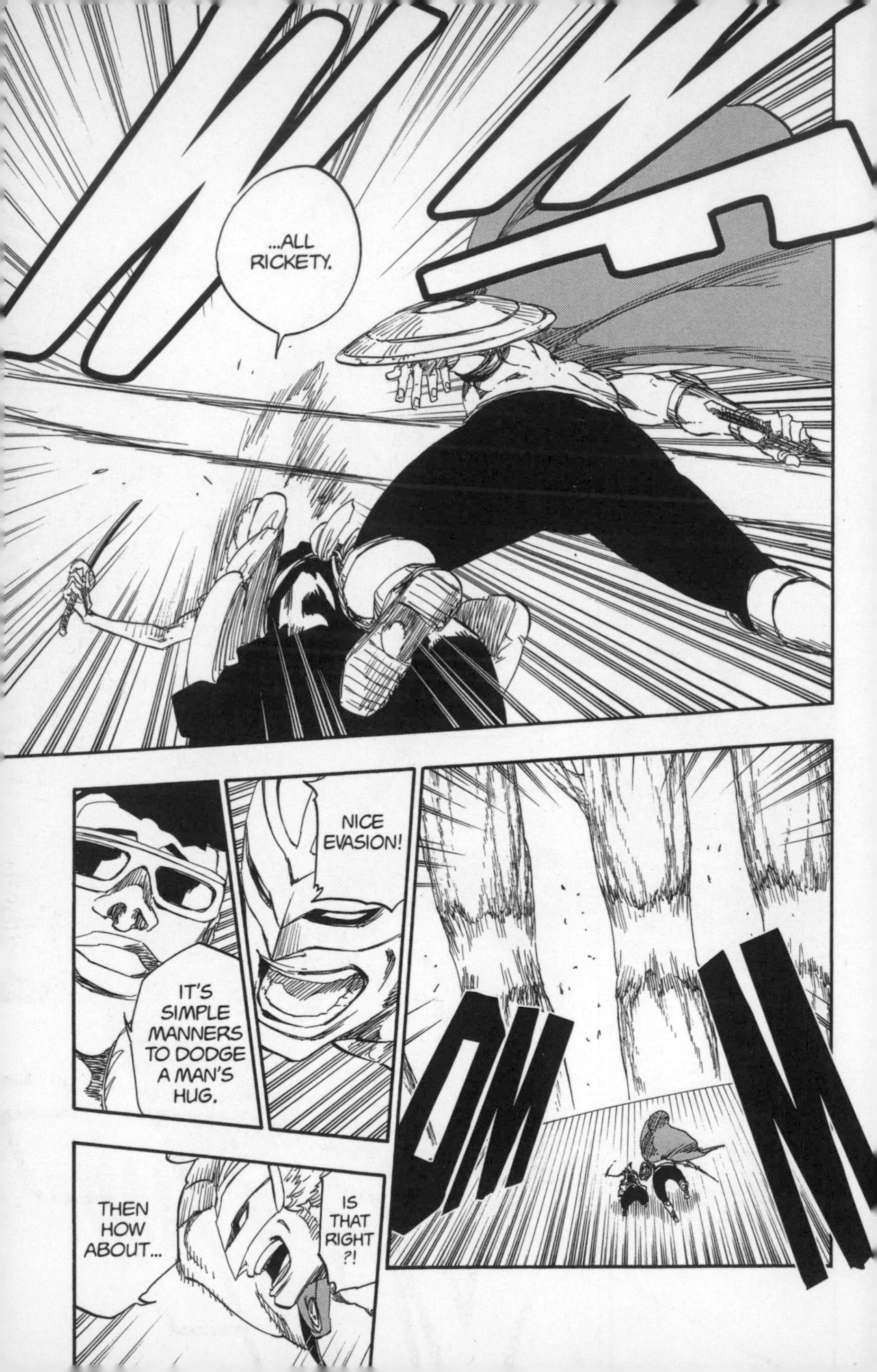
...ALL RICKETY.
NICE EVASION!
IT'S SIMPLE MANNERS TO DODGE A MAN'S HUG.
IS THAT RIGHT?!
THEN HOW ABOUT...

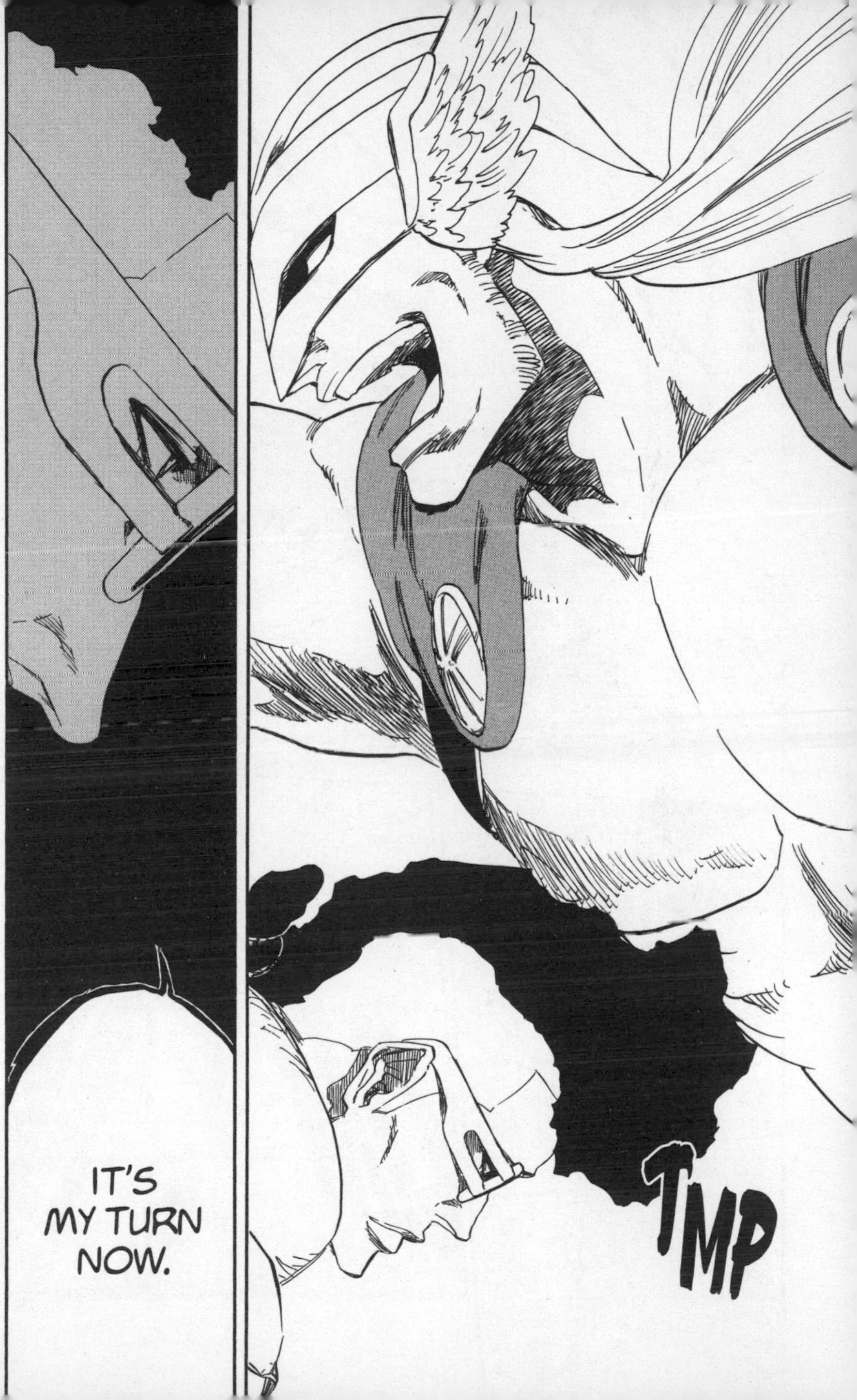
TMP
IT'S MY TURN NOW.

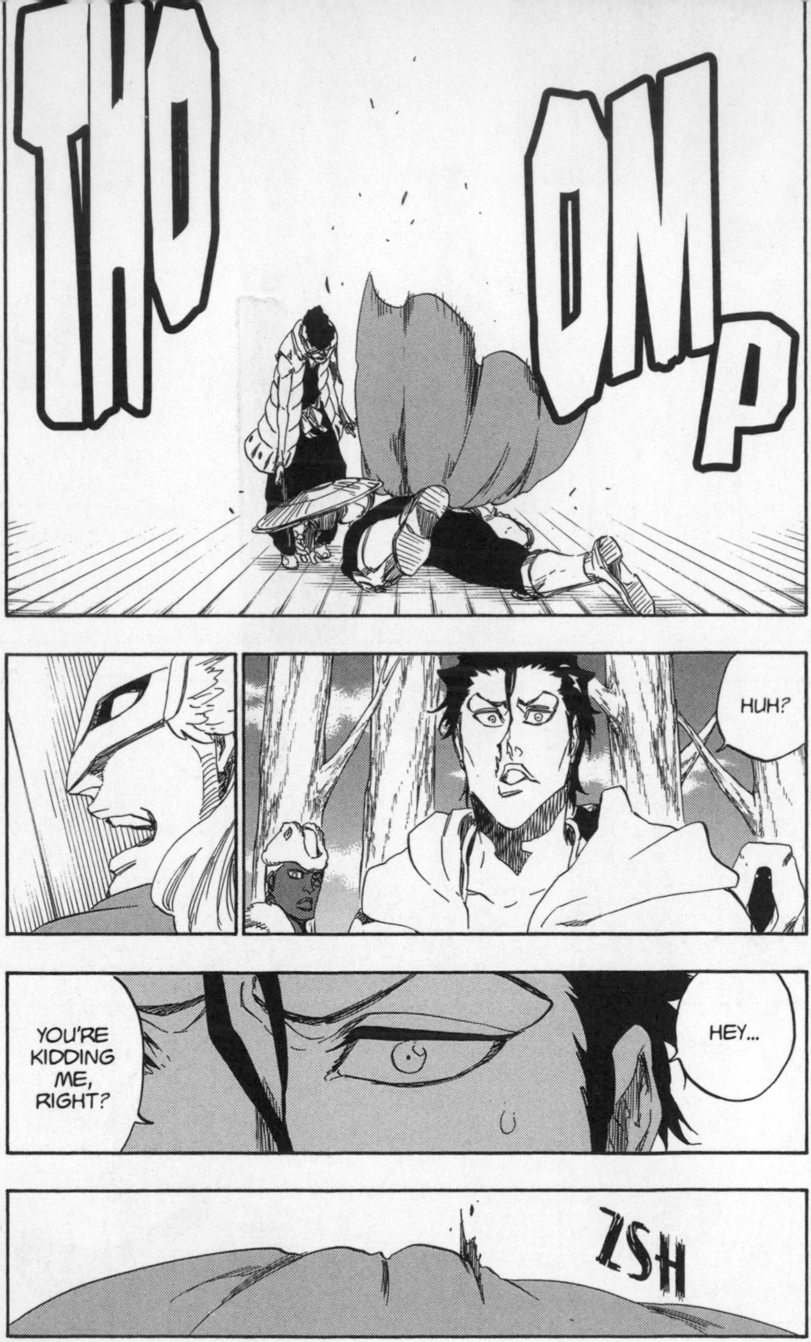
THOOMP
HUH?
HEY...
YOU'RE KIDDING ME, RIGHT?
ZSH

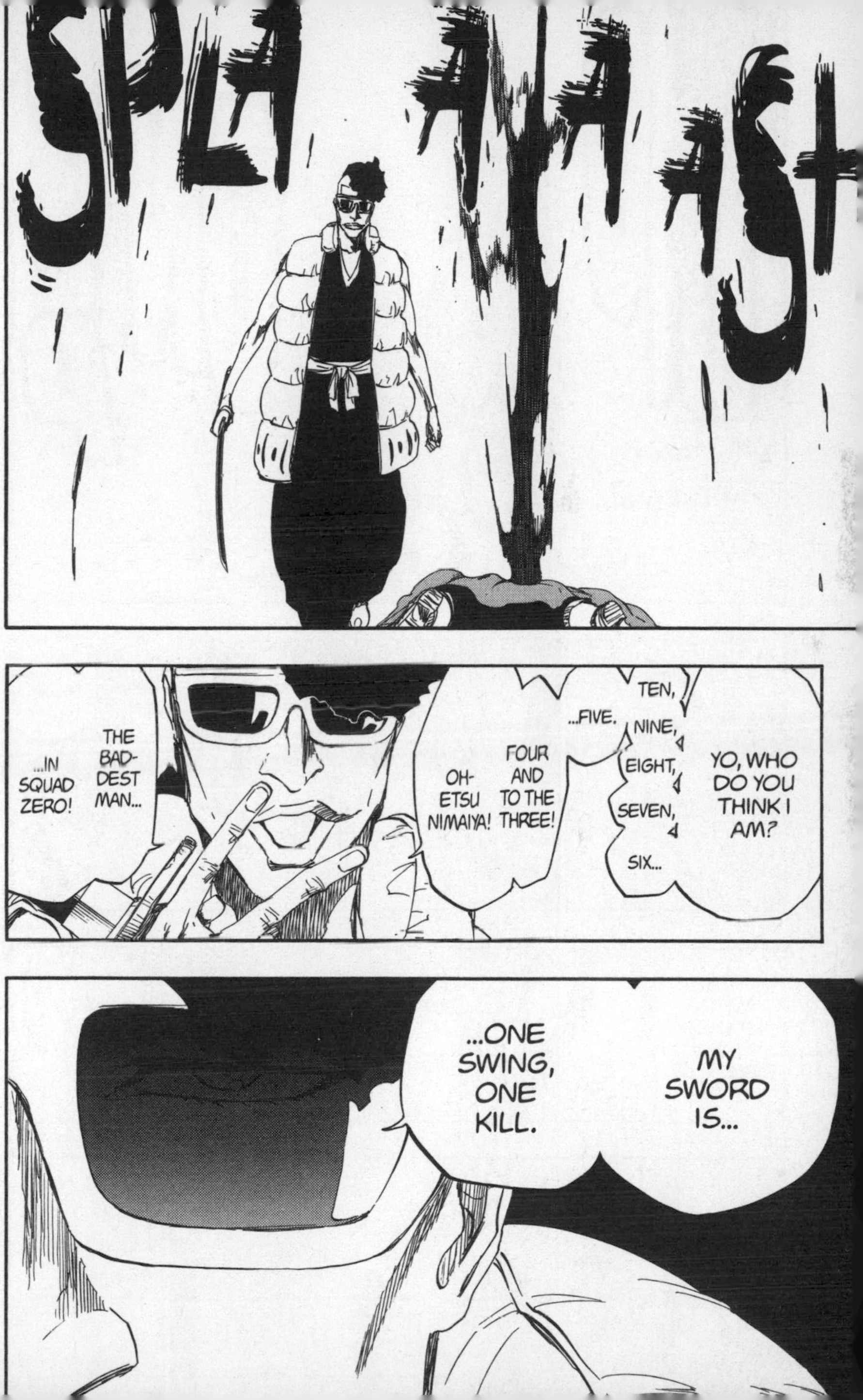
SPLAAAASH
YO, WHO DO YOU THINK I AM?
TEN, NINE, EIGHT, SEVEN, SIX...
...FIVE.
FOUR AND TO THE THREE!
OH-ETSU NIMAIYA!
THE BAD-DEST MAN...
...IN SQUAD ZERO!
MY SWORD IS...
...ONE SWING, ONE KILL.

READ THIS WAY

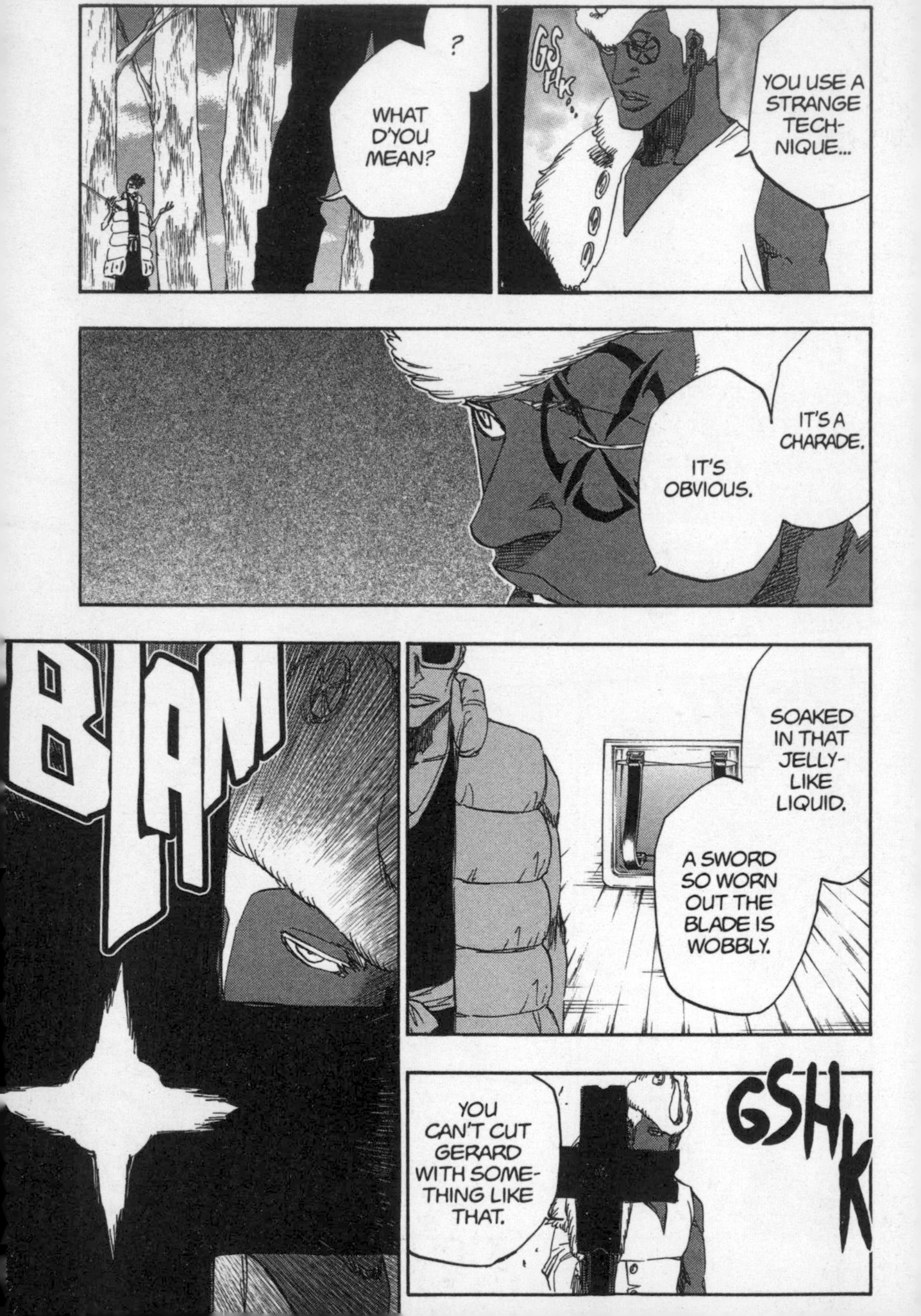
GSHK...
YOU USE A STRANGE TECH-NIQUE...
?
WHAT D'YOU MEAN?
IT'S A CHARADE.
IT'S OBVIOUS.
SOAKED IN THAT JELLY-LIKE LIQUID.
A SWORD SO WORN OUT THE BLADE IS WOBBLY.
GSHK
YOU CAN'T CUT GERARD WITH SOME-THING LIKE THAT.
BLAM

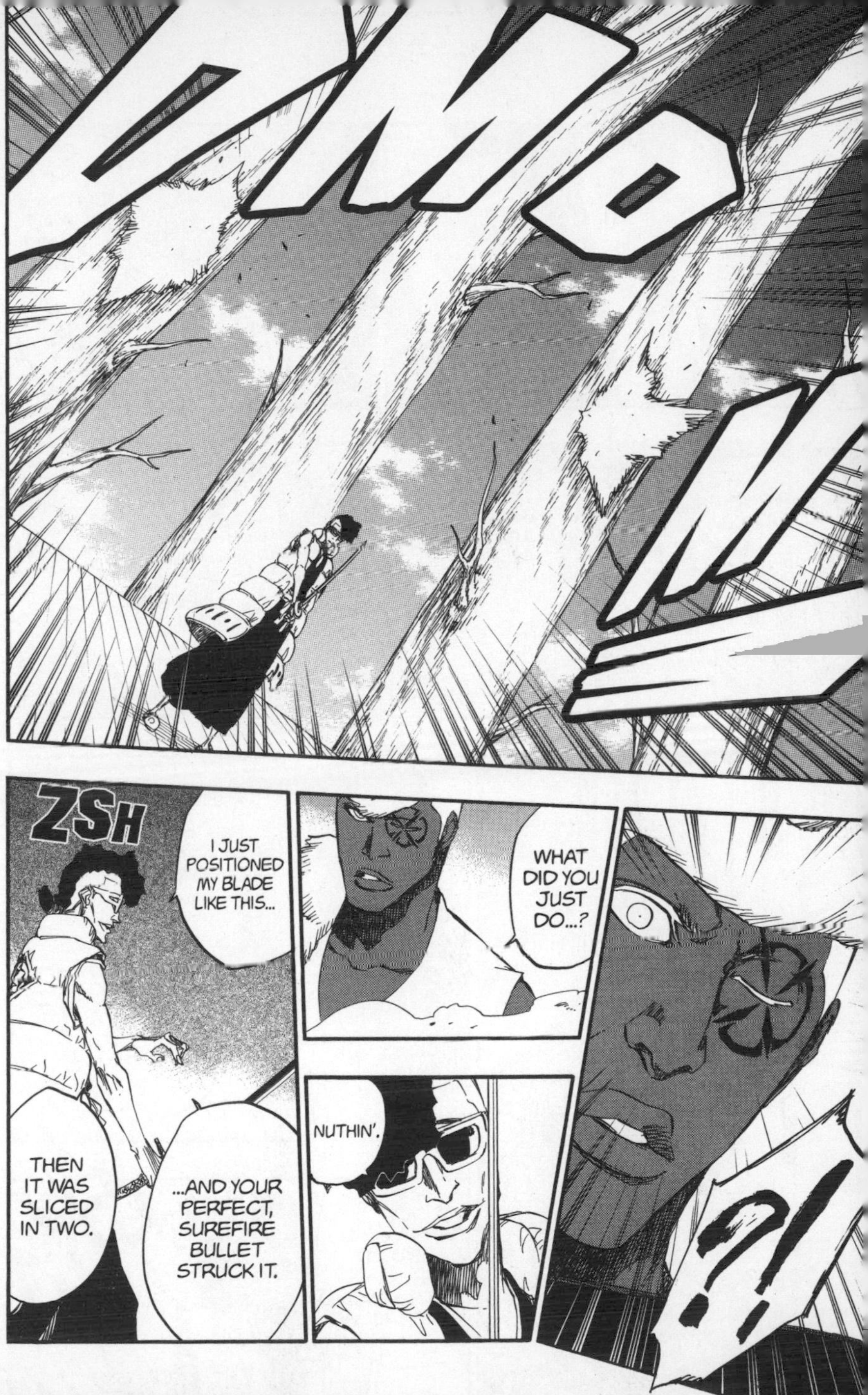
?!
WHAT DID YOU JUST DO...?
NUTHIN'.
ZSH
I JUST POSITIONED MY BLADE LIKE THIS...
...AND YOUR PERFECT, SUREFIRE BULLET STRUCK IT.
THEN IT WAS SLICED IN TWO.

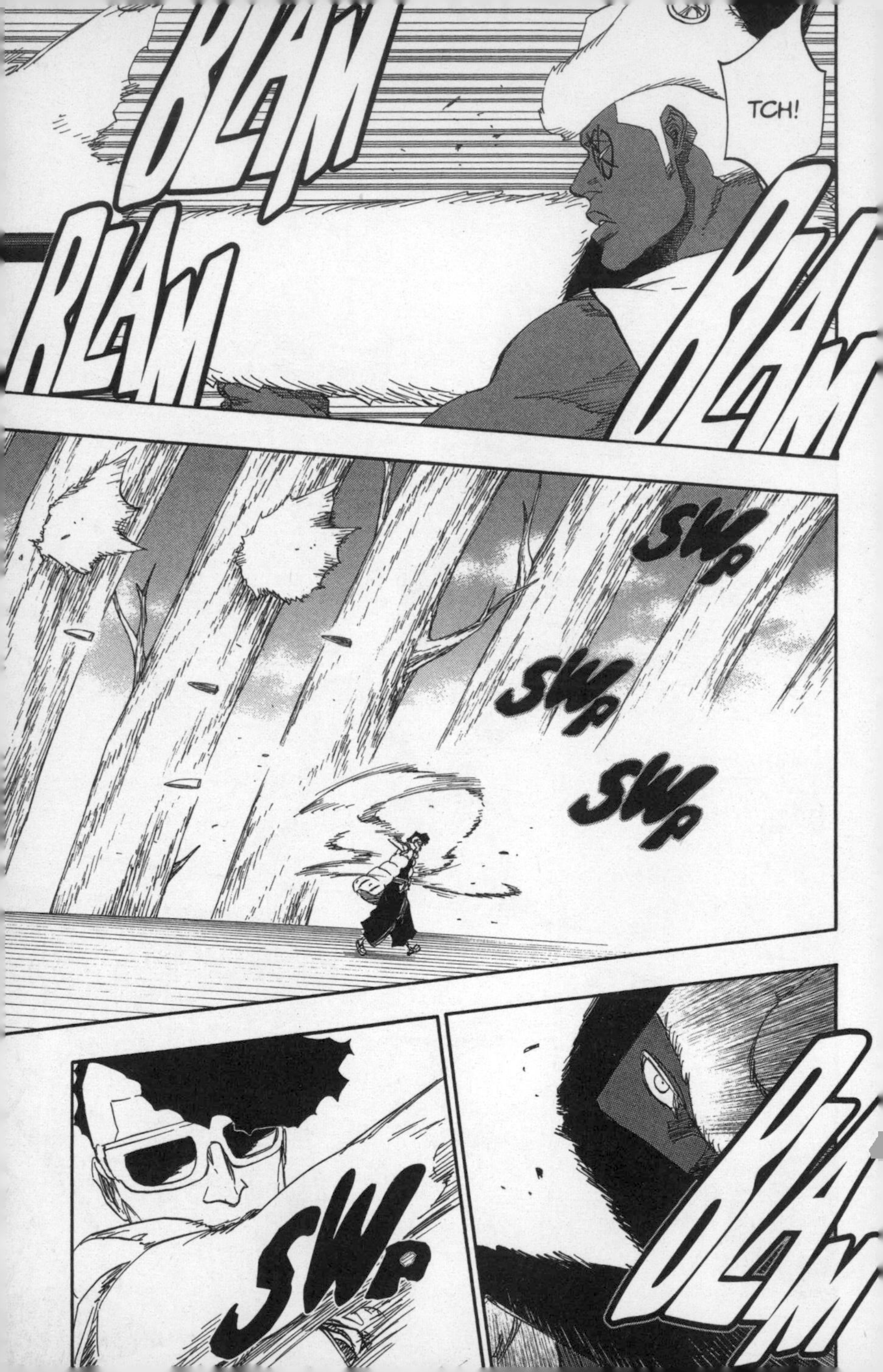
TCH!
BLAM
BLAM
BLAM
SWP
SWP
SWP
BLAM
SWP

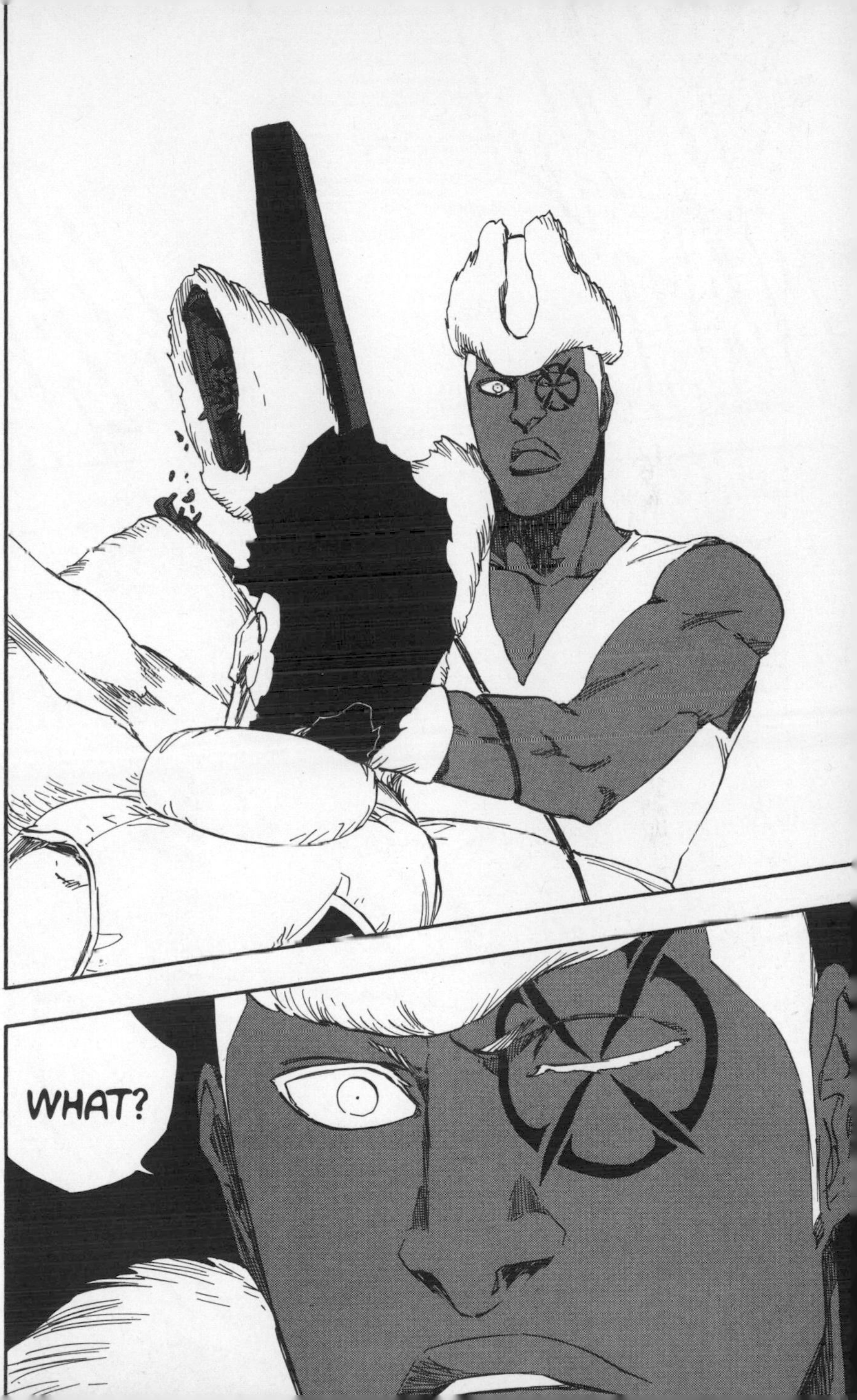
WHAT?

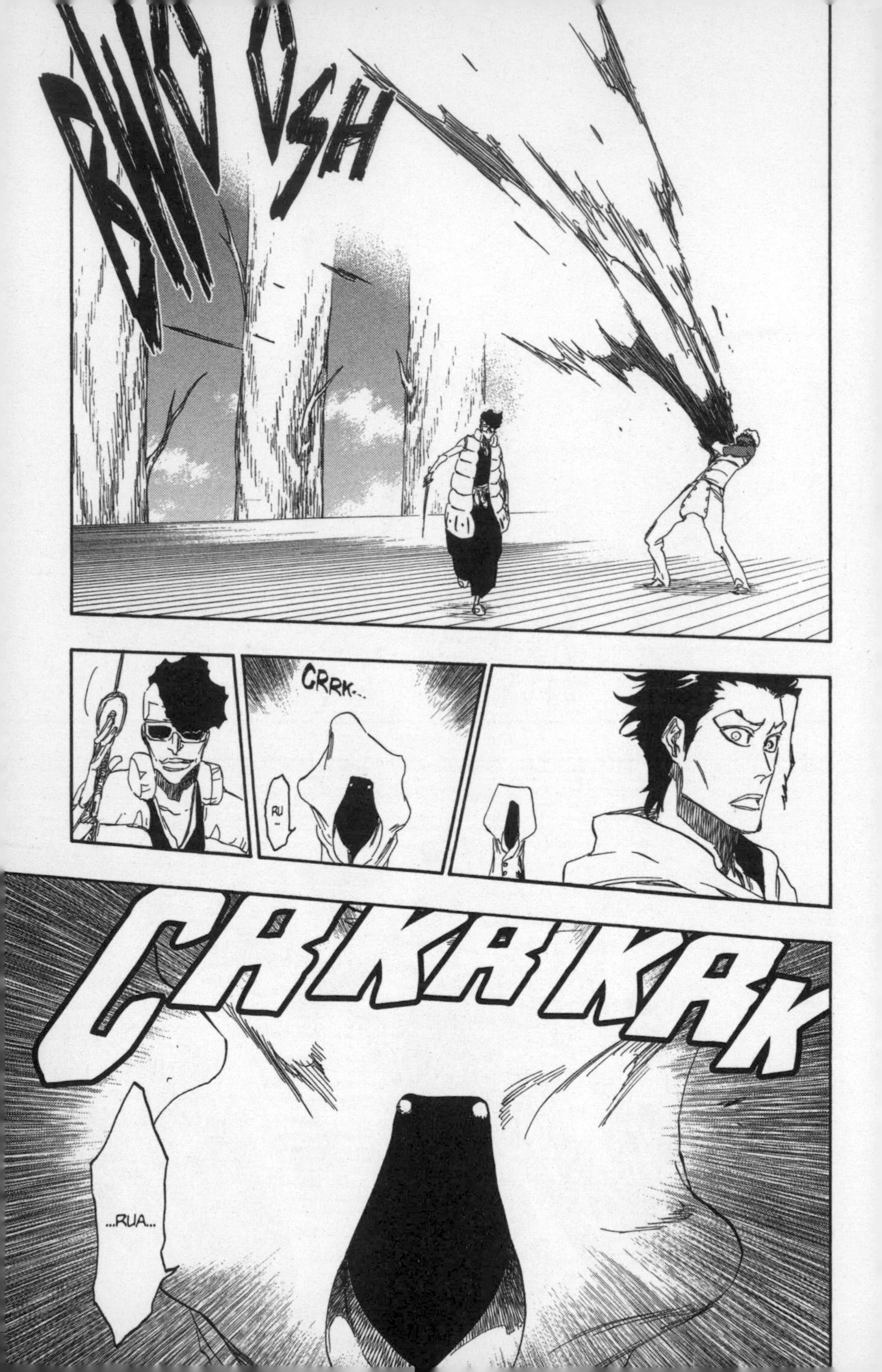
BWOOSH
CRRK...
RU...
CRKRKRK
...RUA...

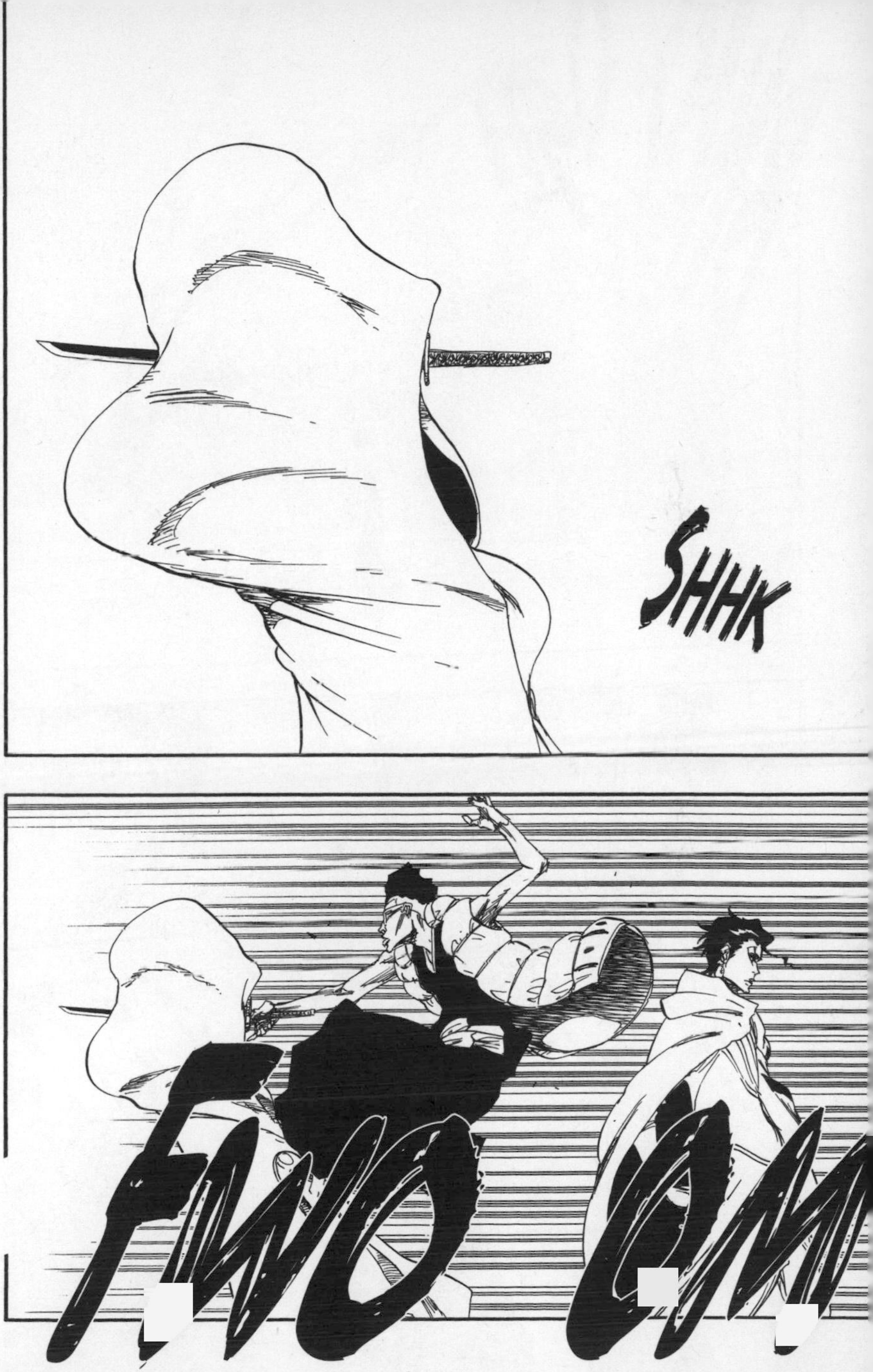
SHHK
FWOOM

READ THIS WAY

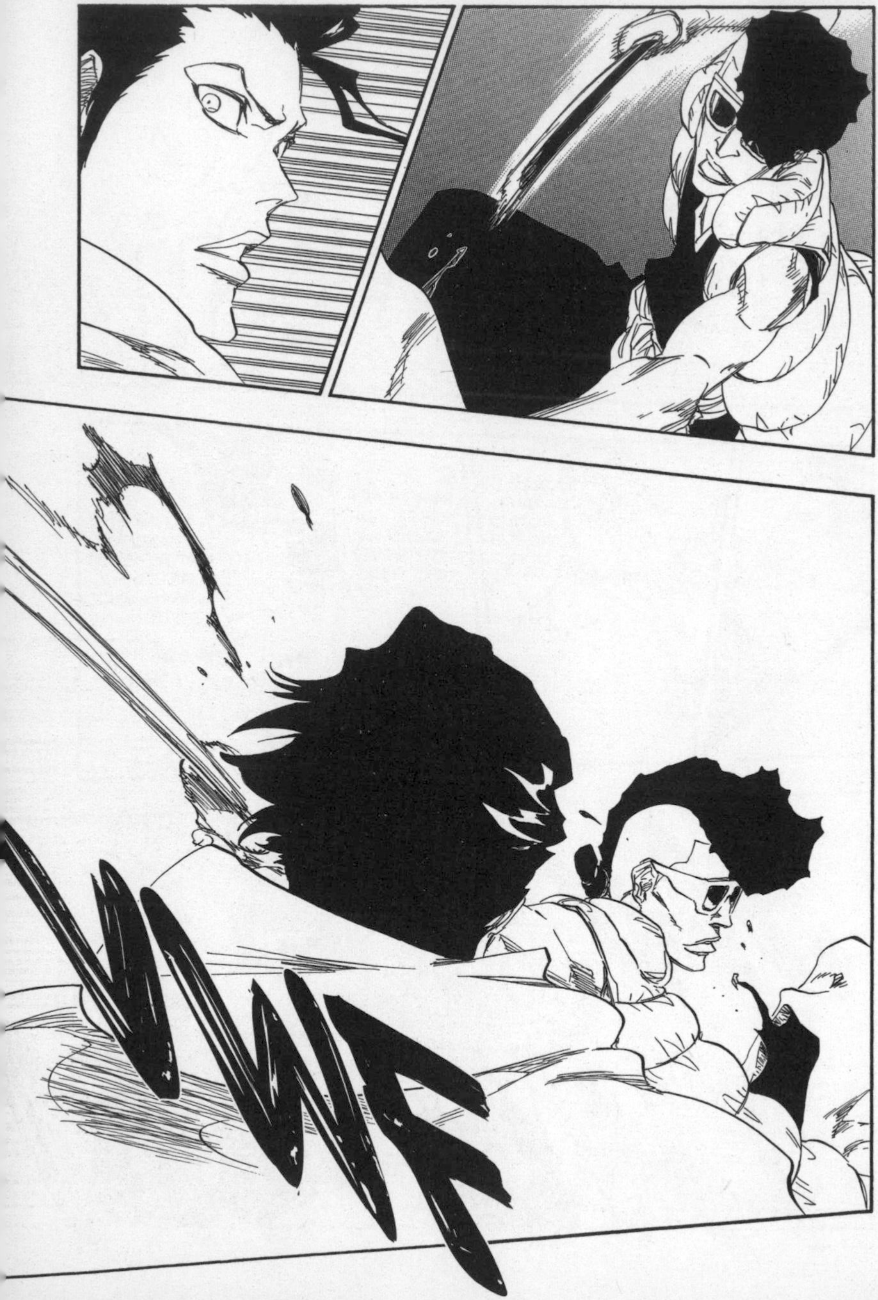

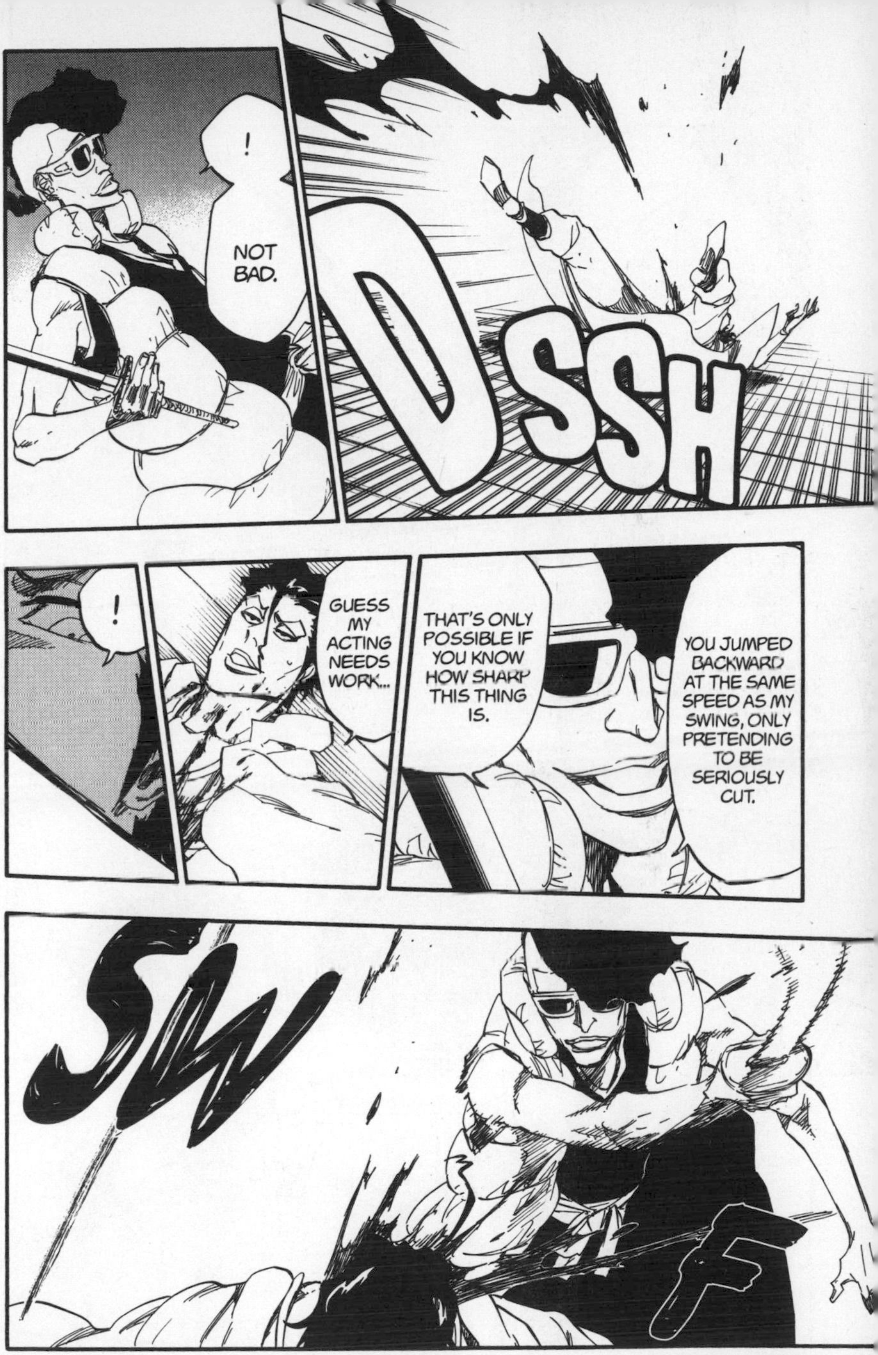
DSSH
!
NOT BAD.
YOU JUMPED BACKWARD AT THE SAME SPEED AS MY SWING, ONLY PRETENDING TO BE SERIOUSLY CUT.
THAT'S ONLY POSSIBLE IF YOU KNOW HOW SHARP THIS THING IS.
GUESS MY ACTING NEEDS WORK...
!
SW
F

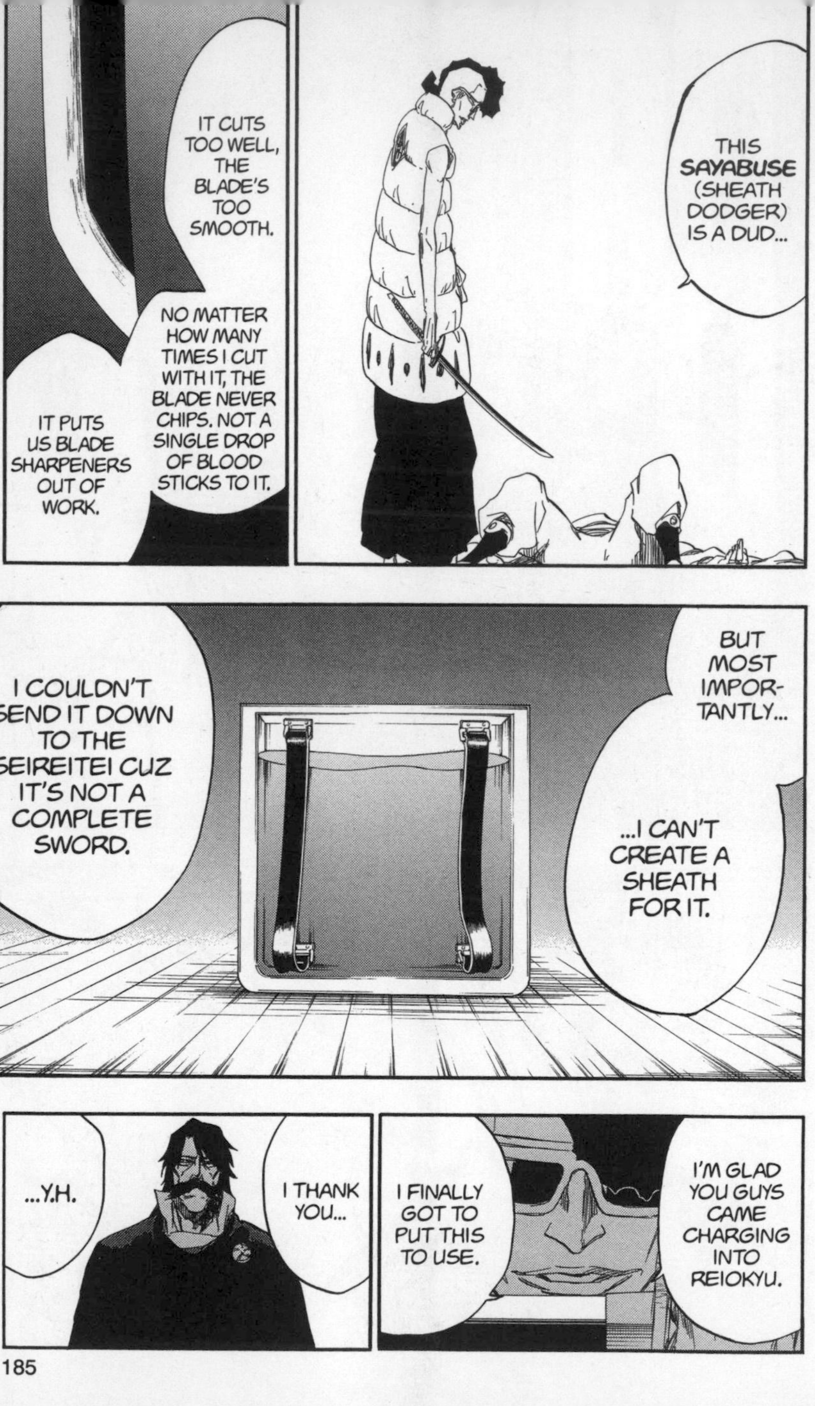
THIS **SAYABUSE** (SHEATH DODGER) IS A DUD...
IT CUTS TOO WELL, THE BLADE'S TOO SMOOTH.
NO MATTER HOW MANY TIMES I CUT WITH IT, THE BLADE NEVER CHIPS. NOT A SINGLE DROP OF BLOOD STICKS TO IT.
IT PUTS US BLADE SHARPENERS OUT OF WORK.
BUT MOST IMPORTANTLY... ...I CAN'T CREATE A SHEATH FOR IT.
I COULDN'T SEND IT DOWN TO THE SEIREITEI CUZ IT'S NOT A COMPLETE SWORD.
I'M GLAD YOU GUYS CAME CHARGING INTO REIOKYU.
I FINALLY GOT TO PUT THIS TO USE.
I THANK YOU...
...Y.H.

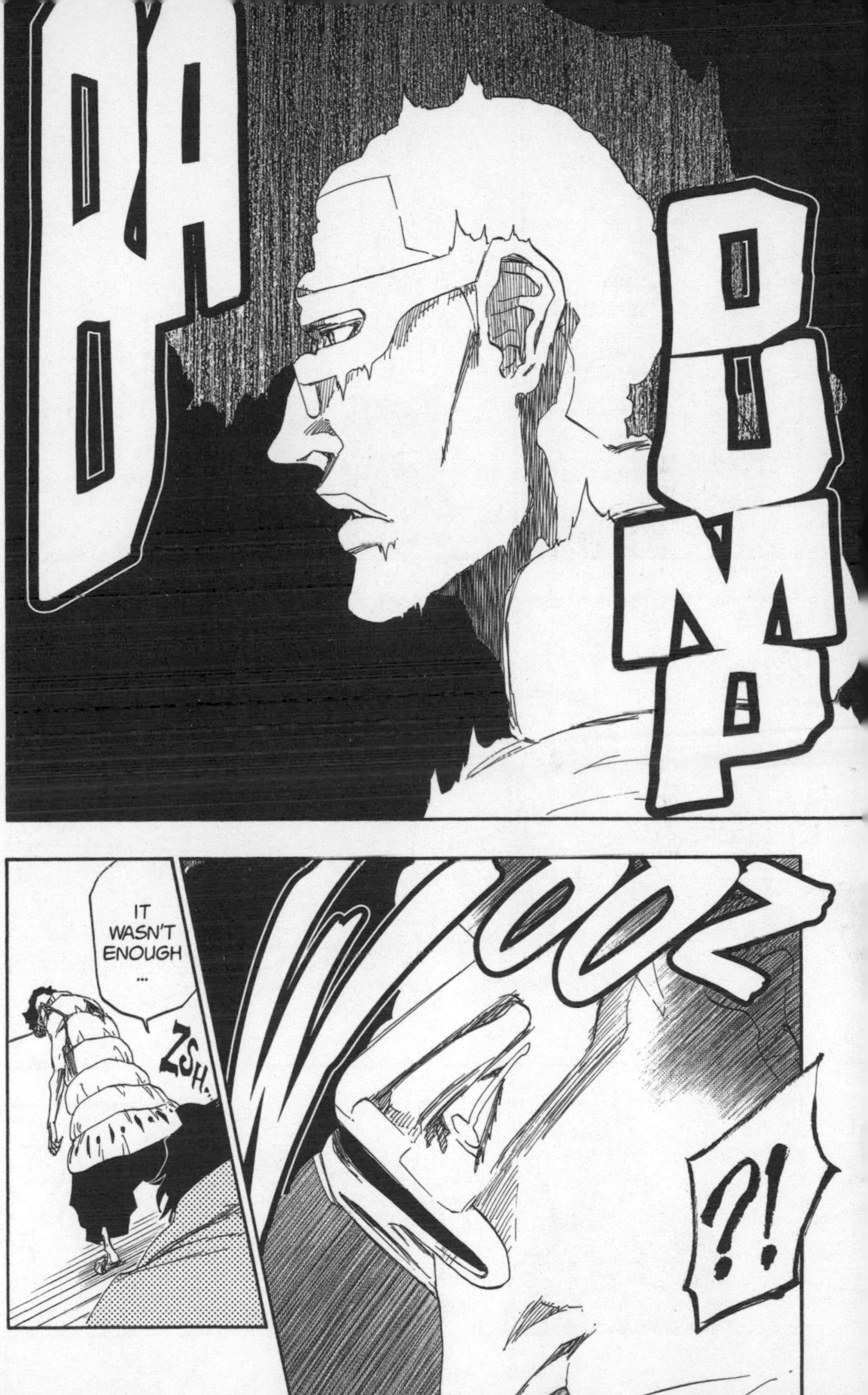
BA
DUMP
?!
IT WASN'T ENOUGH ...
ZSH..

READ THIS WAY

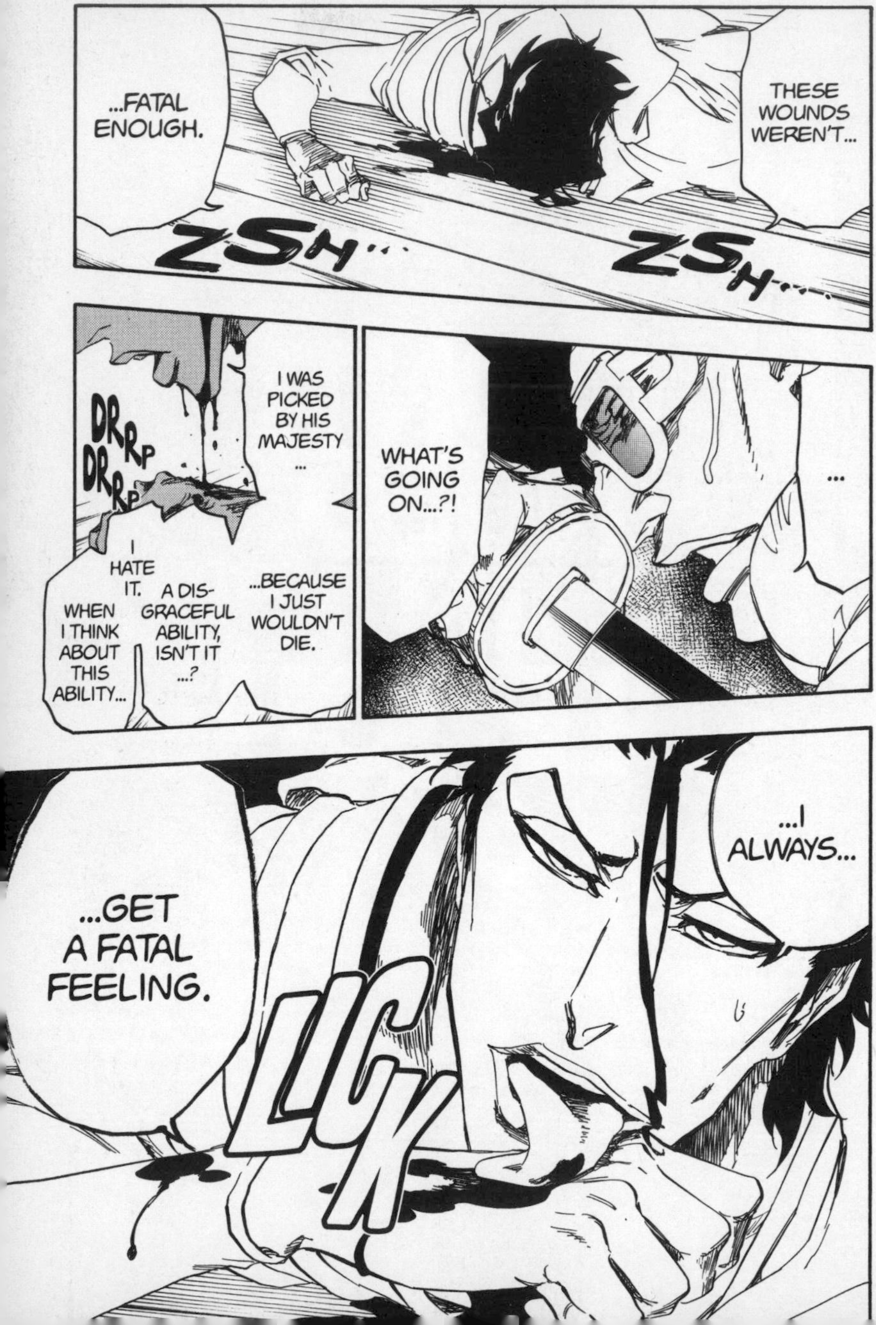
THESE WOUNDS WEREN'T...
...FATAL ENOUGH.
ZSH...
ZSH...
...
WHAT'S GOING ON...?!
I WAS PICKED BY HIS MAJESTY ...
...BECAUSE I JUST WOULDN'T DIE.
DRRP DRRP
A DISGRACEFUL ABILITY, ISN'T IT ...?
I HATE IT.
WHEN I THINK ABOUT THIS ABILITY...
...I ALWAYS...
LICK
...GET A FATAL FEELING.

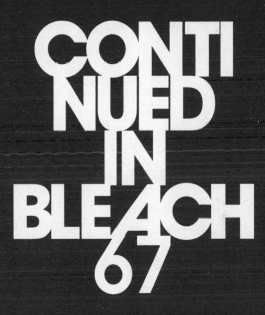

CONTINUED IN BLEACH 67

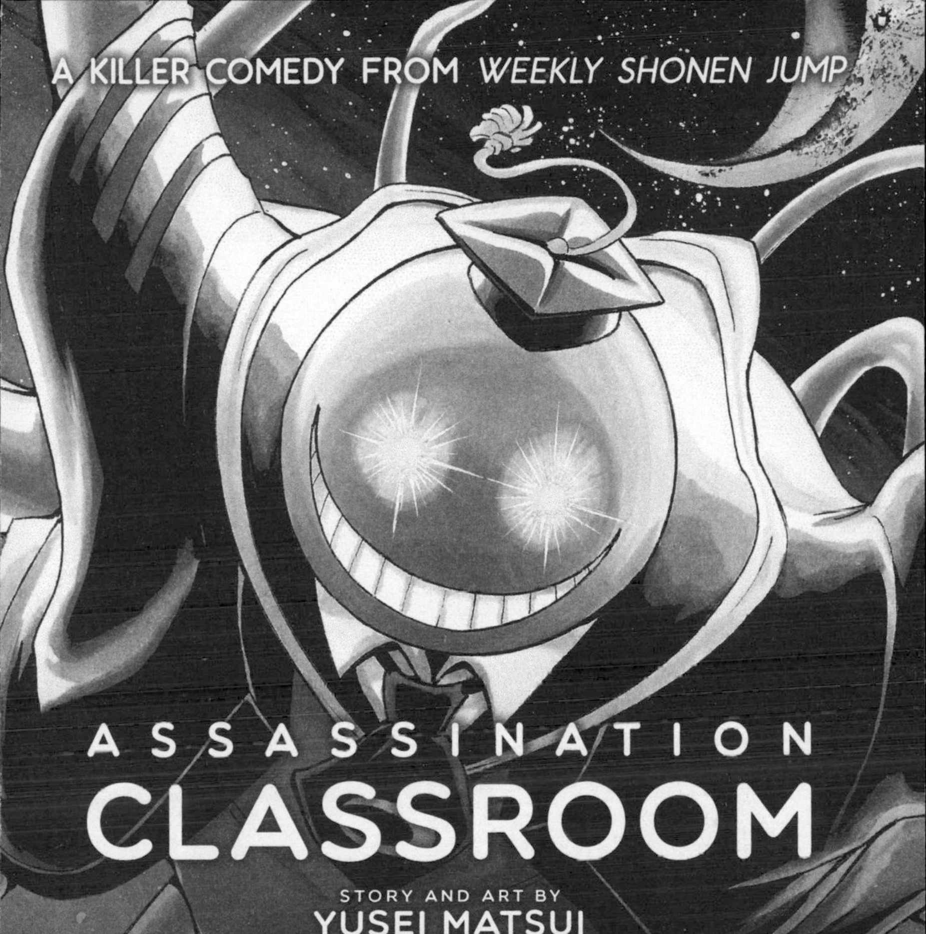

A KILLER COMEDY FROM *WEEKLY SHONEN JUMP*

A S S A S S I N A T I O N
CLASSROOM

STORY AND ART BY
YUSEI MATSUI

Ever caught yourself screaming, "I could just kill that teacher"? What would it take to justify such antisocial behavior and weeks of detention? Especially if he's the best teacher you've ever had? Giving you an "F" on a quiz? Mispronouncing your name during roll call...*again*? How about blowing up the moon and threatening to do the same to Mother Earth—unless you take him out first?! Plus a reward of a cool 100 million from the Ministry of Defense!

Okay, now that you're committed... How are you going to pull this off? What does your pathetic class of misfits have in their arsenal to combat Teach's alien technology, bizarre powers and...*tentacles*?!

ASSASSINATION
CLASSROOM

STORY AND ART BY
YUSEI MATSUI
1

SHONEN JUMP ADVANCED

You're Reading in the Wrong Direction!!

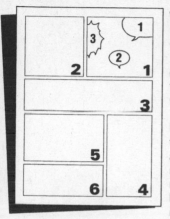

Whoops! Guess what? You're starting at the wrong end of the comic!

...It's true! In keeping with the original Japanese format, **Bleach** is meant to be read from right to left, starting in the upper-right corner.

Unlike English, which is read from left to right, Japanese is read from right to left, meaning that action, sound effects and word-balloon order are completely reversed... something which can make readers unfamiliar with Japanese feel pretty backwards themselves. For this reason, manga or Japanese comics published in the U.S. in English have sometimes been published "flopped"—that is, printed in exact reverse order, as though seen from the other side of a mirror.

By flopping pages, U.S. publishers can avoid confusing readers, but the compromise is not without its downside. For one thing, a character in a flopped manga series who once wore in the original Japanese version a T-shirt emblazoned with "M A Y" (as in "the merry month of") now wears one which reads "Y A M"! Additionally, many manga creators in Japan are themselves unhappy with the process, as some feel the mirror-imaging of their art skews their original intentions.

We are proud to bring you Tite Kubo's **Bleach** in the original unflopped format. For now, though, turn to the other side of the book and let the adventure begin...!

—Editor